B. Hofmann-Wellenhof,
H. Lichtenegger, and J. Collins

Global Positioning System

Theory and Practice

Third, revised edition

Springer-Verlag Wien New York

Dr. Bernhard Hofmann-Wellenhof
Dr. Herbert Lichtenegger
Abteilung für Landesvermessung und Landinformation, Technische Universität Graz
Graz, Austria

Dr. James Collins
GPS Services, Inc.
Rockville, Maryland, U.S.A.

Printed by Novographic, Ing. Wolfgang Schmid, A-1230 Wien
Printed on acid-free and chlorine-free bleached paper

Cover illustration courtesy of Rockwell International

With 39 Figures

ISBN 3-211-82591-6 Springer-Verlag Wien New York

ISBN 3-211-82477-4 2nd ed. Springer-Verlag Wien New York

We dedicate this book to

Benjamin William Remondi

Foreword

This book is dedicated to Dr. Benjamin William Remondi for many reasons. The project of writing a Global Positioning System (GPS) book was conceived in April 1988 at a GPS meeting in Darmstadt. Dr. Remondi discussed with me the need for an additional GPS textbook and suggested a possible joint effort. In 1989, I was willing to commit myself to such a project. Unfortunately, the timing was less than ideal for Dr. Remondi. Therefore, I decided to start the project with other coauthors. Dr. Remondi agreed and indicated his willingness to be a reviewer.

I selected Dr. Herbert Lichtenegger, my colleague from the University of Technology at Graz, Austria, and Dr. James Collins from the United States.

In my opinion, the knowledge of the three authors should cover the wide spectrum of GPS. Dr. Lichtenegger is a geodesist with broad experience in both theory and practice. He has specialized his research to geodetic astronomy including orbital theory and geodynamical phenomena. Since 1986, Dr. Lichtenegger's main interest is dedicated to GPS. Dr. Collins retired from the U.S. National Geodetic Survey in 1980, where he was the Deputy Director. For the past ten years, he has been deeply involved in using GPS technology with an emphasis on surveying. Dr. Collins was the founder and president of Geo/Hydro Inc. My own background is theoretically oriented. My first chief, Prof. Dr. Peter Meissl, was an excellent theoretician; and my former chief, Prof. DDDDr. Helmut Moritz, fortunately, still is.

It is appropriate here to say a word of thanks to Prof. DDDDr. Helmut Moritz, whom I consider my mentor in science. He is – as is probably widely known – one of the world's leading geodesists and is currently president of the International Union for Geodesy and Geophysics (IUGG). In the fall of 1984, he told me I should go to the U.S.A. to learn about GPS. I certainly agreed, although I did not even know what GPS meant. On the same day, Helmut Moritz called Admiral Dr. John Bossler, at that time the Director of the National Geodetic Survey, and my first stay in the U.S.A. was arranged. Thank you, Helmut! I still remember the flight where I started to read the first articles on GPS. I found it interesting but I did not understand very much. Benjamin W. Remondi deserves the credit for providing my GPS instruction. He was a very patient and excellent teacher. I benefited enormously, and I certainly accepted his offer to return to the U.S.A. several times. Aside from the scientific aspect, our families have also become friends.

The selection of topics is certainly different from the original book conceived by Dr. Remondi. The primary selection criteria of the topics were:

relevancy, tutorial content, and the interest and expertise of the authors. The book is intended to be a text on GPS, recognizing the tremendous need for textual materials for professionals, teachers, and for students. The authors believe that it was not necessary to dwell on the latest technical advances. Instead, concepts and techniques are emphasized.

The book can be employed as a classroom text at the senior or graduate levels, depending on the level of specialization desired. It can be read, selectively, by professional surveyors, navigators, and many others who need to position with GPS.

May 1992   B. Hofmann-Wellenhof

Preface

The contents of the book are partitioned into 13 chapters, a section of references, and a very detailed index which should immediately help in finding certain topics of interest.

The first chapter is a historical review. It shows the origins of surveying and how global surveying techniques have been developed. In addition, a short history on the Global Positioning System (GPS) is given.

The second chapter is an overview of GPS. The system is explained by means of its three segments: the space segment, the control segment, and the user segment.

The third chapter deals with the reference systems, such as coordinate and time systems. The inertial and the terrestrial reference frames are explained in the section on coordinate systems, and the transformation between them is shown. The definition of different times is given in the section on time systems, together with appropriate conversion formulas.

The fourth chapter is dedicated to satellite orbits. This chapter specifically describes GPS orbits and covers the determination of the Keplerian and the perturbed orbit, as well as the dissemination of the orbital data.

The fifth chapter covers the satellite signal. It shows the fundamentals of the signal structure with its various components and the principles of the signal processing.

The sixth chapter deals with the observables. The data acquisition comprises code and phase pseudoranges and Doppler data. The chapter also contains the data combinations, both the phase combinations and the phase/code range combinations. Influences affecting the observables are described. Examples are: the atmospheric and relativistic effects, multipath, and the impact of the antenna phase center.

The seventh chapter is dedicated to surveying with GPS. This chapter defines the terminology used and describes the planning of a GPS survey, surveying procedures, and in situ data processing.

The eighth chapter covers mathematical models for positioning. Models for observed data are investigated. Therefore, models for point positioning and relative positioning, based on various data sets, are derived.

The ninth chapter comprises the data processing and deals with the sophisticated cycle slip detection and repair technique. This chapter also includes the resolving of phase ambiguities. The method of least squares adjustment is assumed to be known to the reader and, therefore, only a brief review is included. Consequently, no details are given apart from the linearization of the mathematical models, which are the input for the adjustment procedure.

The tenth chapter links the GPS results to a local datum. The necessary transformations are given. The combination of GPS and terrestrial data is also considered.

The eleventh chapter treats software modules. The intent of this chapter is not to give a detailed description of existing software and how it works. This chapter should help the reader decide which software would best suit his purposes. The very short sections of this chapter try to cover the variety of features which could be relevant to the software.

The twelfth chapter describes some applications of GPS. Global, regional, and local uses are mentioned, as well as the installation of control networks. The compatibility of GPS with other systems, such as Inertial Navigation Systems (INS) and the Global Navigation Satellite System (GLONASS), the Russian equivalent to GPS, is shown.

The thirteenth chapter deals with the future of GPS. Both critical aspects, such as selective availability and anti-spoofing, are discussed, along with positive aspects such as the combination of GPS with GLONASS and the International Maritime Satellite Communication Organization (INMARSAT). Also, some possible improvements in the hardware and software technology are suggested.

The hyphenation is based on Webster's Dictionary. Therefore, some deviations may appear for the reader accustomed to another hyphenation system. For example, the word "measurement", following Webster's Dictionary, is hyphenated mea-sure-ment; whereas, following The American Heritage Dictionary, the hyphenation is meas-ure-ment. The Webster's hyphenation system also contains hyphenations which are sometimes unusual for words with a foreign language origin. An example is the word "parameter". Following Webster's Dictionary, the hyphenation is pa-ram-e-ter. The word has a Greek origin, and one would expect the hyphenation pa-ra-me-ter.

Symbols representing a vector or a matrix are underlined. The inner product of two vectors is indicated by a dot "·". The outer product, cross product, or vector product is indicated by the symbol "×". The norm of a vector, i.e., its length, is indicated by two double-bars "∥".

Many persons deserve credit and thanks. Dr. Benjamin W. Remondi of the National Geodetic Survey at Rockville, Maryland, was a reviewer of the book. He has critically read and corrected the full volume. His many suggestions and improvements, critical remarks and proposals are gratefully acknowledged.

A second technical proofreading was performed by Dipl.-Ing. Gerhard Kienast from the section of Surveying and Landinformation of the University of Technology at Graz. He has helped us with constructive critique and valuable suggestions.

Nadine Collins kindly read and edited the book in its final form, improving the flow and grammar of the text.

The index of the book was produced using a computer program written by Dr. Walter Klostius from the section of Surveying and Landinformation of the University of Technology at Graz. Also, his program helped in the detection of spelling errors.

The book is compiled based on the text system LATEX. Some of the figures included were also developed with LATEX. The remaining figures are drawn by using Autocad 11.0. The section of Physical Geodesy of the Institute of Theoretical Geodesy of the University of Technology at Graz deserves the thanks for these figures. Dr. Norbert Kühtreiber has drawn one of these figures, and the others were carefully developed by Dr. Konrad Rautz. This shows that theoreticians are also well-suited for practical tasks.

We are also grateful to the Springer Publishing Company for their advice and cooperation.

Finally, the inclusion by name of a commercial company or product does not constitute an endorsement by the authors. In principle, such inclusions were avoided whenever possible. Only those names which played a fundamental role in receiver and processing development are included for historical purposes.

May 1992   B. Hofmann-Wellenhof   H. Lichtenegger   J. Collins

Preface to the second edition

The first edition was released in May 1992. Since then, the first and second printing have been completely sold. There was not sufficient time to prepare a revised version for the second edition. Therefore, only a few misspellings and errors were corrected and other minor improvements performed. However, the authors would appreciate your comments for consideration in the case of a fully revised and updated version.

March 1993   B. Hofmann-Wellenhof   H. Lichtenegger   J. Collins

Preface to the third edition

The third edition has been extensively rewritten to accommodate the more recent advances in GPS technology, such as on-the-fly integer ambiguity resolution, Differential GPS (DGPS), the full operational status of the satellite constellation together with the denial of accuracy by Selective Availability and Anti-Spoofing. The overall structure and paragraph numbering have been retained, and new material has been added by extending and shifting the sub-chapter numbering. We continue to request your comments and seek your advise for changes to future editions.

April 1994   B. Hofmann-Wellenhof   H. Lichtenegger   J. Collins

Contents

Abbreviations

AC	Alternating Current
ACS	Active Control System
AFB	Air Force Base
AGREF	Austrian GPS Reference (network)
AOC	Auxiliary Output Chip
A-S	Anti-Spoofing
AVL	Automatic Vehicle Location
BBS	Bulletin Board Service
BC	Ballistic Camera
BDT	Barycentric Dynamic Time
C/A	Coarse/Acquisition
CAD	Computer Aided Design
CEP	Celestial Ephemeris Pole
CGIS	Civil GPS Service Interface Committee
CGS	Civil GPS Service
CIGNET	Cooperative International GPS Network
CIO	Conventional International Origin
CIS	Conventional Inertial System
CSOC	Consolidated Space Operations Center
CTS	Conventional Terrestrial System
DC	Direct Current
DD	Double-Difference
DEC	Digital Equipment Corporation
DGPS	Differential GPS
DLL	Delay Lock Loop
DMA	Defense Mapping Agency
DME	Distance Measuring Equipment
DoD	Department of Defense
DOP	Dilution of Precision
DoT	Department of Transportation
ECEF	Earth-Centered-Earth-Fixed
ERS	Earth Remote Sensing (satellite)
FAA	Federal Aviation Administration
FGCC	Federal Geodetic Control Committee
FM	Frequency Modulated
FMS	Flight Managing System

FOC	Full Operational Capability
FRP	Federal Radionavigation Plan
GDOP	Geometric Dilution of Precision
GIC	GPS Integrity Channel
GIS	Geographic Information System
GLONASS	Global Navigation Satellite System
GNSS	Global Navigation Satellite System
GOTEX	Global Orbit Tracking Experiment
GPS	Global Positioning System
GPSIC	GPS Information Center
GPST	GPS Time
GRS	Geodetic Reference System
HDOP	Horizontal Dilution of Precision
HIRAN	High Range Navigation
HOW	Hand Over Word
IAG	International Association of Geodesy
IAT	International Atomic Time
IBM	International Business Machines (corporation)
IERS	International Earth Rotation Service
IGS	International GPS Geodynamics Service
ILS	Instrument Landing System
INMARSAT	International Maritime Satellite (organization)
INS	Inertial Navigation System
IOC	Initial Operational Capability
ION	Institute of Navigation
IRF	Inertial Reference Frame
ISU	International System of Units
ITRF	IERS Terrestrial Reference Frame
IUGG	International Union for Geodesy and Geophysics
IVHS	Intelligent Vehicle/Highway System
JD	Julian Date
JPL	Jet Propulsion Laboratory
JPO	Joint Program Office
LAN	Local Area Network
LORAN	Long Range Navigation (system)
MIT	Massachusetts Institute of Technology
MITES	Miniature Interferometer Terminals for Earth Survey
MJD	Modified Julian Date
MLS	Microwave Landing System
MMIC	Monolithic Microwave Integrated Circuit
NAD	North American Datum

NASA	National Aeronautics and Space Administration
NAVSTAR	Navigation System with Time and Ranging
NGS	National Geodetic Survey
NNSS	Navy Navigational Satellite System
NSWC	Naval Surface Warfare Center
OCS	Operational Control System
OEM	Original Equipment Manufacturer
OTF	On-the-Fly
P	Precision
PC	Personal Computer
PDOP	Position Dilution of Precision
PDP	Programable Data Processor
PLL	Phase Lock Loop
PPS	Precise Positioning Service
PRN	Pseudorandom Noise
RAIM	Receiver Autonomous Integrity Monitoring
RDS	Radio Data System
RF	Radio Frequency
RINEX	Receiver Independent Exchange (format)
RTCM	Radio Technical Commission for Maritime services
SA	Selective Availability
SD	Single-Difference
SERIES	Satellite Emission Range Inferred Earth Surveying
SLR	Satellite Laser Ranging
SNR	Signal-to-Noise Ratio
SPOT	Satellite Probatoire d'Observation de la Terre
SPS	Standard Positioning Service
SV	Space Vehicle
TACAN	Tactical Air Navigation
TD	Triple-Difference
TDOP	Time Dilution of Precision
TDT	Terrestrial Dynamic Time
TEC	Total Electron Content
TLM	Telemetry
TM	Trade Mark
TOPEX	(Ocean) Topography Experiment
TOW	Time-of-Week (count)
TRF	Terrestrial Reference Frame
UERE	User Equivalent Range Error
USCG	U.S. Coast Guard
USGS	U.S. Geological Survey

UT	Universal Time
UTC	Universal Time Coordinated
UTM	Universal Transverse Mercator (projection)
VDOP	Vertical Dilution of Precision
VHF	Very High Frequency
VHSIC	Very High Speed Integrated Circuit
VLBI	Very Long Baseline Interferometry
VOR	VHF Omnidirectional Range (equipment)
VTS	Vehicle Traffic System
WADGPS	Wide Area Differential GPS
WGS	World Geodetic System

Numerical constants

GPS signal frequencies	
$f_0 =$ 10.23 MHz	fundamental frequency
$L1 = 1\,575.42$ MHz	primary carrier frequency
$L2 = 1\,227.60$ MHz	secondary carrier frequency

WGS-84		
a	$=$ 6 378 137.000 00 m	semimajor axis of ellipsoid
$\bar{C}_{2,0} =$	$-484.166\,85 \cdot 10^{-6}$	normalized spherical harmonic
ω_E	$= 7\,292\,115 \cdot 10^{-11}\,\mathrm{rad\,s}^{-1}$	angular velocity of the earth
$GM =$	$3\,986\,005 \cdot 10^{8}\,\mathrm{m^3\,s^{-2}}$	earth's gravitational constant
b	$=$ 6 356 752.314 25 m	semiminor axis of ellipsoid
f	$=$ $3.352\,810\,664\,74 \cdot 10^{-3}$	flattening of ellipsoid
e^2	$=$ $6.694\,379\,990\,13 \cdot 10^{-3}$	first numerical eccentricity
e'^2	$=$ $6.739\,496\,742\,26 \cdot 10^{-3}$	second numerical eccentricity

Various constants		
c	$=$ $299\,792\,458\,\mathrm{m\,s}^{-1}$	velocity of light
ω_E	$= 7\,292\,115.1467 \cdot 10^{-11}\,\mathrm{rad\,s}^{-1}$	untruncated angular velocity
CD $=$	January 6.0, 1980	Civil date of GPS standard epoch
JD $=$	2 444 244.5	Julian date of GPS standard epoch

1 Introduction

1.1 The origins of surveying

Since the dawn of civilization, man has looked to the heavens with awe searching for portentous signs. Some of these men became experts in deciphering the mystery of the stars and developed rules for governing life based upon their placement. The exact time to plant the crops was one of the events that was foretold by the early priest astronomers who in essence were the world's first surveyors. Today, we know that the alignment of such structures as the pyramids and Stonehenge was accomplished by celestial observations and that the structures themselves were used to measure the time of celestial events such as the vernal equinox. The chain of technical developments from these early astronomical surveyors to the present satellite geodesists reflects man's desire to be able to master time and space and to use science to further his society.

The surveyor's role in society has remained unchanged from the earliest days; that is to determine land boundaries, provide maps of his environment, and control the construction of public works.

Some of the first known surveyors were Egyptian surveyors who used distant control points to replace property corners destroyed by the flooding Nile River. Later, the Greeks and Romans surveyed their settlements. Surveys on a larger scale were conducted by the French surveyors Cassini and Picard, who measured the interior angles of a series of interconnecting triangles in combination with measured baselines, to determine the coordinates of points extending from Dunkirk to Collioure. The triangulation technique was subsequently used by surveyors as the main means of determining accurate coordinates over continental distances.

1.2 Development of global surveying techniques

The use of triangulation (later combined with trilateration and traversing) was limited by the line-of-sight. Surveyors climbed to mountain tops and developed special survey towers to extend this line-of-sight usually by small amounts. The series of triangles was generally oriented or fixed by astronomic points where special surveyors had observed selected stars to determine the position of that point on the surface of the earth. Since these astronomic positions could be in error by hundreds of meters, each continent was virtually (positionally) isolated and their interrelationship was imprecisely known.

1.2.1   Optical global triangulation

Some of the first attempts to determine the interrelationship between the continents were made using the occultation of certain stars by the moon. This method was cumbersome at best and was not particularly successful. The launch of the Russian Sputnik satellite in 1957, however, had tremendously advanced the connection of the various world datums. In the beginning of the era of artificial satellites, an optical method, based (in principle) on the stellar triangulation method developed in Finland as early as 1946, was applied very successfully. The worldwide satellite triangulation program often called the BC-4 program (after the camera that was used) for the first time determined the interrelationships of the major world datums. This method involved photographing special reflective satellites against a star background with a metric camera that was fitted with a specially manufactured chopping shutter. The image that appeared on the photograph consisted of a series of dots depicting each star's path and a series of dots depicting the satellite's path. The coordinates of selected dots were precisely measured using a photogrammetric comparator, and the associated spatial directions from the observing site to the satellite were then processed using an analytical photogrammetric model. Photographing the same satellite from a neighbouring site simultaneously and processing the data in an analogous way yields another set of spatial directions. Each pair of corresponding directions forms a plane containing the observing points and the satellite, and the intersection of at least two planes results in the spatial direction between the observing sites. In the next step, these oriented directions were used to construct a global network with the scale being derived from several terrestrial traverses. An example is the European baseline running from Tromsø in Norway to Catania on Sicily. The main problem in using this optical technique was that clear sky was required simultaneously at a minimum of two observing sites separated by some 4 000 km, and the equipment was massive and expensive. Thus, optical direction measurement was soon supplanted by the electromagnetic ranging technique because of all-weather capability, greater accuracy, and lower cost of the newer technique.

1.2.2   Electromagnetic global trilateration

First attempts to (positionally) connect the continents by electromagnetic techniques was by the use of an electronic High Ranging (HIRAN) system developed during World War II to position aircraft. Beginning in the late

1940's, HIRAN arcs of trilateration were measured between North America and Europe in an attempt to determine the difference in their respective datums. A significant technological breakthrough occurred when scientists around the world experienced that the Doppler shift in the signal broadcast by a satellite could be used as an observable to determine the exact time of closest approach of the satellite. This knowledge, together with the ability to compute satellite ephemerides according to Kepler's laws, led to the present capability of instantaneously determining precise position anywhere in the world.

The immediate predecessor of today's modern positioning system is the Navy Navigational Satellite System (NNSS), also called TRANSIT system. This system was composed of six satellites orbiting at altitudes of about 1 100 km with nearly circular polar orbits. The TRANSIT system was developed by the U.S. military, primarily, to determine the coordinates of vessels and aircraft. Civilian use of this satellite system was eventually authorized, and the system became widely used worldwide both for navigation and surveying. Today, thousands of small vessels and aircraft still use the TRANSIT system to determine their position worldwide.

Some of the early TRANSIT experiments by the U.S. Defense Mapping Agency (DMA) and the U.S. Coast & Geodetic Survey showed that accuracies of about one meter could be obtained by occupying a point for several days and reducing the observations using the postprocessed precise ephemerides. Groups of Doppler receivers in translocation mode could also be used to determine the relative coordinates of points to submeter accuracy using the broadcast ephemerides. This system employed essentially the same Doppler observable used to track the Sputnik satellite; however, the orbits of the TRANSIT satellites were precisely determined by tracking them at widely spaced fixed sites.

1.3 History of the Global Positioning System

The Global Positioning System (GPS) was developed to replace the TRANSIT system because of two major shortcomings in the earlier system. The main problem with TRANSIT was the large time gaps in coverage. Since nominally a satellite would pass overhead every 90 minutes, users had to interpolate their position between "fixes" or passes. The second problem with the TRANSIT system was its relatively low navigation accuracy.

In contrast, GPS answers the questions "What time, what position, and what velocity is it?" quickly, accurately, and inexpensively anywhere on the globe at any time, cf. Remondi (1991c).

1.3.1 Navigating with GPS

The aim of navigation is instantaneous positioning and velocity determination. As stated, one of the main problems with the TRANSIT system was the fact that the six orbiting satellites were not able to provide continuous positioning.

Satellite constellation
To provide a continuous global positioning capability, a scheme to orbit a sufficient number of satellites to ensure that (at least) four were always electronically visible was developed for GPS. Several schemes were proposed and it was found that 21 evenly spaced satellites placed in circular 12-hour orbits inclined 55° to the equatorial plane would provide the desired coverage for the least expense. In any event, this constellation provides a minimum of four satellites in good geometric position 24 hours per day anywhere on the earth. Depending on the selected elevation angle, there are often more than the minimum number of satellites available for use and it is during these periods that surveyors perform kinematic and other special surveys. In fact, assuming a 10° elevation angle, there are brief periods where up to 10 GPS satellites are visible on the earth.

Point positioning
The GPS satellites are configured, primarily, to provide the user with the capability of determining his position, expressed for example by latitude, longitude, and elevation. This is accomplished by the simple resection process using the distances measured to satellites.

Consider the satellites frozen in space at a given instant. The space coordinates $\underline{\varrho}^S$ relative to the center of the earth of each satellite, cf. also Fig. 1.1, can be computed from the ephemerides broadcast by the satellite by an algorithm presented in Chap. 4. If the ground receiver defined by its geocentric position vector $\underline{\varrho}_R$ employed a clock that was set precisely to GPS system time, cf. Sect. 3.3, the true distance or range ϱ to each satellite could be accurately measured by recording the time required for the (coded) satellite signal to reach the receiver. Each range defines a sphere (more precisely: surface of a sphere) with its center at the satellite. Hence, using this technique, ranges to only three satellites would be needed since the intersection of three spheres yields the three unknowns (e.g., latitude, longitude, and height) which could be determined from the three range equations

$$\varrho = \|\underline{\varrho}^S - \underline{\varrho}_R\|. \tag{1.1}$$

GPS receivers apply a slightly different technique. They typically use an inexpensive crystal clock which is set approximately to GPS time. Thus,

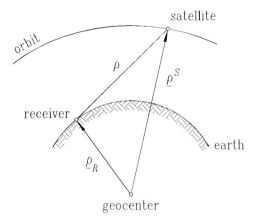

Fig. 1.1. Principle of satellite positioning

the clock of the ground receiver is offset from true GPS time, and because of this offset, the distance measured to the satellite is slightly longer or shorter than the "true" range. The receiver can overcome this problem by measuring the distances to four satellites (simultaneously). These distances are called pseudoranges R since they are the true range plus a small (positive or negative) range correction $\Delta\varrho$ resulting from the receiver clock error or bias δ. A simple model for the pseudorange is

$$R = \varrho + \Delta\varrho = \varrho + c\,\delta \tag{1.2}$$

with c being the velocity of light.

The point position can be solved by resection as before except that now four pseudoranges are needed to solve for the four unknowns; these are three components of position plus the clock bias. It is worth noting that the range error $\Delta\varrho$ could be eliminated in advance by differencing the pseudoranges measured from one site to two satellites or two different positions of one satellite. In the second case, the resulting delta range corresponds to the observable in the TRANSIT system. In both cases, the delta range now defines a hyperboloid with its foci placed at the two satellites or the two different satellite positions for the geometric location of the receiver.

Considering the fundamental observation equation (1.1), one can conclude that the accuracy of the position determined using a single receiver essentially is affected by the following factors:

- Accuracy of each satellite's position.

- Accuracy of pseudorange measurement.

- Geometry.

Systematic errors in the satellite's position and eventual satellite clock biases in the pseudoranges can be reduced or eliminated by differencing the pseudoranges measured from two sites to the satellite. This interferometric approach has become fundamental for GPS surveying as demonstrated below. However, no mode of differencing can overcome poor geometry.

A measure of satellite geometry with respect to the observing site is a factor known as Geometric Dilution of Precision (GDOP). In a geometric approach, this factor is inversely proportional to the volume of a body. This body is formed by points obtained from the intersection of a unit sphere with the vectors pointing from the observing site to the satellites. More details and an analytical approach on this subject are provided in Sect. 9.5.

Velocity determination

The determination of the instantaneous velocity of a moving vehicle is another goal of navigation. This can be achieved by using the Doppler principle of radio signals. Because of the relative motion of the GPS satellites with respect to a moving vehicle, the frequency of a signal broadcast by the satellites is shifted when received at the vehicle. This measurable Doppler shift is proportional to the relative radial velocity. Since the radial velocity of the satellites is known, the radial velocity of the moving vehicle can be deduced from the Doppler observable.

In summary, GPS was designed to solve many of the problems inherent to the TRANSIT system. Above all, GPS provides 24 hours a day instantaneous global navigation. The system as originally designed, however, did not include provision for the accurate surveying that is performed today. This surveying use of GPS resulted from a number of fortuitous developments described below.

1.3.2   Surveying with GPS

From navigation to surveying

As previously described, the use of near-earth satellites for navigation was demonstrated by the TRANSIT system. In 1964, I. Smith filed a patent describing a satellite system that would emit time codes and radio waves that would be received on earth as time delayed transmissions creating hyperbolic lines of position, cf. Smith (1964). This concept would become important in the treatment of GPS observables to compute precise vectors. A few years later, another patent was filed by R. Easton further refining the concept of comparing the phase from two or more satellites, cf. Easton (1970).

In 1972, C. Counselman along with his colleagues from the Massachusetts

Institute of Technology's (MIT) Department of Earth and Planetary Sciences reported on the first use of interferometry to track the Apollo 16 Lunar Rover module, cf. Counselman et al. (1972). The principle they described is in essence the same technique they used later in developing the first geodetic GPS receiver and corresponds to differencing pseudoranges measured from two receivers to one satellite. The present use of the GPS carrier phase to make millimeter vector measurements dates from work by the MIT group using Very Long Baseline Interferometry (VLBI) performed between 1976 and 1978 where they proved millimeter accuracy was obtainable using the interferometric technique, cf. Rogers et al. (1978).

The present GPS survey system is essentially described in a paper by Counselman and Shapiro (1978). The Miniature Interferometer Terminals for Earth Surveying (MITES) detail how a satellite system can be used for precise surveying. This concept was further refined to include the Navigation System with Timing and Ranging (NAVSTAR) in a paper authored by Counselman et al. (1979). This paper also presents a description of the codeless technique that later became important in developing high-accuracy dual frequency receivers. The main significance of the MIT group's contribution to GPS is they demonstrated for the first time that the GPS carrier signal could be processed by differencing the phases, so that vectors between two points could be measured to millimeter accuracy (for short lines).

Observation techniques
It should be noted that when referring to high accuracy, GPS surveying implies the precise measurement of the vector between two (or more) GPS instruments. The observation technique where both receivers involved remain fixed in position is called "static" surveying. The static method formerly required hours of observation and was the technique that was primarily used for early GPS surveys.

A second technique where one receiver remains fixed, while the second receiver moves is called "kinematic" surveying. Remondi (1986) first demonstrated that subcentimeter vector accuracies could be obtained between a pair of GPS survey instruments with as little as a few seconds of data collection using this method. Surveys are performed by first placing a pair of receivers on two points of known location where data are collected from four (or preferably more) satellites for several minutes. Following this brief initialization, one of the receivers may be moved and, as long as four or more satellites are continuously (no loss of lock) tracked, the vector between the fixed and roving instruments can be determined to high accuracies. Remondi also reported a variation of this technique to quickly determine the initial vector for kinematic surveys. This variant has been termed the antenna swap technique since the instruments are swapped between two points at the beginning of the survey to determine the initial vector, cf. Hofmann-Wellenhof and Remondi (1988). An antenna swap can be performed in approximately 1 minute. Nowadays, initialization may be performed by improved techniques as described in Sect. 9.1.3.

Remondi (1988) also first developed another survey technique that is a variant of the normal static method. In this "pseudokinematic" technique a pair of receivers occupies a pair of points for two brief (e.g., 2–5 minutes) periods that are separated in time (e.g., 30–60 minutes). This method has also been called intermittent static or snapshot static and has demonstrated accuracies comparable to the static method.

The "differential" positioning technique involves placing a continuous tracking receiver at a fixed site of known position. Comparing computed ranges with measured pseudoranges, the reference site can transmit corrections to a roving receiver to improve its measured pseudoranges. This technique provides real-time accurate positioning at the one-meter level or even better. Hence, it meets many requirements dictated by the complexity of modern civilization.

Hardware developments

The following sections contain reference to various terms that are more fully described in subsequent chapters. These are the C/A-code (Coarse/Acquisition) and P-code (Precision) which are basically code bits that are modulated on the two carrier signals broadcast by the GPS satellites. Code correlation as well as codeless techniques strip these codes from the carrier so that the phase of the (reconstructed) carrier can be measured. Brand names mentioned in this section are included for historical purposes since they represent the first of a certain class or type of receiver.

An interferometric technology for codeless pseudoranging was developed by P. MacDoran at the California Institute of Technology, Jet Propulsion Laboratory (JPL), with financial support from the National Aeronautics and Space Administration (NASA). This Satellite Emission Range Inferred Earth Surveying (SERIES) technique was later improved for commercial geodetic applications, cf. MacDoran et al. (1985). The culmination of the VLBI interferometric research applied to earth orbiting satellites was the production of a "portable" codeless GPS receiver that could measure short baselines to millimeter accuracy and long baselines to one part per million (ppm), cf. Collins (1982). This receiver, trade-named the Macrometer Interferometric Surveyor™ (Macrometer is a trademark of Aero Service Division, Western Atlas International, Houston, Texas), was tested by the U.S. Federal Geodetic Control Committee (FGCC), cf. Hothem and Fronczek (1983), and was used shortly thereafter in commercial surveys.

A parallel development was being carried out by the DMA in cooperation with the U.S. National Geodetic Survey (NGS) and the U.S. Geological Survey (USGS). In 1981, these agencies developed specifications for a portable dual frequency code correlating receiver that could be used for precise surveying and point positioning. Texas Instruments Company was awarded the contract to produce a receiver later trade-named the TI-4100. The NGS participated in developing specifications for the TI-4100 and their geodesists, C. Goad and B. Remondi, developed software to process its carrier phase data in a manner similar to the method used by the MIT group (i.e., interferometrically).

The physical characteristics of the TI-4100 were significantly different from the Macrometer. The TI-4100 was a dual frequency receiver that used the P-code to track a maximum of four satellites, while the original Macrometer was a rack mounted codeless single frequency receiver that simultaneously tracked up to six satellites. There were also significant logistic differences in performing surveys using these two pioneer instruments. The TI-4100 received the broadcast ephemerides and timing signals from the GPS satellites so units could be operated independently, while the Macrometer required that all units be brought together prior to the survey and after the survey so that the time of the units could be synchronized. Also, the Macrometer required that the ephemerides for each day's tracking be generated at the home office prior to each day's observing session.

The next major development in GPS surveying occurred in 1985 when manufacturers started to produce C/A-code receivers that measured and output the carrier phase. The first of this class of receivers was trade-named the Trimble 4000S. This receiver required the data to be collected on an external (i.e., laptop) computer. The 4000S was the first of the generic C/A-code receivers that eventually were produced by a host of manufacturers. The first Trimble receivers were sold without processing software; however, the company soon retained the services of C. Goad who produced appropriate vector computation software which set the standard for future software developers.

Today's GPS receivers include all features of the early models and additionally have expanded capabilities. By far the major portion of receivers produced today are the C/A-code single frequency type. For precise geodetic work, however, dual frequency receivers are becoming the standard. Many survey receivers now have incorporated the codeless technology to track the second frequency, and other receivers use all three techniques (C/A-code, P-code, codeless) to track satellites on both broadcast frequencies. These advanced receivers provide the greatest accuracy and productivity although they are more expensive than the simpler C/A-code receivers.

Software developments

The development of GPS surveying software has largely paralleled the development of hardware. Most of the receivers that can be used for surveying are sold with a suite of personal computer (PC) programs that use the carrier phase data to compute the vectors between occupied points.

The NGS has been one of the primary organizations in the world in developing independent GPS processing software. As previously mentioned, C. Goad and B. Remondi pioneered the development of receiver independent software.

The NGS first produced processing software that used the Macrometer phase measurements and the precise ephemerides produced by the U.S. Naval Surface Warfare Center (NSWC). Other Macrometer users had to apply the processing software developed by the Macrometer manufacturer which required the use of specially formatted ephemerides produced (and sold) by them. The NGS software was also adapted for the TI-4100 format data and finally for other receivers that were subsequently used.

The original software developed by both the NGS and manufacturers computed individual vectors one at a time. These vectors were then combined in a network or geometric figure, and the coordinates of all points were determined using least squares adjustment programs.

The NGS and the Macrometer manufacturer eventually developed processing software that simultaneously determined all vectors observed during a given period of time (often called session). First, this software fixed the satellite positions in the same way as the vector by vector software. The second generation multibaseline software included the ability to determine corrections to the satellite orbits and is often called orbital relaxation software. This technique was pioneered by G. Beutler's group at the Bernese Astronomical Institute. Although today the majority of surveyors use the single vector computation software run in a "batch" computer mode, the orbit relaxation software is used for special projects requiring the highest accuracy (e.g., 0.01 ppm). Some GPS experts feel that the orbit relaxation software will be used in the future by land surveyors as well as geodesists to provide high accuracy surveys referenced to distant fixed tracking sites.

Ephemerides service

The first GPS surveys performed in late 1982 using Macrometers depended on orbital data derived from a private tracking network. Later, the broadcast ephemerides were used to supplement this private tracking data. The TI-4100 receiver obtained the ephemerides broadcast by the satellites so that processing programs could use this ephemerides to process vectors. The NSWC originally processed the military ephemerides, cf. Swift (1985), obtaining "precise" postprocessed ephemerides which were turned over to the NGS for limited distribution to the public.

Today, various organizations around the world provide satellite tracking data from points that are referenced to a global datum. The NGS, for example, runs the Cooperative International GPS Network (CIGNET). These tracking stations collect code range and phase data for both frequencies for all satellites. The data are sent to the NGS on a daily basis and are available to the public upon request. Theoretically, one could compute highly accurate orbits from this data set (using appropriate software). Precise ephemerides are now available within a few days from the U.S. Coast Guard Bulletin Board Service or can be directly purchased from the NGS.

2 Overview of GPS

2.1 Basic concept

The Global Positioning System is the responsibility of the Joint Program Office (JPO) located at the U.S. Air Force Systems Command's Space Division, Los Angeles Air Force Base (AFB). In 1973, the JPO was directed by the U.S. Department of Defense (DoD) to establish, develop, test, acquire, and deploy a spaceborne positioning system. The present Navigation System with Timing And Ranging (NAVSTAR) Global Positioning System (GPS) is the result of this initial directive.

The Global Positioning System was conceived as a ranging system from known positions of satellites in space to unknown positions on land, sea, in air and space. Effectively, the satellite signal is continually marked with its (own) transmission time so that when received the signal transit period can be measured with a synchronized receiver. Apart from point positioning, the determination of a vehicle's instantaneous position and velocity (i.e., navigation), and the precise coordination of time (i.e., time transfer) were original objectives of GPS. A definition given by Wooden (1985) reads:

"The Navstar Global Positioning System (GPS) is an all-weather, space-based navigation system under development by the Department of Defense (DoD) to satisfy the requirements for the military forces to accurately determine their position, velocity, and time in a common reference system, anywhere on or near the Earth on a continuous basis."

Since the DoD is the initiator of GPS, the primary goals were military ones. But the U.S. Congress, with guidance from the President, directed DoD to promote its civil use. This was greatly accelerated by employing the Macrometer for geodetic surveying. This instrument was in commercial use at the time the military was still testing navigation receivers so that the first productive application of GPS was to establish high-accuracy geodetic networks.

As previously stated, GPS uses pseudoranges derived from the broadcast satellite signal. The pseudorange is derived either from measuring the travel time of the (coded) signal and multiplying it by its velocity or by measuring the phase of the signal. In both cases, the clocks of the receiver and the satellite are employed. Since these clocks are never perfectly synchronized, instead of true ranges "pseudoranges" are obtained where the synchronization error (denoted as clock error) is taken into account, cf. Eq. (1.2). Consequently, each equation of this type comprises four unknowns: the desired three point coordinates contained in the true range, and the clock error. Thus, four satellites are necessary to solve for the four unknowns. Indeed, the GPS concept assumes that four or more satellites are in view at any location on earth 24 hours a day. The solution becomes more complicated when using the measured phase. This observable is ambiguous by an integer number of signal wavelengths so that the model for phase pseudoranges is augmented by an initial bias, also called integer ambiguity.

The all-weather global system managed by the JPO consists of three segments:

- The space segment consisting of satellites which broadcast signals.

- The control segment steering the whole system.

- The user segment including the many types of receivers.

2.2   Space segment

2.2.1   Constellation

With the full constellation, the space segment provides global coverage with four to eight simultaneously observable satellites above 15° elevation at any time of day. If the elevation mask is reduced to 10°, occasionally up to 10 satellites will be visible; and if the elevation mask is further reduced to 5°, occasionally 12 satellites will be visible. This is accomplished by satellites in nearly circular orbits with an altitude of about 20 200 km above the earth and a period of approximately 12 sidereal hours, cf. Perreault (1980), Rutscheidt and Roth (1982). The constellation and the number of satellites used have evolved from earlier plans for a 24-satellite and 3-orbital plane constellation, inclined 63° to the equator, cf. Mueller and Archinal (1981). Later, for budgetary reasons, the space segment was reduced to 18 satellites, with three satellites in each of six orbital planes. This scheme was eventually rejected, since it did not provide the desired 24-hour worldwide coverage. In about 1986, the number of satellites planned was increased to 21, again three each in six orbital planes, and three additional active spares, cf. Wells et al. (1987). The spare satellites were designated to replace malfunctioning "active" satellites, cf. Brunner (1984). According to the present policy, the constellation will consist of 24 operational satellites deployed in six planes with an inclination of 55° and with four satellites per plane. Furthermore, four active spare satellites for replenishment will be operational, cf. Graviss (1992).

2.2.2 Satellites

General remarks

The GPS satellites, essentially, provide a platform for radio transceivers, atomic clocks, computers, and various ancillary equipment used to operate the system. The electronic equipment of each satellite allows the user to measure a pseudorange R to the satellite, and each satellite broadcasts a message which allows the user to determine the spatial position ϱ^S of the satellite for arbitrary instants. Given these capabilities, users are able to determine their position ϱ_R on or above the earth by resection, cf. Fig. 1.1. The auxiliary equipment of each satellite, among others, consists of two $7\,m^2$ solar panels for power supply and a propulsion system for orbit adjustments and stability control, cf. Payne (1982).

The satellites have various systems of identification: launch sequence number, assigned vehicle pseudorandom noise (PRN) code, orbital position number, NASA catalogue number, and international designation. To avoid any confusion, primarily, and in agreement with the satellite navigation message, cf. Wells (1985), the PRN number will be used.

Satellite categories

There are five classes or types of GPS satellites. These are the Block I, Block II, Block IIA, Block IIR, and Block IIF satellites.

Eleven Block I satellites (weighing 845 kg) were launched by JPO in the period between 1978 to 1985 from Vandenberg AFB, California, with Atlas F launch vehicles. With the exception of one booster failure in 1981, cf. Jones (1989), all launches were successful. In April 1994, two of the original Block I satellites with launch dates in 1984 and 1985 remained in operation. This is remarkable considering the 4.5 year design life of Block I satellites, cf. Stein (1986). The remaining Block I satellites have been fully replaced by the satellite launch in March 1994. Thus, the redundant Block I satellites which are in a low power state will be boosted out of orbit and be left for scientific testing purposes as reported in CGSIC (1993b), page 21. For historical reasons, an overview of characteristic data of the Block I satellites is given in Table 2.1.

The Block II constellation is slightly different from the Block I constellation since the inclination of their orbital planes is 55° compared to the former 63° inclination. Apart from orbital inclination, there is an essential difference between Block I and Block II satellites related to U.S. national security. Block I satellite signals were fully available to civilian users, while some Block II satellite signals are restricted.

The Block II satellites were designated for the first operational constella-

Table 2.1. Status of Block I satellites in early 1994

Block I satellites						
Flight No.	PRN No.	Launch date	Available since	Loss of navigation	Reason of loss	Operational (months)
1	04	22 Feb 78	29 Mar 78	25 Jan 80	Clock	21.9
2	07	13 May 78	14 Jul 78	30 Aug 80	Clock	25.5
3	06	6 Oct 78	9 Nov 78	19 Apr 92	Clock	161.3
4	08	11 Dec 78	8 Jan 79	27 Oct 86	Clock	93.6
5	05	9 Feb 80	27 Feb 80	28 Nov 83	Wheels	45.0
6	09	26 Apr 80	16 May 80	10 Dec 90	Wheels	126.8
7	–	18 Dec 81	–	–	Booster	–
8	11	14 Jul 83	10 Aug 83	4 May 93	Power	116.8
9	13	13 Jun 84	19 Jul 84	25 Feb 94	Power	115.2
10	12	8 Sep 84	3 Oct 84			
11	03	9 Oct 85	30 Oct 85	27 Feb 94	Signal	99.9

tion (i.e., 21 active and 3 spare active satellites), cf. Jones (1989). The first Block II satellite, costing approximately $ 50 million and weighing more than 1 500 kg, was launched on February 14, 1989 from the Kennedy Space Center, Cape Canaveral AFB in Florida, using a Delta II Rocket, cf. Stein (1986). The mean mission duration of the Block II satellites is six years, and their design goal is 7.5 years. Individual satellites can easily remain operational as long as 10 years since their consumables will last this long, cf. Payne (1982).

The Block IIA satellites ("A" denotes advanced) are equipped with mutual communication capability. Some of them carry retroreflectors and can be tracked by Laser ranging. The first Block IIA satellite was launched on November 26, 1990. An overview of characteristic data of Block II and Block IIA satellites is given Table 2.2. The orbital position of the satellites is indicated by a letter for the orbital plane and a number for the position within the plane.

The GPS satellites which will replace the Block II's are the Block IIR's which have a design life of 10 years. The "R" denotes replenishment or replacement. These satellites are currently under development, with the first satellites planned for delivery by 1996, see Graviss (1992). The Block IIR's are expected to have on-board hydrogen masers. These atomic clocks are at least one order of magnitude more precise than the atomic clocks in the Block II satellites. The Block IIR satellites will also have improved facilities for communication and improved on-board orbit capability, since intersatellite tracking is provided which strongly improves the autonomy from ground

Table 2.2. Status of Block II/IIA satellites in early 1994

Block II satellites				
Flight No.	PRN No.	Launch date	Available since	Orbital position
12	14	14 Feb 89	14 Apr 89	E1
13	02	10 Jun 89	12 Jul 89	B3
14	16	17 Aug 89	13 Sep 89	E3
15	19	21 Oct 89	14 Nov 89	A4
16	17	11 Dec 89	11 Jan 90	D3
17	18	24 Jan 90	14 Feb 90	F3
18	20	25 Mar 90	19 Apr 90	B2
19	21	2 Aug 90	31 Aug 90	E2
20	15	1 Oct 90	20 Oct 90	D2

Block IIA satellites				
Flight No.	PRN No.	Launch date	Available since	Orbital position
21	23	26 Nov 90	10 Dec 90	E4
22	24	3 Jul 91	30 Aug 91	D1
23	25	23 Feb 92	24 Mar 92	A2
24	28	9 Apr 92	25 Apr 92	C2
25	26	7 Jul 92	23 Jul 92	F2
26	27	9 Sep 92	30 Sep 92	A3
27	32	22 Nov 92	11 Dec 92	F1
28	29	18 Dec 92	5 Jan 93	F4
29	22	2 Feb 93	4 Apr 93	B1
30	31	30 Mar 93	13 Apr 93	C3
31	07	13 May 93	12 Jun 93	C4
32	09	26 Jun 93	21 Jul 93	A1
33	05	30 Aug 93	28 Sep 93	B4
34	04	26 Oct 93	29 Nov 93	D4
35	06	3 Mar 94	28 Mar 94	C1

control. The Block IIR's weigh more than 2 000 kg but are only one-half of the cost of the Block II's, cf. Montgomery (1991). It is planned to orbit the Block IIR satellites using the Space Shuttle. Each Shuttle would be capable of transporting up to three satellites so that rapid replenishment of the constellation is possible; however, these plans may change as the space program develops.

The next generation satellites, the Block IIF satellites ("F" denotes follow on), will be launched in the period between 2001 and 2010. These satellites will have improved on-board capabilities such as inertial navigation systems.

Satellite signal

The actual carrier broadcast by the satellite is a spread spectrum signal that makes it less subject to intentional (or unintentional) jamming. The spread spectrum technique is commonly used today by such diverse equipment as hydrographic positioning ranging systems and wireless Local Area Network (LAN) systems.

The key to the system's accuracy is the fact that all signal components are precisely controlled by atomic clocks. The Block II satellites have four on-board time standards, two rubidium and two cesium clocks. The long-term frequency stability of these clocks reaches a few parts in 10^{-13} and 10^{-14} over one day. The hydrogen masers planned for the Block IIR's have a stability of 10^{-14} to 10^{-15} over one day, cf. Scherrer (1985). These highly accurate frequency standards being the heart of GPS satellites produce the fundamental L-band frequency of 10.23 MHz. Coherently derived from this fundamental frequency are two signals, the $L1$ and the $L2$ carrier waves generated by multiplying the fundamental frequency by 154 and 120 respectively yielding

$$L1 = 1575.42 \text{ MHz}$$

$$L2 = 1227.60 \text{ MHz} .$$

These dual frequencies are essential for eliminating the major source of error, i.e., the ionospheric refraction, cf. Sect. 6.3.2.

The pseudoranges that are derived from measured travel times of the signal from each satellite to the receiver use two pseudorandom noise (PRN) codes that are modulated (superimposed) onto the two base carriers.

The first code is the C/A-code (Coarse/Acquisition-code), also designated as the Standard Positioning Service (SPS), which is available for civilian use. The C/A-code with an effective wavelength of approximately 300 m is modulated only upon $L1$ and is purposely omitted from $L2$. This omission allows the JPO to control the information broadcast by the satellite, and, thus, denies full system accuracy to nonmilitary users.

The second code is the P-code (Precision-code), also designated as the Precise Positioning Service (PPS), which has been reserved for use by the U.S. military and other authorized users. The P-code with an effective wavelength of approximately 30 m is modulated on both carriers $L1$ and $L2$. Unlimited access to the P-code was permitted until the system was declared fully operational.

In addition to the PRN codes, a data message is modulated onto the carriers comprising satellite ephemerides, ionospheric modeling coefficients, status information, system time and satellite clock bias, and drift information. A detailed signal description is given in Sect. 5.1.

2.2.3   Operational capabilities

There are two operational capabilities: (1) Initial Operational Capability (IOC) and (2) Military Full Operational Capability (FOC).

IOC was attained in July 1993 when 24 GPS satellites (Block I/II/IIA) were operating and were available for navigation. Officially, IOC was declared by the DoD on December 8, 1993, see ION Newsletter (1993), 3(4), page 10 and GPS World (1994), 5(1), page 8 and page 10.

FOC will be achieved when 24 operational (Block II/IIA) satellites are operating in their assigned orbits and the constellation has been tested for operational military performance. Even though 24 Block II and Block IIA satellites are available since March 1994, FOC will not be declared until the tests on the military performance have been completed. According to the 1992 Federal Radionavigation Plan, FOC is planned to be declared by the DoD in 1995, see CGSIC (1993a), page 10.

After the March 1994 launch, all subsequent launches are to replace malfunctioning satellites. This fact is reflected in the future moderate launch schedule: two more launches in 1994 after the March date, two launches in 1995, and four launches (Block IIR) in 1996, see Graviss (1992). Problems could also arise when replacing malfunctioning satellites because of the dependence on a launch window. The length of this window varies for the different orbital planes. For the most unfavourable situation, this window is restricted to some 90 days.

2.2.4   Denial of accuracy and access

There are basically two methods for denying civilian users full use of the system. The first is Selective Availability (SA) and the second method is Anti-spoofing (A-S).

Selective availability
Originally, the accuracy expected from C/A-code pseudorange positioning was in the range of some 400 m. Field tests achieved a surprising level of navigation accuracy of 15–40 m for positioning and a fraction of a meter per second for velocity. The goal of SA is to degrade this navigation accuracy by dithering the satellite clock (δ-process) and manipulating the ephemerides

(ε-process). The SA has only been implemented in Block II satellites and has been in force since March 25, 1990 at various levels of accuracy denial.

Following the specifications of the DoD, the accuracy is degraded to 100 m for horizontal position and to 156 m for height. These specifications also imply a velocity error of 0.3 meter per second and an error in time of 340 ns. All numbers are given at the 95% probability level, cf. Olsen (1992). At the 99.99% probability level, the predictable accuracy decreases to 300 m for horizontal position and to 500 m for height, cf. Department of Defense (1993).

The δ-process is achieved by introducing varying errors into the fundamental frequency of the satellite clock. The satellite clock bias has a direct impact on the pseudorange which is derived from a comparison of the satellite clock and the receiver clock. Since the fundamental frequency is dithered, code and carrier pseudoranges are affected in the same way. In Fig. 2.1, the different behavior of satellite clocks with and without SA is shown. With activated SA, there are variations of the pseudoranges with amplitudes of some 50 m and with periods of some minutes. When pseudoranges are differenced between two receivers, the dithering effect is largely eliminated, so that this navigation mode proposed for example by the U.S. Coast Guard (USCG) will remain unaffected.

The ε-process is the truncation of the orbital information in the transmitted navigation message so that the coordinates of the satellites cannot accurately be computed. The error in satellite position roughly translates to a like position error of the receiver. For baselines, the relative satellite position errors are equal to the relative baseline errors. The orbital errors cause pseudorange errors. In Fig. 2.2, the behavior of the radial orbit error with and without SA is shown. In the case of SA, there are variations of the pseudoranges with amplitudes between 50 m and 150 m and with periods of some hours.

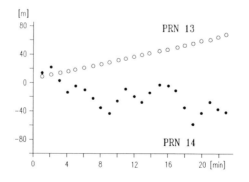

Fig. 2.1. Satellite clock behavior of PRN 13 (without SA) and of PRN 14 (with SA) on day 177 of 1992 after Breuer et al. (1993)

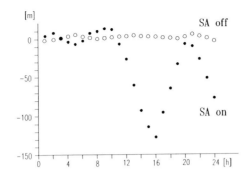

Fig. 2.2. Radial orbit error of PRN 21 on day 177 of 1992 with SA on and on day 184 of 1992 with SA off after Breuer et al. (1993)

Anti-spoofing
The design of GPS includes the ability to essentially "turn off" the P-code or invoke an encrypted code as a means of denying access to the P-code to all but authorized users. The rationale for doing this is to keep adversaries from sending out false signals with the GPS signature to create confusion and cause users to misposition themselves.

A-S is accomplished by the modulo 2 sum of the P-code and an encrypting W-code. The resulting code is denoted as Y-code. Thus, when A-S is active, the P-code on the $L1$ and the $L2$ carrier is replaced by the unknown Y-code. Note that A-S is either on or off. A variable influence of A-S (as is the case with SA) cannot occur.

For testing purposes, A-S was first turned on over the weekend of August 1, 1992 and later for several times. It was expected that A-S would be switched on permanently when FOC has been attained. However, A-S was permanently implemented on January 31, 1994 and affects many of the high accuracy survey uses of GPS. In accordance with the DoD policy, no advance announcement of the implementation date was made, cf. GPS World 1994, 5(3), page 21.

2.3 Control segment

This segment comprises the Operational Control System (OCS) which consists of a master control station, worldwide monitor stations, and ground control stations. The main operational tasks of the control segment are: tracking of the satellites for the orbit and clock determination and prediction modeling, time synchronization of the satellites, and upload of the data message to the satellites. It is also the responsibility of the OCS to steer the level of SA. In principle, SA must always be considered turned on but its effect can be reduced to zero, see Bagley and Lamons (1992). The OCS performs many nonoperational activities, such as procurement and launch, that will not be addressed here.

2.3.1 Master control station

The location of the master control station was formerly at Vandenberg AFB, California, but has been moved to the Consolidated Space Operations Center (CSOC) at Falcon AFB, Colorado Springs, Colorado. CSOC collects the tracking data from the monitor stations and calculates the satellite orbit and clock parameters using a Kalman estimator. These results are then passed to one of the three ground control stations for eventual upload to the satellites. The satellite control and system operation is also the responsibility of the master control station.

2.3.2 Monitor stations

There are five monitor stations located at: Hawaii, Colorado Springs, Ascension Island in the South Atlantic Ocean, Diego Garcia in the Indian Ocean, and Kwajalein in the North Pacific Ocean, cf. Gouldman et al. (1989). Each of these stations is equipped with a precise cesium time standard and receivers which continuously measure pseudoranges to all satellites in view. Pseudoranges are tracked every 1.5 seconds and, using the ionospheric and meteorological data, they are smoothed to produce 15-minute interval data which are transmitted to the master control station.

The tracking network described above is the official network for determining the broadcast ephemerides as well as modeling the satellite clocks. For the precise ephemerides, the data of five additional (DMA) sites are used. Other private tracking networks do exist, however. These private networks generally determine the ephemerides of the satellites after the fact and have no part in managing the system. One such private tracking network has been operated by the manufacturer of the Macrometer since 1983. Another more globally oriented tracking network is the Cooperative International GPS Network (CIGNET). This network is being operated by the NGS with tracking stations located at VLBI sites. More details on this network are provided in Sect. 4.4.1.

2.3.3 Ground control stations

These stations collocated with the monitor stations at Ascension, Diego Garcia, and Kwajalein, cf. Bowen et al. (1986), are the communication links to the satellites and mainly consist of the ground antennas. The satellite ephemerides and clock information, calculated at the master control station and received via communication links, are uploaded to each GPS satellite via S-band radio links, cf. Rutscheidt and Roth (1982). Formerly, uploading to each satellite was performed every eight hours, cf. Stein (1986), at present the rate has been reduced to once (or twice) per day, cf. Remondi (1991b). If a ground station becomes disabled, prestored navigation messages are available in each satellite to support a prediction span so that the positioning accuracy degrades only gradually.

2.4 User segment

2.4.1 User categories

Military user
Strictly speaking, the term "user segment" is related to the DoD concept of GPS as an adjunct to the national defense program. Even during the early days of the system, it was planned to incorporate a GPS receiver into virtually every major defense system. It was envisioned that every aircraft, ship, land vehicle, and even groups of infantry would have an appropriate GPS receiver to coordinate their military activities. In fact, many GPS receivers were used as planned during the 1991 Gulf War under combat conditions. In this war, SA which had been previously invoked was turned off so that troops could use more readily available civilian receivers. Hand-held C/A-code receivers were particularly useful in navigating the desert.

There are various other military uses that have recently been proposed. One manufacturer offers a receiver that can be connected to four antennas. When the antennas are placed in a fixed array (e.g., corners of a square), the three rotation angles of the array can be determined in addition to its position. For example, placing antennas on the bow, stern, and port and starboard points of a ship would result in the determination of pitch, roll, yaw, and position of the vessel.

More unconventional uses of the system include measuring the position of lower altitude satellites. On-board GPS receivers will permit satellites to be accurately positioned with much less effort than the present tracking techniques. For example, the utility of imaging satellites such as the French SPOT satellite would be greatly improved by an on-board GPS receiver to determine the precise position of each image.

Civilian user
The civilian use of GPS occurred several years ahead of schedule in a manner

not envisioned by the system's planners. The primary focus in the first few years of the system's development was on navigation receivers. As previously described in Chap. 1, the SERIES technique at JPL and the development of the Macrometer by C. Counselman started the GPS surveying revolution. The primary concept of using an interferometric rather than Doppler solution model meant that GPS could be used for not only long line geodetic measurements but also for the most exacting short line land survey measurements.

Today, GPS receivers are routinely being used to conduct all types of land and geodetic control surveys, and to precisely position photo-aircraft to reduce the amount of ground control needed for mapping.

The nonsurveyor civilian uses of GPS will significantly outnumber the survey uses of the system. One of the major uses of GPS will be for fleet management and control. Several cities are equipping emergency vehicles with receivers and computers with screens that display the cities' road system. The location of each emergency vehicle can be sent to a dispatcher by radio link so that track can be kept of the resources and vehicles are rerouted when necessary. Similar systems are planned to track trains and freight hauling vehicles. Naturally, all aircraft and vessels will be equipped with GPS in the near future.

GPS is also being used by hikers and boaters to determine their locations. Some manufacturers are presently offering a combined system of GPS and computer graphics for use in automobiles at the cost of a good high fidelity music system.

2.4.2   Receiver types

The uses of GPS described in the previous section are just a sample of the applications of this system. The diversity of the uses is matched by the type of receivers available today. This section will give an overview of the equipment marketed today; however, more details will be provided in Sect. 5.2. Based on the type of observables (i.e., code pseudoranges or carrier phases) and on the availability of codes (i.e., C/A-code, P-code, or Y-code), one can classify GPS receivers into four groups: (1) C/A-code pseudorange, (2) C/A-code carrier phase, (3) P-code carrier phase, and (4) Y-code carrier phase measuring instruments.

C/A-code pseudorange receivers
With this type of receiver only code pseudoranges using the C/A-code are measured. The receiver is usually a hand-held device powered by flashlight batteries. Typical devices have from one to six independent receiver channels

and output the three-dimensional position either in longitude, latitude, and height or in some map projection system (e.g., UTM coordinates and height). Receivers with four or more channels are preferred for applications where the receiver is in motion since simultaneous satellite ranges can be measured to produce more accurate positions. On the other hand, a single channel receiver is adequate for applications where the receiver is at a fixed location and the range measurements can be sequentially determined. The basic multichannel C/A-code pseudorange receiver is the type of receiver that is mostly used by hikers, boaters, and eventually in automobiles.

C/A-code carrier receivers
With this type of receiver only code ranges and carrier phases from the $L1$ carrier can be obtained because the C/A-code is not modulated on $L2$. This means that no dual frequency data are available.

Most of the receivers for surveying in the early stage of GPS used the C/A-code to acquire and lock on to the $L1$ carrier. Most instruments have a minimum of four independent receiver channels and some of the more recent designs have 12 channels. These receivers perform all the functions of the previously described models and, in addition, store the time-tagged code range and carrier phase in some type of memory. Early models used laptop computers and magnetic tapes to store the measured data. Later models store measurement data in memory chips.

This type of receiver has been augmented to measure the phases of the $L2$ carrier by the use of some codeless technique. The drawback is that the signal-to-noise ratio (SNR) of these measurements is considerably lower than the C/A-code measurements on $L1$. Normally, the $L2$ phase is used in combination with the $L1$ measurement to reduce the ionospheric effect on the signal and, thus, provide a more accurate vector determination (especially for long lines).

These receivers can be used for all types of precise surveys including static, kinematic, and pseudokinematic methods.

P-code receivers
This type of receiver uses the P-code and, thus, enables lock on to the $L1$ and $L2$ carrier. The P-code data on the carriers are derived by correlating the signals with a replica of the P-code. To do this, the structure of the code must be known. The cross correlation is performed by matching the received satellite signal with the receiver generated code replica. No carrier phase measurement can be performed before the code components of the received satellite signal are removed, see Ashjaee (1993).

One of the first receivers for surveying, point positioning, and navigation was the P-code receiver TI-4100 completed in 1984. This receiver was developed more from a military perspective than a civilian one and only military-related development could have attempted this. Manufacturers of civilian receivers first were able to justify P-code work around 1989–1990. In the fall of 1991, the U.S. Federal Geodetic Control Committee (FGCC) tested another P-code receiver which was the first receiver to be tested since the earlier TI-4100 FGCC tests. This test demonstrated the two main advantages of the P-code receiver. The first is its capability to measure long (100 km) lines to an accuracy of a few centimeters. The second advantage is that P-code instruments can measure moderate length lines (20 km) to an accuracy of a few centimeters with as little as ten minutes of data using a technique known as wide laning which is based on a linear combination of the measured phases of $L1$ and $L2$.

With A-S activated, the known P-code is replaced by the unknown Y-code and traditional P-code correlation technique can no longer be applied. However, this type of receiver can operate in a codeless or quasi-codeless mode, see Melbourne et al. (1993), providing carrier phase data and code pseudoranges for the $L2$ frequency without knowledge of the Y-code. The $L2$ tracking is accomplished using four techniques which differ in their performance characteristics: signal squaring, cross correlation, code correlation followed by squaring, and the Z-tracking technique. More details on these techniques can be found in Sect. 5.2.

Y-code receivers
This type of receiver provides access to the P-code with A-S invoked. Thus, the code ranges and phases can be derived from $L1$ and $L2$ signals by the P-code correlation technique. The access to the P-code is achieved by installing Auxiliary Output Chips (AOC) in each receiver channel. These chips allow the decryption of the Y-code into the P-code and also correct the degradation imposed by SA. However, only users authorized by the DoD have access to the AOC.

2.4.3 Information services

To provide GPS information and data to the civilian community of users, several governmental and private information services have been established.

In the U.S., the GPS Information Center (GPSIC) is mainly consulted. This service is part of the Civil GPS Service (CGS) and is run by the U.S. Coast Guard. The current service includes operation of a computer Bulletin Board Servive (BBS) and a telephone information service manned by GPS specialists. The BBS is a 24-hour service that contains constellation status report, scheduled outages, an almanac suitable for making GPS coverage and satellite visibility predictions, and general information about GPS including various papers and meetings. Inside the U.S. call (703) 313- to enter the service and dial the extension 5900 for live information, the extension 5907 for GPS status voice recording, and the extension 5910 for modem access to the BBS. The communication parameters for the BBS are: 8 data bits, 1 stop bit, no parity, up to 2400 baud. More details on the GPSIC can be found in, e.g., Brandt (1992).

Outside the U.S., further GPS information sources are available. The actual communication parameters for the BBS as well as the current phone numbers are published regularly for example in the monthly magazine "GPS World".

3 Reference systems

3.1 Introduction

Consider the basic observation equation which relates the range ϱ with the instantaneous position vector $\underline{\varrho}^S$ of a satellite and the position vector $\underline{\varrho}_R$ of the observing site:

$$\varrho = \|\underline{\varrho}^S - \underline{\varrho}_R\| . \tag{3.1}$$

In Eq. (3.1) both vectors must be expressed in a uniform coordinate system. The definition of a three-dimensional Cartesian system requires a convention for the orientation of the axes and for the position of the origin.

For global applications such as satellite geodesy, equatorial coordinate systems are appropriate. According to Fig. 3.1, a space-fixed or inertial system $\underline{X}_i^0$ and an earth-fixed or terrestrial system $\underline{X}_i$ must be distinguished where $i = 1, 2, 3$. The earth's rotational vector $\underline{\omega}_E$ serves as $\underline{X}_3$-axis in both cases. The $\underline{X}_1^0$-axis for the space-fixed system points towards the vernal equinox and is, thus, the intersection line between the equatorial and the ecliptic plane. The $\underline{X}_1$-axis of the earth-fixed system is defined by the intersection line of the equatorial plane with the plane represented by the Greenwich meridian. The angle Θ_0 between the two systems is called Greenwich sidereal time. The $\underline{X}_2$-axis being orthogonal to both the $\underline{X}_1$-axis and the $\underline{X}_3$-axis completes a right-handed coordinate frame.

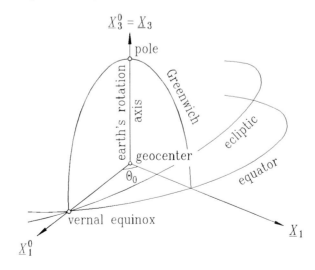

Fig. 3.1. Equatorial coordinate systems

A coordinate system whose origin is located at the barycenter is at rest with respect to the solar system and, thus, conforms to Newtonian mechanics. In a geocentric system, however, accelerations are present because the earth is orbiting the sun. Thus, in such a system the laws of general relativity must be taken into account. But, since the main relativistic effect is caused by the gravity field of the earth itself, the geocentric system is better suited for the description of the motion of a satellite close to the earth. Note that the axes of a geocentric coordinate system remain parallel because the motion of the earth around the sun is described by revolution without rotation.

The earth's rotational vector denoted by $\underline{\omega}_E$ oscillates due to several reasons. The basic differential equations describing the oscillations follow from classical mechanics and are given by

$$\underline{M} = \frac{d\underline{N}}{dt} \tag{3.2}$$

$$\underline{M} = \frac{\partial \underline{N}}{\partial t} + \underline{\omega}_E \times \underline{N} \tag{3.3}$$

where $\underline{M}$ denotes a torque vector, $\underline{N}$ is the angular momentum vector of the earth, and t indicates time, cf. Moritz and Mueller (1988), Eqs. (2-54) and (2-59). The symbol "$\times$" indicates a vector product. The torque $\underline{M}$ originates mainly from the gravitational forces of sun and moon. Therefore, it is closely related to the tidal potential. Equation (3.2) is expressed in a (quasi-) inertial system such as $\underline{X}_i^0$ and Eq. (3.3) holds for the rotating system $\underline{X}_i$. The partial derivative expresses the temporal change of $\underline{N}$ with respect to the earth-fixed system, and the vector product considers the rotation of this system with respect to the inertial system. The earth's rotational vector $\underline{\omega}_E$ is related to the angular momentum vector $\underline{N}$ by the inertia tensor $\underline{C}$ as

$$\underline{N} = \underline{C}\,\underline{\omega}_E \,. \tag{3.4}$$

Introducing for the earth's rotational vector $\underline{\omega}_E$ its unit vector $\underline{\omega}$ and its norm $\omega_E = ||\underline{\omega}_E||$, the relation

$$\underline{\omega}_E = \omega_E\,\underline{\omega} \tag{3.5}$$

can be formed.

The differential equations (3.2) and (3.3) can be separated into two parts. The oscillations of $\underline{\omega}$ are responsible for the variations of the $\underline{X}_3$-axis and are considered in the subsequent section. The oscillations of the norm ω_E cause variations in the speed of rotation which are treated in the section on time systems.

Considering only the homogeneous part (i.e., $\underline{M} = \underline{0}$) of Eqs. (3.2) and (3.3) leads to free oscillations. The inhomogeneous solution gives the forced oscillation. In both cases, the oscillations can be related to the inertial or to the terrestrial system. A further criterion for the solution concerns the inertia tensor. For a rigid earth and neglecting internal mass shifts, this tensor is constant; this is not the case for a deformable earth.

3.2 Coordinate systems

3.2.1 Definitions

Oscillations of axes
The oscillation of $\underline{\omega}$ with respect to the inertial space is called nutation. For the sake of convenience, the effect is partitioned into the secular precession and the periodic nutation. The oscillation with respect to the terrestrial system is named polar motion. A simplified representation of polar motion is given in Fig. 3.2. The image of a mean position of $\underline{\omega}$ is denoted by P in this polar plot of the earth. The free oscillation results in a motion of the rotational axis along a circular cone, with its mean position as axis, and an aperture angle of about $0.''4$. On the earth, this motion is represented by a 6 m radius circle around P. The image of an instantaneous position of the free oscillating earth's rotational axis is denoted by R_0. The period of the free motion amounts to about 430 days and is known as the Chandler period. The forced motion can also be described by a cone. In Fig. 3.2, this cone is mapped by the circle around the free position R_0. The radius of this circle is related to the tidal deformation and amounts to approximately 0.5 m. The nearly diurnal period of the forced motion corresponds to the tesseral part of the tidal potential of second degree since the zonal and sectorial components have no influence.

The respective motions of the angular momentum axis, which is within $0.''001$ of the rotational axis, are very similar. The free motion of the angular momentum axis deserves special attention because the forced motion can be removed by modeling the tidal attractions. The free polar motion is long-periodic and the free position in space is fixed since for $\underline{M} = \underline{0}$ the integration of Eq. (3.2) yields $\underline{N} = $ const. By the way, this result implies the law of conservation of angular momentum as long as no external forces are applied. Because of the above mentioned properties, the angular momentum axis is appropriate to serve as a reference axis and the scientific community has named its free position in space Celestial Ephemeris Pole (CEP). A candidate for serving as reference axis in the terrestrial system is the mean

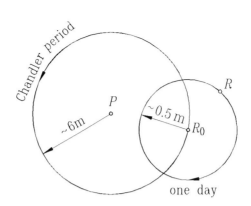

Fig. 3.2. Polar motion of the earth's rotational axis

position of the rotational axis denoted by P, cf. Fig. 3.2. This position is called Conventional International Origin (CIO). For historical reasons, the CIO represents the mean position of $\underline{\omega}$ during the period 1900 until 1905.

Conventional Inertial System
By convention, the $\underline{X}_3^0$-axis is identical to the position of the angular momentum axis at a standard epoch denoted by J2000.0, cf. Sect. 3.3. The $\underline{X}_1^0$-axis points to the associated vernal equinox. This equinox is realized, for example, kinematically by a set of fundamental stars, cf. Fricke et al. (1988). Since this system is defined conventionally and the practical realization does not necessarily coincide with the theoretical system, it is called (conventional) Inertial Reference Frame (IRF). Sometimes the term "quasi-inertial" is used to point out that a geocentric system is not rigorously inertial because of the accelerated motion of the earth around the sun.

Conventional Terrestrial System
Again by convention, the $\underline{X}_3$-axis is identical to the mean position of the earth's rotational axis as defined by the CIO. The $\underline{X}_1$-axis is associated with the mean Greenwich meridian. The realization of this system is named (conventional) Terrestrial Reference Frame (TRF) and is defined by a set of terrestrial control stations serving as reference points. Most of the reference stations are equipped with Satellite Laser Ranging (SLR) or Very Long Baseline Interferometry (VLBI) facilities.

One example for such a terrestrial reference frame is that established by the International Earth Rotation Service (IERS), cf. Boucher and Altamimi (1989). This frame is called ITRF where the first letter indicates the IERS-origin. Note that ITRF is yearly updated, therefore, the acronym is

Table 3.1. Parameters of the WGS-84 ellipsoid

Parameter and Value	Description
$a \quad = 6\,378\,137$ m	Semimajor axis of the ellipsoid
$\bar{C}_{2,0} = -484.166\,85 \cdot 10^{-6}$	Zonal coefficient of second degree
$\omega_E \;= 7\,292\,115 \cdot 10^{-11}$ rad s^{-1}	Angular velocity of the earth
$\mu \quad = 3\,986\,005 \cdot 10^{8}$ m^3 s^{-2}	Earth's gravitational constant

supplemented by the last two digits of the actual year.

Since 1987, GPS has used the World Geodetic System WGS-84 as a reference, cf. Decker (1986). Associated with WGS-84 is a geocentric equipotential ellipsoid of revolution which is defined by the four parameters listed in Table 3.1. Using the theory of the equipotential ellipsoid, numerical values for other parameters such as the geometric flattening ($f = 1/298.2572236$) or the semiminor axis ($b = 6\,356\,752.314$ m) can be derived. Note that the parameter values have been adopted from the Geodetic Reference System 1980 (GRS-80) ellipsoid. However, in GRS-80 the zonal coefficient $J_2 = -\sqrt{5}\,\bar{C}_{2,0}$ was defined by the numerical value $J_2 = 108\,263 \cdot 10^{-8}$. Note that originally the zonal coefficient was defined with six digits, while now it is defined by eight digits. This causes, among others, the slight difference in flattening $\Delta f = f_{\mathrm{GRS}} - f_{\mathrm{WGS}} = 16 \cdot 10^{-12}$.

A vector $\underline{X}$ in the terrestrial system can be represented by Cartesian coordinates X, Y, Z as well as by ellipsoidal coordinates φ, λ, h, cf. Fig. 3.3. The rectangular coordinates are often called Earth-Centered-Earth-Fixed

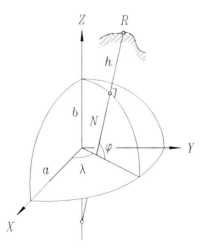

Fig. 3.3. Cartesian and ellipsoidal coordinates

(ECEF) coordinates. The relation between the two sets of coordinates is given by, cf. for example Heiskanen and Moritz (1967), p. 182,

$$
\underline{X} = \begin{bmatrix} X \\ Y \\ Z \end{bmatrix} = \begin{bmatrix} (N+h)\cos\varphi\cos\lambda \\ (N+h)\cos\varphi\sin\lambda \\ \left(\dfrac{b^2}{a^2}N+h\right)\sin\varphi \end{bmatrix} \tag{3.6}
$$

where φ, λ, h are the ellipsoidal latitude, longitude, height, N is the radius of curvature in prime vertical, and a, b are the semimajor and semiminor axis of the ellipsoid. More details on the transformation of Cartesian and ellipsoidal (i.e., geodetic) coordinates are provided in Sect. 10.2.1.

3.2.2 Transformations

General remarks
The transformation between the Conventional Inertial System (CIS) and the Conventional Terrestrial System (CTS) is performed by means of rotations. For an arbitrary vector $\underline{x}$, the transformation is given by

$$
\underline{x}_{\text{CTS}} = \underline{R}^M \underline{R}^S \underline{R}^N \underline{R}^P \underline{x}_{\text{CIS}} \tag{3.7}
$$

where

$$
\begin{array}{ll}
\underline{R}^M & \text{...} \quad \text{rotation matrix for polar motion} \\
\underline{R}^S & \text{...} \quad \text{rotation matrix for sidereal time} \\
\underline{R}^N & \text{...} \quad \text{rotation matrix for nutation} \\
\underline{R}^P & \text{...} \quad \text{rotation matrix for precession.}
\end{array}
$$

The CIS, defined at the standard epoch J2000.0, is transformed into the instantaneous or true system at observation epoch by applying the corrections due to precession and nutation. The $\underline{X}_3^0$-axis of the true CIS represents the free position of the angular momentum axis and, thus, points to the CEP. Rotating this system about the $\underline{X}_3^0$-axis and through the sidereal time by the matrix $\underline{R}^S$ does not change the position of the CEP. Finally, the CEP is rotated into the CIO by $\underline{R}^M$ which completes the transformation.

The rotation matrices in Eq. (3.7) are composed of the elementary matrices $\underline{R}_i\{\alpha\}$ describing a positive rotation of the coordinate system about the $\underline{X}_i$-axis and through the angle α. As it may be verified from any textbook on vector analysis, the rotation matrices are given by

$$\underline{R}_1\{\alpha\} = \begin{bmatrix} 1 & 0 & 0 \\ 0 & \cos\alpha & \sin\alpha \\ 0 & -\sin\alpha & \cos\alpha \end{bmatrix}$$

$$\underline{R}_2\{\alpha\} = \begin{bmatrix} \cos\alpha & 0 & -\sin\alpha \\ 0 & 1 & 0 \\ \sin\alpha & 0 & \cos\alpha \end{bmatrix} \tag{3.8}$$

$$\underline{R}_3\{\alpha\} = \begin{bmatrix} \cos\alpha & \sin\alpha & 0 \\ -\sin\alpha & \cos\alpha & 0 \\ 0 & 0 & 1 \end{bmatrix}.$$

Note that these matrices are consistent with right-handed coordinate systems. The rotation angle α has a positive sign for clockwise rotation as viewed from the origin to the positive $\underline{X}_i$-axis.

Precession
A graphic representation of precession is given in Fig. 3.4. The position of the mean vernal equinox at the standard epoch t_0 is denoted by E_0 and the position at the observation epoch t is denoted by E. The precession matrix $\underline{R}^P$ is composed of three successive rotation matrices

$$\underline{R}^P = \underline{R}_3\{-z\}\,\underline{R}_2\{\vartheta\}\,\underline{R}_3\{-\zeta\} \tag{3.9}$$

where z, ϑ, ζ are the precession parameters. Explicitly, performing the mul-

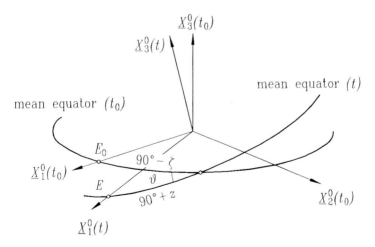

Fig. 3.4. Precession

tiplication,

$$\underline{R}^{P} = \begin{bmatrix} \cos z \cos \vartheta \cos \zeta & -\cos z \cos \vartheta \sin \zeta & -\cos z \sin \vartheta \\ -\sin z \sin \zeta & -\sin z \cos \zeta & \\ \sin z \cos \vartheta \cos \zeta & -\sin z \cos \vartheta \sin \zeta & -\sin z \sin \vartheta \\ +\cos z \sin \zeta & +\cos z \cos \zeta & \\ \sin \vartheta \cos \zeta & -\sin \vartheta \sin \zeta & \cos \vartheta \end{bmatrix} \quad (3.10)$$

is obtained. The precession parameters are computed from the time series, cf. Nautical Almanac Office (1983), p. S19:

$$\zeta = 2306.\!''2181\,T + 0.\!''30188\,T^2 + 0.\!''017998\,T^3$$

$$z = 2306.\!''2181\,T + 1.\!''09468\,T^2 + 0.\!''018203\,T^3 \quad (3.11)$$

$$\vartheta = 2004.\!''3109\,T - 0.\!''42665\,T^2 - 0.\!''041833\,T^3\,.$$

The parameter T represents the timespan expressed in Julian centuries of 36 525 mean solar days between the standard epoch J2000.0 and the epoch of observation. To give a numerical example consider an observation epoch J1990.5 which corresponds to $T = -0.095$. With T and Eq. (3.11), the numerical values $\zeta = -219.\!''0880$, $z = -219.\!''0809$, and $\vartheta = -190.\!''4134$ are obtained. The substitution of these values into Eq. (3.10) gives the following numerical precession matrix:

$$\underline{R}^{P} = \begin{bmatrix} 0.999997318 & 0.002124301 & 0.000923150 \\ -0.002124301 & 0.999997744 & -0.000000981 \\ -0.000923150 & -0.000000981 & 0.999999574 \end{bmatrix}\,.$$

Nutation

A graphic representation of nutation is given in Fig. 3.5. The mean vernal equinox at the observation epoch is denoted by E and the true equinox by

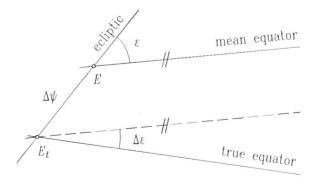

Fig. 3.5. Nutation

E_t. The nutation matrix $\underline{R}^N$ is composed of three successive rotation matrices where both the nutation in longitude $\Delta\psi$ and the nutation in obliquity $\Delta\varepsilon$ can be treated as differential quantities:

$$\underline{R}^N = \underline{R}_1\{-(\varepsilon + \Delta\varepsilon)\}\, \underline{R}_3\{-\Delta\psi\}\, \underline{R}_1\{\varepsilon\}\,. \tag{3.12}$$

Explicitly,

$$\underline{R}^N = \begin{bmatrix} 1 & -\Delta\psi\cos\varepsilon & -\Delta\psi\sin\varepsilon \\ \Delta\psi\cos\varepsilon & 1 & -\Delta\varepsilon \\ \Delta\psi\sin\varepsilon & \Delta\varepsilon & 1 \end{bmatrix} \tag{3.13}$$

is obtained. The mean obliquity of the ecliptic ε has been determined, cf. Nautical Almanac Office (1983), p. S21, as

$$\varepsilon = 23°26'21.''448 - 46.''8150\,T - 0.''00059\,T^2 + 0.''001813\,T^3 \tag{3.14}$$

where T is the same time factor as in Eq. (3.11). The nutation parameters $\Delta\psi$ and $\Delta\varepsilon$ are computed from the harmonic series:

$$\Delta\psi = \sum_{i=1}^{106} a_i \sin\left(\sum_{j=1}^{5} e_j\, E_j\right) = -17.''2\,\sin\Omega_m + \ldots$$
$$\Delta\varepsilon = \sum_{i=1}^{64} b_i \cos\left(\sum_{j=1}^{5} e_j\, E_j\right) = 9.''2\,\cos\Omega_m + \ldots \tag{3.15}$$

The amplitudes a_i, b_i as well as the integer coefficients e_j are tabulated for example in Nautical Almanac Office (1983), pp. S23–S26. The five fundamental arguments E_j describe mean motions in the sun-earth-moon system. The mean longitude Ω_m of moon's ascending node is one of the arguments. The moon's node retrogrades with a period of about 18.6 years and this period appears in the principal terms of the nutation series.

Sidereal time
The rotation matrix for sidereal time $\underline{R}^S$ is

$$\underline{R}^S = \underline{R}_3\{\Theta_0\}\,. \tag{3.16}$$

The computation of the apparent Greenwich sidereal time Θ_0 is shown in the section on time systems, cf. Sect. 3.3.2.

The WGS-84 system is defined by a uniform angular velocity ω_E, cf. Table 3.1. Consequently, the mean sidereal time must be used instead of the apparent sidereal time in the case of GPS for the rotation angle in Eq. (3.16).

Polar motion
The previous computations yield the instantaneous CEP. The CEP must

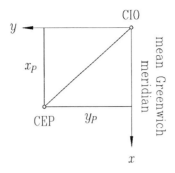

Fig. 3.6. Pole coordinates

still be rotated into the CIO. This is achieved by means of the pole coordinates x_P, y_P which define the position of the CEP with respect to the
CIO, cf. Fig. 3.6. The pole coordinates are determined by the IERS and
are available upon request, cf. Feissel and McCarthy (1994). The rotation
matrix for polar motion $\underline{R}^M$ is given by

$$\underline{R}^M = \underline{R}_2\{-x_P\}\,\underline{R}_1\{-y_P\} = \begin{bmatrix} 1 & 0 & x_P \\ 0 & 1 & -y_P \\ -x_P & y_P & 1 \end{bmatrix}. \tag{3.17}$$

The rotation matrices $\underline{R}^S$ and $\underline{R}^M$ are often combined to a single matrix $\underline{R}^R$
for earth rotation:

$$\underline{R}^R = \underline{R}^M \underline{R}^S. \tag{3.18}$$

In the case of GPS, the space-fixed coordinate system is already related to
the CEP. Hence, $\underline{R}^R$ is the only rotation matrix which must be applied for
the transformation into the terrestrial system. For most of the practical
purposes, the effect of polar motion is also negligible.

3.3 Time systems

3.3.1 Definitions

Several time systems are in current use. They are based on several periodic
processes such as earth's rotation and are listed in Table 3.2.

Solar and sidereal times
A measure of earth rotation is the hour angle which is the angle between
the meridian of a celestial body and a reference meridian (preferably the
Greenwich meridian). Universal Time is defined by the Greenwich hour angle

Table 3.2. Time systems

Periodic process	Time system
Earth rotation	Universal Time (UT)
	Greenwich Sidereal Time (Θ_0)
Earth revolution	Terrestrial Dynamic Time (TDT)
	Barycentric Dynamic Time (BDT)
Atomic oscillations	International Atomic Time (IAT)
	UT Coordinated (UTC)
	GPS Time (GPST)

augmented by 12 hours of a fictitious sun uniformly orbiting in the equatorial plane. Sidereal time is defined by the hour angle of the vernal equinox. Taking the mean equinox as the reference leads to mean sidereal time and using the true equinox as a reference yields true or apparent sidereal time. Both, solar and sidereal time are not uniform since the angular velocity ω_E is not constant. The fluctuations are partly due to changes in the polar moment of inertia exerted by tidal deformation as well as other mass transports. Another reason has to do with the oscillations of the earth's rotational axis itself. In this case the universal time corrected for polar motion is denoted by UT1.

Dynamic times
The time systems derived from planetary motions in the solar system are called dynamic times. The Barycentric Dynamic Time (BDT) is an inertial time system in the Newtonian sense and provides the time variable in the equations of motion. The quasi-inertial Terrestrial Dynamic Time (TDT) was formerly called ephemeris time and serves for the integration of the differential equations for the orbital motion of satellites around the earth.

Atomic times
A practical realization of the dynamic time system is achieved by the atomic time scales. GPS time also belongs to this system. The Universal Time Coordinated (UTC) system is a compromise. The unit of the system is the atomic second, but to keep the system close to UT and approximate civil time, integer leap seconds are inserted at distinct epochs. The GPS time system has nominally a constant offset of 19 seconds with the International Atomic Time (IAT) and was coincident with UTC at the GPS standard epoch 1980, January $6\overset{d}{.}0$.

3.3.2   Conversions

The conversion between the times derived from earth rotation (i.e., the mean solar time corrected for polar motion UT1 and the apparent sidereal time Θ_0) is achieved by the formula

$$\Theta_0 = 1.002\,737\,9093\ \text{UT1} + \vartheta_0 + \Delta\psi\cos\varepsilon\,. \tag{3.19}$$

The first term in Eq. (3.19) accounts for the different scales of solar and sidereal time and the quantity ϑ_0 represents the actual sidereal time at Greenwich midnight (i.e., 0^{h} UT). The third term describes the projection of $\Delta\psi$ onto the equator and, thus, considers the effect of nutation. The mean sidereal time follows from Eq. (3.19) by neglecting the nutation term and is a part of the navigation message broadcast by the GPS satellites, cf. Sect. 4.4.2.

For ϑ_0 a time series has been determined, cf. Nautical Almanac Office (1983), p. S13, as

$$\vartheta_0 = 24\,110\overset{\text{s}}{.}54841 + 8\,640\,184\overset{\text{s}}{.}812866\,T_0$$
$$+ 0\overset{\text{s}}{.}093104\,T_0^2 - 6\overset{\text{s}}{.}2\cdot10^{-6}\,T_0^3 \tag{3.20}$$

where T_0 represents the timespan expressed in Julian centuries of 36 525 mean solar days between the standard epoch J2000.0 and the day of observation at 0^{h} UT.

The time UT1 is related to UTC by the quantity dUT1 which is time dependent and is also reported by the IERS:

$$\text{UT1} = \text{UTC} + \text{dUT1}\,. \tag{3.21}$$

When the absolute value of dUT1 becomes larger than $0\overset{\text{s}}{.}9$, a leap second is inserted into the UTC system.

Instead of the dynamic time system itself, the atomic time system serves as reference in GPS. The following relations are defined:

$$\begin{aligned}
\text{IAT} &= \text{GPS} + 19\overset{\text{s}}{.}000 &\quad &\text{constant offset} \\
\text{IAT} &= \text{TDT} - 32\overset{\text{s}}{.}184 &\quad &\text{constant offset} \\
\text{IAT} &= \text{UTC} + 1\overset{\text{s}}{.}000\,n &\quad &\text{variable offset as leap seconds are substituted.}
\end{aligned} \tag{3.22}$$

The actual integer n is also reported by the IERS. In early 1994, for example, the integer value was $n = 28$ and, thus, GPS time differed by exactly nine seconds from UTC at this time.

3.3.3 Calendar

Definitions
The Julian Date (JD) defines the number of mean solar days elapsed since the epoch 4713 B.C., January $1.^{d}5$.

The Modified Julian Date (MJD) is obtained by subtracting $2\,400\,000.5$ days from JD. This convention saves digits and MJD commences at civil midnight instead of noon. For the sake of completeness, Table 3.3 with the Julian date for two standard epochs is given. This table enables, for example, the calculation of the parameter T for the GPS standard epoch. Subtracting the respective Julian dates and dividing by $36\,525$ (i.e., the number of days in a Julian century) yields $T = -0.199\,876\,7967$.

Date conversions
The relations for date conversions are taken from Montenbruck (1984) and are slightly modified so that they are only valid for an epoch between March 1900 and February 2100.

Let the civilian date be expressed by integer values for the year Y, month M, day D, and a real value for the time in hours UT. Then

$$JD = INT[365.25\,y] + INT[30.6001\,(m+1)]$$
$$+\, D + UT/24 + 1\,720\,981.5 \tag{3.23}$$

is the conversion into Julian date where INT denotes the integer part of a real number and y, m are given by

$$
\begin{aligned}
y = Y - 1 \quad &\text{and} \quad m = M + 12 \qquad &&\text{if} \quad M \le 2 \\
y = Y \quad\;\;\; &\text{and} \quad m = M \qquad\;\;\; &&\text{if} \quad M > 2.
\end{aligned}
$$

The inverse transformation, that is the conversion from Julian date to

Table 3.3. Standard epochs

Civilian date	Julian date	Explanation
1980 January $6.^{d}0$	$2\,444\,244.5$	GPS standard epoch
2000 January $1.^{d}5$	$2\,451\,545.0$	Current standard epoch (J2000.0)

civil date, is carried out stepwise. First, the auxiliary numbers

$$a = \text{INT}[\text{JD} + 0.5]$$
$$b = a + 1537$$
$$c = \text{INT}[(b - 122.1)/365.25]$$
$$d = \text{INT}[365.25\, c]$$
$$e = \text{INT}[(b - d)/30.6001]$$

are calculated. Afterwards, the civil date parameters are obtained from the relations

$$D = b - d - \text{INT}[30.6001\, e] + \text{FRAC}[\text{JD} + 0.5]$$
$$M = e - 1 - 12\, \text{INT}[e/14] \tag{3.24}$$
$$Y = c - 4\,715 - \text{INT}[(7 + M)/10]$$

where FRAC denotes the fractional part of a number. As a by-product of date conversion, the day of week can be evaluated by the formula

$$N = \text{modulo}\{\text{INT}[\text{JD} + 0.5],\ 7\} \tag{3.25}$$

where $N = 0$ denotes Monday, $N = 1$ means Tuesday, and so on. A further task is the calculation of the GPS week which is achieved by the relation

$$\text{WEEK} = \text{INT}[(\text{JD} - 2\,444\,244.5)/7]\,. \tag{3.26}$$

The formulas given here can be used to prove the different dates in Table 3.3 or to verify the fact that the epoch J2000.0 corresponds to Saturday in the 1042nd GPS week.

4 Satellite orbits

4.1 Introduction

The applications of GPS depend substantially on knowing the satellite orbits. For single receiver positioning, an orbital error is highly correlated with the positional error. In relative positioning (according to a rule of thumb), relative orbital errors are equal to relative baseline errors.

Orbital information is either transmitted by the satellite as part of the broadcast message or can be obtained (typically some days after the observation) from several sources. The activation of Selective Availability (SA) in the Block II satellites may lead to a degradation of the broadcast orbit up to 50–100 m. Since some users need more precise ephemerides, the civil community must generate its own precise satellite ephemerides.

This chapter provides a review of orbital theory with emphasis on GPS orbits to acquaint the reader with the problems of computing ephemerides.

4.2 Orbit description

4.2.1 Keplerian motion

Orbital parameters
Assume two point masses m_1 and m_2 separated by the distance r. Considering for the moment only the attractive force between the masses and applying Newtonian mechanics, the movement of mass m_2 relative to m_1 is defined by the homogeneous differential equation of second order

$$\ddot{\underline{r}} + \frac{G\,(m_1 + m_2)}{r^3}\,\underline{r} = \underline{0} \tag{4.1}$$

where

$$\underline{r} \qquad \dots \quad \text{relative position vector with } \|\underline{r}\| = r$$

$$\ddot{\underline{r}} = \frac{d^2\underline{r}}{dt^2} \quad \dots \quad \text{relative acceleration vector}$$

$$G \qquad \dots \quad \text{universal gravitational constant}$$

and the time parameter t being an inertial time realized by the GPS system time.

In the case of motion of an artificial earth satellite, in a first approximation, both bodies can be considered as point masses and the mass of the satellite can be neglected. The product of G and the earth's mass M_E is denoted as μ and is known as one defining parameter of the WGS-84 reference system, cf. Table 3.1:

$$\mu = G\,M_E = 3\,986\,005 \cdot 10^8 \; \mathrm{m}^3 \, \mathrm{s}^{-2} \, .$$

The analytical solution of differential equation (4.1) can be found in textbooks on celestial mechanics, for example Brouwer and Clemence (1961) or Bucerius (1966), and leads to the well-known Keplerian motion defined by six orbital parameters which correspond to the six integration constants of the second-order vector equation (4.1). Satellite orbits may be restricted to elliptic motion, and the six associated parameters are listed in Table 4.1. The point of closest approach of the satellite with respect to the earth's center of mass is called perigee and the most distant position is the apogee. The intersection between the equatorial and the orbital plane with the unit sphere is termed the nodes, where the ascending node denotes the northward crossing of the equator. A graphical representation of the Keplerian orbit is given in Fig. 4.1.

The mean angular satellite velocity n (also known as the mean motion) with revolution period P follows from Kepler's Third Law given by

$$n = \frac{2\pi}{P} = \sqrt{\frac{\mu}{a^3}} \, . \tag{4.2}$$

For GPS orbits, the nominal semimajor axis is $a = 26\,560$ km. The substitution of a into Eq. (4.2) yields an orbital period of 12 sidereal hours. The ground track of the satellites, thus, repeats every sidereal day.

The instantaneous position of the satellite within its orbit is described by an angular quantity known as anomaly (where this notation is used for historical reasons).

Table 4.1. Keplerian orbital parameters

Parameter	Notation
Ω	Right ascension of ascending node
i	Inclination of orbital plane
ω	Argument of perigee
a	Semimajor axis of orbital ellipse
e	Numerical eccentricity of ellipse
T_0	Epoch of perigee passage

Table 4.2. Anomalies of the Keplerian orbit

Notation	Anomaly
$M(t)$	Mean anomaly
$E(t)$	Eccentric anomaly
$v(t)$	True anomaly

Table 4.2 lists commonly used anomalies. The mean anomaly $M(t)$ is a mathematical abstraction, while both the eccentric anomaly $E(t)$ and the true anomaly $v(t)$ are geometrically produceable, cf. Fig. 4.1.

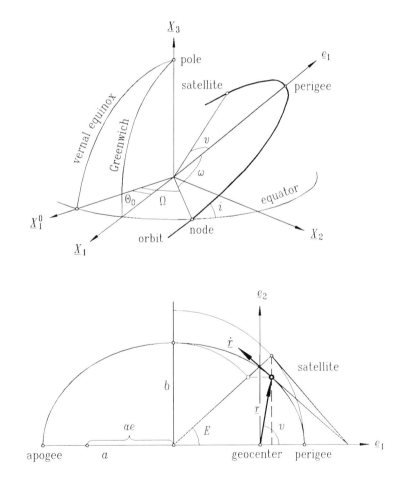

Fig. 4.1. Keplerian orbit

The three anomalies are related by the formulas

$$M(t) = n\,(t - T_0) \tag{4.3}$$

$$E(t) = M(t) + e \sin E(t) \tag{4.4}$$

$$v(t) = 2 \arctan\left[\sqrt{\frac{1+e}{1-e}} \, \tan \frac{E(t)}{2}\right] \tag{4.5}$$

where e denotes the eccentricity. Equation (4.3) holds by definition and shows that the mean anomaly can be used instead of T_0 as a defining parameter. Equation (4.4) is known as Kepler's equation and is obtained in the course of the analytical integration of Eq. (4.1). Finally, Eq. (4.5) follows from purely geometric relations as shown in the following paragraph.

To become more familiar with the various anomalies, assume an orbit with a semidiurnal orbital period and an eccentricity of $e = 0.1$. At an epoch 3 hours after perigee passage, the mean anomaly is $M = 90°\!.0000$. The calculation of the eccentric anomaly requires iteration and gives the value $E = 95°\!.7012$. The true anomaly is obtained as $v = 101°\!.3838$

Orbit representation
The coordinate system $\underline{e}_1$, $\underline{e}_2$ defining the orbital plane is shown in Fig. 4.1. The position vector $\underline{r}$ and the velocity vector $\underline{\dot{r}} = d\underline{r}/dt$ of the satellite can be represented by means of the eccentric as well as the true anomaly:

$$\underline{r} = a \begin{bmatrix} \cos E - e \\ \sqrt{1 - e^2} \sin E \end{bmatrix} = r \begin{bmatrix} \cos v \\ \sin v \end{bmatrix} \tag{4.6}$$

$$r = a\,(1 - e \cos E) = \frac{a\,(1 - e^2)}{1 + e \cos v} \tag{4.7}$$

$$\underline{\dot{r}} = \frac{n\,a^2}{r} \begin{bmatrix} -\sin E \\ \sqrt{1 - e^2} \cos E \end{bmatrix} = \sqrt{\frac{\mu}{a\,(1 - e^2)}} \begin{bmatrix} -\sin v \\ \cos v + e \end{bmatrix} \tag{4.8}$$

$$\dot{r} = \frac{n\,a^2}{r} \sqrt{1 - (e \cos E)^2} = \sqrt{\mu \left(\frac{2}{r} - \frac{1}{a}\right)}. \tag{4.9}$$

The components of the vector $\underline{r}$ are evident from the geometry in Fig. 4.1 where the semiminor axis b of the orbital ellipse is replaced by $a\sqrt{1 - e^2}$. The geocentric distance $r = r(E)$ corresponds to the norm $\|\underline{r}(E)\|$ and follows from simple algebra. The representation $r = r(v)$ is known as polar equation of the ellipse, cf. Bronstein and Semendjajew (1969), p. 184.

Equation (4.5) can now be verified. For this purpose the first components of Eq. (4.6) are equated and Eq. (4.7) is substituted. This leads to $\cos v = (\cos E - e)/(1 - e\cos E)$. The identity $\tan(\alpha/2) = \sqrt{(1 - \cos\alpha)/(1 + \cos\alpha)}$ applied twice and using simple algebra yields Eq. (4.5).

The derivation of the velocity vector $\dot{r} = \dot{r}(E)$ requires knowledge of the time derivative $dE/dt = na/r$. This result is obtained by differentiating Kepler's equation and substituting Eq. (4.7). The derivation of $\dot{r} = \dot{r}(v)$ is much more laborious and the result is given without proof. The norm of $\dot{r}$ (i.e., the velocity $\dot{r}$) can be derived from either representation $\dot{r}(E)$ or $\dot{r}(v)$. The calculation of $\dot{r}(E)$ is straightforward; the proof of $\dot{r}(v)$ is left to the reader. It is worth noting that Eq. (4.9) when squared and divided by two relates kinetic energy on the left-hand side with potential energy on the right-hand side where a by definition is a constant. Hence, Eq. (4.9) can be recognized as the law of energy conservation in the earth-satellite system!

The transformation of r and $\dot{r}$ into the equatorial system X_i^0 is performed by a rotation matrix $\underline{R}$ and results in vectors denoted by ϱ and $\dot{\varrho}$. The superscript "S" generally indicating a satellite is omitted here for simplicity. The vectors expressed in the orbital system must be considered as three-dimensional vectors for the transformation. Therefore, the axes $\underline{e}_1$, $\underline{e}_2$ are supplemented with an $\underline{e}_3$-axis which is orthogonal to the orbital plane. Since r and $\dot{r}$ are vectors in the orbital plane (represented by $\underline{e}_1$, $\underline{e}_2$), their $\underline{e}_3$-component is zero.

The transformation is defined by

$$\varrho = \underline{R}\,r$$
$$\dot{\varrho} = \underline{R}\,\dot{r} \qquad (4.10)$$

where the matrix $\underline{R}$ is composed of three successive rotation matrices, cf. Fig. 4.1, and is given by

$$\underline{R} = \underline{R}_3\{-\Omega\}\,\underline{R}_1\{-i\}\,\underline{R}_3\{-\omega\}$$

$$= \begin{bmatrix} \cos\Omega\cos\omega & -\cos\Omega\sin\omega & \sin\Omega\sin i \\ -\sin\Omega\sin\omega\cos i & -\sin\Omega\cos\omega\cos i & \\ \sin\Omega\cos\omega & -\sin\Omega\sin\omega & -\cos\Omega\sin i \\ +\cos\Omega\sin\omega\cos i & +\cos\Omega\cos\omega\cos i & \\ \sin\omega\sin i & \cos\omega\sin i & \cos i \end{bmatrix} \quad (4.11)$$

$$= \begin{bmatrix} \underline{e}_1, & \underline{e}_2, & \underline{e}_3 \end{bmatrix}.$$

The column vectors of the orthonormal matrix $\underline{R}$ are the axes of the orbital coordinate system represented in the equatorial system X_i^0.

In order to rotate the system $\underline{X}_i^0$ into the earth-fixed system $\underline{X}_i$, an additional rotation through the angle Θ_0, the Greenwich sidereal time, is required. The transformation matrix, therefore, becomes

$$\underline{R}' = \underline{R}_3\{\Theta_0\}\,\underline{R}_3\{-\Omega\}\,\underline{R}_1\{-i\}\,\underline{R}_3\{-\omega\}\,. \qquad (4.12)$$

The product $\underline{R}_3\{\Theta_0\}\,\underline{R}_3\{-\Omega\}$ can be expressed by a simple matrix $\underline{R}_3\{-\ell\}$ where $\ell = \Omega - \Theta_0$. Hence, Eq. (4.12) can be written in the form

$$\underline{R}' = \underline{R}_3\{-\ell\}\,\underline{R}_1\{-i\}\,\underline{R}_3\{-\omega\} \qquad (4.13)$$

and matrix $\underline{R}'$ corresponds to matrix $\underline{R}$ if in Eq. (4.11) the parameter Ω is replaced by ℓ.

For a numerical example assume a satellite orbiting in a Kepler ellipse with the following parameters: $a = 26\,000$ km, $e = 0.1$, $\omega = -140°$, $i = 60°$, $\ell = 110°$. To calculate the position and velocity vector in the earth-fixed equatorial system at an epoch where the eccentric anomaly is $E = 45°$, the vectors are first calculated in the orbital plane using Eqs. (4.6) through (4.9). Then, the transformation into the equatorial system is performed by means of Eq. (4.10) using the rotation matrix $\underline{R}'$. The final result is

$$\underline{\varrho} = [11\,465,\ 3\,818,\ -20\,923]^T \qquad [\text{km}]$$

$$\underline{\dot{\varrho}} = [-1.2651,\ 3.9960,\ -0.3081]^T \quad [\text{km\,s}^{-1}]$$

where "T" denotes transposition.

In addition to the fixed orbital system $\underline{e}_i$, another orthonormal system $\underline{e}_i^*$ may be defined. This system rotates about the $\underline{e}_3$-axis because the $\underline{e}_1^*$-axis always points towards the instantaneous satellite position. Hence, the unit vectors $\underline{e}_i^*$ can be derived from the position and velocity vectors by

$$\underline{e}_1^* = \frac{\underline{\varrho}}{\|\underline{\varrho}\|} \qquad \underline{e}_3^* = \frac{\underline{\varrho} \times \underline{\dot{\varrho}}}{\|\underline{\varrho} \times \underline{\dot{\varrho}}\|} = \underline{e}_3 \qquad \underline{e}_2^* = \underline{e}_3 \times \underline{e}_1\,. \qquad (4.14)$$

Note that the base vectors $\underline{e}_i^*$ correspond to the column vectors of a modified rotation matrix $\underline{R}^*$ in Eq. (4.11) where the parameter ω is replaced by $(\omega + v)$.

The transformation of a change $d\underline{\varrho}$ in the position vector into the orbital system $\underline{e}_i^*$ results in a vector $\underline{e} = [e_i]$ with its components reckoned along the respective axes $\underline{e}_i^*$:

$$e_1 = \underline{e}_1^* \cdot d\underline{\varrho} \qquad \text{radial or across-track component}$$

$$e_2 = \underline{e}_2^* \cdot d\underline{\varrho} \qquad \text{along-track component} \qquad (4.15)$$

$$e_3 = \underline{e}_3^* \cdot d\underline{\varrho} \qquad \text{out-of-plane component.}$$

Inversely, $d\varrho$ is calculated if the vector e is given. The solution follows from the inversion of Eq. (4.15) and leads to

$$d\varrho = \underline{R}^* \, \underline{e} \, . \tag{4.16}$$

For a numerical examination assume a change $d\varrho = [0.1, 1.0, -0.5]^T$ [km] in the satellite's position of the previous example. Applying Eqs. (4.14) and (4.15) gives $e = [0.638, 0.914, 0.128]^T$ [km].

Differential relations
The derivatives of ϱ and $\dot{\varrho}$ with respect to the six Keplerian parameters are required in one of the subsequent sections. The differentiation can be separated into two groups because in Eq. (4.10) the vectors r and $\dot{r}$ depend only on the parameters a, e, T_0, whereas the matrix $\underline{R}$ is only a function of the remaining parameters ω, i, Ω.

In order to obtain the derivatives of r and $\dot{r}$, it is advantageous to differentiate the vectors represented by the eccentric anomaly. As a first step, the derivatives of the quantities n, E, r with respect to the parameters a, e, T_0 are calculated. By differentiating Eq. (4.2) one gets

$$\frac{\partial n}{\partial a} = -\frac{3}{2}\frac{n}{a} \qquad \frac{\partial n}{\partial e} = 0 \qquad \frac{\partial n}{\partial T_0} = 0 \, . \tag{4.17}$$

Differentiating the Kepler equation (4.4) and substituting Eq. (4.17) leads to

$$\frac{\partial E}{\partial a} = -\frac{3}{2}\frac{M}{r} \qquad \frac{\partial E}{\partial e} = \frac{a}{r}\sin E \qquad \frac{\partial E}{\partial T_0} = -n\frac{a}{r} \, . \tag{4.18}$$

Finally, the differentiation of Eq. (4.7) yields

$$\frac{\partial r}{\partial a} = (1 - e\cos E) + ae\sin E \,\frac{\partial E}{\partial a}$$

$$\frac{\partial r}{\partial e} = -a\cos E + ae\sin E\,\frac{\partial E}{\partial e} \tag{4.19}$$

$$\frac{\partial r}{\partial T_0} = ae\sin E\,\frac{\partial E}{\partial T_0} \, .$$

Now, the desired result follows after applying the chain rule to Eqs. (4.6) and (4.8), and after algebraic operations where $dm = -n\, dT_0$ is substituted:

$$\frac{\partial r}{\partial a} = \left[\begin{array}{c} \cos E - e + \dfrac{3}{2}\dfrac{a}{r}M\sin E \\[2mm] \sqrt{1 - e^2}\,(\sin E - \dfrac{3}{2}\dfrac{a}{r}M\cos E) \end{array} \right] \tag{4.20}$$

$$\frac{\partial r}{\partial e} = \begin{bmatrix} -a\left(1 + \dfrac{a}{r}\sin^2 E\right) \\[2ex] \dfrac{a^2 \sin E}{r\sqrt{1-e^2}}\left(\cos E - e\right) \end{bmatrix} \tag{4.21}$$

$$\frac{\partial r}{\partial m} = \begin{bmatrix} -\dfrac{a^2}{r}\sin E \\[2ex] \dfrac{a^2}{r}\sqrt{1-e^2}\cos E \end{bmatrix} \tag{4.22}$$

$$\frac{\partial \dot{r}}{\partial a} = \frac{a\,n}{2r}\begin{bmatrix} \sin E - \dfrac{3a}{r}M\left(\dfrac{a\,e}{r}\sin^2 E - \cos E\right) \\[2ex] \sqrt{1-e^2}\left(\dfrac{3a}{r}M\sin E\left(\dfrac{a\,e}{r}\cos E + 1\right) - \cos E\right) \end{bmatrix} \tag{4.23}$$

$$\frac{\partial \dot{r}}{\partial e} = \frac{a^2 n}{r}\begin{bmatrix} \dfrac{a^2}{2r^2}\left(2e\sin E + \sin(2E)\left(e\cos E - 2\right)\right) \\[2ex] -\dfrac{e}{\sqrt{1-e^2}}\cos E + \dfrac{a}{r}\sqrt{1-e^2}\left(\dfrac{a}{r}\sin^2 E - \cos^2 E\right) \end{bmatrix} \tag{4.24}$$

$$\frac{\partial \dot{r}}{\partial m} = -\frac{n\,a^4}{r^3}\begin{bmatrix} \cos E - e \\[1ex] \sqrt{1-e^2}\sin E \end{bmatrix}. \tag{4.25}$$

Considering Eq. (4.11), the differentiation of the matrix $\underline{R}$ with respect to the parameters ω, i, Ω is simple and does not pose any problem.

Hence, the differential relations are given by

$$\begin{aligned}
d\underline{\rho} &= \underline{R}\,\frac{\partial r}{\partial a}\,da + \underline{R}\,\frac{\partial r}{\partial e}\,de + \underline{R}\,\frac{\partial r}{\partial m}\,dm \\
&\quad + \frac{\partial \underline{R}}{\partial \omega}\,\underline{r}\,d\omega + \frac{\partial \underline{R}}{\partial i}\,\underline{r}\,di + \frac{\partial \underline{R}}{\partial \Omega}\,\underline{r}\,d\Omega \\[2ex]
d\underline{\dot{\rho}} &= \underline{R}\,\frac{\partial \dot{r}}{\partial a}\,da + \underline{R}\,\frac{\partial \dot{r}}{\partial e}\,de + \underline{R}\,\frac{\partial \dot{r}}{\partial m}\,dm \\
&\quad + \frac{\partial \underline{R}}{\partial \omega}\,\underline{\dot{r}}\,d\omega + \frac{\partial \underline{R}}{\partial i}\,\underline{\dot{r}}\,di + \frac{\partial \underline{R}}{\partial \Omega}\,\underline{\dot{r}}\,d\Omega\,.
\end{aligned} \tag{4.26}$$

In Eqs. (4.20) through (4.25), the mean or eccentric anomaly is contained. Hence, these derivatives with respect to the parameters a, e, m are time dependent. Because of the appearance of $\underline{r}$ and $\underline{\dot{r}}$, all terms in Eq. (4.26) are time dependent although the derivatives of the matrix $\underline{R}$ with respect to the parameters ω, i, Ω are constant.

4.2.2 Perturbed motion

The Keplerian orbit is a theoretical orbit and does not include actual perturbations. Consequently, disturbing accelerations $d\ddot{\underline{\varrho}}$ must be added to Eq. (4.1) which is now expressed in the equatorial system. The perturbed motion, thus, is based on an inhomogeneous differential equation of the second order

$$\ddot{\underline{\varrho}} + \frac{\mu}{\varrho^3}\,\underline{\varrho} = d\ddot{\underline{\varrho}}\,. \tag{4.27}$$

One should note that, for GPS satellites, the acceleration $\|\ddot{\underline{\varrho}}\|$ due to the central attractive force μ/ϱ^2 is at least 10^4 times larger than the disturbing accelerations. Hence, for the analytical solution of Eq. (4.27), perturbation theory can be applied where, initially, only the homogeneous part of the equation is considered. This leads to a Keplerian orbit defined by the six parameters p_{i0}, $i = 1,\ldots,6$ at the reference epoch t_0. Each disturbing acceleration $d\ddot{\underline{\varrho}}$ causes temporal variations $\dot{p}_{i0} = dp_{i0}/dt$ in the orbital parameters. Therefore, at an arbitrary epoch t, the parameters p_i describing the so-called osculating ellipse are given by

$$p_i = p_{i0} + \dot{p}_{i0}\,(t - t_0)\,. \tag{4.28}$$

In order to obtain time derivatives $\dot{p}_{i0}$, the Keplerian motion is compared to the perturbed motion. In the first case, the parameters p_i are constant, whereas in the second case they are time dependent. Thus, for the position and velocity vector of the perturbed motion one may write

$$\begin{aligned}\underline{\varrho} &= \underline{\varrho}\{t, p_i(t)\} \\[4pt] \dot{\underline{\varrho}} &= \dot{\underline{\varrho}}\{t, p_i(t)\}\,.\end{aligned} \tag{4.29}$$

Differentiating the above equations with respect to time and taking into account Eq. (4.27) leads to

$$\dot{\underline{\varrho}} = \frac{\partial \underline{\varrho}}{\partial t} + \sum_{i=1}^{6}\left(\frac{\partial \underline{\varrho}}{\partial p_i}\,\frac{dp_i}{dt}\right) \tag{4.30}$$

$$\ddot{\underline{\varrho}} = \frac{\partial \dot{\underline{\varrho}}}{\partial t} + \sum_{i=1}^{6}\left(\frac{\partial \dot{\underline{\varrho}}}{\partial p_i}\,\frac{dp_i}{dt}\right) = -\frac{\mu}{\varrho^3}\,\underline{\varrho} + d\ddot{\underline{\varrho}}\,. \tag{4.31}$$

Since for any epoch t an (osculating) ellipse is defined, the Eqs. (4.30) and (4.31) must also hold for Keplerian motion. Evidently, equivalence is obtained with the following conditions

$$\sum_{i=1}^{6} \left(\frac{\partial \underline{\varrho}}{\partial p_i} \frac{dp_i}{dt} \right) = \underline{0}$$

$$\sum_{i=1}^{6} \left(\frac{\partial \underline{\dot{\varrho}}}{\partial p_i} \frac{dp_i}{dt} \right) = d\underline{\ddot{\varrho}} .$$

(4.32)

In the following, for simplicity, only one disturbing acceleration is considered. The two vector equations (4.32) correspond to six linear equations which, in vector notation, are given by

$$\underline{A}\,\underline{u} = \underline{\ell}$$

(4.33)

where

$$\underline{A} = \begin{bmatrix} \dfrac{\partial \underline{\varrho}}{\partial a} & \dfrac{\partial \underline{\varrho}}{\partial e} & \dfrac{\partial \underline{\varrho}}{\partial m} & \dfrac{\partial \underline{\varrho}}{\partial \omega} & \dfrac{\partial \underline{\varrho}}{\partial i} & \dfrac{\partial \underline{\varrho}}{\partial \Omega} \\[2mm] \dfrac{\partial \underline{\dot{\varrho}}}{\partial a} & \dfrac{\partial \underline{\dot{\varrho}}}{\partial e} & \dfrac{\partial \underline{\dot{\varrho}}}{\partial m} & \dfrac{\partial \underline{\dot{\varrho}}}{\partial \omega} & \dfrac{\partial \underline{\dot{\varrho}}}{\partial i} & \dfrac{\partial \underline{\dot{\varrho}}}{\partial \Omega} \end{bmatrix}$$

$$= \begin{bmatrix} \underline{R}\,\dfrac{\partial \underline{r}}{\partial a} & \underline{R}\,\dfrac{\partial \underline{r}}{\partial e} & \underline{R}\,\dfrac{\partial \underline{r}}{\partial m} & \underline{r}\,\dfrac{\partial \underline{R}}{\partial \omega} & \underline{r}\,\dfrac{\partial \underline{R}}{\partial i} & \underline{r}\,\dfrac{\partial \underline{R}}{\partial \Omega} \\[2mm] \underline{R}\,\dfrac{\partial \underline{\dot{r}}}{\partial a} & \underline{R}\,\dfrac{\partial \underline{\dot{r}}}{\partial e} & \underline{R}\,\dfrac{\partial \underline{\dot{r}}}{\partial m} & \underline{\dot{r}}\,\dfrac{\partial \underline{R}}{\partial \omega} & \underline{\dot{r}}\,\dfrac{\partial \underline{R}}{\partial i} & \underline{\dot{r}}\,\dfrac{\partial \underline{R}}{\partial \Omega} \end{bmatrix}$$

$$\underline{u} = \begin{bmatrix} \dfrac{da}{dt} & \dfrac{de}{dt} & \dfrac{dm}{dt} & \dfrac{d\omega}{dt} & \dfrac{di}{dt} & \dfrac{d\Omega}{dt} \end{bmatrix}^T$$

$$= \begin{bmatrix} \dot{a} & \dot{e} & \dot{m} & \dot{\omega} & \dot{i} & \dot{\Omega} \end{bmatrix}^T$$

$$\underline{\ell} = \begin{bmatrix} \underline{0} \\ d\underline{\ddot{\varrho}} \end{bmatrix} .$$

The 6×6 matrix $\underline{A}$ requires the derivatives of $\underline{\varrho}$ and $\underline{\dot{\varrho}}$ with respect to the Keplerian parameters which have been developed in the preceding section, cf. Eq. (4.26). The 6×1 vector $\underline{\ell}$ contains the disturbing acceleration. Finally, the six unknown time derivatives appear in the 6×1 vector $\underline{u}$. The inversion of the system (4.33) leads to Lagrange's equations where the disturbing potential R, associated with the disturbing acceleration by $d\underline{\ddot{\varrho}} = \operatorname{grad} R$, has been introduced, cf. for example Beutler (1992), Eq. (6.96):

$$\dot{a} = \frac{2}{n\,a}\frac{\partial R}{\partial m}$$

$$\dot{e} = \frac{1-e^2}{n\,a^2\,e}\frac{\partial R}{\partial m} - \frac{\sqrt{1-e^2}}{n\,a^2\,e}\frac{\partial R}{\partial \omega}$$

$$\dot{m} = -\frac{2}{n\,a}\frac{\partial R}{\partial a} - \frac{1-e^2}{n\,a^2\,e}\frac{\partial R}{\partial e}$$

$$\dot{\omega} = \frac{\sqrt{1-e^2}}{n\,a^2\,e}\frac{\partial R}{\partial e} - \frac{\cos i}{n\,a^2\,\sqrt{1-e^2}\,\sin i}\frac{\partial R}{\partial i} \tag{4.34}$$

$$\dot{i} = \frac{\cos i}{n\,a^2\,\sqrt{1-e^2}\,\sin i}\frac{\partial R}{\partial \omega} - \frac{1}{n\,a^2\,\sqrt{1-e^2}\,\sin i}\frac{\partial R}{\partial \Omega}$$

$$\dot{\Omega} = \frac{1}{n\,a^2\,\sqrt{1-e^2}\,\sin i}\frac{\partial R}{\partial i}.$$

Note that the system (4.34) fails for $e = 0$ or $i = 0$. This singularity can be avoided by the substitution of auxiliary parameters, cf. Bucerius (1966), p. 193 or Arnold (1970), p. 28.

The Lagrange equations presuppose that the disturbing potential R is expressed in function of the Keplerian parameters. When the acceleration $d\ddot{\varrho}$ is represented by components K_i along the axes $\underline{e}_i^*$, the system (4.34) can be transformed using the identity

$$\frac{\partial R}{\partial p_i} = \operatorname{grad} R \cdot \frac{\partial \underline{\varrho}}{\partial p_i} = (K_1\,\underline{e}_1^* + K_2\,\underline{e}_2^* + K_3\,\underline{e}_3^*) \cdot \frac{\partial \underline{\varrho}}{\partial p_i}. \tag{4.35}$$

The simple but cumbersome algebra leads to the Gaussian equations. The result is taken from Seeber (1993), Eq. (3.101) where K_1 and K_3 are interchanged and slight modifications are introduced:

$$\dot{a} = \frac{2}{n\sqrt{1-e^2}}\left[e \sin v\, K_1 + (1 + e \cos v)\, K_2\right]$$

$$\dot{e} = \frac{\sqrt{1-e^2}}{n\,a}\left[\sin v\, K_1 + (\cos E + \cos v)\, K_2\right]$$

$$\dot{m} = \frac{1-e^2}{n\,a\,e}\left[\left(\frac{-2e}{1+e\cos v} + \cos v\right) K_1\right.$$
$$\left. - \left(1 + \frac{1}{1+e\cos v}\right)\sin v\, K_2\right]$$

and

$$\dot{\omega} = \frac{\sqrt{1-e^2}}{n\,a\,e} \left[-\cos v\, K_1 + \left(1 + \frac{1}{1+e\cos v}\right) \sin v\, K_2 \right.$$
$$\left. - \frac{e\,\sin(\omega+v)}{1+e\cos v}\, \cot i\, K_3 \right]$$

$$i = \frac{r\,\cos(\omega+v)}{n\,a^2\,\sqrt{1-e^2}}\, K_3$$

$$\dot{\Omega} = \frac{r\,\sin(\omega+v)}{n\,a^2\,\sqrt{1-e^2}\,\sin i}\, K_3 \,.$$

$$(4.36)$$

Note that in the temporal variations i and $\dot{\Omega}$ only the component orthogonal to the orbital plane, K_3, appears, whereas the variations of $\dot{a}$, $\dot{e}$, $\dot{m}$ are affected by both components in the orbital plane, K_1, K_2.

4.2.3 Disturbing accelerations

In reality, many disturbing accelerations act on a satellite and are responsible for the temporal variations of the Keplerian elements. Roughly speaking, they can be divided into two groups, namely those of gravitational and nongravitational origin, see Table 4.3. Because the GPS satellites are orbiting at an altitude of approximately $20\,000$ km, the indirect effects as well as air drag may be neglected. On the other hand, the shape (and, thus, the cross section) of the satellites is irregular which renders the modeling of solar radiation more difficult. The variety of materials used for the satellites each has a different heat-absorption which results in additional and complicated perturbing accelerations. Also, accelerations may arise from leaks in the container for the gas-propellant as mentioned by Lichten and Neilan (1990).

To demonstrate the effect of disturbing accelerations, an example is computed by assuming a constant disturbance $d\ddot{\varrho} = 10^{-9}\,\mathrm{m\,s^{-2}}$ acting on a GPS satellite. The associated shift in the position of the satellite results from

Table 4.3. Sources for disturbing accelerations

Gravitational	Nonsphericity of the earth,
	Tidal attraction (direct and indirect)
Nongravitational	Solar radiation pressure (direct and indirect),
	Air drag,
	Relativistic effects,
	Others (solar wind, magnetic field forces, etc.)

double integration over time t and yields $d\varrho = d\ddot{\varrho}\,(t^2/2)$. Substituting the numerical value $t \approx 12$ hours gives the shift after one revolution which is $d\varrho \approx 1$ m. This can be considered as typical value.

Nonsphericity of the earth
The earth's potential V can be represented by a spherical harmonic expansion, cf. Heiskanen and Moritz (1967), p. 342, by

$$V = \frac{\mu}{r}\left[1 - \sum_{n=2}^{\infty}\left(\frac{a_E}{r}\right)^n J_n\, P_n(\sin\varphi)\right.$$

$$\left. - \sum_{n=2}^{\infty}\sum_{m=1}^{n}\left(\frac{a_E}{r}\right)^n [J_{nm}\cos m\lambda + K_{nm}\sin m\lambda]\, P_{nm}(\sin\varphi)\right]$$

$$(4.37)$$

where a_E is the semimajor axis of the earth, r is the geocentric distance of the satellite, and φ, λ are its latitude and longitude. The J_n, J_{nm}, K_{nm} denote the zonal and tesseral coefficients of the harmonic development known from an earth model. Finally, P_n are the Legendre polynomials and P_{nm} are the associated Legendre functions.

The first term on the right-hand side of Eq. (4.37), μ/r, represents the potential V_0 for a spherical earth, and its gradient, $\mathrm{grad}(\mu/r) = (\mu/r^3)\,\underline{r}$, was considered as the central force for the Keplerian motion. Hence, the disturbing potential R is given by the difference

$$R = V - V_0\,. \qquad (4.38)$$

It is shown below that the disturbing acceleration due to J_2, the term representing the oblateness, is smaller by a factor of 10^4 than the acceleration due to V_0. On the other hand, the oblateness term is approximately three orders of magnitude larger than any other coefficient. Rizos and Stolz (1985) pointed out that a subset of the coefficients complete up to degree and order eight is sufficient for GPS satellite arcs of a few revolutions.

A numerical assessment of the central acceleration of GPS satellites gives $\|\ddot{\underline{r}}\| = (\mu/r^2) \approx 0.57\,\mathrm{m\,s^{-2}}$. The acceleration corresponding to the oblateness term in the disturbing potential R is given by $\|d\ddot{\underline{r}}\| \approx \|\partial R/\partial r\| = 3\mu\,(a_E/r^2)^2\, J_2\, P_2(\sin\varphi)$. The latitude of a satellite can only reach $\varphi = 55°$, the value of its orbital inclination. The maximum of the function $P_2(\sin\varphi) = \frac{1}{2}\,(3\sin\varphi^2 - 1)$, therefore, becomes 0.5. Finally, with $J_2 \approx 1.1 \cdot 10^{-3}$, the numerical value $\|d\ddot{\underline{r}}\| \approx 5 \cdot 10^{-5}\,\mathrm{m\,s^{-2}}$ is obtained.

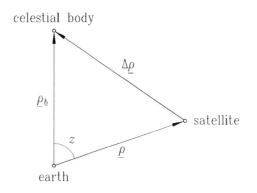

Fig. 4.2. Three-body problem

Tidal effects
Consider a celestial body with pointmass m_b and the geocentric position vector $\underline{\varrho}_b$, see Fig. 4.2. Note that the geocentric angle z between the celestial body and the satellite can be expressed as a function of $\underline{\varrho}_b$ and $\underline{\varrho}$, the latter denoting the geocentric position vector of the satellite, by

$$\cos z = \frac{\underline{\varrho}_b}{\|\underline{\varrho}_b\|} \cdot \frac{\underline{\varrho}}{\|\underline{\varrho}\|} \,. \tag{4.39}$$

The additional mass exerts an acceleration with respect to the earth as well as with respect to the satellite. For the perturbed motion of the satellite around the earth, only the difference of the two accelerations is relevant; consequently, the disturbing acceleration is given by

$$d\underline{\ddot{\varrho}} = G\,m_b \left[\frac{\underline{\varrho}_b - \underline{\varrho}}{\|\underline{\varrho}_b - \underline{\varrho}\|^3} - \frac{\underline{\varrho}_b}{\|\underline{\varrho}_b\|^3} \right]\,. \tag{4.40}$$

Among all the celestial bodies in the solar system, only the sun and the moon must be considered because the effects of the planets are negligible. The geocentric position vector of the sun and the moon are obtained by evaluating known analytical expressions for their motion.

The maximum of the perturbing acceleration is reached when the three bodies in Fig. 4.2 are situated in a straight line. In this case Eq. (4.40) reduces to $\|d\underline{\ddot{\varrho}}\| = G\,m_b\,(1/\|\underline{\varrho}_b - \underline{\varrho}\|^2 - 1/\|\underline{\varrho}_b\|^2)$. For a numerical assessment, the corresponding numerical values for the sun ($G\,m_b \approx 1.3 \cdot 10^{20}$ m^3 s^{-2}, $\varrho_b \approx 1.5 \cdot 10^{11}$ m) and of the moon ($G\,m_b \approx 4.9 \cdot 10^{12}$ m^3 s^{-2}, $\varrho_b \approx 3.8 \cdot 10^8$ m) are substituted. The resulting numerical values for the perturbing acceleration are $2 \cdot 10^{-6}$ m s^{-2} for the sun and $5 \cdot 10^{-6}$ m s^{-2} for the moon.

Apart from the direct effect of the tide generating bodies, indirect effects due to the tidal deformation of the solid earth and the oceanic tides must be taken into account. Considering only the tidal potential W_2 of second degree, the disturbing potential R due to the tidal deformation of the solid earth, cf. Melchior (1978), is given by

$$R = k \left(\frac{a_E}{\varrho}\right)^3 W_2 = \frac{1}{2} k\, G\, m_b \frac{a_E{}^5}{(\varrho\, \varrho_b)^3} (3\cos^2 z - 1) \tag{4.41}$$

with $k \approx 0.3$ being one of the Love numbers. The associated acceleration of the satellite is in the order of $10^{-9}\,\mathrm{m\,s^{-2}}$ as the reader may verify.

The model for the indirect effect due to the oceanic tides is more complicated. Tidal charts with the distribution of the oceanic tides are required. Such charts have been published by Schwiderski (1981). In addition, loading coefficients as computed by Farrell (1972) are needed. These coefficients describe the response of the solid earth to the load of the oceanic water masses. The perturbing acceleration is again in the order of $10^{-9}\,\mathrm{m\,s^{-2}}$.

As a consequence of the tidal deformation and the oceanic loading, the geocentric position vector $\underline{\varrho}_R$ of an observing site varies with time. This variation must be taken into account when modeling receiver dependent biases in the observation equations, cf. for example McCarthy (1992).

Solar radiation pressure
Following Fliegel et al. (1985), the perturbing acceleration due to the direct solar radiation pressure has two components. The principal component $d\underline{\ddot{\varrho}}_1$ is directed away from the sun and the smaller component $d\underline{\ddot{\varrho}}_2$ acts along the satellite's y-axis. This is an axis orthogonal to both the vector pointing to the sun and the antenna which is nominally directed towards the center of the earth.

The principal component is usually modeled by

$$d\underline{\ddot{\varrho}}_1 = \nu\, K\, \varrho_S^2 \frac{\underline{\varrho} - \underline{\varrho}_S}{\|\underline{\varrho} - \underline{\varrho}_S\|^3} \tag{4.42}$$

where $\underline{\varrho}_S$ denotes the geocentric position vector of the sun. The factor K depends linearly on the solar radiation constant P_S, a factor C_r defining the reflective properties of the satellite, and the area-to-mass ratio of the satellite. The quantity ν is an eclipse factor which is zero when the satellite is in the earth's shadow. This occurs twice a year for each satellite when the sun is in or near the orbital plane. Such an eclipse lasts approximately one hour. The eclipse factor equals one when the satellite is in sunlight and for the penumbra regions the relation $0 < \nu < 1$ holds.

The magnitude of $d\underline{\ddot{\varrho}}_1$ is in the order of $10^{-7}\,\mathrm{m\,s^{-2}}$. Hence, an accurate model for the factors K and ν is required even for short arcs. The modeling is extremely difficult since the factor P_S varies unpredictably over the year and a single factor C_r is not adequate for the satellite. Although the mass in orbit is usually well-known, the irregular shape of the satellites does not allow for an exact determination of the area-to-mass-ratio. A further problem is the modeling of the earth's penumbra and the assignment of an eclipse factor, particularly in the transition zone between illumination and shadow. Some models are given in Landau (1988).

The component $d\underline{\ddot{\varrho}}_2$ is often called y-bias and is believed to be caused by a combination of misalignments of the solar panels and thermal radiation along the y-axis. Since the magnitude of this bias can remain constant for several weeks, it is usually introduced as an unknown parameter which is determined in the course of the orbit determination. Note that this bias is two orders of magnitudes smaller than the principal term, cf. Feltens (1988).

That portion of the solar radiation pressure which is reflected back from the earth's surface causes an effect called albedo. In the case of GPS, the associated perturbing accelerations are smaller than the y-bias and can be neglected.

Relativistic effect
The relativistic effect on the satellite orbit is caused by the earth's gravity field and gives rise to a perturbing acceleration which, simplified, is given, cf. Beutler (1991), Eq. (2.5), by

$$d\underline{\ddot{\varrho}} = -\frac{3\mu^2\, a\left(1-e^2\right)}{c^2}\,\frac{\underline{\varrho}}{\varrho^5} \tag{4.43}$$

where c denotes the velocity of light. Numerically assessed, the perturbing acceleration results in an order of $3\cdot 10^{-10}\,\mathrm{m\,s^{-2}}$, cf. Zhu and Groten (1988). This effect is smaller than the indirect effects by one order of magnitude and is only mentioned for the sake of completeness.

4.3 Orbit determination

Here, orbit determination essentially means the determination of orbital parameters and satellite clock biases. In principle, the problem is inverse to the navigational or surveying goal. In the fundamental equation for the range ϱ or the range rate $\dot{\varrho}$ between the observing site R and the satellite S,

$$\varrho = \|\underline{\varrho}^S - \underline{\varrho}_R\| \tag{4.44}$$

$$\dot{\varrho} = \frac{\underline{\varrho}^S - \underline{\varrho}_R}{\|\underline{\varrho}^S - \underline{\varrho}_R\|} \cdot \underline{\dot{\varrho}}^S\,, \tag{4.45}$$

the position vector $\underline{\varrho}^S$ and the velocity vector $\underline{\dot{\varrho}}^S$ of the satellite are considered unknown, whereas the coordinates of the observing site are assumed to be known in a geocentric system. Note that the satellite vectors are indicated with a superscript.

From the observation equations one may state that the position vector $\underline{\varrho}^S$ is a function of ranges, whereas the velocity vector $\underline{\dot{\varrho}}^S$ is determined by range rates. The ranges in Eq. (4.44) are obtained with high precision as outlined in Sect. 6.1. This is particularly true for delta range data since biases are eliminated by differencing the ranges. The range rates in Eq. (4.45) are less accurate and are derived from frequency shifts due to the Doppler effect. At present, the observations for the orbit determination are performed at terrestrial points, but GPS data could also be obtained from orbiting receivers such as the TOPEX/Poseidon mission, cf. Lichten and Neilan (1990).

In the following, the satellite clock biases and other parameters are neglected. The actual orbit determination which is performed in two steps is emphasized. First, a Kepler ellipse is fitted to the observations. In the second step, this ellipse serves as reference for the subsequent improvement of the orbit by taking into account perturbing accelerations.

4.3.1 Keplerian orbit

For the moment, it is assumed that both the position and the velocity vector of the satellite have been derived from observations. Now, the question arises of how to use these data for the derivation of the Keplerian parameters.

The position and velocity vector given at the same epoch t define an initial value problem, and two position vectors at different epochs t_1 and t_2 define a (first) boundary value problem. In principle, also a second and a third boundary value problem could be defined; however, these problems are not of practical importance in the context of GPS and are therefore not treated here.

Initial value problem
As stated previously, the derivation of the Keplerian parameters from position and velocity vectors, both given at the same epoch and expressed in an equatorial system such as $\underline{X}_i$, is an initial value problem for solving the differential equation (4.1). Recall that the two given vectors contain six components which allow for the calculation of the six Keplerian parameters. Since both vectors are given at the same epoch, the time parameter is omitted.

The solution corresponds to a transformation inverse to Eq. (4.10) and makes use of the fact that quantities like distances or angles are invariant with respect to rotation. Hence, the following equations are obtained:

$$\|\underline{\varrho}\| = \|\underline{r}\|$$

$$\|\underline{\dot{\varrho}}\| = \|\underline{\dot{r}}\|$$

$$\underline{\varrho} \cdot \underline{\dot{\varrho}} = \underline{r} \cdot \underline{\dot{r}}$$

$$\|\underline{\varrho} \times \underline{\dot{\varrho}}\| = \|\underline{r} \times \underline{\dot{r}}\| .$$

$$(4.46)$$

In addition, by substituting Eqs. (4.6) and (4.8), the following equations can be derived:

$$\underline{\varrho} \cdot \underline{\dot{\varrho}} = \sqrt{\mu a}\, (e \sin E) \tag{4.47}$$

$$\|\underline{\varrho} \times \underline{\dot{\varrho}}\| = \sqrt{\mu a\,(1 - e^2)}. \tag{4.48}$$

Note that the inner product is denoted by a dot, the cross or vector product by the symbol $\times$, and the norm of a vector by two $\|$ symbols.

Now, the inverse transformation can be solved as follows. First, the geocentric distance r and the velocity $\dot{r}$ are calculated from the given $\underline{\varrho}$ and $\underline{\dot{\varrho}}$. Based on these two quantities, the semimajor axis a follows from Eq. (4.9). With a and r determined, $e \cos E$ can be established using Eq. (4.7) and $e \sin E$ can be established using Eq. (4.47). Hence, the eccentricity e and the eccentric anomaly E, and consequently the mean and true anomalies M and v, can be calculated. The vector product of $\underline{\varrho}$ and $\underline{\dot{\varrho}}$ is equivalent to the vector of angular momentum and is directed orthogonal to the orbital plane. Therefore, this vector after normalisation is identical to the vector $\underline{e}_3$ in Eq. (4.11) from which the parameters i and ℓ can be deduced. According to Eq. (4.48), the norm of the vector product allows for a check of the previously calculated parameters a and e. For the determination of ω, the unit vector $\underline{k} = [\cos \ell, \sin \ell, 0]^T$ directed to the ascending node is defined. From Fig. 4.1 one can obtain the relations $\underline{\varrho} \cdot \underline{k} = r \cos(\omega + v)$ and $\underline{\varrho} \cdot \underline{X}_3 = r \sin i \sin(\omega + v)$. And, since r, v, i are already known, the two equations can be uniquely solved for ω.

For a numerical example start with a position vector $\underline{\varrho}$ and the corresponding velocity vector $\underline{\dot{\varrho}}$

$$\underline{\varrho} = [11\,465,\ 3\,818,\ -20\,923]^T \qquad [\text{km}]$$

$$\underline{\dot{\varrho}} = [-1.2651,\ 3.9960,\ -0.3081]^T \quad [\text{km\,s}^{-1}]$$

to determine the Keplerian parameters. This is a task inverse to the numerical example in Sect. 4.2.1 and the result can be read from there.

Boundary value problem

Now, it is assumed that two position vectors $\underline{\varrho}^S(t_1)$ and $\underline{\varrho}^S(t_2)$ at epochs t_1 and t_2 are available. Note that position vectors are preferred for orbit determination since they are more accurate than velocity vectors. The given data correspond to boundary values in the solution of the basic second-order differential equation, cf. Eq. (4.1).

An approximate method for the derivation of the Keplerian parameters makes use of initial values defined for an averaged epoch $t = \frac{1}{2}(t_1 + t_2)$:

$$\underline{\varrho}^S(t) = \frac{\underline{\varrho}^S(t_2) + \underline{\varrho}^S(t_1)}{2}$$

$$\underline{\dot{\varrho}}^S(t) = \frac{\underline{\varrho}^S(t_2) - \underline{\varrho}^S(t_1)}{t_2 - t_1} \, . \tag{4.49}$$

The rigorous solution starts with the computation of the geocentric distances

$$r_1 = r(t_1) = \|\underline{\varrho}^S(t_1)\|$$

$$r_2 = r(t_2) = \|\underline{\varrho}^S(t_2)\| \, . \tag{4.50}$$

The unit vector $\underline{e}_3$, orthogonal to the orbital plane, is obtained from a vector product by

$$\underline{e}_3 = \frac{\underline{\varrho}^S(t_1) \times \underline{\varrho}^S(t_2)}{\|\underline{\varrho}^S(t_1) \times \underline{\varrho}^S(t_2)\|} \tag{4.51}$$

and produces the longitude ℓ and the inclination angle i, cf. Eqs. (4.11) and (4.13). As demonstrated earlier, the argument of the latitude $u = \omega + v$ is defined as the angle between the satellite's position and the ascending node vector $\underline{k} = [\cos\ell, \sin\ell, 0]^T$. Hence, the relation

$$r_i \cos u_i = \underline{k} \cdot \underline{\varrho}^S(t_i), \qquad i = 1,2 \tag{4.52}$$

holds from which the u_i with $u_2 > u_1$ can be deduced uniquely. Now, there are two equations, cf. Eq. (4.7),

$$r_i = \frac{a(1 - e^2)}{1 + e \cos(u_i - \omega)}, \qquad i = 1,2 \tag{4.53}$$

where the parameters a, e, ω are unknown. The system can be solved for a and e after assigning a preliminary value such as the nominal one to ω, the argument of the perigee. Based on the assumed ω and the u_i, the true anomalies v_i and subsequently the mean anomalies M_i are obtained. Therefore, the mean angular velocity n can be calculated twice by the formulas

$$n = \sqrt{\frac{\mu}{a^3}} = \frac{M_2 - M_1}{t_2 - t_1}, \tag{4.54}$$

cf. Eqs. (4.2) and (4.3). The equivalence is achieved by varying ω. This iterative procedure is typical for boundary value problems. Finally, the epoch of perigee passage T_0 follows from the relation

$$T_0 = t_i - \frac{M_i}{n} . \qquad (4.55)$$

For a numerical solution of the boundary value problem assume two position vectors $\underline{\varrho}(t_1)$ and $\underline{\varrho}(t_2)$, both represented in the earth-fixed equatorial system $\underline{X}_i$ and with $\Delta t = t_2 - t_1 = 1$ hour:

$$\underline{\varrho}(t_1) = [11\,465, \quad 3\,818, \quad -20\,923]^T \quad [\text{km}]$$

$$\underline{\varrho}(t_2) = [\ 5\,220, \ 16\,754, \ -18\,421]^T \quad [\text{km}].$$

The application of the Eqs. (4.50) through (4.55) results, apart from rounding errors, in the following set of parameters for the associated Kepler ellipse: $a = 26\,000\,\text{km}$, $e = 0.1$, $\omega = -140°$, $i = 60°$, $\ell = 110°$, and $T_0 = t_1 - 1^{\text{h}}3183$.

Orbit improvement
If there are redundant observations, the parameters of an instantaneous Kepler ellipse can be improved. The position vector $\underline{\varrho}_0^S$ associated to the reference ellipse can be computed. Each observed range, for example, gives rise to an equation

$$\varrho = \varrho_0 + d\varrho = \|\underline{\varrho}_0^S - \underline{\varrho}_R\| + \frac{\underline{\varrho}_0^S - \underline{\varrho}_R}{\|\underline{\varrho}_0^S - \underline{\varrho}_R\|} \cdot d\underline{\varrho}^S . \qquad (4.56)$$

The vector $d\underline{\varrho}^S$ can be expressed as a function of the Keplerian parameters, cf. Eq. (4.26). Thus, Eq. (4.56) actually contains the differential increments for the six orbital parameters.

An orbit improvement is often performed in the course of GPS data processing when, in addition to terrestrial position vectors $\underline{\varrho}_R$, the solution also allows for the determination of the increments dp_{0i}. Of course, the procedure becomes unstable or even fails for small networks. Sometimes only three degrees of freedom are assigned to the orbit by a shift vector. This procedure is called orbit relaxation.

4.3.2 Perturbed orbit

Analytical solution
As known from previous sections, the perturbed motion is characterized by temporal variations of the orbital parameters. The analytical expressions for these variations are given by the Eqs. (4.34) or (4.36).

In order to be applicable for Lagrange's equations, the disturbing potential must be expressed as a function of the Keplerian parameters. For the effects of the nonsphericity of the earth, the Legendre functions in Eq. (4.37) must be transformed which first has been performed by Kaula (1966). The resulting relation is

$$R = \sum_{n=2}^{\infty} \sum_{m=0}^{n} A_n(a) \sum_{p=0}^{n} F_{nmp}(i)$$
$$\cdot \sum_{q=-\infty}^{\infty} G_{npq}(e) S_{nmpq}(\omega, \Omega, M; \Theta_0, J_{nm}, K_{nm}).$$

(4.57)

Recall that n denotes the degree and m the order of the spherical harmonics in the disturbing potential development. Each of the functions A_n, F_{nmp}, G_{npq} contains only one parameter of a Kepler ellipse. However, the function S_{nmpq} is composed of several parameters and can be expressed by

$$S_{nmpq} = \quad J_{nm} \cos \psi + K_{nm} \sin \psi \quad \text{for } n - m \text{ even}$$
$$S_{nmpq} = -K_{nm} \cos \psi + J_{nm} \sin \psi \quad \text{for } n - m \text{ odd}.$$

(4.58)

The frequency $\dot\psi$ associated to the argument ψ is given by

$$\dot\psi = (n - 2p)\,\dot\omega + (n - 2p + q)\,\dot M + m\,(\dot\Omega - \dot\Theta_0)$$

(4.59)

and is a measure of the spectrum of the perturbations.

The conditions $(n - 2p) = (n - 2p + q) = m = 0$ lead to $\dot\psi = 0$ and, thus, to secular variations. Because of $m = 0$, they are caused by zonal harmonics. If $(n - 2p) \neq 0$, then the variations depend on ω and are, therefore, generally long-periodic. Finally, the conditions $(n - 2p + q) \neq 0$ and/or $m \neq 0$ result in short-periodic variations. The integer value $(n - 2p + q)$ gives the frequency in cycles per revolution and m the frequency in cycles per (sidereal) day.

A rough overview of the frequency spectrum in the Keplerian parameters due to the gravity field of the earth is given in Table 4.4. Summarizing, one can state that the even degree zonal coefficients produce primarily secular variations and the odd degree zonal coefficients give rise to long-periodic perturbations. The tesseral coefficients are responsible for short-periodic terms. From Table 4.4 one can read that short-periodic variations occur in each parameter. With the exception of the semimajor axis, the parameters are also affected by long-periodic perturbations. Secular effects are only contained in Ω, ω, M. The analytical expression for the secular variations

Table 4.4. Perturbations due to the earth's gravity field

Parameter	Secular	Long-periodic	Short-periodic
a	no	no	yes
e	no	yes	yes
i	no	yes	yes
Ω	yes	yes	yes
ω	yes	yes	yes
M	yes	yes	yes

in these parameters due to the oblateness term J_2 is given as an example:

$$\dot{\Omega} = -\frac{3}{2}\, n\, a_E^2\, \frac{\cos i}{a^2\,(1-e^2)^2}\, J_2$$

$$\dot{\omega} = \frac{3}{4}\, n\, a_E^2\, \frac{5\cos^2 i - 1}{a^2\,(1-e^2)^2}\, J_2 \qquad\qquad (4.60)$$

$$\dot{m} = \frac{3}{4}\, n\, a_E^2\, \frac{3\cos^2 i - 1}{a^2\,\sqrt{(1-e^2)^3}}\, J_2\,.$$

The first equation describes the regression of the node in the equatorial plane, the second equation expresses the rotation of the perigee, and the third equation contributes to the variation of the mean anomaly by $\dot{M} = n + \dot{m}$. In the case of GPS satellites, the numerical values $\dot{\Omega} \approx -0°03$ per day, $\dot{\omega} \approx 0°01$ per day, and $\dot{m} \approx 0$ are obtained. The result for $\dot{m}$ is verified immediately since for the nominal inclination $i = 55°$ the term $3\cos^2 i - 1$ becomes approximately zero. A graphical representation of the secular perturbations is given in Fig. 4.3. Special attention must be paid to resonance effects which occur when the period of revolution corresponds to a harmonic in the gravity potential. This is why the GPS satellites are raised into slightly higher orbits to preclude an orbital period very close to half a sidereal day.

The tidal potential also has a harmonic representation. Analogously, the tidal perturbations can be analytically modeled. This was done first by Kozai (1959) and, analogously to the earth's potential effect, has led to analytical expressions for the secular variations of the node's right ascension Ω and of the perigee's argument ω. The reader is referred to the publication of Kozai (1959) for formulas specified.

Numerical solution
If the disturbing acceleration cannot be expressed in analytical form, one has

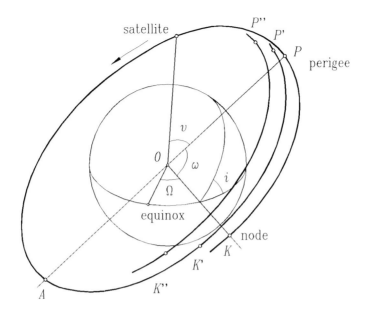

Fig. 4.3. Secular perturbations caused by the oblateness term J_2

to apply numerical methods for the solution. Therefore, in principle, with initial values such as the position and velocity vectors $\underline{\varrho}(t_0)$ and $\underline{\dot{\varrho}}(t_0)$ at a reference epoch t_0, a numerical integration of Eq. (4.27) could be performed. This simple concept can be improved by the introduction of a Kepler ellipse as a reference. By this means only the smaller difference between the total and the central acceleration must be integrated. The integration results in an increment $\delta\underline{\varrho}$ which, when added to the position vector computed for the reference ellipse, gives the actual position vector.

The second-order differential equation is usually transformed to a system of two differential equations of the first order for the numerical integration. This system is given by

$$\underline{\dot{\varrho}}(t) = \underline{\dot{\varrho}}(t_0) + \int_{t_0}^{t} \underline{\ddot{\varrho}}(t_0)\,dt$$

$$= \underline{\dot{\varrho}}(t_0) + \int_{t_0}^{t} \left[d\underline{\ddot{\varrho}}(t_0) - \frac{\mu}{\varrho^3(t_0)}\,\underline{\varrho}(t_0)\right] dt \qquad (4.61)$$

$$\underline{\varrho}(t) = \underline{\varrho}(t_0) + \int_{t_0}^{t} \underline{\dot{\varrho}}(t_0)\,dt\,.$$

The numerical integration of this coupled system can be performed by applying the standard Runge-Kutta algorithm, cf. for example Kreyszig (1968), p. 89. This method is shortly outlined. Let $y(x)$ be a function defined in the interval $x_1 \leq x \leq x_2$ and denote by $y' = dy/dx$ its first derivative with respect to the argument x. The general solution of the ordinary differential equation of the first order

$$y' = \frac{dy}{dx} = y'(y, x) \tag{4.62}$$

follows from integration. The particular solution is found after assigning the given numerical initial value $y_1 = y(x_1)$ to the integration constant. For the application of numerical integration, first the integration interval is partitioned into n equal and sufficiently small $\Delta x = (x_2 - x_1)/n$ where n is an arbitrary integer number > 0. Then, the difference between successive functional values is obtained by the weighted mean

$$\begin{aligned} \Delta y &= y(x + \Delta x) - y(x) \\ &= \frac{1}{6} \left[\Delta y^{(1)} + 2 \left(\Delta y^{(2)} + \Delta y^{(3)} \right) + \Delta y^{(4)} \right] \end{aligned} \tag{4.63}$$

where

$$\Delta y^{(1)} = y'(y, \ x) \, \Delta x$$

$$\Delta y^{(2)} = y'(y + \frac{\Delta y^{(1)}}{2}, \quad x + \frac{\Delta x}{2}) \, \Delta x$$

$$\Delta y^{(3)} = y'(y + \frac{\Delta y^{(2)}}{2}, \quad x + \frac{\Delta x}{2}) \, \Delta x$$

$$\Delta y^{(4)} = y'(y + \Delta y^{(3)}, \quad x + \Delta x) \, \Delta x \, .$$

Hence, starting with the initial value y_1 for the argument x_1, the function can be calculated for the successive argument $x_1 + \Delta x$ and so on.

Numerical methods can also be applied to the integration of the disturbing equations of Lagrange or Gauss. These equations have the advantage of being differentials of the first order and, therefore, must only be integrated once over time.

This section is concluded with an example for numerical integration. Assume the ordinary first-order differential equation $y' = y - x + 1$ with the initial value $y_1 = 1$ for $x_1 = 0$. The differential equation should be solved for the argument $x_2 = 1$ with increments $\Delta x = 0.5$. Starting with the initial values for the first interval, successively the values $\Delta y^{(1)} = 1.000$, $\Delta y^{(2)} = 1.125$, $\Delta y^{(3)} = 1.156$, and $\Delta y^{(4)} = 1.328$ are obtained. The corresponding weighted mean is $\Delta y = 1.148$. Replacing the initial values in the second interval by $x = x_1 + \Delta x = 0.5$ and $y = y_1 + \Delta y = 2.148$ and proceeding as before yields $\Delta y = 1.569$ and, thus, the final result $y_2 = y_1 + \Sigma \Delta y = 3.717$. Note that the function $y = e^x + x$, satisfying the differential equation, gives the true value $y_2 = 3.718$. With an increment $\Delta x = 0.1$ the numerical integration would provide an accuracy in the order of 10^{-6}.

4.4 Orbit dissemination

4.4.1 Tracking networks

Objectives and strategies
The broadcast ephemerides for Block I satellites with cesium clocks were accurate to about 5 m (assuming three uploads per day) as demonstrated by Remondi and Hofmann-Wellenhof (1989a). For the Block II satellites, the accuracy for nonauthorized users can be degraded up to 50–100 m by SA. However, an orbital accuracy of about 20 cm is required for specific missions such as TOPEX/Poseidon or for investigations which require an accuracy at the level of 10^{-9}. Moreover, the geodetic community should become independent from the vagaries of the Department of Defense (DoD). The need for civil tracking networks for orbit determination is evident.

Global networks result in higher accuracy and reliability of the orbits compared to those determined from regional networks. The tie of the orbital system to terrestrial reference frames is achieved by the collocation of GPS receivers with VLBI and SLR trackers. The distribution of the GPS sites is essential to achieve the highest accuracy. Two different approaches can be compared. In the first case, the sites are regularly distributed around the globe; in the second case each network site is surrounded by a cluster of additional points to facilitate ambiguity resolution and, thus, to strengthen the solution of the orbital parameters by a factor of three to five, cf. Counselman and Abbot (1989). If a configuration is desired where at least two satellites can be tracked simultaneously any time from two sites, the minimum number of sites in a global network is six, cf. Lichten and Neilan (1990). A densified version should contain approximately 20 sites with clusters around them.

Examples
Apart from the GPS control segment, several networks have been established for orbit determination. Without mentioning the numerous networks on a regional or even continental scale such as the Australian GPS orbit determination pilot project reported by Rizos et al. (1987), some examples of global networks are given.

The Cooperative International GPS Network (CIGNET) is being operated by the U.S. National Geodetic Survey (NGS) with tracking stations

Table 4.5. CIGNET sites (status in early 1991)

	Site	Country
	Hartebeesthoek	South Africa
*	Hobart	Australia
*	Kokee Park	Hawaii, USA
	Madrid	Spain
*	Mojave/Goldstone	California, USA
	Natal	Brazil
*	Onsala	Sweden
	Port Harcourt	Nigeria
*	Richmond	Florida, USA
	Santiago	Chile
	Tidbinbilla	Australia
*	Townsville	Australia
*	Tromsø	Norway
*	Tsukuba-Kashima	Japan
	Useda	Japan
*	Wellington	New Zealand
*	Westford	Massachusetts, USA
*	Wettzell	Germany
	Yaragadee	Australia
*	Yellowknife	Canada

Fig. 4.4. CIGNET sites (status in early 1991)

located at VLBI sites. In early 1991, about 20 stations were participating, cf. Fig. 4.4. These tracking sites are listed in Table 4.5, cf. Chin (1991). Today (early 1994), 48 stations are involved. Some of the CIGNET participants (marked by an asterisk in Table 4.5) download their tracking data every night to the processing center located at the NGS facility in Rockville, Maryland. The NGS processes these data and makes it available on the following morning to participants by means of a file server computer connected to modems. Data from the remaining stations are received at NGS with a delay of two to seven days and are processed and made available within one day.

The CIGNET is different from the official tracking network in several aspects. First and most important, these stations observe and record the phase as well as the code range data from all satellites. Thus, they observe the C/A-code and P-code pseudoranges on the $L1$ frequency and the P-code pseudorange on the $L2$ frequency as well as the carrier phase on both frequencies. A second major difference in the CIGNET is the fact that the tracking data are immediately available to users, whereas the official precise ephemerides are subject to a delay. Furthermore, the coordinates of the CIGNET sites refer to ITRF, while the official ephemerides are represented in WGS-84.

Participants (and possibly others) can access the tracking data from CIGNET and, if they are equipped with appropriate programs, they would be able to compute their own ephemerides. Another application of the tracking data is to combine it with data from a local survey and use orbit relaxation software to compute the coordinates of local points. The NGS has tested this concept using data from the U.S. CIGNET stations and obtained a few centimeters accuracy for points in the mid-continent.

The first Global Orbit Tracking Experiment (GOTEX) was performed in the fall of 1988 and aimed at the collocation of GPS at existing VLBI and SLR sites. The data should permit a close connection between the WGS-84 and the VLBI/SLR systems. About 25 sites, distributed worldwide, were occupied during the three weeks of the campaign. The data were reformatted into the CIGNET format and may be obtained from the NGS.

In 1990, the International Association of Geodesy (IAG) decided to install an International GPS Geodynamics Service (IGS). After a test campaign in 1992, routine activities started at the beginning of 1994. The main purpose of this service is dedicated to geodynamical applications which require highest accuracy. Another task is the establishment of an orbit determination activity similar to CIGNET. The network consists of a permanent core network with about 25 control stations supplemented by more than 100 intermittent fiducial stations. Further details can be found in Mueller (1991).

4.4.2   Ephemerides

Three sets of data are available for the determination of position and velocity vectors of the satellites in a terrestrial reference frame at any instant. These sets are almanac data, broadcast ephemerides, and precise ephemerides. The data differ in accuracy, cf. Table 4.6, and are either available in real time or after the fact.

Table 4.6. Overview of ephemerides uncertainties

Ephemerides	Uncertainty	Comment
Almanac	Some kilometers	Depending on the age of data
Broadcast (SA on)	$2 - 50\,\text{m}$	Depending on the level of SA
Broadcast (SA off)	$2 - 5\,\text{m}$	Or even better
Precise	$0.5 - 1\,\text{m}$	Or even better

Almanac data

The purpose of the almanac data is to provide the user with less precise data to facilitate receiver satellite search or for planning tasks such as the computation of visibility charts. The almanac data are transmitted via the satellite message, cf. Sect. 5.1.2, which essentially contains parameters for the orbit representation, satellite clock correction parameters, and some other information, cf. Table 4.7. The parameter ℓ_0 denotes the difference between

Table 4.7. Almanac data

Parameter	Explanation
ID	Satellite PRN number
HEALTH	Satellite health status
WEEK	Current GPS week
t_a	Reference epoch in seconds within the current week
$\sqrt{a}$	Square root of semimajor axis
e	Eccentricity
M_0	Mean anomaly at reference epoch
ω	Argument of perigee
δi	Offset from 0.3 semicircles ($\hat{=} 54°$)
ℓ_0	Longitude of node at weekly epoch
$\dot{\Omega}$	Rate of node's right ascension
a_0	Clock phase bias
a_1	Clock frequency bias

the node's right ascension at epoch t_a and the Greenwich sidereal time at t_0, the beginning of the current GPS week. The reduction of the Keplerian parameters to the observation epoch t is obtained by the formulas

$$M = M_0 + n\,(t - t_a)$$

$$i \;\; = 54° + \delta i \tag{4.64}$$

$$\ell \;\; = \ell_0 + \dot{\Omega}\,(t - t_a) - \omega_E\,(t - t_0)$$

where $\omega_E = 7\,292\,115.1467 \cdot 10^{-11}\,\mathrm{rad\,s^{-1}}$ is the (untruncated) angular velocity of the earth. The other three Keplerian parameters a, e, ω remain unchanged. Note that in the formula for ℓ in Eq. (4.64) the second right-hand side term considers the node's regression and the third term expresses the uniform change in the sidereal time since epoch t_0. An estimate for the satellite clock bias is given by

$$\delta^S = a_0 + a_1\,(t - t_a)\,. \tag{4.65}$$

Broadcast ephemerides
The broadcast ephemerides in Table 4.8 are based on observations at the five monitor stations of the GPS control segment. The most recent of these data are used to compute a reference orbit for the satellites. Additional tracking data are entered into a Kalman filter and the improved orbits are used for extrapolation, cf. Wells et al. (1987). As reported by Remondi and Hofmann-Wellenhof (1989b), these orbital data could be accurate to approximately 5 m based on three uploads per day; with a single daily update one might expect

Table 4.8. Broadcast ephemerides

Parameter	Explanation
AODE	Age of ephemerides data
t_e	Ephemerides reference epoch
$\sqrt{a},\,e,\,M_0,$ $\omega_0,\,i_0,\,\ell_0$	Keplerian parameters at t_e
Δn	Mean motion difference
$\dot{i}$	Rate of inclination angle
$\dot{\Omega}$	Rate of node's right ascension
$C_{uc},\,C_{us}$	Correction coefficients (argument of perigee)
$C_{rc},\,C_{rs}$	Correction coefficients (geocentric distance)
$C_{ic},\,C_{is}$	Correction coefficients (inclination)

an accuracy of 10 m. The Master Control Station is responsible for the computation of the ephemerides and the upload to the satellites. Essentially, the ephemerides contain six parameters to describe a smoothed Kepler ellipse at a reference epoch and some secular and periodic correction terms. The most recent parameters listed in Table 4.8 are broadcast (mostly) every hour and should only be used during the prescribed period of approximately four hours to which they refer.

The perturbation effects due to the nonsphericity of the earth, the direct tidal effect, and the solar radiation pressure are considered by the last nine terms in Table 4.8. In order to compute the satellite's position at the observation epoch t, the following quantities, apart from the parameters a and e, are needed

$$M = M_0 + \left[\sqrt{\frac{\mu}{a^3}} + \Delta n \right] (t - t_e)$$

$$\ell = \ell_0 + \dot{\Omega} (t - t_e) - \omega_E (t - t_0)$$

$$\omega = \omega_0 + C_{uc} \cos(2u) + C_{us} \sin(2u) \qquad (4.66)$$

$$r = r_0 + C_{rc} \cos(2u) + C_{rs} \sin(2u)$$

$$i = i_0 + C_{ic} \cos(2u) + C_{is} \sin(2u) + i(t - t_e)$$

where $u = \omega + v$ is the argument of latitude. The geocentric distance r_0 is calculated by Eq. (4.7) using a, e, E at the observation epoch. Based on the reference epoch t_e, the computation of ℓ is analogous to that in Eq. (4.64). Note that again the untruncated value for the earth's rotation rate must be used.

Precise ephemerides
The precise ephemerides are based on observed data obtained in tracking networks and are computed by several institutions. The results are available with some delay (from 4 to 14 days) after data collection and are expressed as satellite positions and velocities at equidistant epochs. As an example, the NGS format according to Remondi (1989) is described here.

The complete NGS format consists of a header containing general information (epoch interval, orbit type, etc.) followed by the data section for successive epochs. These data are reported for each satellite and represent the position vector $\underline{\varrho}$ [km] and the velocity vector $\underline{\dot{\varrho}}$ [km s^{-1}].

The reduced NGS format contains only positions since it is shown by Remondi (1989) and Remondi (1991b) that, in general, velocity is superfluous. The velocity information can, with sufficient precision, be computed from the position data by differentiating an interpolating polynomial. Hence, only the half storage amount is needed compared to the complete format.

Originally, the NGS results have been based on dual frequency P-code range data obtained from the CIGNET. Later, the NGS has switched to a carrier phase observable. The orbits are computed using the IERS station coordinates which approximate the WGS-84 values. The internal precision of the orbits is at the level of a few parts in 10^{-7}. NGS disseminates the data as ASCII and binary files. The latter is formatted for IBM compatible PC's, saves storage capacity, and facilitates electronic data transfer. The position and velocity vectors between the given epochs are obtained by interpolation where the Lagrange interpolation based on polynomial base functions is used.

Note that Lagrange interpolation is also applicable to variable epoch series and that the coefficients determined can be applied to considerably longer series without updating the coefficients. This interpolation method is a fast procedure and can be easily programmed. Extensive studies by Remondi (1989) concluded that for GPS satellites a 30-minute epoch interval and a 9th-order interpolator suffices for an accuracy of about 10^{-8}. A more recent study by Remondi (1991b) using a 17th-order interpolator demonstrates that millimeter-level (10^{-10}) can be achieved based on a 40-minute epoch interval.

For those not familiar with Lagrange interpolation, the principle of this method and a numerical example is given, cf. for example Moritz (1977). Let the epochs t_j, $j = 0, \ldots, n$ be where the associated functional values $f(t_j)$ are given. Then,

$$\ell_j(t) = \frac{(t - t_0)(t - t_1) \cdots (t - t_{j-1})(t - t_{j+1}) \cdots (t - t_n)}{(t_j - t_0)(t_j - t_1) \cdots (t_j - t_{j-1})(t_j - t_{j+1}) \cdots (t_j - t_n)}$$

$$(4.67)$$

is the definition of the corresponding base functions $\ell_j(t)$ of degree n related to an arbitrary epoch t. The interpolated functional value at epoch t follows from the summation

$$f(t) = \sum_{j=0}^{n} f(t_j) \ell_j(t). \qquad (4.68)$$

The following numerical example assumes the functional values $f(t_j)$ given at the epochs t_j:

$$\underline{f} = [f(t_j)] = [13, 17, 85]^T$$

$$\underline{t} = [t_j] \quad = [-3, 1, 5]^T.$$

The base functions are polynomials of second degree

$$\ell_0(t) = \frac{(t - t_1)(t - t_2)}{(t_0 - t_1)(t_0 - t_2)} = \frac{1}{32}(t^2 - 6t + 5)$$

$$\ell_1(t) = \frac{(t - t_0)(t - t_2)}{(t_1 - t_0)(t_1 - t_2)} = -\frac{1}{16}(t^2 - 2t - 15)$$

$$\ell_2(t) = \frac{(t - t_0)(t - t_1)}{(t_2 - t_0)(t_2 - t_1)} = \frac{1}{32}(t^2 + 2t - 3)$$

and, according to Eq. (4.68), the interpolated value for $t = 4$ is $f(t) = 62$. The result is immediately verified since the given functional values were generated by the polynomial $f(t) = 2t^2 + 5t + 10$.

5 Satellite signal

5.1 Signal structure

5.1.1 Physical fundamentals

Operational satellite geodesy is based upon data transmitted from the satellite to the user by means of electromagnetic waves. Some of the factors describing the physical behavior of these waves are presented in Table 5.1 together with their symbols and dimensions. A fundamental constant is the speed of light in the vacuum and its numerical value is given by

$$c = 299\,792\,458 \text{ m s}^{-1}. \tag{5.1}$$

Note that integer cycles are equivalent to multiples of 2π radians. Another unit for cycles per second (cps) is Hertz (Hz) or decimal multiples according to the rules of the International System of Units (ISU). Equation (5.2) relates the parameters shown in Table 5.1:

$$f = 2\pi \frac{1}{P} = \frac{c}{\lambda}. \tag{5.2}$$

The instantaneous circular frequency f is also defined by the derivation of the phase φ with respect to time

$$f = \frac{d\varphi}{dt}, \tag{5.3}$$

Table 5.1. Physical quantities

Quantity	Symbol	Dimension
Circular frequency	f	cycle s^{-1}
Phase	φ	cycle
Wavelength	λ	m cycle^{-1}
Period	P	s
Speed of light	c	m s^{-1}

and the phase is obtained from integrating the frequency between the epochs t_0 and t

$$\varphi = \int_{t_0}^{t} f \, dt \, . \tag{5.4}$$

Assuming a constant frequency, setting the initial phase $\varphi(t_0) = 0$, and taking into account the time span t_ϱ which the signal needs to propagate through the distance ϱ from the emitter to the receiver yields the phase equation for electromagnetic waves as observed at the receiving site:

$$\varphi = f\left(t - t_\varrho\right) = f\left(t - \frac{\varrho}{c}\right) . \tag{5.5}$$

For a numerical example consider an electromagnetic wave with frequency $f = 1.5\,\text{GHz}$ and calculate the instantaneous phase at an antenna $20\,000\,\text{km}$ distant from the transmitter source. With $c = 3 \cdot 10^5\,\text{km s}^{-1}$ a (continuous) phase of exactly 10^8 cycles results. The observable (fractional) phase within one cycle, thus, is zero.

In the case of a moving emitter or a moving receiver, the received frequency is Doppler shifted. This means that the received frequency f_r differs from the emitted frequency f_e by an amount Δf which, apart from relativistic effects, is proportional to the radial velocity $v_\varrho = d\varrho/dt = \dot{\varrho}$ of the emitter with respect to the receiver:

$$\Delta f = f_r - f_e = -\frac{1}{c} \, v_\varrho \, f_e \, . \tag{5.6}$$

It can be verified by Eq. (4.9) that GPS satellites are orbiting with the mean velocity $\dot{r} = n\,a \approx 3.9\,\text{km s}^{-1}$. With respect to a stationary terrestrial receiver, there is a zero radial velocity and, thus, no Doppler effect at the epoch of closest approach. The maximum radial velocity appears when the satellite crosses the horizon and amounts to $0.9\,\text{km s}^{-1}$. Assuming a transmitted frequency $f_e = 1.5\,\text{GHz}$, the Doppler frequency shift is $\Delta f = 4.5 \cdot 10^3\,\text{Hz}$. This frequency shift leads to a phase change of 4.5 cycles after one millisecond which corresponds to a change in range of $90\,\text{cm}$. The result can be verified by multiplying the radial velocity or range rate with the time span of one millisecond.

5.1.2   Components of the signal

General remarks
The oscillators on board the satellites generate a fundamental frequency f_0 with a stability in the range of 10^{-13} over one day for the Block II satellites. Two carrier signals in the L-band, denoted $L1$ and $L2$, are generated by

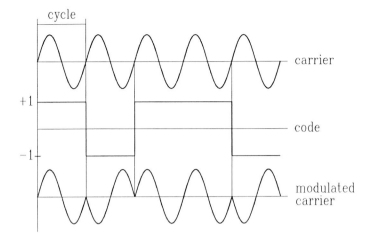

Fig. 5.1. Biphase modulation of carrier wave

Table 5.2. Components of the satellite signal

Component	Frequency (MHz)		
Fundamental frequency	f_0	$= 10.23$	
Carrier $L1$	$154\,f_0$	$= 1\,575.42$	$(\hat{=} 19.0\,\text{cm})$
Carrier $L2$	$120\,f_0$	$= 1\,227.60$	$(\hat{=} 24.4\,\text{cm})$
P-code	f_0	$= 10.23$	
C/A-code	$f_0/10$	$= 1.023$	
W-code	$f_0/20$	$= 0.5115$	
Navigation message	$f_0/204\,600 = 50 \cdot 10^{-6}$		

integer multiplications of f_0. These carriers are modulated by codes to provide satellite clock readings to the receiver and to transmit information such as the orbital parameters. The codes consist of a sequence with the states $+1$ or -1, corresponding to the binary values 0 or 1. The so-called biphase modulation is performed by a 180° shift in the carrier phase whenever a change in the code state occurs, cf. Fig. 5.1.

The components of the signal and their frequencies are summarized in Table 5.2. Note that the nominal fundamental frequency f_0 is intentionally reduced by about 0.005 Hz to compensate for relativistic effects. More details on this subject are provided in Sect. 6.4.3.

Two codes are used for the satellite clock readings, both characterized by a pseudorandom noise (PRN) sequence. The coarse/acquisition (or clear/access) code (C/A-code) has the frequency $f_0/10$ and is repeated every millisecond. The precision (or protected) code (P-code) has the frequency f_0 and is repeated approximately once every 266.4 days. The W-code is used to encrypt the P-code to the Y-code when A-S is implemented. The frequency $f_0/20$ of the W-code has not yet been verified. The coding of the navigation message requires 1 500 bits and, at the frequency of 50 Hz, is transmitted in 30 seconds.

Both the $L1$ and $L2$ carrier are modulated by the P-code (more precisely, by the Y-code). The C/A-code is placed on the $L1$ carrier in phase quadrature (i.e., 90° offset) with the P-code. Denoting unmodulated carrier by $Li(t) = a_i \cos(f_i t)$ and the state sequences of the P-code, the C/A-code, and the navigation message by $P(t)$, $C/A(t)$, and $D(t)$ respectively, the modulated carriers are represented by the equations, cf. Spilker (1980),

$$L1(t) = a_1 P(t) D(t) \cos(f_1 t) + a_1 C/A(t) D(t) \sin(f_1 t)$$
$$L2(t) = a_2 P(t) D(t) \cos(f_2 t) \,.$$

$$(5.7)$$

Note that the broadcast signal is a spread spectrum signal which ensures more communication security.

Pseudorandom noise codes
The generation of the PRN sequences in the codes is based on the use of hardware devices called tapped feedback shift registers, cf. Wells et al. (1987), Sect. 6.4. As illustrated in Fig. 5.2, such a device consists of a number of storage cells (here labeled 1–5) comprising one bit. Associated with each clock pulse is a shift of the bits to the right where the content of the rightmost cell is read as output. The new value of the leftmost cell is determined by the binary sum of two defined cells where a binary 0 is set if the bits in these two cells are equal. The choice of the defining cells is arbitrary and determines the property of the resulting code.

In order to make the procedure more clear consider cells 2 and 3 as defining pair in Fig. 5.2. After one clock pulse, the initial state would deliver a binary 0 as output and a binary 1 would be set in cell 1 of the successive

Number of cell	1	2	3	4	5
Initial state	1	0	1	1	0
Successive state	1	1	0	1	1

Fig. 5.2. Principle of a tapped feedback shift register

state. Continuing in an analogous way, the bit sequence 1101110010... would be delivered.

The bits of the PRN sequences are often called chips to underscore that these codes do not carry data.

The C/A-code is generated by the combination of two 10-bit tapped feedback shift registers where the output of both registers are added again by binary operation to produce the code sequence. The codes of the two registers are not classified, and the C/A-code is available to civilian users. A unique code is assigned to each satellite depending on the defining cells. The frequency of 1.023 MHz and the repetition rate of 1 millisecond results in a code length of 1 023 chips. Hence, the time interval between two chips is just under 1 microsecond which approximately corresponds to a 300 m chip length.

The P-code is also not classified and originates from a combination of two bit sequences, again each generated by two registers. The first bit sequence repeats every 1.5 second and, because of the frequency f_0, has a length of $1.5345 \cdot 10^7$ bits. The second sequence has 37 more bits. The combination of both sequences, thus, results in a code with approximately $2.3547 \cdot 10^{14}$ bits which corresponds to a time span of approximately 266.4 days as stated earlier. The total code length is partitioned into 37 unique one-week segments and each segment is assigned to a satellite defining its PRN number. The codes are restarted at the beginning of every GPS week at Saturday midnight. The chip length of the P-code is about 30 m. In order to illustrate the P-code generation, an example is given, cf. Fig. 5.3. Consider the two sequences $S1$ and $S2$ containing the bit sequences 010 and 10110 respectively. The combination of $5 * S1$ with $3 * S2$ using binary addition results in a code with a length of 15 chips. Since $S2$ comprises 2 bits more than $S1$, the combined code can be partitioned into two unique segments where their length is two times the length of $S1$.

In order to protect the P-code against spoofing (i.e., the deliberate transmission of incorrect information by an adversary), the P-code is encrypted to the Y-code by A-S, cf. Sect. 2.2.4. Since the Y-code is the modulo two sum of the P-code and the encrypting W-code, access to the P-code is only possible when the secret conversion algorithm is known.

$5 * S1$	0 1 0 0 1 0 0 1 0 0 1 0 0 1 0
$3 * S2$	1 0 1 1 0 1 0 1 1 0 1 0 1 1 0
Combination	1 1 1 1 1 1 0 0 1 0 0 0 1 0 0

Fig. 5.3. Principle of P-code generation

Navigation message

The navigation message essentially contains information about the satellite clock, the satellite orbit, the satellite health status, and various correction data. As shown schematically in Table 5.3, the total message consisting of 1 500 bits is subdivided into five subframes. One subframe is transmitted in 6 seconds and contains 10 words with 30 bits. The transmission time needed for a word is therefore 0.6 seconds.

Each subframe starts with the telemetry word (TLM) containing a synchronization pattern and some diagnostic messages. The second word in each subframe is the hand-over word (HOW). Apart from a subframe identification and some flags, this word contains a number which, when multiplied by four, gives the time-of-week (TOW) count for the epoch at the start (leading edge) of the next subframe. The TOW count is a multiple number of 1.5-second intervals since the beginning of the current GPS week.

The first subframe contains the GPS week number, a prediction for the user range accuracy, indicators on the satellite health and on the age of the data, an estimation for the group delay of the signal, and the three coefficients for a quadratic polynomial to model the satellite clock correction.

The second and third subframe transmit the broadcast ephemerides of the satellite as described in Sect. 4.4.2.

The contents of the fourth and the fifth subframe are changed in every message and have a repetition rate of 25. The total information, thus, is packed into 25 pages and needs 12.5 minutes for transmission. Many pages of the fourth subframe are reserved for military use; the rest contains information on the ionosphere, UTC data, various flags, and the almanac data (i.e., low-accuracy orbital data) for all the satellites exceeding the nominal constellation. The pages of the fifth subframe are mainly dedicated to the almanac data and the health status for the first 24 satellites in orbit. The pages of the fourth and fifth subframe are broadcast by each satellite. Therefore, by tracking only one satellite one receives the almanac data of all the other satellites in orbit.

Table 5.3. Scheme of navigation message

	Number of bits	Transmission time
Total message	1 500	30 seconds
Subframe (1–5)	300	6 seconds
Word (1–10)	30	0.6 seconds

For more information concerning the data of the navigation message, the reader is referred to Sect. 4.4 on orbit dissemination. A detailed description of the data format is given in Dierendonck et al. (1980), Rockwell International Corporation (1984), Nieuwejaar (1988), and Department of Defense (1993).

5.2   Signal processing

The signal emitted from the satellite is represented by Eq. (5.7) and contains three components in the symbolic form $(L1, C/A, D)$, $(L1, P, D)$, and $(L2, P, D)$. Note that the C/A-code signal on $L1$ is twice as powerful as the P-code signal on $L1$. The same ratio exists between the P-code signals on $L1$ and $L2$, cf. Hatch et al. (1992).

The goal of signal processing by the GPS receiver is the recovery of the signal components, including the reconstruction of the carrier wave and the extraction of the codes for the satellite clock readings and the navigation message. The principle is illustrated in Fig. 5.4.

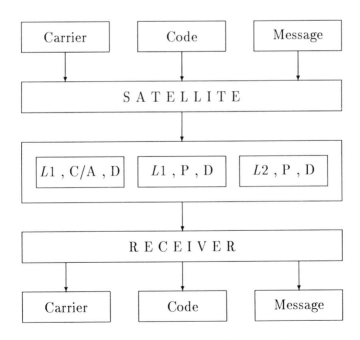

Fig. 5.4. Principle of signal processing

5.2.1 Receiver design

General features
Presently, there are more than 100 receivers on the market used for different
purposes (navigation, surveying, time transfer) and with different features.
Despite this variety, all the receivers show certain common principles which
are presented in this section.

Following Langley (1991), the receiver unit contains elements for signal
reception and signal processing. The basic concept is shown in Fig. 5.5.

An omnidirectional antenna receives the signals of all satellites above the
horizon and, after preamplification, transmits them to the radio frequency
section. It is worth noting that the signals are very resistant to interferences
since the PRN codes are unique for each satellite and have very low cross
correlations. The antenna may be designed for only the primary carrier $L1$
or for both $L1$ and $L2$ carriers. Today, most of the antennas on the market
are microstrip antennas. The important design criterion of the antenna is the
sensitivity of the phase center. The electronic center should be close to its
geometric center and should be insensitive to rotation and inclination. This
becomes particularly important in kinematic applications where the antenna
is moved while in operation. Additionally, the antenna should have a gain
pattern which filters low elevation or multipath signals. At present, this is
best achieved by chokering antennas. Additional details on these subjects
are provided in Sects. 6.5 and 6.6.

The microprocessor controls the entire system and enables real-time navigation by means of code pseudoranges. The control device provides inter-
active communication with the receiver. Commands can be keyed in and
diagnostic or other messages can be displayed. Therefore, this device is

Fig. 5.5. Basic concept of a receiver unit

usually designed as keyboard display unit.

A storage device is necessary for storing the observables and the navigation message so that they are available for later processing. Various media are presently used: microchips, cassette drives, magnetic bubbles or other nonvolatile storage. Additionally, the receiver can be interfaced to an external computer.

Many receivers have an (optional) internal power supply such as rechargeable batteries; but, there is always a provision for external batteries or other power supplies.

Radio frequency section

The radio frequency (RF) section forms the heart of the receiver. After signal input from the antenna, the discrimination of the signals is achieved by the C/A-codes, for example. These are, as previously mentioned, unique for each satellite. Another logic to discriminate between satellites is the monitoring of the Doppler shift.

The RF section processes the incoming signals in channels. Single frequency units process only the $L1$ signal, while dual frequency instruments process both the $L1$ and $L2$ signals. The data collected by a dual frequency receiver enables a combination where the ionospheric refraction can eventually be eliminated. This subject is treated in Sect. 6.3.2.

An important feature of the RF section is the number of channels and, hence, the number of satellites which can be tracked simultaneously. Older instruments used a limited number of physical channels and alternated satellite tracking by rapidly sequencing (20 milliseconds) satellites on the same channel. Today, most receivers assign one satellite each to a physical channel where the satellites are continuously tracked. Multichannel receivers are more accurate and less sensitive to loss of signal lock but show interchannel biases. However, with modern receivers these biases can be completely calibrated out at the level of less than 0.1 mm. Receivers with sequencing channels are less expensive but slower. The combination of both concepts can be found in hybrid receivers.

The basic elements of the RF section are oscillators to generate a reference frequency, multipliers to obtain higher frequencies, filters to eliminate undesired frequencies, and mixers. In the latter, two oscillations y_1, y_2 with different amplitudes a_1, a_2 and different frequencies f_1, f_2 are mathematically multiplied. In simplified form, this gives

$$
\begin{aligned}
y = y_1\, y_2 &= a_1 \cos(f_1\, t)\, a_2 \cos(f_2\, t) \\
&= \frac{a_1\, a_2}{2} \left[\cos\left((f_1 - f_2)\, t\right) + \cos\left((f_1 + f_2)\, t\right) \right]
\end{aligned}
\tag{5.8}
$$

and results in an oscillation y consisting of a low-frequency part and a high-frequency part. After applying a low-pass filter, the high-frequency part is eliminated. The remaining low-frequency signal is processed. The difference $f_1 - f_2$ between the frequencies is often called intermediate or beat frequency.

5.2.2   Processing techniques

The actual pseudorange measurements are performed in tracking loop circuits. The code ranges are determined in the delay lock loop (DLL) by using the code correlation technique. After removing the PRN code from the incoming signal and some filtering, the unmodulated (Doppler shifted) carrier wave is obtained. This carrier wave is then passed to the phase lock loop (PLL) where the phase measurement is conducted. The result is the (fractional) phase offset between the received signal and the reference signal generated in the receiver.

The code correlation technique provides all components of the satellite signal: the satellite clock reading, the navigation message, and the unmodulated carrier. The drawback is that the procedure requires the knowledge of one PRN code. The correlation technique is performed in several steps. First, a reference carrier is generated in the receiver which then is biphase modulated with a replica of the known PRN code. In a second step, the resulting reference signal is correlated with the received satellite signal. The signals are shifted with respect to time so that they optimally match (based on a mathematical correlation). The necessary time shift Δt, neglecting clock biases, corresponds to the signal travel time from the satellite antenna to the phase center of the receiving antenna. After removal of the PRN code, the received signal still contains the navigation message which can be decoded and eliminated by high-pass filtering. The final result is the Doppler shifted carrier on which a phase measurement can be performed. Since a PRN code is required, the code correlation technique is generally only applicable to the C/A-code with only the $L1$ carrier being reconstructed. If the P-code (more precisely, the Y-code) is available, both carriers can be reconstructed by the code correlation technique. Normally, the C/A-code is used to lock onto the signal and to initialize the tracking loop. This is performed in a short time since this code repeats every millisecond and is computationally simple. One result of the C/A-code correlation is the decoded navigation message which contains the HOW in each subframe which tells the receiver where to start the search in the P-code for signal matching.

Without knowledge of the Y-code, one has to apply codeless or quasi-codeless techniques for the reconstruction of the unmodulated carrier wave from which the phase of the base carrier is measured. Most of the receivers provide a hybrid technique. The $L1$ carrier is reconstructed by code correlation using the C/A-code, and a codeless technique is applied to reconstruct the $L2$ carrier. These techniques are subsequently described in more detail since they are essential because of A-S.

Squaring technique
This codeless technique was first presented in Counselman (1981). The procedure is based on autocorrelating the received signal. In other words, the received signal is mixed (i.e., multiplied) with itself and, hence, all modulations are removed. This happens because a 180° phase shift during modulation is equivalent to a change in the sign of the signal. The result is the unmodulated carrier with twice the frequency, cf. Eq. (5.8), and, thus, half the wavelength. In general, it is more difficult to resolve the ambiguities of the squared signals with halved wavelength.

This technique has the advantage of being independent of PRN codes. The drawback of squaring is that the satellite clock and the satellite orbit information are lost in the process. Additionally, the signal-to-noise ratio (SNR) is substantially reduced in the squaring process, cf. Ashjaee (1993). For example, compared to the code correlation technique, the SNR is reduced by 30 dB.

Cross correlation technique
This is another codeless technique which was first described by MacDoran et al. (1985). The technique is based on the fact that the unknown Y-code is identical on both carriers which enables cross correlation of the $L1$ and $L2$ signal. Due to the frequency dependent propagation of an electromagnetic wave through the ionosphere, the Y-code on $L2$ is slightly slower than the Y-code on $L1$. The time delay necessary to match the $L1$ signal with the $L2$ signal in the receiver is a measure of the travel time difference of the two signals. The delay of the $L2$ signal is variable and must be adjusted appropriately to achieve maximum correlation between the $L1$ and the $L2$ signal. The observables resulting from the correlation process are the range difference between the two signals obtained from the time delay of the Y-code on the two carriers, that is $R_{L2,Y} - R_{L1,Y}$, and a phase difference $\Phi_{L2} - \Phi_{L1}$ obtained from the beat frequency carrier.

The cross correlation outputs may be used to derive the $L2$ code range and phase by forming

$$R_{L2} = R_{L1,C/A} + (R_{L2,Y} - R_{L1,Y}) \tag{5.9}$$

and

$$\Phi_{L2} = \Phi_{L1,C/A} + (\Phi_{L2} - \Phi_{L1}) \tag{5.10}$$

where the subscripts of $R_{L1,C/A}$ and $\Phi_{L1,C/A}$ indicate that this code range and phase have been derived via the C/A-code on the $L1$ signal.

Since the power of the $L1$ ranging signal is twice that of the corresponding $L2$ signal, the cross correlation of the $L1$ and the $L2$ signal leads to an improvement of 3 dB compared to the squaring of the $L2$ signal, cf. Ashjaee and Lorenz (1992). However, compared to the code correlation technique, a SNR degradation of 27 dB occurs.

Code correlation plus squaring technique
This improved squaring technique was patented by Keegan (1990). The method is also denoted code-aided squaring and involves correlating the received Y-code on $L2$ signal with a locally generated replica of the P-code. This correlation is possible because the Y-code originates from a modulo two sum of the P-code and the encrypting W-code. Since the frequency (or chipping rate) of the W-code is about 20 times less the frequency of the Y-code, there always exist Y-code portions which are identical to the original P-code portions, see Eissfeller (1993). Therefore, the replica of the P-code is shifted to match with the underlying P-code portion of the satellite Y-code, see Ashjaee (1993). After the correlation, a low-pass filter is applied by narrowing the bandwidth and, subsequently, the signal is squared to get rid of the code. The technique provides code range and, because of squaring, half-wavelength carrier phase. The correlation with the P-code yields a better jamming immunity and an improvement in the multipath performance, see Ashjaee and Lorenz (1992).

The subsequent squaring results in 20 times more power (i.e., 13 dB) than by directly squaring the Y-code signal, because the SNR of a squared signal is inversely proportional to its bandwidth, cf. Hatch et al. (1992). Compared to the code correlation technique, however, a SNR degradation of 17 dB occurs.

Z-tracking technique
The most recent quasi-codeless technique is denoted Z-tracking[TM] and has been reported in Ashjaee and Lorenz (1992). At the moment this technique offers the best performance in the presence of A-S.

The Y-code on both the $L1$ signal and the $L2$ signal is separately correlated with a receiver generated replica of the P-code. Since there is a separate correlation on $L1$ and $L2$, the W-code on each frequency is obtained. The subsequent procedure is explained by Ashjaee (1993) in the following way: "The carriers on each frequency also contain the underlying encrypting code. At this time, with enough integration of signal, the encrypting signal bit is estimated for each frequency and is fed to the other frequency. This estimation is used to remove the encrypting code from the signal." The above mentioned integration is performed by a low-pass filtering where the bandwidth may be reduced to that of the encrypting W-code. There is no need to know the W-code because it is only used for synchronization purposes, cf. Breuer et al. (1993). The removal of the encrypting code leads, as far as the availability is concerned, to the same signals as in the case of no A-S. Thus, the code ranges and full wavelength $L1$ and $L2$ carrier phases are available. Note that the Y-code pseudoranges are "precisely the same observables as obtained by code correlation with the P-code", see Ashjaee and Lorenz (1992). Analogously, the output pseudoranges $R_{L1,Y}$ and $R_{L2,Y}$ of the Z-tracking technique are pseudoranges in the original P-code sense (since the characteristics of the P-code and the Y-code are the same).

Compared to the previous code correlation plus squaring technique, the SNR is improved by 3 dB; however, compared to the code correlation technique, a SNR degradation of 14 dB occurs.

All four approaches to recover the $L2$ carrier in the presence of A-S suffer from a substantial degradation in the SNR. Without exception, no codeless or quasi-codeless technique recovers GPS signal information as well as the code correlation technique. Also, weaker signals are more sensitive to high ionospheric activities and interfering (jamming) signals which may even cause a loss of lock.

The numerical values in Table 5.4 summarize the SNR degradation compared to the code correlation technique. Note that SNR increased by 3 dB is equivalent to an increase in signal power by a factor 2.

Table 5.5 summarizes the characteristics of the four techniques. The graphical diagrams are adapted from Ashjaee and Lorenz (1992) and Eissfeller (1993). The symbol $\otimes$ indicates the process of correlation.

Table 5.4. SNR degradation compared to code correlation technique

Squaring	-30 dB
Cross correlation	-27 dB
Code correlation plus squaring	-17 dB
Z-tracking	-14 dB

Table 5.5. Techniques to recover carrier and code on the $L2$ signal when A-S is on

Technique	Input	Operation	Output
Squaring	Y-code on $L2$		$\Phi_{L2}(\lambda_{L2}/2)$ no code range
Cross correlation	Y-code on $L1$ Y-code on $L2$		$\Phi_{L2} - \Phi_{L1}$ $R_{L2,Y} - R_{L2,Y}$
Code correlation plus squaring	Y-code on $L2$ P-code replica		$\Phi_{L2}(\lambda_{L2}/2)$ $R_{L2,P}$
Z-tracking	Y-code on $L1$ P-code replica Y-code on $L2$ P-code replica		Φ_{L1} $R_{L1,Y}$ Φ_{L2} $R_{L2,Y}$

6 Observables

6.1 Data acquisition

In concept, the GPS observables are ranges which are deduced from measured time or phase differences based on a comparison between received signals and receiver generated signals. Unlike the terrestrial electronic distance measurements, GPS uses the "one way concept" where two clocks are used, namely one in the satellite and the other in the receiver. Thus, the ranges are biased by satellite and receiver clock errors and, consequently, they are denoted as pseudoranges.

6.1.1 Code pseudoranges

Let us denote by t^S the reading of the satellite clock at emission time and by t_R the reading of the receiver clock at signal reception time. Analogously, the delays of the clocks with respect to GPS system time will be termed δ^S and δ_R. Recall that the satellite clock reading t^S is transmitted via the PRN code. The difference between the clock readings is equivalent to the time shift Δt which aligns the satellite and reference signal during the code correlation procedure in the receiver. Thus,

$$\Delta t = t_R - t^S = [t_R(\text{GPS}) - \delta_R] - [t^S(\text{GPS}) - \delta^S]$$
$$= \Delta t(\text{GPS}) + \Delta\delta \, ,$$

(6.1)

where $\Delta t(\text{GPS}) = t_R(\text{GPS}) - t^S(\text{GPS})$ and $\Delta\delta = \delta^S - \delta_R$. The bias δ^S of the satellite clock can be modeled by a polynomial with the coefficients being transmitted in the first subframe of the navigation message. Assuming the δ^S correction is applied, $\Delta\delta$ equals the negative receiver clock delay. The time interval Δt multiplied by the speed of light c yields the pseudorange R and, hence,

$$R = c\,\Delta t = c\,\Delta t(\text{GPS}) + c\,\Delta\delta = \varrho + c\,\Delta\delta \, . \tag{6.2}$$

Note that the C/A-code repeats every millisecond which corresponds to 300 km in range. Since the satellites are at a distance of about 20 000 km from the earth, C/A-code pseudoranges are ambiguous. However, this ambiguity can be easily resolved during initial satellite acquisition by introducing approximate (within some few hundred kilometers) position coordinates of the receiver, cf. Lachapelle (1991).

The range ϱ is calculated from the true signal travel time. In other words, ϱ corresponds to the distance between the position of the satellite at epoch $t^S(\text{GPS})$ and the position of receiver's antenna at epoch $t_R(\text{GPS})$. Since ϱ is a function of two different epochs, it is often expanded into a Taylor series with respect to, e.g., the emission time

$$
\begin{aligned}
\varrho = \varrho(t^S, t_R) &= \varrho(t^S, (t^S + \Delta t)) \\
&= \varrho(t^S, t^S) + \dot\varrho(t^S, t^S)\,\Delta t
\end{aligned}
\tag{6.3}
$$

where $\dot\varrho$ denotes the time derivative of ϱ or the radial velocity of the satellite relative to the receiving antenna. All epochs in Eq. (6.3) are expressed in GPS system time.

The maximum radial velocity for GPS satellites in the case of a stationary receiver is $\dot\varrho \approx 0.9\,\text{km s}^{-1}$, and the travel time of the satellite signal is about 0.07 seconds. The correction term in Eq. (6.3), thus, amounts to 60 m.

The precision of a pseudorange derived from code measurements has been traditionally about 1% of the chip length. Thus, a precision of roughly 3 m and 0.3 m is achieved with C/A-code and P-code pseudoranges respectively. However, recent developments demonstrate that a precision of about 0.1% of the chip length is possible.

6.1.2   Phase pseudoranges

Let us denote by $\varphi^S(t)$ the phase of the received and reconstructed carrier with frequency f^S and by $\varphi_R(t)$ the phase of a reference carrier generated in the receiver with frequency f_R. Here, the parameter t is an epoch in the GPS time system reckoned from an initial epoch $t_0 = 0$. According to Eq. (5.5), the following phase equations are obtained

$$
\begin{aligned}
\varphi^S(t) &= f^S\, t - f^S \frac{\varrho}{c} - \varphi_0^S \\
\varphi_R(t) &= f_R\, t - \varphi_{0R}.
\end{aligned}
\tag{6.4}
$$

The initial phases φ_0^S, φ_{0R} are caused by clock errors and are equal to

$$
\begin{aligned}
\varphi_0^S &= f^S\, \delta^S \\
\varphi_{0R} &= f_R\, \delta_R.
\end{aligned}
\tag{6.5}
$$

Hence, the beat phase $\varphi_R^S(t)$ is given by

$$
\begin{aligned}
\varphi_R^S(t) &= \varphi^S(t) - \varphi_R(t) \\
&= -f^S \frac{\varrho}{c} - f^S\, \delta^S + f_R\, \delta_R + (f^S - f_R)\, t.
\end{aligned}
\tag{6.6}
$$

The deviation of the frequencies f^S, f_R from the nominal frequency f is only in the order of some fractional parts of Hz. This may be verified by considering for instance a short-time stability in the frequencies of $df/f = 10^{-12}$. With the nominal carrier frequency $f \approx 1.5\,\text{GHz}$, the frequency error, thus, becomes $df = 1.5 \cdot 10^{-3}\,\text{Hz}$. Such a frequency error may be neglected because during signal propagation (i.e., $t = 0.07$ seconds) a maximum error of 10^{-4} cycles in the beat phase is generated which is below the noise level. The clock errors are in the range of milliseconds and are, thus, less effective. Summarizing, Eq. (6.6) may be written in the simplified form

$$\varphi_R^S(t) = -f\,\frac{\varrho}{c} - f\,\Delta\delta \tag{6.7}$$

where again $\Delta\delta = \delta^S - \delta_R$ has been introduced. If the assumption of frequency stability is incorrect and the oscillators are unstable, then their behavior has to be modeled by, for example, polynomials where clock and frequency offsets and a frequency drift are determined. A complete carrier phase model which includes the solution of large (e.g., 1 second) receiver clock errors was developed by Remondi (1984). Adequate formulas can also be found in King et al. (1987), pp. 55. No further details are given here because in practice eventual residual errors will be eliminated by differencing the measurements.

Switching on a receiver at epoch t_0, the instantaneous fractional beat phase is measured. The initial integer number N of cycles between satellite and receiver is unknown. However, when tracking is continued without loss of lock, the number N, also called integer ambiguity, remains the same and the beat phase at epoch t is given by

$$\varphi_R^S(t) = \Delta\varphi_R^S\,\Big|_{t_0}^{t} + N \tag{6.8}$$

where $\Delta\varphi_R^S$ denotes the (measurable) fractional phase at epoch t augmented by the number of integer cycles since the initial epoch t_0. A geometrical interpretation of Eq. (6.8) is provided in Fig. 6.1 where $\Delta\varphi_i$ is a shortened notation for $\Delta\varphi_R^S\,|_{t_0}^{t_i}$ and, for simplicity, the initial fractional beat phase $\Delta\varphi_0$ is assumed to be zero. Substituting Eq. (6.8) into Eq. (6.7) and denoting the negative observation quantity by $\Phi = -\Delta\varphi_R^S$ yields the equation for the phase pseudoranges

$$\Phi = \frac{1}{\lambda}\,\varrho + \frac{c}{\lambda}\,\Delta\delta + N \tag{6.9}$$

where the wavelength λ has been introduced according to Eq. (5.2). Multiplying the above equation by λ scales the phase expressed in cycles to a

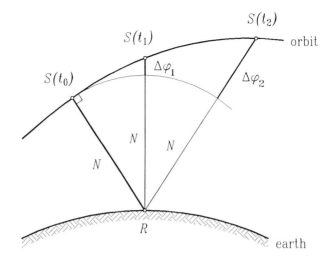

Fig. 6.1. Geometrical interpretation of phase range

range which only differs from the code pseudorange by the integer multiples of λ. Again, the range ϱ represents the distance between the satellite at emission epoch t and the receiver at reception epoch $t + \Delta t$. The phase of the carrier can be measured to better than 0.01 cycles which corresponds to millimeter precision.

It should be noted that a plus sign convention has been chosen for Eq. (6.9). This choice is somehow arbitrary since quite often the phase Φ and the distance ϱ show different signs. Actually, the sign is receiver dependent because the beat phase is generated in the receiver and the combination of the satellite and the receiver signal differs for various receiver types.

6.1.3 Doppler data

Some of the first solution models proposed for GPS were to use the Doppler observable as with the TRANSIT system. This system used the integrated Doppler shifts (i.e., phase differences) which were scaled to delta ranges. The raw Doppler shift, cf. Eq. (5.6), being linearly dependent on the radial velocity and, thus, allowing for velocity determination in real time is important for navigation. Considering Eq. (6.9), the equation for the observed Doppler shift scaled to range rate is given by

$$D = \lambda \, \dot{\Phi} = \dot{\varrho} + c \, \Delta \dot{\delta} \tag{6.10}$$

where the derivatives with respect to time are indicated by a dot. The raw Doppler shift is less accurate than integrated Doppler, cf. Hatch (1982). To obtain an estimate of the achievable accuracy, Ashjaee et al. (1989) mention 0.001 Hz. This corresponds to $0.3 \, \mathrm{m \, s^{-1}}$ if the Doppler shift is measured in the C/A-code tracking loop.

A detailed derivation of Doppler equations within the frame of GPS is given in Remondi (1984) where even relativistic effects are accounted for. It is worth noting here that the raw Doppler shift is also applied to determine integer ambiguities in kinematic surveying, cf. Remondi (1991a), or is used as an additional independent observable for point positioning, cf. Ashjaee et al. (1989).

6.1.4   Biases and noise

The code pseudoranges, cf. Eq. (6.2), and phase pseudoranges, cf. Eq. (6.9), are affected by both, systematic errors or biases and random noise. Note that Doppler measurements are affected by the rate of change of the biases only. The error sources can be classified into three groups, namely satellite related errors, propagation medium related errors, and receiver related errors. Some range biases are listed in Table 6.1.

Some of the systematic errors can be modeled and give rise to additional terms in the observation equations which will be explained in detail in subsequent sections. As mentioned earlier, systematic effects can also be eliminated by appropriate combinations of the observables. Differencing between receivers eliminates satellite-specific biases, and differencing between satellites eliminates receiver-specific biases. Thus, double-differenced pseudoranges are, to a high degree, free of systematic errors originating from the satellites and from the receivers. With respect to refraction, this is only true for short baselines where the measured ranges at both endpoints are affected equally. In addition, ionospheric refraction can be virtually eliminated by an

Table 6.1. Range biases

Source	Effect
Satellite	Clock bias, Orbital errors
Signal propagation	Ionospheric refraction, Tropospheric refraction
Receiver	Antenna phase center variation, Clock bias, Multipath

adequate combination of dual frequency data. Antenna phase center variations are treated in Sect. 6.5. Multipath is caused by multiple reflections of the signal (which can also occur at the satellite during signal emission). The interference between the direct and the reflected signal is largely not random; however, it may also appear as a noise. Wells et al. (1987) report a similar effect called "imaging" where a reflecting obstacle generates an image of the real antenna which distorts the antenna pattern. Both effects, multipath and imaging, can be considerably reduced by selecting sites protected from reflections (buildings, vehicles, trees, etc.) and by an appropriate antenna design. It should be noted that multipath is frequency dependent. Therefore, carrier phases are less affected than code ranges where multipath can amount to the meter level as stated by Lachapelle (1990). More details on the multipath problems are given in Sect. 6.6.

The random noise mainly contains the actual observation noise plus random constituents of multipath (especially for kinematic applications). The pseudorange noise is summarized in Table 6.2.

The measurement noise, an estimation of the satellite biases, and the contributions from the wave propagation are combined in the User Equivalent Range Error (UERE). This UERE is transmitted via the navigation message. In combination with a DOP factor, explained in Sect. 9.5, UERE allows for an estimation of the achievable point positioning precision.

6.2   Data combinations

GPS observables are obtained from the code information or the carrier wave in the broadcast satellite signal. Recall that the P-code is modulated on both carriers $L1$ and $L2$, whereas the C/A-code is modulated on $L1$ only. Consequently, one could measure the code ranges R_{L1}, R_{L2}, the carrier phases Φ_{L1}, Φ_{L2}, and the corresponding Doppler shifts D_{L1}, D_{L2} for a single epoch. Note that the $L1$ observables may either be derived from the C/A-code or from the P-code. In general, not all observables are available because, for ex-

Table 6.2. Range noise

Range	Noise
Code range (C/A-code)	$10 - 300\,\mathrm{cm}$
Code range (P-Code)	$10 -30\,\mathrm{cm}$
Phase range	$0.5 - 5\,\mathrm{mm}$

ample, a single frequency receiver delivers only data from the $L1$ frequency. Furthermore, the Doppler observables are not considered here.

The objectives of this section are to show how linear combinations are developed for dual frequency phases, and how code range smoothing by means of carrier phases is performed.

6.2.1 Linear phase combinations

Generally, the linear combination of two phases φ_1 and φ_2 is defined by

$$\varphi = n_1 \varphi_1 + n_2 \varphi_2 \tag{6.11}$$

where n_1 and n_2 are arbitrary numbers. The substitution of the relations $\varphi_i = f_i\, t$ for the corresponding frequencies f_1 and f_2 gives

$$\varphi = n_1 f_1\, t + n_2 f_2\, t = f\, t\,. \tag{6.12}$$

Therefore,

$$f = n_1 f_1 + n_2 f_2 \tag{6.13}$$

is the frequency and

$$\lambda = \frac{c}{f} \tag{6.14}$$

is the wavelength of the linear combination.

In the case of GPS, the linear combination of $L1$ and $L2$ carrier phases Φ_{L1} and Φ_{L2} for the simplest nontrivial cases in Eq. (6.11) are $n_1 = n_2 = 1$, yielding the sum

$$\Phi_{L1+L2} = \Phi_{L1} + \Phi_{L2} \tag{6.15}$$

and $n_1 = 1$, $n_2 = -1$, leading to the difference

$$\Phi_{L1-L2} = \Phi_{L1} - \Phi_{L2}\,. \tag{6.16}$$

The corresponding wavelengths according to Eq. (6.14) are

$$\lambda_{L1+L2} = 10.7 \text{ cm}$$
$$\tag{6.17}$$
$$\lambda_{L1-L2} = 86.2 \text{ cm}$$

where the numerical values for the carrier frequencies f_{L1} and f_{L2}, see Table 5.2, have been substituted. The combination Φ_{L1+L2} is denoted as narrow lane and Φ_{L1-L2} as wide lane, cf. for example Beutler et al. (1988), Wübbena (1988).

A slightly more complicated linear combination results from the choice

$$n_1 = 1 \qquad n_2 = -\frac{f_{L2}}{f_{L1}} \tag{6.18}$$

which is frequently denoted as $L3$ signal, thus

$$\Phi_{L3} = \Phi_{L1} - \frac{f_{L2}}{f_{L1}}\,\Phi_{L2}\,. \tag{6.19}$$

Now that the most significant linear combinations have been defined, the advantage of these combinations will be shown. The $L3$ combination, for example, is used to reduce ionospheric effects, cf. Sect. 6.3.2., and the ambiguity resolution combines wide and narrow lane signals, cf. Sect. 9.1.3.

Assuming a certain noise level for the phase measurements, it is seen that the noise level will increase for these linear combinations. Applying the error propagation law and assuming the same noise for both phases, the noise of the sum or the difference formed by Φ_{L1} and Φ_{L2} is higher by the factor $\sqrt{2}$ than the noise of a single phase. Of course, to compute this factor correctly, one must take into account the different noise levels.

6.2.2   Phase and code pseudorange combinations

The objective here is to show the principle of the smoothing of code pseudoranges by means of phase pseudoranges. A first extensive investigation on this subject was provided by Hatch (1982). Applications and improvements were proposed later by the same author and are given in Hatch and Larson (1985) and Hatch (1986). Other slight variations can be found in, e.g., Lachapelle et al. (1986) or Meyerhoff and Evans (1986). Today, phase and code pseudorange combinations are an important part of real-time trajectory determination.

Assuming dual frequency measurements for epoch t_1, the code pseudoranges $R_{L1}(t_1)$, $R_{L2}(t_1)$ and the carrier phase pseudoranges $\Phi_{L1}(t_1)$, $\Phi_{L2}(t_1)$ are obtained. Assume also, the code pseudoranges are scaled to cycles (but still denoted as R) by dividing them by the corresponding carrier wavelength. Using the two frequencies f_{L1}, f_{L2}, the combination

$$R(t_1) = \frac{f_{L1}\,R_{L1}(t_1) - f_{L2}\,R_{L2}(t_1)}{f_{L1} + f_{L2}} \tag{6.20}$$

is formed for the code pseudoranges and the wide lane signal

$$\Phi(t_1) = \Phi_{L1}(t_1) - \Phi_{L2}(t_1) \tag{6.21}$$

for the carrier phase pseudoranges. From Eq. (6.20) one can see that the noise of the combined code pseudorange $R(t_1)$ is reduced by a factor of 0.7

compared to the noise of the single code measurement. The increase of the noise in the wide lane signal by a factor of $\sqrt{2}$ has no effect because the noise of the carrier phase pseudoranges is essentially lower than the noise of the code pseudoranges. It is worth noting that both signals $R(t_1)$ and $\Phi(t_1)$ have the same frequency and, thus, the same wavelength as the reader may verify by applying Eq. (6.13). This is not the case with the approach given in Hatch (1986) where a plus sign is chosen for the code pseudorange combination (this can be regarded as a weighted mean).

Combinations of the form (6.20) and (6.21) are formed for each epoch. Additionally, for all epochs t_i after t_1, extrapolated values of the code pseudoranges $R(t_i)_{\mathrm{ex}}$ can be calculated from

$$R(t_i)_{\mathrm{ex}} = R(t_1) + (\Phi(t_i) - \Phi(t_1)). \tag{6.22}$$

The smoothed value $R(t_i)_{\mathrm{sm}}$ is finally obtained by the arithmetic mean

$$R(t_i)_{\mathrm{sm}} = \frac{1}{2}\left(R(t_i) + R(t_i)_{\mathrm{ex}}\right). \tag{6.23}$$

Generalizing the above formulas for an arbitrary epoch t_i (with the preceding epoch t_{i-1}), a recursive algorithm is given by

$$R(t_i) = \frac{f_{L1}\,R_{L1}(t_i) - f_{L2}\,R_{L2}(t_i)}{f_{L1} + f_{L2}}$$

$$\Phi(t_i) = \Phi_{L1}(t_i) - \Phi_{L2}(t_i)$$

$$R(t_i)_{\mathrm{ex}} = R(t_{i-1})_{\mathrm{sm}} + (\Phi(t_i) - \Phi(t_{i-1}))$$

$$R(t_i)_{\mathrm{sm}} = \frac{1}{2}\left(R(t_i) + R(t_i)_{\mathrm{ex}}\right)$$

which works under the initial condition $R(t_1) = R(t_1)_{\mathrm{ex}} = R(t_1)_{\mathrm{sm}}$ for all $i > 1$.

The above algorithm assumes the data is free of gross errors. However, carrier phase data is sensitive to changes in the integer ambiguity (i.e., cycle slips). To circumvent this problem, a variation of the algorithm is given in Lachapelle et al. (1986). Using the same notations as before for an epoch t_i, the smoothed code pseudorange is obtained by

$$R(t_i)_{\mathrm{sm}} = w\,R(t_i) + (1 - w)\,(R(t_{i-1})_{\mathrm{sm}} + \Phi(t_i) - \Phi(t_{i-1})) \tag{6.24}$$

where w is a time dependent weight factor. For the first epoch $i = 1$, the weight is set $w = 1$; thus, putting the full weight on the measured code pseudorange. For consecutive epochs, the weight is reduced continuously and, thus, emphasizes the influence of the carrier phases. To obtain an estimate of the reduction factor, Lachapelle et al. (1986) proposed a reduction

of the weight by 0.01 from epoch to epoch for a kinematic experiment with
a data sampling rate of 1 Hz. After 100 seconds, only the smoothed value
of the previous epoch (augmented by the carrier phase difference) is taken
into account. Again, in the case of cycle slips, the algorithm would fail. A
simple check of the carrier phase difference for two consecutive epochs by the
Doppler shift multiplied by the time interval may detect data irregularities
such as cycle slips. After the occurrence of a cycle slip, the weight is reset
to $w = 1$ which fully eliminates the influence of the erroneous carrier phase
data. The key of this approach is that cycle slips must be detected but do
not have to be corrected, cf. Hein et al. (1988).

Another smoothing algorithm for code pseudoranges is given by Meyerhoff and Evans (1986). Here, the phase changes obtained by the integrated
Doppler shift between the epochs t_i and t_1 are denoted by $\Delta\Phi(t_i, t_1)$ with t_1
being the starting epoch for the integration. Note that these phase changes
are insensitive to cycle slips. From each code pseudorange $R(t_i)$ at epoch t_i,
an estimate of the code pseudorange at epoch t_1 can be given by

$$R(t_1)_i = R(t_i) - \Delta\Phi(t_i, t_1) \tag{6.25}$$

where the subscript i on the left-hand side indicates the epoch that the
code pseudorange $R(t_1)$ is computed from. Obtaining consecutively for each
epoch an estimate, the arithmetic mean $R(t_1)_\mathrm{m}$ of the code pseudorange for
n epochs is calculated by

$$R(t_1)_\mathrm{m} = \frac{1}{n} \sum_{i=1}^{n} R(t_1)_i \tag{6.26}$$

and the smoothed code pseudorange for an arbitrary epoch results from

$$R(t_i)_\mathrm{sm} = R(t_1)_\mathrm{m} + \Delta\Phi(t_i, t_1) . \tag{6.27}$$

The advantage of this procedure lies in the reduction of the noise in the
initial code pseudorange by averaging an arbitrary number n of measured
code pseudoranges. Note from the three formulas (6.25) through (6.27) that
the algorithm may also be applied successively epoch by epoch where the
arithmetic mean must be updated from epoch to epoch. Using the above
notations, formula (6.27) also works for epoch t_1, where, of course, $\Delta\Phi(t_1, t_1)$
is zero and there is no smoothing effect.

All the smoothing algorithms are also applicable if only single frequency
data are available. In this case, $R(t_i)$, $\Phi(t_i)$, and $\Delta\Phi(t_i, t_1)$ denote the single
frequency code pseudorange, carrier phase pseudorange, and phase difference
respectively.

6.3   Atmospheric effects

6.3.1   Phase and group velocity

Consider a single electromagnetic wave propagating in space with wavelength λ and frequency f. The velocity of its phase

$$v_{\rm ph} = \lambda f \tag{6.28}$$

is denoted phase velocity. For GPS, the carrier waves $L1$ and $L2$ are propagating with this velocity.

For a group of waves with slightly different frequencies, the propagation of the resultant energy is defined by the group velocity

$$v_{\rm gr} = -\frac{df}{d\lambda}\lambda^2 \tag{6.29}$$

according to Bauer (1992), p. 97. This velocity has to be considered for GPS code measurements.

A relation between phase and group velocity may be derived by forming the total differential of Eq. (6.28) resulting in

$$dv_{\rm ph} = f\,d\lambda + \lambda\,df \tag{6.30}$$

which can be rearranged to

$$\frac{df}{d\lambda} = \frac{1}{\lambda}\frac{dv_{\rm ph}}{d\lambda} - \frac{f}{\lambda}. \tag{6.31}$$

The substitution of (6.31) into (6.29) yields

$$v_{\rm gr} = -\lambda\frac{dv_{\rm ph}}{d\lambda} + f\lambda \tag{6.32}$$

or finally the Rayleigh equation

$$v_{\rm gr} = v_{\rm ph} - \lambda\frac{dv_{\rm ph}}{d\lambda}. \tag{6.33}$$

Note that the differentiation (6.30) implicitly contains the dispersion, cf. Joos (1956), p. 57, which is defined as a dependence of the phase velocity on the wavelength or the frequency. Phase and group velocity are equal in nondispersive media and correspond to the speed of light in vacuum.

The wave propagation in a medium depends on the refractive index n. Generally, the propagation velocity is obtained from

$$v = \frac{c}{n}. \tag{6.34}$$

Applying this expression to the phase and group velocity, one gets appropriate formulas for the corresponding refractive indices n_{ph} and n_{gr}:

$$v_{\text{ph}} = \frac{c}{n_{\text{ph}}} \tag{6.35}$$

$$v_{\text{gr}} = \frac{c}{n_{\text{gr}}} . \tag{6.36}$$

Differentiation of the phase velocity with respect to λ, that is

$$\frac{dv_{\text{ph}}}{d\lambda} = -\frac{c}{n_{\text{ph}}^2} \frac{dn_{\text{ph}}}{d\lambda} , \tag{6.37}$$

and substitution of the last three equations into (6.33) yields

$$\frac{c}{n_{\text{gr}}} = \frac{c}{n_{\text{ph}}} + \lambda \frac{c}{n_{\text{ph}}^2} \frac{dn_{\text{ph}}}{d\lambda} \tag{6.38}$$

or

$$\frac{1}{n_{\text{gr}}} = \frac{1}{n_{\text{ph}}} \left(1 + \lambda \frac{1}{n_{\text{ph}}} \frac{dn_{\text{ph}}}{d\lambda} \right) . \tag{6.39}$$

This equation may be inverted to

$$n_{\text{gr}} = n_{\text{ph}} \left(1 - \lambda \frac{1}{n_{\text{ph}}} \frac{dn_{\text{ph}}}{d\lambda} \right) \tag{6.40}$$

where the approximation $(1 + \varepsilon)^{-1} = 1 - \varepsilon$ has been applied accordingly. Thus,

$$n_{\text{gr}} = n_{\text{ph}} - \lambda \frac{dn_{\text{ph}}}{d\lambda} \tag{6.41}$$

is the modified Rayleigh equation. A slightly different form is obtained by differentiating the relation $c = \lambda f$ with respect to λ and f, that is

$$\frac{d\lambda}{\lambda} = -\frac{df}{f} , \tag{6.42}$$

and by substituting the result into (6.41):

$$n_{\text{gr}} = n_{\text{ph}} + f \frac{dn_{\text{ph}}}{df} . \tag{6.43}$$

6.3.2 Ionospheric refraction

The ionosphere, extending in various layers from about 50 km to 1 000 km above earth, is a dispersive medium with respect to the GPS radio signal. Following Seeber (1993), p. 44, the series

$$n_{\text{ph}} = 1 + \frac{c_2}{f^2} + \frac{c_3}{f^3} + \frac{c_4}{f^4} + \dots \tag{6.44}$$

approximates the phase refractive index. The coefficients c_2, c_3, c_4 do not depend on frequency but on the quantity N_e denoting the number of electrons per m^3 (i.e., the electron density) along the propagation path. Using an approximation by cutting off the series expansion after the quadratic term, that is

$$n_{\text{ph}} = 1 + \frac{c_2}{f^2}, \tag{6.45}$$

differentiating this equation

$$dn_{\text{ph}} = -\frac{2c_2}{f^3} \, df, \tag{6.46}$$

and substituting (6.45) and (6.46) into (6.43) yields

$$n_{\text{gr}} = 1 + \frac{c_2}{f^2} - f \frac{2c_2}{f^3} \tag{6.47}$$

or

$$n_{\text{gr}} = 1 - \frac{c_2}{f^2}. \tag{6.48}$$

It can be seen from (6.45) and (6.48) that the group and the phase refractive indices deviate from unity with opposite sign. With an estimate for c_2, cf. Seeber (1993), p. 44,

$$c_2 = -40.3 \, N_e \quad [\text{Hz}^2] \tag{6.49}$$

the relation $n_{\text{gr}} > n_{\text{ph}}$ and, thus, $v_{\text{gr}} < v_{\text{ph}}$ follows because the electron density N_e is always positive. As a consequence of the different velocities, a group delay and a phase advance occur, cf. for example Young et al. (1985). In other words, GPS code measurements are delayed and the carrier phases are advanced. Therefore, the code pseudoranges are measured too long and the carrier phase pseudoranges are measured too short compared to the geometric range between the satellite and the receiver. The amount of the difference is in both cases the same.

According to Fermat's principle, the measured range s is defined by

$$s = \int n \, ds \tag{6.50}$$

where the integral must be extended along the path of the signal. The geometric range s_0 along the straight line between the satellite and the receiver may be obtained analogously by setting $n = 1$:

$$s_0 = \int ds_0 \,. \tag{6.51}$$

The difference Δ^{Iono} between measured and geometric range is called ionospheric refraction and follows from

$$\Delta^{\text{Iono}} = \int n \, ds - \int ds_0 \tag{6.52}$$

which may be written for a phase refractive index n_{ph} from (6.45) as

$$\Delta_{\text{ph}}^{\text{Iono}} = \int \left(1 + \frac{c_2}{f^2}\right) ds - \int ds_0 \tag{6.53}$$

and for a group refractive index n_{gr} from (6.48) as

$$\Delta_{\text{gr}}^{\text{Iono}} = \int \left(1 - \frac{c_2}{f^2}\right) ds - \int ds_0 \,. \tag{6.54}$$

A simplification is obtained when allowing the integration for the first term in (6.53) and (6.54) along the geometric path. In this case ds becomes ds_0 and the formulas

$$\Delta_{\text{ph}}^{\text{Iono}} = \int \frac{c_2}{f^2} \, ds_0 \qquad \Delta_{\text{gr}}^{\text{Iono}} = -\int \frac{c_2}{f^2} \, ds_0 \tag{6.55}$$

result which can also be written as

$$\Delta_{\text{ph}}^{\text{Iono}} = -\frac{40.3}{f^2} \int N_e \, ds_0 \qquad \Delta_{\text{gr}}^{\text{Iono}} = \frac{40.3}{f^2} \int N_e \, ds_0 \tag{6.56}$$

where (6.49) has been substituted. Defining the total electron content (TEC) by

$$\text{TEC} = \int N_e \, ds_0 \,, \tag{6.57}$$

and substituting TEC into (6.56) yields

$$\Delta_{\text{ph}}^{\text{Iono}} = -\frac{40.3}{f^2} \text{TEC} \qquad \Delta_{\text{gr}}^{\text{Iono}} = \frac{40.3}{f^2} \text{TEC} \tag{6.58}$$

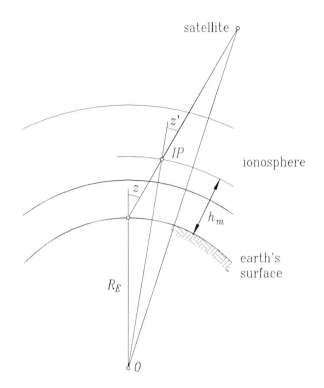

Fig. 6.2. Geometry for the ionospheric path delay

as the final result which has the dimension of length. Usually, the TEC is measured in units of 10^{16} electrons per m^2.

Note that TEC as introduced in (6.57) is the total electron content along the signal path between the satellite and the receiver. The integral is assumed to include the electrons in a column with a cross-section of $1\,m^2$ and extending from the receiver to the satellite. Usually, the total vertical electron content (TVEC) is modeled. More figuratively, Friedrich et al. (1989) denote this quantity as total overhead electron content. If TVEC is introduced in (6.58), the quantities suffice only for satellites at zenith. For arbitrary lines of sight, cf. Fig. 6.2, the zenith angle of the satellite must be taken into account by

$$\Delta_{\text{ph}}^{\text{Iono}} = -\frac{1}{\cos z'}\frac{40.3}{f^2}\,\text{TVEC} \qquad \Delta_{\text{gr}}^{\text{Iono}} = \frac{1}{\cos z'}\frac{40.3}{f^2}\,\text{TVEC} \qquad (6.59)$$

since the path length in the ionosphere varies with a changing zenith angle.

These two quantities differ only with respect to the sign. Introducing the notation

$$\Delta^{\text{Iono}} = \frac{1}{\cos z'}\frac{40.3}{f^2}\,\text{TVEC} \qquad\qquad\qquad (6.60)$$

for the (positive) amount of the ionospheric influence on a measured pseudorange allows the omission of the subscripts "ph" or "gr" but requires the
consideration of the correct sign for the appropriate models. This means that
the ionospheric influence for the code pseudorange is modeled by $+\Delta^{\text{Iono}}$,
whereas for the phase model by $-\Delta^{\text{Iono}}$.

From Fig. 6.2, the relation

$$\sin z' = \frac{R_E}{R_E + h_m} \sin z \tag{6.61}$$

can be read where R_E is the mean radius of the earth, h_m is a mean value
for the height of the ionosphere, and z' and z are the zenith angles at the
ionospheric point IP and at the observing site. The zenith angle z can be
calculated for a known satellite position and approximate coordinates of the
observation location. For h_m a value in the range between 300 km and 400 km
is typical. Gervaise et al. (1985) use 300 km, Wild et al. (1989) take 350 km,
and Finn and Matthewman (1989) recommend an average value of 400 km
but prefer an algorithm for calculating individual mean heights. Anyway,
the height is only sensitive for low satellite elevations.

As shown by (6.58), the change of range caused by the ionospheric refraction may be restricted to the determination of the TEC. However, the
TEC itself is a fairly complicated quantity because it depends on sunspot
activities (approximately 11-year cycle), seasonal and diurnal variations, the
line of sight which includes elevation and azimuth of the satellite, and the
position of the observation site, cf. Finn and Matthewman (1989). Taking all
of these effects into account, a GPS pseudorange may be wrong from about
0.15 m to 50 m, cf. Clynch and Coco (1986). The TEC may be measured,
estimated, its effect computed by models, or eliminated.

Measuring the TEC
Considering as an example Japan, Kato et al. (1987) describe one facility in
Tokyo that directly measures the TEC. However, since there is a correlation
between the TEC and the critical plasma frequency, the TEC may also be
calculated by the five Japanese ionospheric observatories which make available critical plasma frequency results on an hourly basis. Using instead of
the measured the calculated TEC induces an error of about 20%; but by
interpolation any arbitrary location in Japan can be covered.

Estimating the TEC
A straightforward estimation of the TEC is described by Wild et al. (1989)
where a Taylor series expansion as function of the observation latitude and
the local solar time is set up and substituted into (6.58). The coefficients in

the Taylor series are introduced as unknowns in the pseudorange equations and estimated together with the other unknowns during data processing.

Computing the effect of the TEC
Here, the entire vertical ionospheric refraction is approximated by the model of Klobuchar (1986) and yields the vertical time delay for the code measurements. Although the model is an approximation, it is nevertheless of importance because it uses the ionospheric coefficients broadcast within the fourth subframe of the navigation message, cf. Sect. 5.1.2. Following Jorgensen (1989), the Klobuchar model is

$$\Delta T_v^{\text{Iono}} = A_1 + A_2 \cos\left(\frac{2\pi(t - A_3)}{A_4}\right) \tag{6.62}$$

where

$$A_1 = 5 \cdot 10^{-9} \text{ s} = 5 \text{ ns}$$

$$A_2 = \alpha_1 + \alpha_2\,\varphi_{IP}^m + \alpha_3\,\varphi_{IP}^{m\,2} + \alpha_4\,\varphi_{IP}^{m\,3}$$

$$A_3 = 14^{\text{h}} \text{ local time} \tag{6.63}$$

$$A_4 = \beta_1 + \beta_2\,\varphi_{IP}^m + \beta_3\,\varphi_{IP}^{m\,2} + \beta_4\,\varphi_{IP}^{m\,3}\,.$$

The values for A_1 and A_3 are constant, the coefficients α_i, β_i, $i = 1, \ldots, 4$ are uploaded daily to the satellites and broadcast to the user. The parameter t in (6.62) is the local time of the ionospheric point IP, cf. Fig. 6.2, and may be derived from

$$t = \frac{\lambda_{IP}}{15} + t_{UT} \tag{6.64}$$

where λ_{IP} is the geomagnetic longitude positive to East for the ionospheric point in degrees and t_{UT} is the observation epoch in Universal Time, cf. Walser (1988). Finally, φ_{IP}^m in Eq. (6.63) is the spherical distance between the geomagnetic pole and the ionospheric point. Denoting the coordinates of the geomagnetic pole by φ_P, λ_P and those of the ionospheric point by φ_{IP}, λ_{IP}, then φ_{IP}^m is obtained by

$$\cos\varphi_{IP}^m = \sin\varphi_{IP}\,\sin\varphi_P + \cos\varphi_{IP}\,\cos\varphi_P\,\cos(\lambda_{IP} - \lambda_P) \tag{6.65}$$

where at present, cf. Walser (1988), the coordinates of the geomagnetic pole are

$$\varphi_P = 78°\!.3$$

$$\lambda_P = 291°\!.0\,. \tag{6.66}$$

Summarizing, the evaluation of the Klobuchar model may be performed by the following steps, cf. also Jorgensen (1989):

- For epoch t_{UT} compute the azimuth a and the zenith angle z of the satellite.

- Choose a mean height of the ionosphere and compute the distance s between the observing site and the ionospheric point obtained from the triangle origin-observation site-ionospheric point, cf. Fig. 6.2.

- Compute the coordinates φ_{IP}, λ_{IP} of the ionospheric point by means of the quantities a, z, s.

- Calculate φ_{IP}^m from (6.65).

- Calculate A_2 and A_4 from (6.63) where the coefficients α_i, β_i, $i = 1, \ldots, 4$ are received via the satellite navigation message.

- Use (6.63) and (6.64) and compute the vertical delay ΔT_v^{Iono} by (6.62).

- By calculating z' from (6.61) and applying $\Delta T^{\text{Iono}} = \frac{1}{\cos z'} \Delta T_v^{\text{Iono}}$, the transition from the vertical delay to the delay along the wave path is achieved. The result is obtained as a time delay in seconds which must be multiplied by the speed of light to convert it to a change of range.

Eliminating the effect of the TEC

It is difficult to find a satisfying model for the TEC because of the various time dependent influences. The most efficient method, thus, is to eliminate the ionospheric refraction by using two signals with different frequencies. This dual frequency method is the main reason why the GPS signal has two carrier waves $L1$ and $L2$.

Starting with the code pseudorange model (6.2) and adding the frequency dependent ionospheric refraction (6.60), gives

$$
\begin{aligned}
R_{L1} &= \varrho + c\,\Delta\delta + \Delta^{\text{Iono}}(f_{L1}) \\
R_{L2} &= \varrho + c\,\Delta\delta + \Delta^{\text{Iono}}(f_{L2})
\end{aligned}
\tag{6.67}
$$

where the frequencies of the two carriers are denoted by f_{L1} and f_{L2}.

A linear combination is now formed by

$$
R_{L1,L2} = n_1\,R_{L1} + n_2\,R_{L2}
\tag{6.68}
$$

where n_1 and n_2 are arbitrary factors to be determined. The objective is to find a combination so that the ionospheric refraction cancels out. Substituting (6.67) into (6.68) leads to the postulate

$$
n_1\,\Delta^{\text{Iono}}(f_{L1}) + n_2\,\Delta^{\text{Iono}}(f_{L2}) \stackrel{!}{=} 0
\tag{6.69}
$$

where the exclamation mark stresses that the expression must become zero. Equation (6.69) comprises two unknowns; therefore, one unknown may be chosen arbitrarily. Assuming $n_1 = 1$,

$$n_2 = -\frac{\Delta^{\text{Iono}}(f_{L1})}{\Delta^{\text{Iono}}(f_{L2})} \tag{6.70}$$

follows or, by using (6.60), this may be written as

$$n_2 = -\frac{f_{L2}^2}{f_{L1}^2} . \tag{6.71}$$

Substituting these values for n_1 and n_2, Eq. (6.69) is fulfilled and the linear combination (6.68) becomes

$$R_{L1,L2} = R_{L1} - \frac{f_{L2}^2}{f_{L1}^2} R_{L2} . \tag{6.72}$$

This is the ionospheric-free linear combination for code ranges. A similar ionospheric-free linear combination for carrier phases may be derived. The carrier phase models can be written as

$$\lambda_{L1}\Phi_{L1} = \varrho + c\,\Delta\delta + \lambda_{L1}N_{L1} - \Delta^{\text{Iono}}(f_{L1})$$
$$\lambda_{L2}\Phi_{L2} = \varrho + c\,\Delta\delta + \lambda_{L2}N_{L2} - \Delta^{\text{Iono}}(f_{L2}) \tag{6.73}$$

or, divided by the corresponding wavelengths,

$$\Phi_{L1} = \frac{1}{\lambda_{L1}}\varrho + f_{L1}\,\Delta\delta + N_{L1} - \frac{1}{\lambda_{L1}}\Delta^{\text{Iono}}(f_{L1})$$
$$\Phi_{L2} = \frac{1}{\lambda_{L2}}\varrho + f_{L2}\,\Delta\delta + N_{L2} - \frac{1}{\lambda_{L2}}\Delta^{\text{Iono}}(f_{L2}) \tag{6.74}$$

which is linearly combined by

$$\Phi_{L1,L2} = n_1\,\Phi_{L1} + n_2\,\Phi_{L2} \tag{6.75}$$

or explicitly

$$\Phi_{L1,L2} = \varrho\left(\frac{n_1}{\lambda_{L1}} + \frac{n_2}{\lambda_{L2}}\right) + \Delta\delta\,(n_1 f_{L1} + n_2 f_{L2})$$
$$+ n_1 N_{L1} + n_2 N_{L2} \tag{6.76}$$
$$- \frac{n_1}{\lambda_{L1}}\Delta^{\text{Iono}}(f_{L1}) - \frac{n_2}{\lambda_{L2}}\Delta^{\text{Iono}}(f_{L2}) .$$

For an ionospheric-free linear phase combination the postulate

$$\frac{n_1}{\lambda_{L1}} \Delta^{\text{Iono}}(f_{L1}) + \frac{n_2}{\lambda_{L2}} \Delta^{\text{Iono}}(f_{L2}) \overset{!}{=} 0 \tag{6.77}$$

must be fulfilled where again one of the two unknowns n_1, n_2 may be arbitrarily chosen, thus

$$n_1 = 1$$
$$\tag{6.78}$$
$$n_2 = -\frac{\lambda_{L2}}{\lambda_{L1}} \frac{\Delta^{\text{Iono}}(f_{L1})}{\Delta^{\text{Iono}}(f_{L2})}$$

is a possible solution. Substituting Eq. (6.60) and the relation $c = \lambda f$, one obtains

$$n_1 = 1$$
$$\tag{6.79}$$
$$n_2 = -\frac{f_{L2}}{f_{L1}},$$

and the ionospheric-free linear phase combination is

$$\Phi_{L1,L2} = \Phi_{L1} - \frac{f_{L2}}{f_{L1}} \Phi_{L2}. \tag{6.80}$$

This result corresponds to Eq. (6.19). Note that the choice of this linear combination is somewhat arbitrary since $n_1 = 1$ was taken. For another choice see, e.g., Beutler et al. (1988). However, since the noise of the ionospheric-free combination is increased compared to the raw phase, the choice of one of the two unknowns is restricted.

The elimination of the ionospheric refraction is the major advantage of the two ionospheric-free linear combinations (6.72) and (6.80). Remembering the derivation, it should be clear that the term "ionospheric-free" is not fully correct because there are some approximations involved, for instance Eq. (6.45), the integration is not along the true signal path (6.55), etc.

In the case of carrier phases, the ionospheric-free linear combination also has a significant disadvantage: if the ambiguities N_{L1} and N_{L2} in (6.74) are assumed to be integer numbers, then the linear combination gives a number $N = n_1 N_{L1} + n_2 N_{L2} = N_{L1} - (f_{L2}/f_{L1}) N_{L2}$ which is no longer an integer.

6.3.3 Tropospheric refraction

The effect of the neutral atmosphere (i.e., the nonionized part) is denoted as tropospheric refraction, tropospheric path delay or simply tropospheric delay. As Elgered et al. (1985) mention, the notations are slightly incorrect because they hide the stratosphere which is another constituent of the neutral atmosphere. However, the dominant contribution of the troposphere explains the notation.

The neutral atmosphere is a nondispersive medium with respect to radio waves up to frequencies of 15 GHz, cf. for example Bauersima (1983), and, thus, the propagation is frequency independent. Consequently, a distinction between carrier phases and code ranges derived from different carriers $L1$ or $L2$ is not necessary. The disadvantage is that an elimination of the tropospheric refraction by dual frequency methods is not possible.

The tropospheric path delay is defined by

$$\Delta^{\text{Trop}} = \int (n-1)\, ds \qquad (6.81)$$

which is analogous to the ionospheric formula (6.52). Again an approximation is introduced so that the integration is performed along the geometric path of the signal. Usually, instead of the refractive index n the refractivity

$$N^{\text{Trop}} = 10^6 \, (n-1) \qquad (6.82)$$

is used so that Eq. (6.81) becomes

$$\Delta^{\text{Trop}} = 10^{-6} \int N^{\text{Trop}}\, ds \,. \qquad (6.83)$$

Hopfield (1969) shows the possibility of separating N^{Trop} into a dry and a wet component

$$N^{\text{Trop}} = N_d^{\text{Trop}} + N_w^{\text{Trop}} \qquad (6.84)$$

where the dry part results from the dry atmosphere and the wet part from the water vapor. Correspondingly, the relations

$$\Delta_d^{\text{Trop}} = 10^{-6} \int N_d^{\text{Trop}}\, ds \qquad (6.85)$$

$$\Delta_w^{\text{Trop}} = 10^{-6} \int N_w^{\text{Trop}}\, ds \qquad (6.86)$$

and

$$\begin{aligned} \Delta^{\text{Trop}} &= \Delta_d^{\text{Trop}} + \Delta_w^{\text{Trop}} \\ &= 10^{-6} \int N_d^{\text{Trop}}\, ds + 10^{-6} \int N_w^{\text{Trop}}\, ds \end{aligned} \qquad (6.87)$$

are obtained. About 90% of the tropospheric refraction arise from the dry and about 10% from the wet component, cf. Janes et al. (1989). In practice, models for the refractivities are introduced in Eq. (6.87) and the integration is performed by numerical methods or analytically after, e.g., series expansions of the integrand. Models for the dry and wet refractivity at the earth's surface have been known for some time, cf. for example Essen and Froome (1951). The corresponding dry component is

$$N_{d,0}^{\text{Trop}} = \bar{c}_1 \, \frac{p}{T} \,, \qquad\qquad \bar{c}_1 = 77.64 \ \text{K mb}^{-1} \qquad\qquad (6.88)$$

where p is the atmospheric pressure in millibar (mb) and T is the temperature in Kelvin (K). The wet component was found to be

$$N_{w,0}^{\text{Trop}} = \bar{c}_2 \, \frac{e}{T} + \bar{c}_3 \, \frac{e}{T^2} \,, \qquad\qquad \bar{c}_2 = -12.96 \ \text{K mb}^{-1}$$
$$\bar{c}_3 = 3.718 \cdot 10^5 \ \text{K}^2 \, \text{mb}^{-1} \qquad\qquad (6.89)$$

where e is the partial pressure of water vapor in mb and T again the temperature in K. The overbar in the coefficients only stresses that there is absolutely no relationship to the coefficients for the ionosphere in, e.g., (6.55).

The values for $\bar{c}_1$, $\bar{c}_2$, and $\bar{c}_3$ are empirically determined and, certainly, cannot fully describe the local situation. An improvement is obtained by measuring meteorological data at the observation site. The following paragraphs present several models where meteorological surface data are taken into account.

Hopfield model
Using real data covering the whole earth, Hopfield (1969) has empirically found a representation of the dry refractivity as a function of the height h above the surface by

$$N_d^{\text{Trop}}(h) = N_{d,0}^{\text{Trop}} \left[\frac{h_d - h}{h_d} \right]^4 \qquad\qquad (6.90)$$

under the assumption of a single polytropic layer with thickness

$$h_d = 40\,136 + 148.72\,(T - 273.16) \quad [\text{m}] \,, \qquad\qquad (6.91)$$

see Janes et al. (1989) and cf. Fig. 6.3. Substitution of (6.90) and (6.91) into (6.85) yields (for the dry part) the tropospheric path delay

$$\Delta_d^{\text{Trop}} = 10^{-6} \, N_{d,0}^{\text{Trop}} \int \left[\frac{h_d - h}{h_d} \right]^4 ds \,. \qquad\qquad (6.92)$$

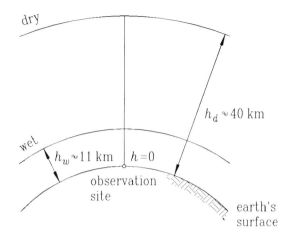

Fig. 6.3. Thickness of polytropic layers for the troposphere

The integral can be solved if the delay is calculated along the vertical direction and if the curvature of the signal path is neglected. Extracting the constant denominator, Eq. (6.92) becomes

$$\Delta_d^{\text{Trop}} = 10^{-6}\, N_{d,0}^{\text{Trop}}\, \frac{1}{h_d{}^4} \int_{h=0}^{h=h_d} (h_d - h)^4\, dh \tag{6.93}$$

for an observation site on the earth's surface (i.e., $h = 0$) and gives after integration

$$\Delta_d^{\text{Trop}} = 10^{-6}\, N_{d,0}^{\text{Trop}}\, \frac{1}{h_d{}^4} \left[-\frac{1}{5}(h_d - h)^5 \Big|_{h=0}^{h=h_d} \right]. \tag{6.94}$$

The evaluation of the expression between the brackets gives $h_d^5/5$ so that

$$\Delta_d^{\text{Trop}} = \frac{10^{-6}}{5}\, N_{d,0}^{\text{Trop}}\, h_d \tag{6.95}$$

is the dry portion of the tropospheric path delay at the zenith.

The wet portion is much more difficult to model because of the strong variations of the water vapor with respect to time and space. Nevertheless, due to lack of an appropriate alternative, the Hopfield model assumes the same functional model for both the wet and dry components. Thus,

$$N_w^{\text{Trop}}(h) = N_{w,0}^{\text{Trop}} \left[\frac{h_w - h}{h_w} \right]^4 \tag{6.96}$$

where the mean value

$$h_w = 11\,000 \text{ m} \tag{6.97}$$

is used. Sometimes other values such as $h_w = 12\,000\,\text{m}$ have been proposed, cf. Fell (1980). Unique values for h_d and h_w cannot be given because of their dependence on location and temperature. Kaniuth (1986) investigated a local situation with radio sonde data over 4.5 years and calculated for the region of the observation site $h_d = 41.6\,\text{km}$ and $h_w = 11.5\,\text{km}$. The effective troposphere heights are given as $40\,\text{km} \leq h_d \leq 45\,\text{km}$ and $10\,\text{km} \leq h_w \leq 13\,\text{km}$.

The integration of (6.96) is completely analogous to (6.92) and, thus, results in

$$\Delta_w^{\text{Trop}} = \frac{10^{-6}}{5} N_{w,0}^{\text{Trop}} h_w \,. \tag{6.98}$$

Therefore, the total tropospheric path delay at zenith is

$$\Delta^{\text{Trop}} = \frac{10^{-6}}{5} \left[N_{d,0}^{\text{Trop}} h_d + N_{w,0}^{\text{Trop}} h_w \right] \tag{6.99}$$

with the dimension meters. The model in its present form does not account for an arbitrary zenith angle of the signal. Considering the line of sight, an obliquity factor must be applied which in its simplest form is the projection from the zenith onto the line of sight given by $1/\cos z$, cf. also (6.59). Frequently, the transition of the zenith delay with $z = 0$ to a delay with arbitrary zenith angle z is denoted as the application of a mapping function, cf. for example Lanyi (1984), Janes et al. (1989), Kaniuth et al. (1989).

A slight variation of the Hopfield model contains an arbitrary elevation angle E (expressed in degrees) at the observing site. Seeber (1993), p. 47, presents the formulas where for the dry component $1/\sin(E^2 + 6.25)^{1/2}$ and for the wet component $1/\sin(E^2 + 2.25)^{1/2}$ are used as mapping functions:

$$\Delta^{\text{Trop}}(E) = \frac{10^{-6}}{5} \left[\frac{N_{d,0}^{\text{Trop}} h_d}{\sin \sqrt{E^2 + 6.25}} + \frac{N_{w,0}^{\text{Trop}} h_w}{\sin \sqrt{E^2 + 2.25}} \right] \,. \tag{6.100}$$

In more compact form, Eq. (6.100) can be represented as

$$\Delta^{\text{Trop}}(E) = \Delta_d^{\text{Trop}}(E) + \Delta_w^{\text{Trop}}(E) \tag{6.101}$$

where

$$\begin{aligned}
\Delta_d^{\text{Trop}}(E) &= \frac{10^{-6}}{5} \frac{N_{d,0}^{\text{Trop}} h_d}{\sin \sqrt{E^2 + 6.25}} \\[2ex]
\Delta_w^{\text{Trop}}(E) &= \frac{10^{-6}}{5} \frac{N_{w,0}^{\text{Trop}} h_w}{\sin \sqrt{E^2 + 2.25}}
\end{aligned} \tag{6.102}$$

or, by substituting (6.88), (6.91) and (6.89), (6.97) respectively,

$$\Delta_d^{\text{Trop}}(E) = \frac{10^{-6}}{5} \frac{77.64 \frac{p}{T}}{\sin \sqrt{E^2 + 6.25}} [40\,136 + 148.72\,(T - 273.16)]$$

$$\Delta_w^{\text{Trop}}(E) = \frac{10^{-6}}{5} \frac{-12.96\,T + 3.718 \cdot 10^5}{\sin \sqrt{E^2 + 2.25}} \frac{e}{T^2}\,11\,000$$

$$(6.103)$$

results. Measuring p, T, e at the observation location and calculating the elevation angle E, the total tropospheric path delay is obtained in meters by (6.101) after evaluating (6.103).

Modified Hopfield models
The empirical function (6.90) is now rewritten by introducing lengths of position vectors instead of heights. Denoting the earth's radius by R_E, the corresponding lengths are $r_d = R_E + h_d$ and $r = R_E + h$, cf. Fig. 6.4. Thus, the dry refractivity in the form

$$N_d^{\text{Trop}}(r) = N_{d,0}^{\text{Trop}} \left[\frac{r_d - r}{r_d - R_E} \right]^4 \tag{6.104}$$

is equivalent to (6.90). Applying Eq. (6.85) and introducing a mapping

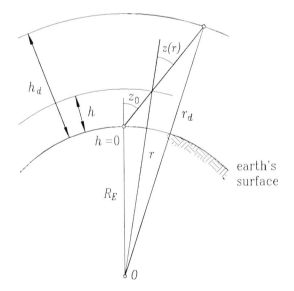

Fig. 6.4. Geometry for the tropospheric path delay

function gives

$$\Delta_d^{\text{Trop}}(z) = 10^{-6} \int\limits_{r=R_E}^{r=r_d} N_d^{\text{Trop}}(r) \frac{1}{\cos z(r)} \, dr \tag{6.105}$$

for the dry path delay. Note that the zenith angle $z(r)$ is variable. Denoting the zenith angle at the observation site by z_0, the sine-law

$$\sin z(r) = \frac{R_E}{r} \sin z_0 \tag{6.106}$$

can be applied, cf. Fig. 6.4. From Eq. (6.106) follows

$$\cos z(r) = \sqrt{1 - \frac{R_E^2}{r^2} \sin^2 z_0} \tag{6.107}$$

which is equivalent to

$$\cos z(r) = \frac{1}{r} \sqrt{r^2 - R_E^2 \sin^2 z_0} \,. \tag{6.108}$$

Substituting (6.108) and (6.104) into (6.105) yields

$$\Delta_d^{\text{Trop}}(z) = \frac{10^{-6} \, N_{d,0}^{\text{Trop}}}{(r_d - R_E)^4} \int\limits_{r=R_E}^{r=r_d} \frac{r \, (r_d - r)^4}{\sqrt{r^2 - R_E^2 \sin^2 z_0}} \, dr \tag{6.109}$$

where the terms being constant with respect to the integration variable r have been extracted from the integral. Assuming the same model for the wet portion, the corresponding formula is given by

$$\Delta_w^{\text{Trop}}(z) = \frac{10^{-6} \, N_{w,0}^{\text{Trop}}}{(r_w - R_E)^4} \int\limits_{r=R_E}^{r=r_w} \frac{r \, (r_w - r)^4}{\sqrt{r^2 - R_E^2 \sin^2 z_0}} \, dr \,. \tag{6.110}$$

Instead of the zenith angle z the elevation angle $E = 90° - z$ could also be used. Many modified Hopfield models have been derived, depending solely on the method to solve the integral. Among them, Janes et al. (1989) mention for instance the models of Yionoulis (1970), Goad and Goodman (1974), Black (1978), Black and Eisner (1984). Here, one model is presented based on a series expansion of the integrand. Details can be found for example in Goad and Goodman (1974). The resulting formulas can be found, e.g., in Remondi (1984) where a subscript i is introduced which reflects either the dry component (replace i by d) or the wet component (replace i by w). With

$$r_i = \sqrt{(R_E + h_i)^2 - (R_E \cos E)^2} - R_E \sin E \tag{6.111}$$

the tropospheric delay in meters is

$$\Delta_i^{\mathrm{Trop}}(E) = 10^{-12} N_{i,0}^{\mathrm{Trop}} \left[\sum_{k=1}^{9} \frac{\alpha_{k,i}}{k} r_i^k \right] \qquad (6.112)$$

where

$$\alpha_{1,i} = 1 \qquad\qquad\qquad \alpha_{6,i} = 4a_i\, b_i\, (a_i^2 + 3b_i)$$

$$\alpha_{2,i} = 4a_i \qquad\qquad\qquad \alpha_{7,i} = b_i^2\, (6a_i^2 + 4b_i)$$

$$\alpha_{3,i} = 6a_i^2 + 4b_i \qquad\qquad \alpha_{8,i} = 4a_i\, b_i^3 \qquad\qquad (6.113)$$

$$\alpha_{4,i} = 4a_i\, (a_i^2 + 3b_i) \qquad\quad \alpha_{9,i} = b_i^4$$

$$\alpha_{5,i} = a_i^4 + 12a_i^2\, b_i + 6b_i^2$$

and

$$a_i = -\frac{\sin E}{h_i}$$

$$ \qquad\qquad\qquad\qquad\qquad (6.114)$$

$$b_i = -\frac{\cos^2 E}{2h_i\, R_E} .$$

Substituting $i = d$, the dry part results where in (6.112) for $N_{d,0}^{\mathrm{Trop}}$ Eq. (6.88) and for h_d Eq. (6.91) must be introduced. Analogously, Eqs. (6.89) and (6.97) must be used for $N_{w,0}^{\mathrm{Trop}}$ and for h_w.

Saastamoinen model
The refractivity can alternatively but equivalently be deduced from gas laws. The interrelationship is demonstrated, e.g., in Janes et al. (1989). The Saastamoinen model is based on this approach where again some approximations have been employed. Here, any theoretical derivation is omitted. Saastamoinen (1973) models the tropospheric delay, expressed in meters,

$$\Delta^{\mathrm{Trop}} = \frac{0.002277}{\cos z} \left[p + \left(\frac{1255}{T} + 0.05 \right) e - \tan^2 z \right] \qquad (6.115)$$

as a function of z, p, T and e. As before, z denotes the zenith angle of the satellite, p the atmospheric pressure in millibar, T the temperature in Kelvin, and e the partial pressure of water vapor in millibar. Saastamoinen has also refined this model by adding two correction terms, one being dependent on the height of the observing site and the other on the height and on the zenith angle. Bauersima (1983) gives the refined formula as

$$\Delta^{\mathrm{Trop}} = \frac{0.002277}{\cos z} \left[p + \left(\frac{1255}{T} + 0.05 \right) e - B\, \tan^2 z \right] + \delta R \quad (6.116)$$

Table 6.3. Correction term B for the
refined Saastamoinen model

Height [km]	B [mb]
0.0	1.156
0.5	1.079
1.0	1.006
1.5	0.938
2.0	0.874
2.5	0.813
3.0	0.757
4.0	0.654
5.0	0.563

Table 6.4. Correction term δR in meters for refined Saastamoinen model

Zenith angle	Station height above sea level [km]							
	0	0.5	1.0	1.5	2.0	3.0	4.0	5.0
60°00′	0.003	0.003	0.002	0.002	0.002	0.002	0.001	0.001
66°00′	0.006	0.006	0.005	0.005	0.004	0.003	0.003	0.002
70°00′	0.012	0.011	0.010	0.009	0.008	0.006	0.005	0.004
73°00′	0.020	0.018	0.017	0.015	0.013	0.011	0.009	0.007
75°00′	0.031	0.028	0.025	0.023	0.021	0.017	0.014	0.011
76°00′	0.039	0.035	0.032	0.029	0.026	0.021	0.017	0.014
77°00′	0.050	0.045	0.041	0.037	0.033	0.027	0.022	0.018
78°00′	0.065	0.059	0.054	0.049	0.044	0.036	0.030	0.024
78°30′	0.075	0.068	0.062	0.056	0.051	0.042	0.034	0.028
79°00′	0.087	0.079	0.072	0.065	0.059	0.049	0.040	0.033
79°30′	0.102	0.093	0.085	0.077	0.070	0.058	0.047	0.039
79°45′	0.111	0.101	0.092	0.083	0.076	0.063	0.052	0.043
80°00′	0.121	0.110	0.100	0.091	0.083	0.068	0.056	0.047

where the correction terms B and δR can be interpolated from Tables 6.3
and 6.4.

A numerical assessment using parameters of a standard atmosphere at
sea level results in a vertical tropospheric delay of about 2.3 m.

Tropospheric problems
There are many other tropospheric models which are similar to the models given here, e.g., Lanyi (1984), Chao (1972), Marini and Murray (1973),

Elgered et al. (1985), Davis et al. (1985), Rahnemoon (1988). Although the list is not complete, the question arises why there are so many different approaches. One reason is the difficulty in modeling the water vapor. The simple use of surface measurements cannot give the utmost accuracy so that water vapor radiometers have been developed. These instruments measure the sky brightness temperature by radiometric microwave observations along the signal path enabling the calculation of the wet path delay, cf. Elgered et al. (1985). The hardware components of a water vapor radiometer are described, for example, in Reichert (1986). Accurate water vapor radiometers are expensive and experience problems at low elevation angles, see Lanyi (1984), since the tropospheric path delay at zenith is amplified by the mapping function.

The difficulty in modeling the tropospheric effect will require continuation of research and development for some years. The best solution, in the opinion of Lanyi (1984), is to combine surface and radio sonde meteorological data, water vapor radiometer measurements and statistics. This is a major task and an appropriate model has not yet been found.

6.4 Relativistic effects

6.4.1 Special relativity

Lorentz transformation
Consider two four-dimensional systems $S(x, y, z, t)$ and $S'(x', y', z', t')$ where the union of space coordinates x, y, z and the time coordinate t is characterized by space-time coordinates. The system S is at rest and, relatively to S, the system S' is uniformly translating with velocity v. For simplicity, it is assumed that both systems coincide at an initial epoch $t = 0$ and that the translation takes place along the x-axis.

The transformation of the space-time coordinates is given by

$$x' = \frac{x - v\,t}{\sqrt{1 - \frac{v^2}{c^2}}}$$

$$y' = y$$

$$z' = z$$

$$t' = \frac{t - \frac{v}{c^2}\,x}{\sqrt{1 - \frac{v^2}{c^2}}}$$

(6.117)

where c is the speed of light. Note that the equations above describe the moving system S' with respect to the system S at rest (more figuratively:

as viewed from the moving system). Equivalently, the system S at rest
may be described with respect to the moving system S' (more figuratively:
as viewed from the system at rest). The corresponding formulas follow by
solving Eq. (6.117) for the space-time coordinates in the system S at rest (or
simply by interchanging the role of the primed and the unprimed coordinates
and reversing the sign of the velocity v. Thus, the relations

$$
\begin{aligned}
x &= \frac{x' + v\,t'}{\sqrt{1 - \frac{v^2}{c^2}}} \\[2mm]
y &= y' \\
z &= z' \\[2mm]
t &= \frac{t' + \frac{v}{c^2}\,x'}{\sqrt{1 - \frac{v^2}{c^2}}}
\end{aligned}
\tag{6.118}
$$

are obtained. Equations (6.117) and (6.118) are known as Lorentz transformation. An elegant and simple derivation of these formulas can be found in
Joos (1956), pp. 217–218. Using Eqs. (6.117) or (6.118), the relation

$$
x^2 + y^2 + z^2 - c^2 t^2 = x'^2 + y'^2 + z'^2 - c^2 t'^2
\tag{6.119}
$$

may be verified. This means that the norm of a vector in space-time coordinates is invariant with respect to the choice of its reference system. Note
that in the case of $c = \infty$, the Lorentz transformation (6.117) converts to
the Galilei transformation

$$
\begin{aligned}
x' &= x - v\,t \\
y' &= y \\
z' &= z \\
t' &= t
\end{aligned}
\tag{6.120}
$$

which is fundamental in classical mechanics.

The theory of special relativity is, by definition, restricted to inertial
systems. The application of the Lorentz transformation reveals some features
of that theory.

Time dilation

Consider an observer moving with the system S'. At a specific location x'
the time events t'_1 and t'_2 are recorded. The corresponding time events t_1

and t_2 in the system S at rest, according to Lorentz transformation (6.118), are

$$t_1 = \frac{t_1' + \frac{v}{c^2} x'}{\sqrt{1 - \frac{v^2}{c^2}}} \qquad\qquad t_2 = \frac{t_2' + \frac{v}{c^2} x'}{\sqrt{1 - \frac{v^2}{c^2}}} . \tag{6.121}$$

The time interval $\Delta t' = t_2' - t_1'$ in the moving system is called proper time and the time interval $\Delta t = t_2 - t_1$ in the system at rest is called coordinate time. The relation between proper and coordinate time is found by the difference of the two expressions in (6.121)

$$\Delta t = \frac{\Delta t'}{\sqrt{1 - \frac{v^2}{c^2}}} \tag{6.122}$$

which means that as viewed at the system at rest, the time interval recorded by the moving observer is lengthened or dilated. The same holds for the inverse situation: a time interval recorded by an observer in the system at rest is dilated for an observer in the moving system. The result $\Delta t' = \Delta t / \sqrt{1 - v^2/c^2}$ may be verified by the reader by using Eqs. (6.117) or is simply obtained by interchanging the role of the primed and the unprimed coordinates in (6.122) (reversing the sign of v has here no effect because this quantity is squared). The time dilation is the reason why moving clocks run slower than clocks at rest.

Lorentz contraction
The derivation of the Lorentz contraction is similar to that of time dilation. Consider now two locations x_1' and x_2' in the moving system S' at a specific epoch t'. The corresponding locations x_1 and x_2 in the system S at rest, according to the Lorentz transformation (6.118), are

$$x_1 = \frac{x_1' + v\,t'}{\sqrt{1 - \frac{v^2}{c^2}}} \qquad\qquad x_2 = \frac{x_2' + v\,t'}{\sqrt{1 - \frac{v^2}{c^2}}} . \tag{6.123}$$

With the abbreviations $\Delta x = x_2 - x_1$ and $\Delta x' = x_2' - x_1'$, the difference of the two expressions in (6.123) gives

$$\Delta x = \frac{\Delta x'}{\sqrt{1 - \frac{v^2}{c^2}}} \tag{6.124}$$

which means that as viewed from the system S at rest, $\Delta x'$ is lengthened to Δx. Expressing it in another way, the dimension of a body moving with the observer in the system S' seems to be contracted.

Second-order Doppler effect

Since frequency is inversely proportional to time, one can deduce immediately from the considerations on time dilation that the frequency f' of a moving emitter would be reduced to f given by the formula

$$f = f' \sqrt{1 - \frac{v^2}{c^2}} \, . \tag{6.125}$$

This is the second-order Doppler effect.

Mass relation

Special relativity also affects masses. Denoting the masses in the two reference frames S and S' by m and m' respectively, then

$$m = \frac{m'}{\sqrt{1 - \frac{v^2}{c^2}}} \tag{6.126}$$

is the corresponding mass relation, cf. for example Heckmann (1985).

Each of the formulas (6.122) to (6.126) comprises the same square root which may be expanded into binomial series:

$$\frac{1}{\sqrt{1 - \frac{v^2}{c^2}}} = 1 + \frac{1}{2}\left(\frac{v}{c}\right)^2 \dots$$

$$\sqrt{1 - \frac{v^2}{c^2}} = 1 - \frac{1}{2}\left(\frac{v}{c}\right)^2 \dots \tag{6.127}$$

Substituting these expansions into Eqs. (6.122) to (6.126), each related to an observer at rest, then

$$\frac{\Delta t' - \Delta t}{\Delta t} = \frac{\Delta x' - \Delta x}{\Delta x} = -\frac{f' - f}{f} = \frac{m' - m}{m} = -\frac{1}{2}\left(\frac{v}{c}\right)^2 \tag{6.128}$$

accounts for the mentioned effects of the special relativity in one formula.

6.4.2 General relativity

The theory of general relativity includes accelerated reference systems too, where the gravitational field plays the key role. Formulas analogous to (6.128) may be derived when one replaces the kinetic energy $\frac{1}{2}v^2$ in special relativity by the potential energy ΔU. Thus,

$$\frac{\Delta t' - \Delta t}{\Delta t} = \frac{\Delta x' - \Delta x}{\Delta x} = -\frac{f' - f}{f} = \frac{m' - m}{m} = -\frac{\Delta U}{c^2} \tag{6.129}$$

represents the relations in general relativity, cf. Heckmann (1985), where ΔU is the difference of the gravitational potential in the two reference frames under consideration.

6.4.3   Relevant relativistic effects for GPS

The reference frame (relatively) at rest is located in the center of the earth and an accelerated reference frame is attached to each GPS satellite. Therefore, the theory of special and general relativity must be taken into account. Relativistic effects are relevant for the satellite orbit, the satellite signal propagation, and both the satellite and receiver clock. An overview of all these effects is given for example in Zhu and Groten (1988). The relativistic effects on rotating and gravitating clocks is also treated in Grafarend and Schwarze (1991). With respect to general relativity, Ashby (1987) shows that only the gravitational field of the earth must be considered. Sun and moon and consequently all other masses in the solar system are negligible. Deines (1992) investigates the uncompensated effects if the noninertial GPS observations are not transformed to an inertial frame.

Relativity affecting the satellite orbit
The gravitational field of the earth causes relativistic perturbations in the satellite orbits. An approximate formula for the disturbing acceleration is given by Eq. (4.43). For more details the reader is referred to Zhu and Groten (1988).

Relativity affecting the satellite signal
The gravitational field gives rise to a space-time curvature of the satellite signal. Therefore, a propagation correction must be applied to get the Euclidean range for instance. Following Holdridge (1967), the range correction takes the form

$$\delta^{\text{rel}} = \frac{2\mu}{c^2} \, \ln \frac{\varrho^j + \varrho_i + \varrho_i^j}{\varrho^j + \varrho_i - \varrho_i^j} \tag{6.130}$$

where μ is the earth's gravitational constant. The geocentric distances of satellite j and observing site i are denoted ϱ^j and ϱ_i, and ϱ_i^j is the distance between the satellite and the observing site. In order to estimate the maximum effect for a point on the earth's surface take the mean radius $R_E = 6\,370\,\text{km}$ and a mean altitude of $h = 20\,200\,\text{km}$ for the satellites. The maximum distance ϱ_i^j results from the Pythagorean theorem and is about $25\,800\,\text{km}$. Substituting these values, the maximum range error $\delta^{\text{rel}} = 18.7\,\text{nm}$ results from (6.130). Note that this maximum value only applies to point positioning. In relative positioning the effect is much smaller and amounts to $0.001\,\text{ppm}$, cf. Zhu and Groten (1988).

Relativity affecting the satellite clock
The fundamental frequency f_0 of the satellite clock is $10.23\,\text{MHz}$. All the

signals are based on this frequency which is influenced by the motion of the satellite and by the difference of the gravitational field at the satellite and the observing site. The corresponding effects of special and general relativity are small and may be linearly superposed. Thus,

$$\delta^{\mathrm{rel}} \equiv \frac{f_0' - f_0}{f_0} = \frac{1}{2} \left(\frac{v}{c} \right)^2 + \frac{\Delta U}{c^2}$$
$$\text{special} + \text{general}$$
$$\text{relativity}$$

(6.131)

is the effect on the frequency of the satellite clock where Eqs. (6.128) and (6.129) have been used. To get a numerical value, circular orbits and a spherical earth with the observing site on its surface are assumed. Backing on these simplifications, (6.131) takes the form

$$\delta^{\mathrm{rel}} \equiv \frac{f_0' - f_0}{f_0} = \frac{1}{2} \left(\frac{v}{c} \right)^2 + \frac{\mu}{c^2} \left[\frac{1}{R_E + h} - \frac{1}{R_E} \right]$$

(6.132)

with v being the satellite's mean velocity. Substituting numerical values yields

$$\frac{f_0' - f_0}{f_0} = -4.464 \cdot 10^{-10}$$

(6.133)

which, despite the simplifications, is sufficiently accurate. Ashby (1987) for instance takes into account the J_2-term for the potential and the centrifugal forces and gets the only slightly different result $-4.465 \cdot 10^{-10}$. Recall that f_0' is the emitted frequency and f_0 is the frequency received at the observation site. Thus, it can be seen that the satellite transmitted nominal frequency would be increased by $df = 4.464 \cdot 10^{-10} f_0 = 4.57 \cdot 10^{-3}$ Hz. However, it is desired to receive the nominal frequency. This is achieved by an offset df in the satellite clock frequency, so that 10.22999999543 MHz are emitted, cf. Spilker (1980).

Another periodic effect arises due to the assumption of a circular orbit (which is almost true for the Block II satellites). An adequate correction formula is given by Gibson (1983) as

$$\delta^{\mathrm{rel}} = \frac{2}{c} \sqrt{\mu a}\, e \sin E$$

(6.134)

where e denotes the eccentricity, a the semimajor axis, and E the eccentric anomaly. This relativistic effect is taken into account by the clock polynomial broadcast via the navigation message, cf. Sect. 4.4.2, where the time dependent eccentric anomaly E is expanded into a Taylor series. Thus,

Eq. (6.134) gives slightly more accurate results. However, the decision to use this formula must be correlated with a correction of the clock polynomial coefficients with respect to the built in accounting for the periodic effect. Van Dierendonck et al. (1980) present the necessary formulas. In the case of relative positioning, the effect cancels, cf. Zhu and Groten (1988).

Relativity affecting the receiver clock
A receiver clock located at the earth's surface is rotating with respect to the resting reference frame at the geocenter. The associated linear velocity at the equator is approximately $0.5 \, \text{km} \, \text{s}^{-1}$ and, thus, roughly one tenth of the satellite's velocity. Substituting this value into the special relativistic part of Eq. (6.131) yields a relative frequency shift in the order of 10^{-12} which after 3 hours corresponds to a clock error of 10 nanoseconds ($1 \, \text{ns} = 10^{-9} \, \text{s} \doteq 30 \, \text{cm}$). Ashby (1987) presented the correction formula for this Sagnac effect; however, since usually the correction is performed by the receiver software the formula is not explicitly given here.

6.5   Antenna phase center offset and variation

The phase center of the antennas is the point to which the radio signal measurement is referred and generally is not identical with the geometric antenna center. The offset depends on the elevation, the azimuth, and the intensity of the satellite signal and is different for $L1$ and $L2$. Two effects must be distinguished: the offset and the variation of the antenna phase center. The precision of an antenna should be based on the antenna phase center variation and not on the offset. A constant offset could easily be determined and taken into account.

First, the true antenna phase center may be different from the manufacturer indicated center. This antenna offset may simply arise from inaccurate production series. An investigation to determine this offset was, e.g., performed by Sims (1985) and was based on test measurements by rotating the antenna in a laboratory environment. Second, the antenna phase center varies with respect to the incoming satellite signals. The variation is systematic and may be investigated by test series. Sims (1985) found variations amounting to 1–2 cm. However, it is fairly difficult to model the antenna phase center variation because it is different for each antenna and also for various types. Geiger (1988) shows the different characteristics of conical spiral antennas, microstrip antennas, dipole antennas (crossed pair of horizontal, half-wavelength dipole), and helices. As a consequence, the direct computation of the antenna effects on the distance measurements with respect to azimuth and elevation was proposed. Simple functions for an appropriate modeling may also be found by laboratory tests, cf. Schupler and Clark (1991).

6.6 Multipath

The effect is well described by its name: a satellite emitted signal arrives at the receiver via more than one path. Multipath is mainly caused by reflecting surfaces near the receiver, cf. Fig. 6.5. Secondary effects are reflections at the satellite during signal transmission.

Referring to Fig. 6.5, the satellite signal arrives at the receiver on three different paths, one direct and two indirect ones. As a consequence, the received signals have relative phase offsets and the phase differences are proportional to the differences of the path lengths, cf. Tranquilla (1986). There is no general model of the multipath effect because of the arbitrarily different geometric situations. The influence of the multipath, however, can be estimated by using a combination of $L1$ and $L2$ code, and carrier phase measurements, cf. Evans (1986). The principle is based on the fact that the troposphere, clock errors, and relativistic effects influence code and carrier phases by the same amount. This is not true for ionospheric refraction and multipath which are frequency dependent. Taking ionospheric-free code ranges and carrier phases, and forming corresponding differences, all aforementioned effects except for multipath cancel. The residuals, apart from the noise level, thus reflect the multipath effect. The most effective countermeasure to multipath is to avoid sites where it could be a problem (e.g., near chain link fence). Considering Fig. 6.5, placing the antenna directly on the reflecting ground without tripod would eliminate one of the two indirect

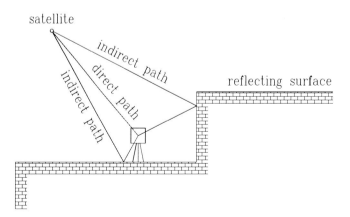

Fig. 6.5. Multipath effect

paths; however, the vertical reflecting surface would still contaminate the results. The general recommendation is, therefore, to avoid, as far as possible, reflecting surfaces in the neighbourhood of the receivers.

The elimination of multipath signals is also possible by selecting an antenna that takes advantage of the signal polarization. GPS signals are right-handed circularly polarized, whereas the reflected signals are left-handed polarized, cf. Scherrer (1985). A reduction of the multipath effect may also be achieved by digital filtering, wideband antennas, cf. Bletzacker (1985), and radio frequency absorbent antenna ground planes, cf. Tallqvist (1985). The absorbent antenna ground plane reduces the interference of satellite signals with low or even negative elevation angles which occur in case of multipath.

Purely from geometry it is clear that signals received from low satellite elevations are more susceptible to multipath than signals from high elevations. It should be noted that code ranges are more highly affected by multipath than carrier phases, cf. Evans (1986). Comparing single epochs, the multipath effect may amount to 10–20 m for code pseudoranges, cf. Wells et al. (1987) and Evans (1986). Under certain circumstances, the error resulting from multipath may grow to about 100 m in the vicinity of buildings, cf. Nee (1992). Tranquilla and Carr (1990/91) group the multipath errors of code pseudoranges into three classes: (1) diffuse forward scattering from a widely distributed area (e.g., the signal passes through a cluttered metallic environment) causing range errors of about 10 m, (2) specular reflection from well-defined objects or reflective surfaces in the vicinity of the antenna with range errors of 2–6 m, (3) fluctuations of very low frequency, usually associated with reflection from the surface of water causing range errors of about 10 m. In severe cases of multipath, loss of lock may even occur.

The effect of multipath on carrier phases may be estimated by the following considerations, cf. Fig. 6.5. The direct and indirect signals interfere at the antenna center and may be represented by

$$
\begin{aligned}
a \cos \varphi \quad &\ldots \quad \text{direct signal} \\
\beta\, a \cos (\varphi + \Delta\varphi) \quad &\ldots \quad \text{indirect signal}
\end{aligned}
\tag{6.135}
$$

where a and φ denote the amplitude and the phase of the direct signal. The amplitude of the indirect signal is reduced by the damping factor β because of the reflection at a surface, see Seeber (1993), p. 308. The phase of the indirect signal is delayed by the phase shift $\Delta\varphi$ which is a function of the geometric configuration. The superposition of the signals in (6.135) is represented by

$$
a \cos \varphi + \beta\, a \cos (\varphi + \Delta\varphi).
\tag{6.136}
$$

Applying the cosine-theorem yields

$$a \cos \varphi + \beta \, a \cos \varphi \cos \Delta\varphi - \beta \, a \sin \varphi \sin \Delta\varphi \qquad (6.137)$$

which is slightly rearranged to

$$(1 + \beta \cos \Delta\varphi) \, a \cos \varphi - (\beta \sin \Delta\varphi) \, a \sin \varphi. \qquad (6.138)$$

This resultant signal may also be represented, see Joos (1956), p. 44, in the form

$$\beta_M \, a \cos (\varphi + \Delta\varphi_M) \qquad (6.139)$$

where the subscript M indicates multipath. The cosine-theorem gives

$$(\beta_M \cos \Delta\varphi_M) \, a \cos \varphi - (\beta_M \sin \Delta\varphi_M) \, a \sin \varphi. \qquad (6.140)$$

Comparing the coefficients for $a \sin \varphi$ and $a \cos \varphi$ of Eqs. (6.138) and (6.140) leads to the relations

$$\begin{aligned} \beta_M \sin \Delta\varphi_M &= \beta \sin \Delta\varphi \\ \beta_M \cos \Delta\varphi_M &= 1 + \beta \cos \Delta\varphi \end{aligned} \qquad (6.141)$$

which represent two equations for the desired quantities β_M and $\Delta\varphi_M$. An explicit expression for β_M follows by squaring and adding the two equations. Thus,

$$\beta_M = \sqrt{1 + \beta^2 + 2\beta \cos \Delta\varphi} \qquad (6.142)$$

is obtained. An explicit expression for $\Delta\varphi_M$ follows by dividing the two equations in (6.141). Thus,

$$\tan \Delta\varphi_M = \frac{\beta \sin \Delta\varphi}{1 + \beta \cos \Delta\varphi} \qquad (6.143)$$

is the solution.

The damping factor β may vary between 0 and 1. The substitution of $\beta = 0$ (i.e., there is no reflected signal and no multipath) into (6.142) and (6.143) gives $\beta_M = 1$ and $\Delta\varphi_M = 0$. This means that the "resultant" signal is identical to the direct signal. The strongest possible reflection is defined by $\beta = 1$. The substitution of this value into (6.142) and (6.143) leads to

$$\beta_M = \sqrt{2(1 + \cos \Delta\varphi)} = 2 \cos \frac{\Delta\varphi}{2} \qquad (6.144)$$

and

$$\tan \Delta\varphi_M = \frac{\sin \Delta\varphi}{1 + \cos \Delta\varphi} = \tan \frac{\Delta\varphi}{2} \qquad (6.145)$$

yielding

$$\Delta\varphi_M = \frac{1}{2}\Delta\varphi. \qquad (6.146)$$

Examples for numerical values for β_M and $\Delta\varphi_M$ as a function of $\Delta\varphi$ are

$\Delta\varphi$	β_M	$\Delta\varphi_M$
$0°$	2	$0°$
$90°$	$\sqrt{2}$	$45°$
$180°$	0	$90°$

which shows that the maximum effect of multipath on phase measurements occurs for $\Delta\varphi_M = 90° = 1/4$ cycle. Converting this phase shift to range gives $\lambda/4$ or, with $\lambda = 20$ cm, the maximum change in range of about 5 cm. However, it should be noted that this value may increase if linear phase combinations are used.

The multipath effects on carrier phases for relative positioning with short baselines, should, generally, not be greater than 1 cm (good satellite geometry and a reasonably long observation interval), cf. Counselman (1981). But even in those cases, as Rocken and Meertens (1989) show, a simple change of the height of the receiver may increase the multipath and, thus, deteriorate the results.

Li et al. (1993) propose the detection and reduction of multipath in the spectral domain. The measured data are transformed by the Fast Fourier Transform into the spectral domain. The detection and reduction of multipath is carried out by amplitude filtering. Afterwards, the inverse Fast Fourier Transform outputs the filtered data.

In the practice of surveying, multipath may not be much of a problem. One must use common sense and a certain amount of judgement in selecting sites for GPS occupation. Sites near wire mesh fences and metal buildings should be avoided as a matter of course. When a point is in or near a fenceline, the antenna can be elevated above the fence to get above its reflecting surface. When performing static surveys where the observation times tend to be relatively long, intermittent periods of multipath contamination are not a problem. Such situations occur when the receiver is set up in the center of a highway and large metal trucks continually pass by the antenna. Rapid static surveys may be more contaminated in such cases, and longer observation times would be appropriate.

7 Surveying with GPS

7.1 Introduction

This chapter mainly concerns the practical aspects of GPS surveying and addresses planning, performance, and in situ data processing. Overlapping with other chapters is intentional to provide complete information in a single chapter for readers more interested in practical considerations.

7.1.1 Terminology definitions

The enormous interest in GPS is reflected by the numerous papers published today. Unfortunately, a standard terminology is not used at this time; although, several authors, e.g., Wells (1985), have attempted to provide a list of terms used. To avoid confusion in the following sections, some of more important definitions are given here and are used throughout the entire text.

Code range versus carrier phase
Typically, GPS observables are pseudoranges derived from code or carrier phase measurements. Generally speaking, the accuracy of code ranges is at the meter level, whereas the accuracy of carrier phases is in the millimeter range. However, the accuracy of code ranges can be improved by smoothing techniques. Unlike the carrier phases, the code ranges are virtually unambiguous. This makes code ranges immune from cycle slips (i.e., changes of the phase ambiguities) and to some extent from site obstructions. The ambiguities of the phases can be determined by various methods (e.g., initialization procedures).

Real-time processing versus postprocessing
To qualify as real-time GPS, the position results must be available in the field immediately or while still on station. The results are denoted as "instantaneous" if the observables of a single epoch are used for the position computation and the processing time is negligible. A different and less stringent definition is "real-time" which includes computing results after more than one observation epoch. The original concept of GPS is the feature of instantaneous navigation which is the determination of the position of a moving vehicle (i.e., a ship, a car, an aircraft) by unsmoothed code pseudoranges, cf. for example Yiu et al. (1984). Postprocessing occurs when data are collected and processed after the fact. Typically, the data are not pro-

cessed in the field and measurements from different sites are combined.

Point positioning versus relative positioning

The coordinates of a single point are determined for point positioning using a single receiver which measures code ranges to (normally four or more) satellites. Instead of "point positioning" the term "single point positioning", cf. for example Lachapelle et al. (1982) or Prilepin (1989), or the term "absolute point positioning", cf. for example Gouldman et al. (1986) or Hartl et al. (1985), is used. Here, the term "absolute" reflects the opposite of "relative".

Relative positioning is possible if two receivers are used and (code or carrier phase) measurements, to the same satellites, are simultaneously made at two sites. The accuracy is better than in the case of point positioning as a consequence of processing the data from two sites. Normally, the coordinates of one site are known and the position of the other site is to be determined relatively to the known site (i.e., the vector between the two sites is determined). In general, the receiver placed on the known site is stationary while observing. In a more stringent definition the term "relative" is used in the case of carrier phase observations, whereas in the case of code range observations, the term "differential" is used, cf. for example Strange (1985); Oswald et al. (1986); Blackwell (1986).

Another definition associates point positioning with navigation and relative positioning with surveying.

Static versus kinematic

Static denotes a stationary observation location, while kinematic implies motion. A temporary loss of signal lock in static mode is not as critical as in kinematic mode.

Attention should be paid to the difference between the terms "kinematic" and "dynamic". A very intuitive example given in Schwarz et al. (1987) points up the difference: "Modeling the movement of a vehicle in three-dimensional space requires either the knowledge of the forces causing the motion or the measurement of the vehicle motion in a given three-dimensional coordinate system. The first type of modeling will be called dynamic, the second kinematic." The modeling of the orbit for GPS satellites is a dynamic procedure. Hein et al. (1988) consider this as the only case of dynamic modeling with respect to the analysis of GPS observations. As soon as the positions of the satellites are assumed to be known and given, positioning of a moving vehicle can be considered as kinematic procedure.

The terms "static" and "kinematic" must be considered in the context of point or relative positioning. Typical examples of these modes are given to acquaint the reader with these terms.

Static point positioning is useful if points are needed with moderate accuracy. Without SA, an accuracy of about 10 m could be achieved after a fairly short observation time. Numerical examples are given, e.g., in Wells and Lachapelle (1981), Lachapelle et al. (1982), Ashjaee (1986). With SA on, the observation time must be extended to obtain the same level of accuracy.

Kinematic point positioning can be used to determine a vehicle's three-dimensional trajectory as a function of time. Because of SA, the positional accuracy may be degraded up to about 300 m. Some examples for kinematic point positioning are vehicle navigation, airborne gravimetry, and gravity vector determination using a land vehicle, cf. Schwarz (1987).

Static relative positioning by carrier phases, at present, is the most frequently used method by surveyors and is also called *static surveying*. The principle is based on determining the vector between two stationary receivers. This vector is often called "baseline" or simply "line" because of its similarity to triangulation baselines. According to this terminology, the process is called single or multipoint baseline determination. Obviously, the multipoint solution concerns more than two sites. In static surveying 1 ppm to 0.1 ppm accuracies are achievable which is equivalent to millimeter accuracy for baselines up to some kilometers.

Kinematic relative positioning involves one stationary and one moving receiver. The two receivers perform the observations simultaneously. The possible applications are basically the same as for kinematic point positioning but the accuracies are higher. The accuracy in differential positioning (i.e., by code ranges) is at the meter level, and in relative positioning (i.e., by carrier phases) centimeter accuracy is achievable, cf. Cannon et al. (1986).

7.1.2   Observation technique

The selection of the observation technique in a GPS survey depends upon the project's particular requirements; especially the desired accuracy plays a dominant role.

Single point positioning
When using a single receiver, only point positioning with code pseudoranges makes sense. For single point positioning, GPS will provide two levels of service: (1) the Standard Positioning Service (SPS) and (2) the Precise Positioning Service (PPS).

For the SPS only the C/A-code is available and SA is incorporated into the service. This limits the (real-time) accuracy in horizontal position to 100 m and the vertical accuracy to 156 m at the 95% probability level. Increasing the probability level to 99.99% degrades the accuracy in horizontal position to 300 m and the vertical accuracy to 500 m.

The PPS has access to both codes. The horizontal accuracy is within 16 m and vertical accuracy within 23 m at the 95% probability level. The availability of PPS is primarily designed for U.S. military use. However, it will also be available to U.S. Federal and Allied Government (civil and military) users through special agreements with DoD. Furthermore, limited nongovernmental civil use of GPS, domestic and foreign, will be considered upon request, see Olsen (1992).

Differential GPS

When two (or more) receivers are used, Differential GPS (DGPS) can be applied where one reference or fixed receiver is located at a known station and the position of the mostly moving receiver is to be determined. At least four common satellites are tracked simultaneously at both sites. The known position of the fixed receiver is used to calculate corrections to the GPS derived position or to the observed code ranges. These corrections are then transmitted via telemetry (i.e., controlled radio link) to the roving receiver and allow the computation of its position which is far more accurate than that in the single point positioning mode.

An alternative to the navigation mode is the surveillance mode where the remote receivers broadcast the raw data to the (fixed) monitor station where the correct position is computed. The surveillance mode has the advantage that the roving (e.g., airborne) receiver does not have to perform a large number of computations, cf. Kasties and Harrer (1991).

As previously mentioned, for real-time DGPS two correction methods are in use. In the first method, the reference receiver at a known location calculates its position using the same set of satellites as the roving receiver. The difference of the known position from the calculated one yields position corrections. These values are then applied to the roving receiver to obtain an improved position. This method is easily performed but requires more complex satellite selection. The second method is based on pseudorange corrections which are derived from the difference between calculated ranges and observed code pseudoranges at the fixed site. Using this method, the observed code ranges at the roving site can be corrected by applying the fixed station corrections. This method is more flexible and gives higher precision. The disadvantage is that more computing effort is needed for the algorithms, cf. Lindemann and Haverland (1991).

The accuracy requirements of GPS users are very different and vary between several hundred meters and centimeter level. A very large group of users is interested in a real-time accuracy level of 1–10 m. This accuracy cannot be obtained in single point positioning mode (because of SA) but can be achieved by DGPS. This capability is primarily based on the fact that GPS error sources are very similar over a region of say 500 km and are, therefore, virtually eliminated by the differential technique.

With C/A-code ranges, one can routinely achieve accuracies at the 3–5 m level. To obtain submeter level one has to use phase smoothed code ranges or high performance C/A-code receivers, cf. Lachapelle (1992). An even higher accuracy level can be reached by the use of carrier phases. This technique (generally) requires the use of dual frequency receivers which perform kinematic relative positioning in real time where accuracies at the decimeter level (or less) over ranges up to 20 km can be obtained, cf. for instance De-Loach and Remondi (1991). To achieve this accuracy, the ambiguities must be resolved on-the-fly.

An essential aspect of DGPS is the data communication link. The radio link requires compatible hardware at the monitor and remote sites. High data transfer rates may be needed to maintain a high accuracy in the presence of SA, which in turn requires that a significant amount of information has to be transmitted in a short time. SA may be characterized by variations of the pseudorange error with an amplitude of about 100 m and a period of about 10 minutes. Thus, correction update rates of 10 seconds or better are adequate to remove SA effects at the 2 m accuracy level.

It is beyond the scope of this book to describe in detail problems concerning the frequency selection for the communication link. Here the reader is referred to, e.g., Langley (1993). Nevertheless, it should be mentioned that existing radio positioning chains with data transmission capability could be used. An example is the Radio Data System (RDS) which is a standardized method for distributing digital data on broadcast FM along with the conventional program, cf. Weber and Tiwari (1994). An interesting future possibility is the use of "pseudolites". The name is a contraction of the words "pseudo" and "satellite" and refers to a transmitter that emits radio signals like a GPS satellite. One could also modulate the differential corrections onto the signal. Pseudolites would be located at fixed sites or in geostationary satellites and could contribute to better GPS integrity. The ultimate use of DGPS will likely occur when the planned worldwide telecommunications satellite program is operational. This program will use numerous low orbit satellites that will provide mobile telephone service anywhere in the world.

For reasons of compatibility between (fixed) monitor and (roving) remote receivers, a standard format for data transmission has been proposed and is widely used. It has been developed by the Radio Technical Commission for Maritime Services, Special Committee 104, and is, thus, named RTCM SC-104. For more details see Wells et al. (1987) or Kalafus (1992).

Relative positioning

At present, geodetic accuracies are only obtained in the relative positioning mode with observed carrier phases. Processing a baseline vector requires the phases be simultaneously observed at both baseline endpoints. Hence, relative positioning originally was only possible by postprocessing data. Today, real-time data transfer on short baselines is routinely possible. This enables real-time computation of baseline vectors, cf. for example Hofmann-Wellenhof et al. (1990).

Static relative positioning

The static surveying method is the most commonly used since the only basic requirement is a relatively unobstructed view of the sky for the occupied points. Conventional static surveys generally, require 10 to 120-minute observation periods depending on the baseline length, the number of visible satellites, the geometric configuration, and the method used. For practical applications, an accuracy of ± 1 ppm or 1 mm for a 1 km baseline can be achieved.

Static relative positioning also includes the shorter (e.g., 2-minute) rapid static technique based on fast ambiguity resolution approaches. These techniques generally use code and carrier phase combinations on both frequencies. Thus, dual frequency receivers and optimum satellite geometry are required. When restricting the method to say 10 km baselines, accuracies of $\pm(5 \text{ mm} + 1 \text{ ppm})$ can be achieved. This has first been demonstrated in a P-code receiver test by the FGCC in 1991 using 10 minutes of data and applying the wide lane technique.

Typical uses of static surveying include: state, county, and local control surveys; photo-control surveys, boundary surveys; and deformation surveys.

Kinematic relative positioning

Kinematic surveys are the most productive in that the greatest number of points can be determined in the least time. Whereas the conventional static GPS method requires that the satellites move in the sky, the conventional kinematic method does not require this motion. Because of this fact, the proposed interoperation of GPS with geostationary satellites will be useful for kinematic surveys, cf. Sect. 13.2.3. Kinematic surveys require considerable reconnaissance since not only the occupied sites but also the route taken to travel between sites should be free of obstructions. The kinematic technique requires that lock be maintained on four or more satellites throughout the entire survey. This means, in practical terms, that the roving receiver cannot travel under a tree or too close to a utility pole. The kinematic method is best suited for wide open areas (such as cleared construction sites) where there are few obstructions. Areas such as suburban subdivisions can also be surveyed by the kinematic technique if there are not too many large trees overhanging the roads. The kinematic technique can be used to position a receiver that is mounted on an all-terrain vehicle that travels across a given area in a series of cross section lines. The three-dimensional coordinates of this vehicle-mounted receiver can be determined to high accuracy (few centimeters) so that an accurate topographic map of the area can be prepared.

The semikinematic, cf. Cannon and Schwarz (1989), or stop-and-go technique, cf. Minkel (1989), is characterized by alternatively stopping and moving one receiver with the main interest being in the stopped positions. The most important feature of this method is the increase in accuracy when several measurement epochs at the stop locations are accumulated and averaged. This technique is often referred to as simply kinematic survey.

On-the-fly kinematic relative positioning is nearly identical to the rapid static technique. This method can use single frequency receivers if the pseudorange error is sufficiently small, e.g. 10 cm (this is achievable with the narrow correlator spacing technique which reduces both noise and multipath). The method works best with dual frequency full wavelength receivers where the carrier phase and code phase is measured on both frequencies. The initial vector is determined using the differential pseudorange data and employing a Kalman filter. The carrier phase ambiguities are then found by using a search algorithm that chooses the best fit from a number of candidates. In the case of single frequency receivers, this would then be the final solution. For dual frequency receivers, the initial solution is used to aid the search for the wide lane ambiguities, followed by the computation of the $L1$ ambiguity biases. Tests with this procedure show that 20 km baselines can be determined to centimeter accuracy in as little as three minutes. This technique is described in more detail in Sect. 9.1.3.

Pseudokinematic relative positioning
The technique most nearly like the static method is the pseudokinematic survey. This technique, developed by Remondi (1988), is also named intermittent static or reoccupation method. These surveys require less occupation time but one must occupy the "point-pair" two times. A typical scenario would involve occupying a pair of points for five minutes, moving to other points, and finally returning to the first point pair about one hour after the initial occupation for a second 5-minute occupation. The advantage of the (total) 10-minute occupation versus, e.g., a 60-minute occupation for conventional static surveying is somewhat offset by the time lost in traveling to the points a second time. The best use of the pseudokinematic method is when the points to be occupied are along a road where the observers can

move quickly between setups. Subcentimeter accuracy is achievable with the pseudokinematic method. This is mainly accomplished by the changed satellite configuration. The main advantage of the pseudokinematic method is that for a given observation time more sites can be occupied than with conventional static surveying. Compared to the kinematic method, a loss of lock may occur and the number of satellites does not play that essential role. There is no requirement for maintaining signal lock between the reoccupation of points. The receiver may even be turned off while moving. The main weakness is the necessity of the site revisiting. This restricts the method to local applications. The main competitor is therefore the rapid static positioning approach where each site has to be occupied only once. Typical pseudokinematic applications include: photo-control, lower-order control surveys, and mining surveys.

In practice, it is best to use a mixture of the three methods. For example, static and pseudokinematic methods can be used to establish a broad framework of control and to set points on either side of obstructions such as bridges. Kinematic surveys can then be employed to determine the coordinates of the major portion of points, using the static points as control and check points. A thorough reconnaissance is required for these mixed surveys.

In order to serve as a reference datum for subsequent surveys and to enable the transformation of GPS results into national datums, two types of GPS control networks are in use: passive control networks and active control systems. The passive concept is to tie GPS surveys to existing triangulation monuments and vertical benchmarks. The disadvantage is that many sites have to be occupied and maintained. This system is appropriate where dense national triangulation networks exist and when the control network serves other purposes such as geodynamical investigations. Such a dense passive control network is being established, e.g., in Austria as reported by Stangl et al. (1991).

The objectives of an active control system are the computation and real-time dissemination of differential corrections for single-receiver users, and the computation of precise ephemerides for postmission processing. The collection and dissemination of the data is performed by the use of high-speed terrestrial, and satellite-based communication links. More details on this subject are provided in Sect. 12.5.

7.1.3   Impact of SA on positioning

As mentioned in Sect. 2.2.4, there are two different SA techniques. The dither technique manipulates the satellite clock frequency, and the epsilon technique truncates the ephemerides data in the navigation message. Both techniques induce variations in the code and phase pseudoranges which in turn translate into like position errors. The variations caused by dithering have periods of some minutes and amplitudes of some tens of meters, whereas the variations due to the manipulation of the ephemerides data have periods of some hours and larger amplitudes.

Theoretically, the simplest method to circumvent SA is to be an authorized user (the chance of becoming an authorized user is very limited). Authorized users read the encrypted correction data from the navigation message and decrypt it so that data are obtained without the effect of SA. Another effective method to overcome SA is to use differential techniques. Other efforts aim at modeling the behavior of SA and to remove its effect by appropriate filters, see, e.g., Braasch (1990/91), Feigl et al. (1991), Rocken and Meertens (1991), True Time (1993).

Impact on single point positioning
The activation of SA primarily affects the navigation users of the system. When considering the dithering effect only, the range residuals typically amount to some 10 m. This value would reduce to about 1 m in the absence of SA, see Jahn (1992). Translating this effect to the (horizontal) position shows the same characteristic. In the case of SA, the position accuracy decreases by about one order of magnitude.

When the dithering effect is removed, the remaining effect on point positioning due to SA is a slow variation of the position on a circle with a radius between 75 m and 100 m, see Fantou (1993) and Kremer et al. (1990) respectively. Since the epsilon-process degrades the broadcast ephemerides, SA can be obviated by postprocessing using precise ephemerides.

An example in Georgiadou and Doucet (1990) shows the effect of SA on single point positioning where data are collected with SA off and on respectively. With SA off, the position errors are at the 15 m level. With SA on, the position errors are at the 100 m level.

Impact on DGPS
The errors induced by SA are similar for the (fixed) monitor station and the (roving) remote receiver over distances of say 500 km. In the case of the short-periodic dithering, this is only true as long as no time lag is present. However in practice, a time delay can never be completely avoided because of (1) the time necessary for calculating the differential corrections at the monitor station and (2) the signal propagation delay in transmitting these corrections to the remote receiver. Thus, the differential corrections received at the remote station are aged. The age of the correction data plays a

much less stringent role in the absence of SA because the pseudoranges
do not show the short variations caused by the dithering process. From
a simulation study performed by the U.S. Department of Transportation
(DoT), a range rate error of roughly $0.1\,\mathrm{m\,s^{-1}}$ was analyzed. The range rate
error translates approximately linearly with time into range errors. Thus,
the differential pseudorange corrections accumulate an error of about 1 m
after 10 s. This is a valuable relationship for analyzing the update rate
inherent in DGPS. Considering the 1 m error level as limiting boundary for
the pseudorange corrections relayed to the unknown station, an update rate
of at least once per every ten seconds would be required. This demand may
be somewhat relieved by transmitting not only the pseudorange corrections
ΔR but also the range rate corrections $d\Delta R/dt$. The pseudorange correction
at the remote receiver for an epoch t may then be calculated by

$$\Delta R(t) = \Delta R(t_0) + \frac{d\Delta R}{dt}(t - t_0) \tag{7.1}$$

where t_0 is the epoch of the data used for the computation of the corrections
$\Delta R(t_0)$ at the monitor station and $t - t_0$ may be regarded as the age of
the corrections. The equation could further be refined by, e.g., taking into
account a possible different satellite almanac data set at the two receivers,
cf. Scott (1993). When applying the range rate corrections, the error of the
pseudorange corrections would still be negligible after 10 s and accumulate
to some 1.5 m after 30 s, see Kremer et al. (1990). Considering that the error
in horizontal position is always a multiple of the pseudorange error leads to
the conclusion that with SA on the position accuracy achievable with DGPS
will typically be in the range of a few meters.

Impact on relative positioning
The lack of broadcast ephemerides accuracy can be overcome by the establishment of private tracking stations or active control points. In the case
of geodetic surveys where some days can be tolerated between the measurements and final computations, postprocessed ephemerides will suffice. In
cases where it is imperative that precise coordinates be determined immediately, the use of active control stations is more appropriate. Some manufacturers have already demonstrated the real-time broadcast of carrier phase
data between a fixed and roving receiver so that the coordinates of the roving receiver can be determined instantaneously by the kinematic technique
to at least centimeter accuracy, cf. Ferguson and Veatch (1990) or Euler et
al. (1992). This mode could be refined and applied to active control points
so that the precise coordinates could be determined in the field without reference to the official ephemerides and, consequently, would negate the effect

of ephemerides denial. The error which results from imprecise ephemerides is quite different for point positioning and differential or relative positioning. In general, point positioning errors are of the same magnitude as the satellite (orbital) errors. In the case of relative positioning, relative baseline errors correspond to relative orbital errors.

A clock error and, thus, the dithering component of SA is completely eliminated when differencing the phase between receivers. However, there is one slight restriction: the measurements combined to form a difference must refer to epochs which may differ only to a small amount (few milliseconds). Melbourne et al. (1993) mention that even in cases when epochs are nonsynchronized to a larger extent, the dithering effect cancels to a high degree by a quadratic interpolation procedure to a common epoch, see also Wu et al. (1990). In Feigl et al. (1991) the following rule of thumb is set up: the satellite clock dithering causes an error on (single-) differenced phases which is proportional to both the frequency of deviation and the difference in transmission time between the wavefronts sampled at the two stations at a specific epoch. Omitting the unknown proportionality factor, the relation reads

$$\Delta \Phi_{AB}^j(\mathrm{SA}) = \Delta f^j(\mathrm{SA})\,\Delta t \tag{7.2}$$

where $\Delta \Phi_{AB}^j(\mathrm{SA})$ is the error induced by SA of satellite j on the difference of phases between station A and B, $\Delta f^j(\mathrm{SA})$ is the frequency change with respect to the nominal frequency due to dithering, and Δt is the difference in transmission time of the measured wavefronts which may also be interpreted as wave propagation delay difference. Generally, a receiver being closer to the satellite will receive a phase that left the satellite later than the phase received by a receiver being at a greater distance from the satellite if the data are recorded at the same epoch.

In principle, this effect would vanish if the receivers could sample the same wavefront at the same epoch. In practice, this would only be the case for zero baselines where the distance of the two receivers to the satellite is the same.

The (theoretical) maximum amount of the time difference Δt occurs if satellite j and stations A and B lie on a straight line (which will rarely happen) and is then given by

$$\Delta t = \frac{b_{AB}}{c} \tag{7.3}$$

where b_{AB} is the distance between the two stations A and B, and c is the velocity of light. For a baseline of 300 km, a delay $\Delta t = 0.001\,\mathrm{s}$ results.

The dithering level of $\Delta f^j(\text{SA})$ is set by the control segment. The investigation of a specific data set by Rocken and Meertens (1991) shows that the dithering amounts to $\pm 2\,\text{Hz}$ but may reach several Hz, see Feigl et al. (1991). Substituting the numerical values into (7.2) gives $\Delta\Phi^j_{AB}(\text{SA}) = 2\,\text{Hz} \cdot 0.001\,\text{s} = 0.002\,\text{cycles}$ for the 300 km baseline. This translates to

$$\Delta\Phi^j_{AB}(\text{SA}) = 0.4\,\text{mm} \tag{7.4}$$

after multiplication by the approximate carrier phase wavelength of 20 cm. Note that this amount is the theoretical maximum error on a (single-) difference phase for a 300 km baseline and the satellite aligned with the baseline. In conclusion, the impact of the satellite clock dithering due to SA is negligible with respect to the wave propagation delay difference.

This small error only considered the time difference Δt due to the difference in transmission time resulting from the different distances from satellite j to the stations A and B. Implicitly, perfect clock synchronization of the two receiver clocks was assumed. Investigating the effect of nonsynchronous receiver clocks, relation (7.2) may be used again if Δt is now interpreted as the time difference in recording data. Usually, this problem will not arise if receivers of the same type record the data, because they should sample the data at the same epochs (e.g., integer minutes). When working with different receivers, there might typically occur differences in the order of 1 ms. Therefore, the effect on single-differenced phases is again 0.4 mm (with a 2 Hz clock dithering).

One receiver which deviates considerably from the 1 ms size is the TI-4100 which records 0.92 s before the integer minute, cf. Feigl et al. (1991). Combining the TI-4100 with another receiver, the nonsynchronization will lead to a phase difference error of $\Delta\Phi^j_{AB}(\text{SA}) = 368\,\text{mm}$ based again on a 2 Hz dithering. This is certainly an unacceptable amount!

The preceding discussion of the SA clock dithering effect on relative positioning may be summarized in the following way. For all terrestrial baselines, the SA clock dithering effect is negligible (less than one millimeter) if phase differences are processed and if the GPS receivers are synchronized to better than 2 ms. This yields 0.8 mm SA effect as long as the amount of dithering is about $\pm 2\,\text{Hz}$.

7.1.4 Field equipment

The field equipment includes receiver units and auxiliary devices such as meteorological sensors, tribrachs, tripods, bipods, and other ancillary equipment. Geodetic receivers which perform precise baseline vector measurements are mainly considered in this section. The selection of an appropriate receiver depends on the special project requirements. Therefore, only some general considerations will be given in this section.

For moderate length baselines up to about 20 km, single frequency receivers may be used because the influence of the ionospheric refraction (mostly) cancels by differencing the phase measurements between the baseline sites. Baseline distances must be reduced in periods of high sunspot activity. This activity cycle has a repetition rate of about 11 years with a maximum in early 1991. Dual frequency receivers compensate (and virtually eliminate) ionospheric refraction by the ionospheric-free combination of the two carrier phases, cf. Sect. 6.3.2.

Receivers with P-code capability are essential for the most precise positioning applications. Using P-code survey receivers that measure both code ranges and carrier phases, the baseline vectors can be determined more accurately and rapidly than with other types of receivers. One reason is that P-code receivers guarantee a better code range resolution and that they are less affected by multipath and imaging. Another reason is that the P-code (if A-S is off) enables the reconstruction of both carriers by the code correlation technique. Accurate phase measurements on $L1$ and $L2$ can be combined to produce the wide lane signal with a wavelength of about 86 cm. The integer ambiguity of this combined wavelength is more easily resolved than the shorter 19 cm base carrier wavelength.

The disadvantage of P-code receivers is that with A-S on the P-code is encrypted to the Y-code and that makes it impossible to lock onto the P-code broadcast on both the $L1$ and $L2$ carriers. In this event, the $L1$ carrier is obtained by C/A-code correlation and for the reconstruction of the $L2$ carrier a codeless or quasi-codeless technique must be applied which degrades the SNR as described in Sect. 5.2.

An important aspect of receiver design is the data sampling rate. A fast rate produces a large volume of data and requires a significant amount of storage. This fast rate is necessary for kinematic applications, and in static techniques it facilitates cycle slip detection and repair. Also, the use of receivers with more than the minimum four channels is appropriate, since the additional satellites provide redundant information.

Another important feature for receiver selection (particularly for kinematic surveys) is its capability of bandwidth selection in the tracking loops. The bandwidth should be wide enough to prevent loss of signal, but narrow enough to provide a high SNR. Therefore, receivers that are able to adapt the bandwidth depending on the dynamics will provide optimum results.

Different receiver types involved in a survey may cause problems due to incompatibility (e.g., different number of channels, different signal processing techniques). The receiver time tagging of observations is of critical importance. The interpolation of measurements to a common reference epoch proposed by Gurtner et al. (1989a) may prove difficult because of the dithering of the time signal when SA is turned on. One (cumbersome) method to ensure common time tagging is to use external oscillators as proposed by Landau (1990). The best technique is to use compatible receivers.

The phase center of the antenna should be stable and repeatable which seems to be best realized in microstrip antennas. When different antenna types are used, the phase center of each type must be calibrated. It should be noted that the phase center depends on frequency and is, therefore, different for $L1$ and $L2$ carrier observations, cf. Prescott et al. (1989). Most of the GPS receiver manufacturers offer coaxial antenna cables with different lengths up to 60 m where 10 m is standard. A long cable provides more versatility for site access; however, manufacturers' recommendations on cable size (type) should be followed to avoid signal loss. Large diameter low loss cable is available for tracking sites where the cable length exceeds 60 m.

Today, a number of weather-proof, lightweight (4–5 kg), small (6 000–7 000 cm^3), and low power consuming (less than 10 W) receivers which are capable of tracking "all-in-view" satellites (6–12 channels) are readily available. New technologies such as MMIC (Monolithic Microwave Integrated Circuits) or VHSIC (Very High Speed Integrated Circuit) will further miniaturize the receivers as pointed out by Cannon (1990).

All comparable GPS equipment being marketed today gives excellent results so the decision of which equipment to use is usually made based upon ease of use and monetary considerations. The cost of GPS receivers is decreasing rapidly and their capability is constantly increasing. The TI-4100 produced in 1984 was priced at $ 170 000. Today, a simple C/A-code receiver costs about $ 15 000 and this price will still decrease to less than $ 10 000 in the near future. When comparing equipment costs, the user should determine if the processing software cost is included. Some years ago, Henstridge (1991) estimated the initial capital and start-up costs for three GPS receivers and related items such as software and computers to amount $ 100 000; today, however, this amount is much lower.

The final factor that should be considered is the primary use of the equipment. For example, if one plans to use the equipment for kinematic surveys or in heavily treed areas, a receiver should be chosen that has a separate antenna that can be mounted on a prism pole or survey mast. Equipment with built-in antennas have optional antennas that can be purchased. Another important feature if kinematic surveys on foot are planned, is the weight of the receiver and its power requirements. A heavy, very power consuming receiver is not the type of instrument to carry for extended periods.

The number of surveying receiver manufacturers is constantly increasing and their products are continuously being improved. To obtain actual information on a particular product, the reader should contact the manufacturer directly. The addresses are provided in regularly compiled lists such as by Chan and Schorr (1994).

7.2 Planning a GPS survey

7.2.1 General remarks

Designing a GPS network gives rise to several practical questions which are just as important as the theoretical aspects of GPS as stated by Bevis (1991). The issues of equipment, observation technique, and organization are all important. In this section the last item will be addressed.

GPS surveying differs essentially from classical surveying because it is weather independent and there is no need for intervisibility between the sites. Because of these differences, GPS surveys require different planning, execution, and processing techniques. At present, only a few organizations such as U.S. Federal Geodetic Control Committee (FGCC) (1988) have published standards and specifications for GPS surveys.

Planning a GPS survey may or may not be appropriate for a particular application or project. Before deciding whether or not to expend resources on planning, one must decide the ultimate purpose of the survey and the accuracy of the desired results (coordinates). The FGCC classifies surveys by designating orders for the various proportional accuracies desired. Generally, surveys of the highest order (A and B) are reserved for special purposes such as state and county control networks and scientific studies. The remaining first-, second-, and third-order surveys are the classifications normally specified for mapping, surveying, and engineering projects. There is no question that a substantial planning effort is required to successfully complete a high-order survey; however, first-order and lower-order surveys may not require extensive planning except in heavily treed or obstructed areas.

The optimum planning of a GPS survey has to consider several parameters such as site or satellite configurations, the number and the type of receivers to be used, and economic aspects. Contrary to the design of triangulation or trilateration networks which involves considerable effort to maintain the geometric strength, for GPS networks geometry and line length are not so critical. The planning phase should also include some data processing considerations, for instance whether the available software allows for the computation of single baseline vectors or for multipoint solutions.

For large projects with many sites and many receivers, planning a GPS survey could be aided by the use of computer programs to save time and resources. The Geodetic Survey of Canada for instance has developed an appropriate software package, cf. Klees (1990). This program plans vehicle routes, the selection of satellites, and the delineation of the network design.

7.2.2 Presurvey planning

Point selection
The first step in planning a GPS survey is to obtain the largest scale map of the area upon which the desired points can be plotted. Topographic maps from 1:25 000 to 1:100 000 scale are excellent for this purpose, also county road maps are quite useful. All desired survey points are plotted on the map along with the known control points. In most instances it is not worth using control points that are not included in the national system. Using the coordinates of points of unknown accuracy can create many problems so that it is better to choose a national network point even if it is at a greater distance from the project site than other control monuments.

In planning a GPS survey, there are only three basic considerations in choosing a point:

1. No obstruction above 20° elevation to avoid satellite signal blockage.

2. No reflecting surfaces (e.g., metal structures, fences, water surfaces) in the vicinity of the antenna to avoid multipath.

3. No nearby electrical installation (e.g., transmitters, high-tension cables) to avoid signal disturbances.

The requirements above are of primary importance; however, the proximity to a road is a convenience that increases production. Further desirable GPS site characteristics are: mark on publicly owned land and not likely to be disturbed, clear site for visible azimuth mark, and space for parked vehicle.

The complete tie of a GPS network to the national datum requires the occupation of three or more control points. Many areas now have supernets which provide convenient reference monuments for GPS surveys. If supernet points are available, one may not even have to visit them prior to beginning field work since the network points have been selected for GPS occupation. A reasonable horizontal tie would consist of measurements to national control points on either side of the project area. Ties to the vertical datum normally require more planning. Three benchmarks at the corners of the project area would provide the minimum acceptable vertical datum reference.

Observation window
The second step of presurvey planning is to determine the optimum daily

observation period and to decide how it should be subdivided into sessions (i.e., periods where two or more receivers simultaneously track the same satellites).

The optimum "window" of satellite availability is the period when a maximum of satellites can be observed simultaneously. The windows of satellite availability are shifted by four minutes each day, due to the difference between sidereal time and Universal Time (UT). For example, if some of the satellites appeared in a given geometric configuration at 9:00 UT today, they would be roughly in the same position in the sky at 8:56 UT the following day. The length of the window is a function of the location. The optimum window is found by inspecting azimuth-elevation charts which are produced by the software of GPS equipment manufacturers.

The calculation of azimuth and elevation is based on the projection of the unit vector $\Delta\underline{\varrho}$, pointing from the observing site to the instantaneous satellite position, onto the orthogonal axes of the local coordinate frame. The unit vector $\Delta\underline{\varrho}$ is defined by

$$\Delta\underline{\varrho} = \frac{\underline{\varrho}^S - \underline{\varrho}_R}{\|\underline{\varrho}^S - \underline{\varrho}_R\|} \tag{7.5}$$

with $\underline{\varrho}^S$ being the geocentric position vector of the satellite and $\underline{\varrho}_R$ being the geocentric position vector of the observing site which is needed only approximately (i.e., coordinates from a map are sufficient). The vector $\underline{\varrho}^S$ can be calculated by procedures described in Chap. 4 and the vector $\underline{\varrho}_R$ corresponds to the vector $\underline{X}$ defined by Eq. (3.6).

With φ and λ being the ellipsoidal latitude and longitude of the observing site, the axes $\underline{i}$, $\underline{j}$, $\underline{k}$ of the local coordinate frame are given by

$$\underline{i} = \begin{bmatrix} -\sin\varphi\cos\lambda \\ -\sin\varphi\sin\lambda \\ \cos\varphi \end{bmatrix} = \frac{\partial\underline{k}}{\partial\varphi}$$

$$\underline{j} = \begin{bmatrix} -\sin\lambda \\ \cos\lambda \\ 0 \end{bmatrix} = \frac{1}{\cos\varphi}\frac{\partial\underline{k}}{\partial\lambda} \tag{7.6}$$

$$\underline{k} = \begin{bmatrix} \cos\varphi\cos\lambda \\ \cos\varphi\sin\lambda \\ \sin\varphi \end{bmatrix}.$$

Hence, adequate equations for the zenith angle z and the azimuth a, reckoned from north towards east positively, follow from the inner products,

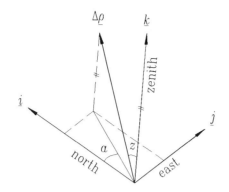

Fig. 7.1. Satellite's zenith angle z and azimuth a

cf. Fig. 7.1,

$$\Delta \varrho \cdot \underline{i} = \sin z \cos a$$

$$\Delta \varrho \cdot \underline{j} = \sin z \sin a \qquad\qquad (7.7)$$

$$\Delta \varrho \cdot \underline{k} = \cos z \, .$$

Table 7.1 is part of a typical tabular listing of satellite locations. The leftmost column shows the Universal Time (UT) and each subsequent column shows the vertical (elevation) angle $E = 90° - z$ and azimuth a for several satellites.

A graphical representation of the complete elevation-azimuth list, based on an elevation cut off angle of 15°, is given in Fig. 7.2. This figure indicates the satellites in view (shown on the ordinate of the coordinate system and indicated as space vehicle SV with the corresponding PRN number) for a certain epoch. No matter what observation technique is used or the precision desired, only periods with four or more satellites in view are considered to provide viable satellite coverage.

An improved representation of visibility is given by the "sky plots". These polar or orthogonal plots show the satellite path as a function of elevation angle and azimuth, cf. Fig. 7.3. Such sky plots are often supplemented by time tags and by the image of the local horizon. The latter may be obtained from field reconnaissance (e.g., fish-eye photos) or can be generated by the computer from a digital terrain model.

Apart from visibility, the tracked satellites should be geometrically well distributed with (ideally) one in each of the four quadrants. This is only a guideline however, but not a firm requirement. In static surveys, poor satellite geometry and even lack of the fourth satellite can often be offset by observing for a longer period of time. The movement of the satellites with

Table 7.1. Part of elevation E and azimuth a list (both in degrees) for Graz, Austria, on October 1, 1993 (cut off elevation: 15 degrees)

SV	02		16		18		19		24		26		27	
UT	E	a	E	a	E	a	E	a	E	a	E	a	E	a
18:30			43	304	44	85	73	78	29	249			68	208
18:45			49	301	38	90	67	66	24	244			75	208
19:00	17	170	54	294	33	95	61	61	19	238			82	204
19:15	24	169	59	285	27	99	54	59					88	111
19:30	31	167	62	272	21	103	48	59					81	56
19:45	38	165	63	256	16	107	41	60			19	293	74	53
20:00	45	162	61	240			35	62			25	295	67	55
20:15	52	157	57	228			29	64			31	298	61	57
20:30	58	151	52	219			23	67			37	300	54	60

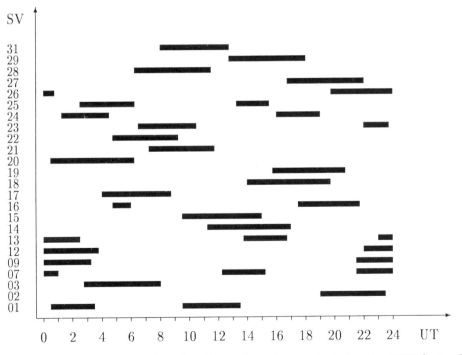

Fig. 7.2. Satellite visibility for Graz, Austria, on October 1, 1993 (cut off elevation: 15 degrees)

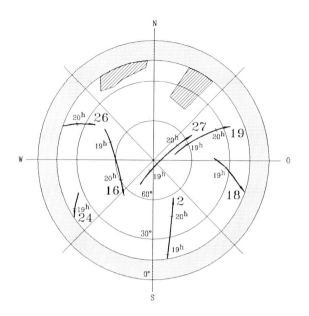

Fig. 7.3. Polar sky plot for Table 7.1

respect to each other improves the geometry and, thus, the solution. Manufacturers' recommendations should be followed especially regarding the use
of three satellites, since it is critical to ensure that the observation time tags
are correct. The surest method of selecting periods of adequate satellite
coverage is to make test observations over known (or determined) baseline
vectors for the full period being considered. This large data set can then be
divided into smaller subsets for processing during periods being considered
for observations. This method allows one to test the acceptability of both the
specific period of coverage and the chosen length of observation time. A measure for satellite geometry is the Geometric Dilution of Precision (GDOP)
factor. Normally, GDOPs under six are considered good and those above
six are considered as being too high. The GDOPs reflect only the instantaneous geometry related to a single point. Therefore, factors for baseline
vectors, accumulated over the time span of a session, are more appropriate
precision indicators, cf. Merminod et al. (1990). It has been proposed that
quality factors can be computed by the receiver itself, and the selection of
the optimum configuration could be automated. Appropriate formulas for
GDOP calculation are provided in Sect. 9.5 where also details on the de-
composition of GDOP into several components such as Position Dilution of
Precision (PDOP) are given.

Another aspect for the selection of the window concerns the ionospheric
refraction. Observations during night hours may be appropriate because the

ionospheric effect is usually quieter during this time. Normally, however, daylight hours are preferred for organizational reasons.

Sessions

The specific time period chosen for an observation is called a session. The first observation of the day would be designated session "a", the second observation session "b", and so on. Some manufacturers use number designation but numbers have the disadvantage of requiring two digits for sessions in excess of 10. Normally, the session designator begins with "a" again each day, and days are expressed as the consecutive calendar day (1 to 365 or, in leap years, 366). For example, session 105c means the third session of day 105.

A good time to begin the first session of static surveys is when four or more satellites are above the 15 to 20 degree elevation angle, and the last observation of this session should, generally, end when the fourth satellite drops below 15 to 20 degrees. This is only a general rule since three-satellite time prior to rise of the fourth satellite and after the fourth satellite has set is useful. There are four factors that determine the length of a particular observation. These are:

1. The length of the baseline.

2. The number of visible satellites (effects geometry).

3. The relative geometry of the satellites and the change in the geometry.

4. The SNR of the received satellite signal.

In general, the more satellites that are available, the better the geometry, and the shorter the length of observation required. The length of a session may also be reduced in the case of shorter baselines. For example, sessions with lines 1–2 km in length could be as short as 30 minutes with five satellites and using single frequency receivers. Longer lines between control points might, on the other hand, require 90 minutes of data to achieve good results. For conventional static surveying, Table 7.2 may be used as a general guide to plan the length of observation when four or more satellites are available and the ionospheric conditions are normal.

What is the reason for needing these relatively long sessions? Chapter 6 discusses the observables and it is seen that at each observation epoch the carrier phase is measured to millimeter accuracy or even better. In effect, a single observation would be sufficient to provide the precision required for a geodetic survey. The difficulty is that one can measure the decimeters, centimeters, and millimeters precisely; however, the observation must last

Table 7.2. Session length in function of baseline length for
conventional static surveying and single frequency receivers

Baseline [km]	Session [min]
0 – 1	10 – 30
1 – 5	30 – 60
5 – 10	60 – 90
10 – 20	90 – 120

long enough to determine the meters by resolving the integer number of
cycles. On a short (less than 1 km) baseline, the integer cycles can often be
resolved in 5–10 minutes using $L1$ only phase. With dual frequency receivers
using the wide lane technique, long (15 km) lines can be accurately measured
with as little as two minutes data.

The best method of determining optimum observation times for large
projects is to make longer than normal observations on the first day to
obtain typical data sets. For example, observations lasting 90 minutes for
short (1–5 km) lines and 120 minutes for longer (5–20 km) lines would be
made. These data sets when processed would yield excellent results. The
observations could then be reprocessed using portions of the data set to
determine the point where good results can no longer be obtained. For
example, consecutive 30-minute data sets could be processed and compared
with the full data set to determine if the shorter observation times were
sufficient to achieve good results.

As discussed previously, a session should be long enough to guarantee
the required accuracy; but, one should also consider that longer sessions
cost more. In any case, the time between the sessions should be long enough
to transport the equipment to another site and allow for accurate setup.
Older receivers may also require oscillator warm up.

In order to reference the single sessions to a common datum, at least
one site of the network must be occupied during the entire project (radial
surveying), or subsequent sessions must contain at least one reoccupied site
(leap frogging). The reoccupation of more than one site improves the precision and reliability of the network. When planning sessions for kinematic
surveys, there are two factors to consider. Normally, times are selected when
five or more satellites are above 20 degrees and when the satellites have a
GDOP of less than six. For most locations, the GDOP condition is satisfied
when five or more satellites are available. Problems occur when one of the
satellites is obstructed during the survey and the remaining four satellites
have a high GDOP. This problem is solved by keeping the roving receiver
stationary until the fifth satellite is reacquired.

Nonplanned surveys

Before proceeding with descriptions of the planning steps, a brief discussion of nonplanned surveys will be given. Not all surveys require extensive planning. Some surveyors are now using GPS as they would use other survey equipment and are not necessarily planning a geodetic "campaign". A good example of a survey requiring a minimum of planning is certain types of photo-control surveys. Since many types of GPS surveys require that points be placed in locations where there may be substantial obstructions, the major planning effort is to layout a scheme and select sites that are relatively free from obstructions. Some types of photo-control surveys do not present the typical obstruction planning problem.

If the area being mapped is a suburban or residential area with clearings well-scattered throughout the area, one can perform the GPS (and photo) point selection during the actual survey. In this type of area, the only reconnaissance or presurvey activity required is to locate both horizontal and vertical control used to reference or tie the survey to the national datum.

Assuming that a photo-control project is performed in a fairly obstruction free area and that acceptable horizontal and vertical control points are nearby, the field crew can be sent to the area with the approximate desired photo-control sites plotted on a county road map or some other relatively small-scale map. A good plan is to begin the survey in a portion of the project area where the sites are close together so the project manager can quickly coordinate the start of the survey. During the first session, the observers setup on their assigned points, while the project manager selects and "monuments" the next set of points. The monumentation may be an iron pin driven into the ground or it may be a nail driven into the pavement. Following selection of the second set of points and completion of the first session, the GPS observers are instructed to proceed to the second session, and the project manager selects the third set of points. Upon conclusion of the local scheme, the ties to existing control can be made to complete the survey.

A second example of nonplanned GPS surveys would be the establishment of control at a construction site. Many times, survey crews are sent to construction sites with plans, coordinate lists, and other supporting data, and the crew chief makes decisions and plans the field work on-site. The same procedure could be followed when using GPS equipment. The crew chief would design the network on-site and establish points in areas where they were needed. Immediately following the observations, the data can be transferred from the GPS receivers to a laptop computer (for example in the survey vehicle). Modern laptop computers are able to process GPS data in a matter of minutes per line so that the data from several sessions (occupations) could be completed in less than one hour. The crew chief would then have accurate (first-order) coordinates of control on-site which could be used to layout desired construction stakes.

7.2.3   Field reconnaissance

After the GPS points have been plotted on a map and descriptions of how to reach the existing control have been obtained, one is ready to perform a field reconnaissance. This is also a good time to assign each point a unique identifier. The most obvious method is to consecutively assign each point a number. Points can have more descriptive (full name) identifiers as well, but a simple consecutive number facilitates future reference to each point. The reconnaissance surveyor visits each site to check its suitability based on the factors listed in Sect. 7.2.2.

First of all, static GPS surveys need an unobstructed view of the sky above an elevation of 15 to 20 degrees and a nonreflective environment. This is a critical requirement for kinematic applications where the path of the roving antenna should be selected carefully in advance. Easy access of the site is desired to save time between the sessions. This may be less important when cross-country vehicles are used or by observing eccentric sites. The latter may often become necessary in the case of forests or urban areas. Sites that have many obstructions require additional consideration. At these sites the reconnaissance surveyor should prepare a polar plot showing the vertical angle and azimuth to obstructions over 20 degrees. This plot is then overlayed the polar sky plot of the satellites, cf. Fig. 7.3. The obstruction problem is solved in two ways. The first is to place the antenna on top of a survey mast so that the desired 20 degree visibility angle is obtained. The Geodetic Survey of Sweden for instance has devised 30 meter (guyed) survey masts that are quickly erected and plumbed over the mark by two offset theodolites. Several manufacturers produce prism poles that extend to 10 meters which also can be used for this purpose. The second technique for overcoming the problem of obstructions is to choose a time when a sufficient number of satellites is electronically visible at the site. The example in Fig. 7.3 shows shaded portions that depict areas obstructed by trees, buildings, hills, etc. It is seen that these obstructions do not effect the observations at this one site. The data used to process a baseline vector consists of the common observations between two points; so the same obstruction check must be made for both ends of a line. Blockage of a satellite at one end of a line effectively eliminates that satellite from the solution; so care must be used in performing the analysis. The manual method of making this analysis is to produce satellite sky plots for every hour of the useable satellite span and then visually compare the site obstruction plots with the various one-hour plots. Another more automated method is to use the software produced by the manufacturers to perform this analysis on the computer.

Field reconnaissance is a must prior to conducting a kinematic survey. Each site must be checked for sky visibility and the route taken to travel between points also must have good sky visibility. Since the kinematic method requires that lock be continuously maintained on four or more satellites, good sky visibility practically means obstruction free (above 20 degrees elevation angle) situations. When obstructions on the route of travel (such as bridges) occur, static points can be placed on either side of the obstruction so that the roving receiver can be reinitialized. The path that the surveyor is to follow between points should be clearly marked on a large-scale map to make sure that unwanted cycle slips do not occur.

Reconnaissance for pseudokinematic surveys is not as important because this technique only requires the revisited sites being unobstructed. In the case of differential (navigation) surveys where code ranges are measured, reconnaissance is not critical at all because the receivers can be simply turned on and measurements made when desired. This mode would be used more as a precise navigation system than a survey system.

Apart from obstructions, it is important to consider the multipath problem. Multipath (more fully discussed in Sect. 6.6) is the effect of unwanted reflected satellite signals that are received by the antenna. This problem is most severe when the antenna is placed near a chain link fence or other metal structure. The satellite signals are reflected by the metal structure and corrupt the direct signals causing phase errors. In the case of chain link fences, the antenna can be elevated above the fence to eliminate the problem. When the point is close to a metal building, the only practical solution is to move the point to another location. Multipath does not appear to be a problem for points located in the median of highways where large trucks pass by at high speed. The multipath caused when a truck is near the antenna is of too brief duration to cause significant problems. However, one should avoid having a large metal transport truck parked next to the antenna.

When the site meets all requirements, the point can be marked for the marksetters to set the monument. The reconnaissance surveyor should plot the location of the chosen site on the largest scale map of the area and prepare a preliminary "to reach" description that describes how to reach the point from a known prominent location (e.g., local post office). This description will save hours in wasted time in the future since it will allow the marksetters and observers to quickly find the point. In cases where a different crew sets the actual monument, this mark setting crew completes the "to reach" description adding the final specific location of the mark and ties to nearby prominent objects. Surveys performed for inclusion in national networks require that a "to reach" description be prepared, and in some cases that a sketch of the site be made. The final site documentation should also include photos of the station surroundings, name and address of the owner, preliminary coordinates, power supply, etc.

7.2.4 Monumentation

The monumentation normally set eventually will become unnecessary when active control networks have been established. For the present, monumentation is still specified for projects where the sites are planned to be reoccupied (e.g., geodynamical studies), cf. Avdis et al. (1990). Note that monuments set other than in solid rock or by deep concrete pillars are not adequate for high precision surveys.

Monumentation is a general term to describe any object used to mark a point. Land surveyors and others commonly use sections of steel reinforcing bar upon which a cap is crimped to monument a point. Each surveyor must decide which particular type of mark is appropriate for the project. A steel rod may be appropriate to mark a photo-panel point; whereas, a massive concrete monument would be more appropriate for a county geodetic survey. The main consideration is the mark should be easily found, at least for the duration of the survey.

7.2.5 Organizational design

The planning phase for static surveys ends with the layout of an organizational design for the project. First, each field crew is allocated a number of personnel and appropriate vehicle and survey equipment. Each crew is then assigned sites to occupy during specific sessions. Field crews should be fully acquainted with the area and should be able to move quickly between points. Today, the operation of GPS receivers no longer requires highly qualified survey personnel. Still, malfunctions are better solved by trained crews.

The minimum number n of sessions in a network with s sites and using r receivers is given by

$$n = \frac{s - o}{r - o} \tag{7.8}$$

where o denotes the number of overlapping sites between the sessions. Equation (7.8) makes only sense for $o \geq 1$ and $r > o$. In the case of a real number, n must be rounded to the next higher integer.

Another approach for the design implies that each network site should be occupied m times. In this case, the minimum number of sessions equals

$$n = \frac{m\,s}{r} \tag{7.9}$$

where n again must be rounded to the next higher integer.

The number s_r of redundant occupied sites with respect to the minimum overlapping $o = 1$ is given by

$$s_r = n\,r - [s + (n-1)]. \tag{7.10}$$

Consider a squared network consisting of nine sites $(P1, \ldots, P9)$ equally spaced and assume that three receivers (A, B, C) are available. If the "leap frogging" method with one-point overlapping between the sessions is the observation technique selected, Eq. (7.8) gives $n = 4$ as minimum number of sessions. The first four sessions in Table 7.3 represent one possible solution for the corresponding organizational design where the sites $P4, P5$, and $P6$ are reoccupied. When each point should be occupied twice then $m = 2$ and Eq. (7.9) gives $n = 6$ which is reflected by two more sessions in Table 7.3. The chosen design has the property that all short baseline vectors between adjacent sites are observed which provides a homogeneous accuracy in the network. For the elimination of receiver or antenna biases, an interchange of the equipment between the sessions is recommended.

Table 7.3. Principles of organizational design

Receiver	Session	a	b	c	d	e	f
A		P2	P4	P4	P6	P7	P1
B		P5	P5	P1	P3	P8	P2
C		P8	P6	P7	P9	P9	P3

The organizational design also depends upon the type of the network (i.e., the distribution of the sites), cf. Snay (1986) or Unguendoli (1990). There are two basic types of GPS networks: (1) radial and (2) closed geometric figures.

Radial surveys
Radial (or cartwheel) surveys are performed by placing one receiver at a fixed site, and measuring lines from this fixed site to receivers placed at other locations. A typical radial survey configuration is shown in Fig. 7.4.

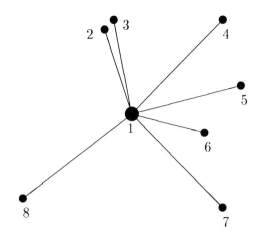

Fig. 7.4. Radial survey

There is no geometric consideration for planning this type of survey except that points in close proximity should be connected by direct observation. Consider in Fig. 7.4 the points 2 and 3 located 10 km from fixed point 1 and 100 m distant from one another. If they were surveyed at different times, the error between the two points could be considerable. A relative baseline error of 10 ppm, for example, produces a 0.1 m error in the points 2 and 3. Therefore, the expected error between the two points would be 0.14 m (as obtained from $\sqrt{0.1^2 + 0.1^2}$) which corresponds to a relative error of 1:714. This large relative error would not be tolerated by most surveyors since it would give a bad impression on the accuracy of the overall survey.

In general, kinematic surveys are radial surveys, and many pseudokinematic surveys are performed in the radial mode. Each point established by the radial method is a "no check" position since there is only one determination of the coordinates and there is no geometric check on the position. An appropriate use of radial surveys might be to establish photo-control since the photogrammetrist is able to make an independent check on the coordinates using analytical bridging. Other uses would be to provide positions for wells or geological features where precise coordinates may generally not be needed.

Network survey
GPS surveys performed by static (and pseudokinematic) methods where accuracy is a primary consideration require that observations be performed in a systematic manner and that closed geometric figures be formed to pro-

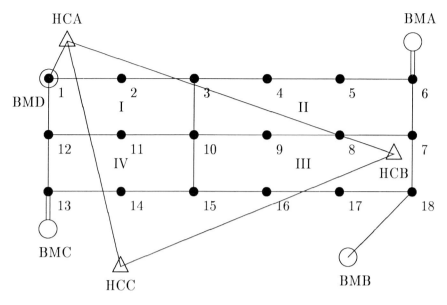

Fig. 7.5. Static network design

vide closed loops. Figure 7.5 shows a typical scheme consisting of 18 points. The preferred observation scheme is to occupy adjacent points consecutively and traverse around the figure. For example, the scheme shown in Fig. 7.5 would be approached in the following manner if three receivers were used. Receiver A would be placed on point 1, receiver B on point 2, and receiver C on point 3 for the first session. Data would be collected from the three receivers for the chosen session length of time. The receivers would then be turned off and receiver A would be moved to point 11, and receiver B to point 10, while receiver C remains on point 3 to overlap between the first two sessions. Following the period during which the receivers were being moved, the three receivers would be turned on for the second session and data collection would be continued. An alternative to this approach is to move all three receivers so that receiver A would occupy point 3, receiver B point 11, and receiver C point 10 for the second session. Either plan works equally well; however, the second approach would eliminate eventual receiver biases, since the overlapping point 3 is occupied by different receivers in consecutive sessions. The leapfrog traversing technique is the preferred method because it provides the required loop checks and gives the maximum productivity. In general, the goal in devising a measuring scheme is to directly connect as many adjacent points as possible.

When national datum coordinates and elevations are desired for points in a scheme, ties to existing control must be made. In Fig. 7.5, horizontal control points are marked by triangles and denoted HCA, HCB, HCC. Proper connection to control points requires that direct measurements be made between the existing control. The purpose of this measurement is to both verify the accuracy of the existing control and to determine scale, shift, and rotation between the control and the new GPS network. After the horizontal control has been occupied, measurements are made between the control and the nearest network point. For example, the points HCA, HCB, and HCC in Fig. 7.5 would be occupied during one session and the tie between HCA and point 1 would be made during another session (using three receivers).

Ties to vertical control points are performed somewhat differently than ties to horizontal points. There is no geometric reason for measuring between existing benchmarks (vertical control) since the error in the geoidal height masks any possible GPS error. Vertical ties are normally made from the benchmark to the closest GPS point. In Fig. 7.5, the benchmarks are shown as BMA, BMB, BMC, and BMD. In this figure, BMD was selected to be point 1. Thus, the need of a tie for this point is eliminated. Existing monuments should be chosen as GPS points, whenever possible, to save placing a mark in the ground. In the figure, BMA and BMC were assumed to be close to points 6 and 13 respectively so that a conventional level (loop) tie was made between benchmark and GPS point. Benchmark BMB was assumed to be far enough away from point 18 so that a GPS measurement was used to connect the two points. In the case of this benchmark, FGCC specifications call for two determinations of the vector between point 18 and point BMB.

Figure 7.5 is an idealized scheme; however, the basic principles apply for all control network schemes. In summary, the following are the major points of network design:

1. The network should consist of closed loops or other geometric figures.

2. Ties should be made to at least three horizontal control points which should also be directly occupied.

3. Ties should be made to at least four vertical control points (benchmarks) by the most direct means.

In addition to these general specifications, other measurements may be prescribed by various agencies, such as making a certain percentage of repeat measurements and setups.

In the case of one-point overlapping per session and using three receivers, a network consisting of 22 sites (i.e., 18 GPS points, 3 horizontal control points, 1 benchmark) would require 11 sessions where one baseline is measured twice, cf. Eqs. (7.8) and (7.10). With 15 sessions, nine loop closures

Table 7.4. Organizational design for the configuration in Fig. 7.5

Session	Receiver		
	A	B	C
a	HCA	HCB	HCC
b	HCA	1	2
c	3	10	2
d	11	10	12
e	1	13	12
f	HCC	13	14
g	15	10	14
h	3	4	5
i	6	7	5
j	9	7	8
k	9	10	15
l	16	17	15
m	BMB	17	18
n	BMB	HCB	18
o	8	7	18

can be formed. One possible occupation schedule for determining the coordinates of the 22 points is listed in Table 7.4.

Under the assumption of 60-minute sessions and 30 minutes for site change, the fifteen sessions would require two days under ideal conditions. A more realistic schedule would be to take three days to make the sessions longer than one hour.

7.3   Surveying procedure

The actual execution of GPS surveys is greatly facilitated by good planning. A well-planned survey normally progresses quite smoothly. This section will discuss the various aspects of conducting a GPS survey and provide information to make the effort more productive.

7.3.1   Preobservation

Antenna setup
To avoid the multipath or imaging effects, it is recommended that any vehicle be parked as far away as possible from the antenna. Parking the survey vehicle the full 10 m (antenna cable length) away from the point should be adequate.

The antennas are mounted on pillars, tripods (with tribrach), or on a range (or prism) pole equipped with steadying legs. This range pole with legs is called a bipod and its use can materially speed up the conduct of a survey. When performing kinematic or pseudokinematic surveys, the bipod is essential so that the antenna is maintained at a fixed height, and to speed the setup time. The use of a bipod for static surveys is not critical; however, its use reduces the possibility of an undetected blunder in measuring the antenna height (since the height of the rod is fixed).

A rather minor problem using GPS should not be overlooked: the calibration of tribrachs. A survey will only be as accurate as the surveyor's ability to center the antenna over the survey point. The best way to avoid this problem is to use two-piece collimating tribrachs that can be rotated to check the centering. A more cost effective approach is to hang a plumb bob from the tribrach at each setup to check the optical centering device.

The antenna phase center offset discussed in Sect. 6.5 is due to the fact that the geometric center of the antenna is not at the electronic center. This problem is virtually eliminated by pointing all antennas in the same direction. In the surveying mode, differences between points are measured so that any systematic offset will be canceled by uniform antenna orientation.

The measurement of the antenna's phase center above the reference point is an important aspect which is often overlooked. Experience has shown that the mismeasured antenna height is the single most vexing problem in conducting GPS surveys and causes the greatest number of errors. The best way to avoid this problem (when using tripods) is to measure the antenna height twice, at the beginning and after completion of the survey. Some manufacturers are providing special rods to facilitate antenna height measurements. When using tripods, the setup at "swing" or repeat points should be broken during the move and the tripod reset over the point at a different height.

Receiver calibration

In general, GPS receivers are considered to be self-calibrating and users do not normally perform equipment calibration. One simple test that can be performed, however, is a zero baseline measurement. This measurement is made by connecting two or more receivers to one antenna. Care should be taken in doing this to use a special device that blocks the voltage from all but one receiver being fed to the antenna. Also, a signal splitter must be used to divide the incoming signal to the multiple receivers.

A normal session (e.g., 60 minutes) is observed and the baseline is computed in the normal manner. Since a single antenna is used, the baseline components should all be zero. This measurement essentially checks the functioning of the receiver circuits and electronics and is a convenient method of trouble shooting receiver problems independent from antenna biases. The zero baseline test is also one way to satisfy specifications which call for equipment calibration.

Initialization

In static surveying, the initialization of some receivers requires the preprogramming or the on-site input of parameters. Some of these are: the selection of the sampling rate, the bandwidth, the minimum number of satellites to track, the start and stop time for the session, the cut off elevation angle, the assignment of a data file. Most of the modern receivers have several channels and track all satellites in view. A preselection is, thus, only necessary to disregard a satellite. The almanac data are generally stored or are gathered after first lock on.

In the kinematic mode, the phase ambiguities are determined during initialization by different techniques. First, one can start from a short known baseline which allows ambiguity resolution after a few observation epochs. Another method is to perform a static survey to determine the vector between the fixed point and the unknown starting point for the kinematic survey. A third method is to perform an antenna swap between the fixed point and starting point, cf. Hofmann-Wellenhof and Remondi (1988). The most advanced technique to resolve phase ambiguities is the on-the-fly (OTF) technique which is described in detail in Sect. 9.1.

Logistically, if the fixed receiver antenna were at a remote location such as the roof of the surveyor's office, the survey starting point at a given site would be located by a static survey. On the other hand, if the fixed point were at the project site, the starting point could be placed near (i.e., 10 m) the fixed site and surveyed by the antenna swap method. This method is accomplished by placing receiver A at the fixed point and receiver B on the starting point. After a few epochs of observation, receiver A is moved to the starting point and receiver B is moved to the fixed point. During this move, both receivers must continuously track a minimum of four satellites. The antenna swap is completed by moving receiver A back to the fixed point and receiver B back to the starting point. By this antenna swap, the vector between the two points is determined to millimeter accuracy for short lines.

7.3.2 Observation

Communications between survey crews are desirable and generally increase efficiency. Even though communication can be critical, today, the major portion of geodetic surveys, where lines average 20 km in length, are performed without communication between observers. In these cases when an observer is late reaching the point, the lines to that point may have to be resurveyed. The use of portable telephones may eliminate this problem since the schedule could be revised on the spot if all parties could communicate. Land (as opposed to geodetic) GPS surveys normally measure lines averaging 5 km so that normal frequency modulated (FM) transceivers (hand-held radios) can be used to communicate between observers. The need for communications is most critical when conducting pseudokinematic surveys because it is important that all receivers collect data during the same time span (except a fixed full time running reference receiver is used).

Most static observations can be performed in an automated mode so that an operator is not required, cf. for example Pesec and Stangl (1990). However, it is good practice to perform data checks during the session, and any irregularity should be noted in the field log. Also, an operator is often needed to keep the receiver from harm or loss. When conducting geodetic surveys (campaigns) of highest accuracy, meteorological data (wet and dry temperature, air pressure) should be collected during the session at each site as far above the ground as possible. In extreme cases, backscatter radiometers may be used to measure the atmospheric water vapor. The inclusion of observed meteorological data does not improve the results for short baselines as opposed to using standard tropospheric refraction models. The data may possibly be used for future studies.

In kinematic surveying applications, after initialization, the fixed receiver and the roving receiver are placed on the fixed and (now known) starting point for a few epochs of observation. Then the roving receiver proceeds to the points for which coordinates are desired. As long as four or more satellites (with low PDOP) are continuously tracked by both receivers, vectors from the fixed point can be measured to a high degree of accuracy. If (in the case of four satellites) the signal lock is lost or a cycle slip occurs, the initialization must be repeated. This may happen due to shadowing (i.e., obstruction) of the satellite signal by buildings, bridges, trees, or other objects. In this case, the roving receiver must return to a point of known position for a reinitialization. In practice, points surveyed should be visited twice so that a check on the determination can be made. Also, several points whose coordinates are known (i.e., from static surveys) should be included in the survey, when possible, to provide additional checks.

The roving receiver normally remains at a point for a few epochs so that observations can be averaged to obtain a more accurate position. A second way to perform kinematic surveys is to alternate the fixed and roving receivers by leapfrogging units. For example, consider consecutive points $1, 2, 3, \ldots, n$ along an open highway. Receiver A would be placed at point 1 and receiver B at starting point 2 near point 1. The two receivers would perform an antenna swap to obtain the starting coordinates of point 2. Receiver B would then move to point 3, with receiver A remaining at point 1. Receiver B would then remain fixed at point 3, while receiver A was moved to point 4. In this way, the vectors 2–3, and 3–4 will be measured. The survey could continue in this manner building a geometric traverse of kinematically surveyed points.

Precaution is recommended during thunderstorms. Lightning strikes may destroy the instrument. Therefore, the receivers should be switched off and the antenna disconnected.

7.3.3   Postobservation

At the completion of a session, a check of the antenna position including a remeasurement of its height above the reference is recommended. Older instruments with external recording devices require the labeling of the data storage media.

A final recommendation is to prepare a site occupation sheet that should be completed at the end of the session. This sheet should contain at least the following information:

1. Project and station name.

2. Date and session number.

3. Start and stop times.

4. Station identifier used for file name.

5. Observer's name.

6. Receiver and antenna serial number.

7. Height of antenna and eccentricities in position.

8. Meteorological data.

9. Problems experienced.

In addition to this minimum amount of information, it is good practice to make a "rubbing" of the top of the survey mark or make a photograph of the mark and to prepare a site sketch of the mark's location (or check existing sketch).

7.3.4   Ties to control monuments

The practice of connecting a GPS network to a horizontal control point is most simple when the control point is in a clear location so that the GPS antenna is placed directly upon the mark. In many cases, however, this is not possible because the control monument is located in an area with many obstructions or where multipath is a problem. In these instances, the point must be occupied eccentrically.

Figure 7.6 shows a typical eccentric occupation. In this figure, it is assumed that the control point C is obstructed and that the GPS receiver can be placed on A, a nearby eccentric point. A conventional azimuth mark and second auxiliary point B are also shown. When an azimuth mark exists at the control point, the problem is simplified because the azimuth to the eccentric point can be determined by measuring the angle at the control point between the azimuth mark and the eccentric point. An alternative method would be to measure the astronomic (third-order) azimuth to the eccentric point. A second auxiliary point such as point B should be used as a check on the measured distance from the control point to the eccentric point, and all angles and distances should be measured in the triangle ABC. A second technique can be used when there is no azimuth mark at the control point. Referring to Fig. 7.6, one GPS antenna would be placed on the eccentric mark A and a second receiver placed upon point B. In this case, the distance between the eccentric and the auxiliary point should exceed the distance from the eccentric point to the control station. From the GPS baseline vector, the azimuth of the line from A to B can be derived and the azimuth from A to the control point C can be computed by the angle measured at A. The azimuth from the control point to the eccentric point is determined in one iteration by subtracting the convergence from the reverse azimuth.

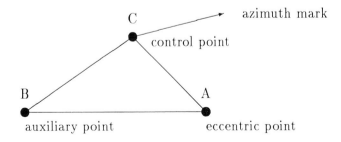

Fig. 7.6. Eccentric occupation

Occupying a benchmark eccentrically is accomplished by setting an eccentric point in a clear area near the benchmark and double running levels between the two marks. It should be remembered when occupying horizontal control points eccentrically, where the control point has an accurate elevation, to level between the marks.

7.4   In situ data processing

7.4.1   Data transfer

Most modern equipments store the GPS observations internally, while some of the older instruments write the observations to floppy disk or tape. The first step in processing is to transfer the data from the receiver to a computer hard disk. This transfer is accomplished using software provided by the manufacturer. Observation files for a given session contain the phase and other observables as the main file, in addition broadcast ephemerides and site data consisting of station identifier, antenna height, and possibly navigation position. The main task in transferring files is to make sure the files are named correctly and that the antenna height is correct.

A good procedure to ensure that the file names and antenna heights are correct is to prepare an abstract form, cf. Table 7.5, containing the assignment of sites to sessions, the measured antenna heights, and the start and stop times of the sessions.

Many times, an observer will enter the incorrect site identifier. This identifier must be immediately corrected before proceeding with the processing. The controlling document should be the site occupation sheets from which the information in Table 7.5 was abstracted. With this information one knows for instance that point 001 was occupied by receiver B from 02:29 to 03:30 UT. If this point were misidentified, one could look at the start and stop times in the given data file also noting the navigation latitude and lon-

Table 7.5. Control abstract

Session	Receiver						Time (UT)	
	A		B		C		Start	Stop
	Site	Height	Site	Height	Site	Height		
a	HCA	1.234	HCB	1.574	HCC	1.342	01:00	02:00
b	HCA	0.987	001	1.782	002	1.543	02:29	03:30
c	003	1.344	010	1.328	002	1.452	04:01	05:00
d	011	1.324	010	1.563	012	1.437	05:31	06:30
e	001	1.564	013	1.453	012	1.455	06:59	08:00

gitude. This start and stop time and position contained in each data file pinpoints that particular file to a given time and location which can then be matched with the data in Table 7.5. Using this technique, one can identify and rename files that have been misnamed.

Most of the batch file processing software automatically extracts the antenna height from the site file data stored in the receiver. After correcting the names of the various files, one should then check and correct all antenna heights. Again a form such as Table 7.5 will be helpful in keeping track of the various antenna heights. Also, a table listing the various occupations and antenna heights is useful for inclusion in the project report.

As soon as all files have been corrected, the observed data should be backed up on at least two sets of storage medium (i.e., floppies). A good practice is to keep one set of original data in a different secure location. Today, many organizations keep a complete set of storage medium in a vault.

7.4.2   Data processing

In the case of remote and extended GPS surveys, a quality control check of the data at least once per day should be made. This control may also include cycle slip detection and repair which, when not performed in the receiver during operation, is normally part of the preprocessing procedure, see Sect. 9.1. The quality control check could also include preliminary computations of baseline vectors in the field before leaving the survey area. The on-site vector processing on a daily basis helps that adequate measurements are being made.

Today, most of the routine processing is performed by batch file processing. All batch files are generated using the three or four digit site identification so that the first task in processing GPS data is to ensure that all sites are properly named. A good practice is to first number the control points and then consecutively assign numbers to adjacent points. This numbering should have been accomplished during the planning and reconnaissance phase to facilitate record keeping.

Processing of static surveys
Modern processing software uses batch processing to compute baseline vectors. Usually, the data for a given day are loaded into a subdirectory on a hard disk. Processing software is normally in another directory and the "path" of the computer has to be set to access the programs. Once the software has been initiated (generally by menu commands), the lines are computed in order, automatically. There are two types of processing software: (1) vector by vector and (2) multipoint solutions.

The vector by vector or single baseline solution type is presently the most common, and in any case should be used prior to processing with the multipoint software. In some instances, one of the points in an observation session will be corrupted and if all points are processed together, the errors from the bad point are distributed among the vectors and the error is masked. The single vector software provides a better check on bad lines or points. The bad point can be more easily isolated by noting that the statistics (i.e., root mean square error, standard error) to lines leading to this one point are worse than the statistics for the other lines. Additionally, the vectors can be summed for the lines in the session, and if the sum around the perimeter is not a small value (e.g., 1 ppm), this indicates that one of the points in the session is bad.

The individual vector processing software performs the following steps:

1. Generation of orbit files.

2. Computation of the best fit value for point positions from code pseudoranges.

3. Creation of undifferenced phase data from receiver carrier phase readings and satellite orbit data. Time tags may also be corrected.

4. Creation of differenced phase data and of computation of their correlations.

5. Computation of an estimate of the vector using triple-difference processing. This method is insensitive to cycle slips but provides least accurate results.

6. Computation of the double-difference solution solving for vector and (real) values of phase ambiguities.

7. Estimation of integer values for the phase ambiguities computed in the previous step, and decision whether to continue with fixed ambiguities.

8. Computation of the fixed bias solution based upon best ambiguity estimates computed in the previous step.

9. Computation of several other fixed bias solutions using integer values differing slightly (e.g., by 1) from selected values.

10. Computation of the ratio of statistical fit between chosen fixed solution and the next best solution. This ratio should be at least two to three indicating that the chosen solution is at least two to three times better than next most likely solution.

Processing of kinematic surveys

The basic steps are similar for static and kinematic processing. The data files are downloaded from the receiver to the computer and the file names and antenna heights are checked. The actual processing differs depending on the software used; however, much of the newer software is automated so that hands-on interaction is not needed. The main check for kinematic vectors is to compute positions of the roving receiver and check that similar values are obtained on separate visits to the same point. Also, it is good survey practice to visit points whose coordinates are known during the survey as a further check of the method.

Differential code range processing

Processing code pseudorange data is accomplished using software provided by manufacturers and third party vendors. Most programs are automated so that only the precise position of the fixed station is entered and the coordinates of the second point are computed. The data seems to have a strong central tendency so that averaging several observations rapidly improves the determined position. Positions can be determined for either fixed or moving receivers. Most uses of this technique are radial surveys so that no check of the results is possible.

7.4.3   Trouble shooting and quality control

Single baseline vectors

There are various quality numbers that indicate how well the survey was performed. The first analysis involves inspecting the statistics of individual vectors. The key for determining which vectors are bad is to compare the statistics of a good line with those of a bad line.

The two baselines shown in Table 7.6 are actual data collected in Texas by single frequency receivers. Both lines were of 30 minutes duration, and

Table 7.6. Baseline statistics

1	2 DX [m]	3 DY [m]	4 DZ [m]	5 σ_{DX} [m]	6 σ_{DY} [m]	7 σ_{DZ} [m]	8 Ratio	9 rms [m]
TRP	−303.457	135.317	158.292	1.419	1.011	0.520		0.003
FLT	−303.431	135.314	158.284	0.068	0.062	0.027		0.003
FIX	−303.437	135.327	158.263	0.003	0.006	0.004	30.1	0.004
TRP	−191.888	−343.451	−546.721	6.686	0.699	1.488		0.004
FLT	−192.221	−343.366	−546.721	0.538	0.069	0.102		0.007
FIX	−192.217	−343.192	−546.689	0.027	0.107	0.051	1.7	0.052

five satellites were in view for nearly the entire period. The sampling rate was 20 seconds.

The results were abstracted from the output or solution files. The first column in Table 7.6 indicates the type of solution: triple-difference (TRP), double-difference with real valued (float) ambiguities (FLT), and double-difference with the ambiguity biases fixed to integers (FIX). The next three columns are the components of the baseline vector (i.e., differences of ECEF coordinates, cf. Chap. 3). The fifth through the seventh column are the standard errors of the three coordinate differences listed in columns two through four. Column eight (single number) is the ratio between the chosen fixed bias solution and the next best solution. The last column is the root mean square (rms) error of fit in meters.

The basic line statistics in Table 7.6 indicate both a good baseline and a problem baseline. The single most important number in the solution output is the ratio shown in column eight. This number is a strong indicator of both good and bad lines, and should be greater than three, especially for short baselines up to about 5 km. When the ratio is a large number as in the first solution, the line is an accurate measurement. In this case, the difference between the fixed and float solutions is small and the change in the rms between the fixed and float solutions is not dramatic. The first baseline is included in Table 7.6 as an example of a good line with "normal" statistics. The second baseline in Table 7.6 is a bad line which is clearly shown by several indicators. First, note that the ratio (column 8) is 1.7 compared to a similar line with a ratio of 30.1. Both baselines are of similar length and both have observations to satellites for 30 minutes. The standard error of the vector components (columns 5 to 7) are substantially greater for the second line although the number of observations was actually greater for this baseline. The critical numbers in Table 7.6 are the differences between the fixed and float solutions. Note that the difference in the DY-value for the second baseline is 0.174 m. In the computation of this line, the software default was chosen to compute the fixed bias solution even though the ratio did not indicate the fixed solution would be a valid one. This "forced" computation of the fixed bias often yields valid solutions, but particularly on short lines with brief observations, the forced solution yields bad results. Another indicator that the observations do not fit the solution model is the large jump in the rms shown in the last column. The rms of the second baseline jumped from 0.007 to 0.052, a sevenfold increase. Compare this change to the rms of the first line which shows the normal slight increase of the three types of solutions.

The statistics of the second line clearly indicate that the fixed bias solution is invalid. This fact is further demonstrated by the inconclusive bias

Table 7.7. Float ambiguity solution

First baseline		Second baseline	
Satellites	Ambiguities	Satellites	Ambiguities
12-24	−970431.089	03-16	−184540.781
13-24	−832899.977	17-16	−155781.542
16-24	2235113.884	20-16	29969.388
20-24	61256.060	24-16	12931.837

values. The computed ambiguities are compared in Table 7.7. Satellite 24 and satellite 16 are the reference satellites for the double-differences of the first and the second baseline respectively. It is clearly seen that the ambiguities of the first baseline are obvious by inspection since the values are close to integers. On the other hand, the integer biases of the second line are not obvious. The bias 17-16 could be rounded either up or down, and the biases 03-16, and 20-16 are too close to 0.5 to be clearly defined. It is a good practice, when in doubt, to inspect the ambiguities to determine if there is an obvious problem. If the measured line is short and sufficient observations are available, one can try reprocessing the line using a different reference satellite, or try eliminating satellites with troublesome bias values. In the case of the second line, there was simply an insufficient amount of data.

Networks

For networks the best single tool for finding problem lines is to use loop closure software that sums the vector components around a loop to determine misclosures. Most GPS software packages have this type of software.

The first step in checking loops is to prepare a simple sketch showing the measured lines. Depending upon the software, the lines should then be numbered to correspond with the data file used by the software, or, in some cases, the path through the network can be chosen by referring to certain node points in the network. Bad lines in a loop are found by computing different combinations that both include and exclude the bad line. For example, if the line from point 10 to 11 (Fig. 7.5) were a bad line, it would be discovered by a high misclosure in the loops I and IV. When the larger loop around both small loops is computed (i.e., 1–3–15–13–1), the loop would have an acceptable closure. Therefore, the bad line could be narrowed to either line 10–11, or line 11–12. Normally, one would then inspect the output files for these lines more closely to determine if one or the other was more suspect. At this point, either the suspect line would be remeasured or point 11 would be dropped or downweighted.

The second quality control procedure in a network is to compute a minimally constrained least squares adjustment (often called free adjustment). This adjustment should normally be performed only after bad lines have been eliminated using the loop closure programs. There are numerous (PC compatible) adjustment programs available today, and possibly many more in the future. Chapter 9 gives a more complete description of least squares adjustment and only some practical uses will be discussed here. Each software package contains programs that prepare the necessary input files automatically from the various manufacturers' GPS output files.

Least squares adjustment programs perform three basic tasks: (1) they first shift all vectors so that they are connected in a contiguous network, (2) they add small corrections to each vector component to obtain a "flat" geometric figure closure, and (3) they compute coordinates and elevations of all points. The network design is important in obtaining useful information from an adjustment. A single loop would provide the minimum required information, while a network such as the one in Fig. 7.5 would provide a high degree of redundancy needed for network analysis.

In the batch processing of GPS data, the navigation position is often used as the starting coordinate for the vector computation and the solution is linearized around this value. When performing a minimally constrained adjustment, the datum coordinates of one point are normally entered, and the coordinates of all vectors are shifted to agree with the chosen coordinates of the one point. Therefore, a listing of the amounts each point was shifted to be consistent with the fixed point is available and can be printed. It is good practice to scan this list of shifts to determine if the starting coordinates for any of the vectors was in error by more than a reasonable amount. For example, if one of the shifts were 200 meters, you would probably wish to recompute that particular vector using a better starting coordinate (e.g., obtained from preliminary adjustment). Also, these shifts give a good indication of how well the C/A-code pseudorange positions agree with the datum position.

The proper weighting of observations (vectors) is always a problem. Many of the adjustment programs build a weight matrix based upon the vector correlation matrix and standard errors in the GPS output file. The formal standard errors of the vector computation are generally optimistic by a factor of three to ten times. Therefore, the weight matrix composed of these optimistic values must be scaled to arrive at a true estimate of the network errors. The problem is to determine what scale factor to use. Experience with the various software packages will show how large a scale factor is appropriate. Also, the adjustment software or the GPS software documentation should indicate the various scaling factors to use.

Adjustment software that does not use the vector correlation matrix requires the a priori estimates of the vector errors. The allowable error for first-order surveys, that is 1 : 100 000, according to the specifications of the Federal Geodetic Control Committee at the two sigma confidence level is 10 mm + 10 ppm of the distance. This error can be chosen as the a priori value for the adjustment, but first must be halved to express the value in terms of the one sigma or standard error level. When this 5 mm + 5 ppm a priori error is used, and the adjustment yields a standard error of unit weight of one or less, one knows that the work meets first-order specifications.

Another method for checking the quality of the GPS network is to inspect the residuals which result from the adjustment. Normally, there are two residual lists. One comprises the actual amounts that vector components have been corrected to achieve (exact) closure of the network. These residuals should consist of small values for short lines and larger values for longer lines. Blunders or large errors will be distributed throughout a general area and may be difficult to isolate. A better way to isolate large errors is to use the loop closure software in combination with appropriate adjustment programs.

The second list of residuals provided by most programs comprises the normalized or standardized residuals. These values are unitless and are the actual residuals scaled. A value of 1.0 for a normalized residual would indicate that the residual was as large as expected using the a priori weight model. A value less than one indicates the residual is less than expected and a value greater than one indicates a larger than expected value. In an adjustment, a few normalized residuals as high as 2.0 are to be expected. When more than 5% of the residuals are greater than 2.0 and for any value over 3.0, further investigations should be performed, and some lines possibly eliminated.

A typical case where redundant lines should be eliminated from a least squares adjustment result from surveying according to the scheme previously described for Fig. 7.5. For example, if receivers were placed on points 1, 2, 3, and 4. The vectors 1–2, 2–3, and 3–4 could have accurate fixed bias solutions, while the vector 1–4 could be a float bias solution. This difference would result from the fact that integer biases are more easily fixed on short lines but are difficult to fix on long lines. In this case, it would be appropriate to eliminate vector 1–4 from the adjustment.

When a kinematic survey has been performed using the leapfrog traversing technique, the traverse or geometric figure can be adjusted in a manner similar to a static survey. The same procedure should be followed to isolate bad lines, or bad elevations, or horizontal points.

7.4.4   Datum transformations

To this point only the computation of vectors and the analysis of their accuracy have been dealt with. After having successfully isolated and eliminated bad lines, the coordinates of points in the network can be computed. The first such computation is the final minimally constrained adjustment using all good vectors. The network shown in Fig. 7.5 has three horizontal control points. One of these points would be designated as fixed and one of the vertical points would be fixed in the free adjustment. If the point HCA were held fixed, the horizontal coordinates of the other two points would be determined. These (free adjusted) values should agree with the known values within a reasonable amount. If, for example, one point agreed well with the adjusted value while the other point disagreed, one could isolate the bad control point.

In most cases, the fixed control agrees quite well and the final adjustment is then performed. The constrained (fixed) adjustment results when two or more horizontal points are held fixed (also three vertical discussed in next section). In Fig. 7.5, the horizontal coordinates of HCA, HCB, and HCC would be fixed and the GPS network would be rotated and scaled to fit these values. Rotation values of 1 or 2 arcseconds and scales of up to 10 ppm are common when the fixed control has been established by triangulation, and less than 1 arcsecond and a few ppm are expected when the fixed control is established by dual frequency GPS (e.g., supernets).

Horizontal datum
The coordinates of points in a GPS network are computed in the same manner as coordinates of triangulation or traverse points. Network coordinates are, essentially, interpolated between the fixed control points using the measured vectors to apportion the values. Geodetic coordinates are, thus, referenced to the values of the fixed control and are, therefore, on the same datum as the fixed control. Proper ellipsoidal parameters should be used when performing the least squares adjustment. For example, when North American Datum 1983 (NAD-83) coordinates are used in an adjustment, the Geodetic Reference System 1980 (GRS-80) ellipsoid should be used. When the computation of coordinates for a survey on a different datum is desired, the coordinates of the fixed control and the proper ellipsoidal values must be used for the new adjustment.

Vertical datum
The computation of elevations with GPS is complicated by the fact that GPS heights are purely geometric and referenced to a surface known as the

ellipsoid, while elevations measured with leveling equipment are referenced to a surface known as the geoid, cf. Sect. 10.2.3. Geodesists at various universities and national geodetic organizations have developed a mathematical model that approximates the shape of the geoid (which is quite irregular). These models are based on data from satellites, astronomic observations, and gravity measurements. These geoid models have been used to compute geoid-ellipsoid separation values (i.e., geoidal heights) on regular grids. For example, the NGS distributes a file containing these geoidal heights for every three minutes of arc in latitude and longitude for the conterminous United States. These theoretical geoidal heights may be used to provide (theoretically) more accurate adjusted elevations.

In general, the ellipsoid and geoid are separated from one another (e.g., some 30 m in U.S.) and are also tilted to one another. Over a moderate size area (10 km × 10 km) with smooth topography, one can simply assume that the geoid has a similar curvature as the ellipsoid and compute the rotation angles and translation distance between the two surfaces, cf. Sect. 10.3.3.

In practice, more than the minimum three required elevations may be available for points in a GPS network, and a least squares adjustment could be performed. Referring to Fig. 7.5, the elevations of points 1, 6, and 13 have been determined and a vector has been measured (twice) to BMB, so that there are four known elevations connected by a network. The transformation of ellipsoidal heights to elevations is accomplished by holding the vertical component of the four points fixed in the adjustment. The adjustment will rotate and translate the entire network so that the elevations of all points are quite close to the true values. This technique works well where the geoid is similar in shape to the ellipsoid; however, in mountainous areas, this assumption is not valid and the difference must be accounted for.

In certain cases, many more than the minimum required elevations may be available for points in a GPS network. For example, a 100 point network covering a county sized area may have 10 elevations scattered throughout the area. Out of the 10 known elevations, there may be as many as five or six combinations of three points that satisfy the "well distributed geometrically" criterion. Therefore, to check for badly known elevations, five to six preliminary adjustments of the 100 station network would have to be performed. Another way of isolating bad elevations can be found in Collins (1989) where an example is given. This method first involves performing a minimally constrained or "free" adjustment holding one of the vertical points fixed (and at least one horizontal point). The geoidal heights are included in this free adjustment so that all points in the network now have so-called pseudoelevations. For example, in Fig. 7.5, the elevation of BMD could be fixed and the pseudoelevations of the remaining points computed by using the geoidal height differences (derived from the geoid model) and the ellipsoidal height differences (determined from the adjustment). The pseudoelevations approximate the true elevations although they contain a systematic error. In a moderate size nonmountainous area (10 km × 10 km), the pseudoelevations are normally within 10 to 20 cm of the true elevations. Many times, the pseudoelevations will be within a few centimeters of the true elevations. The rotation angles can now be computed separately by a simple "regression" program. A convenient way to write such a program is to use a spread sheet program. A list of each point's plane coordinates and pseudoelevation is placed in the first columns and rows of the spread sheet. The difference between the pseudoelevation and true elevation is placed in another column, and zeroes are placed in the cells of this column for points not being held fixed. The normal equation matrix can now be formed automatically by ignoring data in rows where zeroes appear, using only the coordinates and height difference in rows where differences between the true and the pseudoelevations are given. Standard regression or least squares adjustment formulas are employed to compute the 3 × 3 normal equation matrix used to determine the transformation parameters. The five or six combinations of various elevations can easily be computed in a few minutes using this technique. Bad elevations can be quickly isolated in this way since the rotated elevations for the redundant points should agree within a few centimeters of the fixed elevation. After all given elevations have been checked for blunders, the final elevations of points in the network are computed. This is easily accomplished by fixing a minimum of three (geometrically diverse) elevations and performing a fixed adjustment. For example, the elevations at points 1, 6, and 18 in Fig. 7.5 would be fixed in the adjustment, and the elevation of point 13 would serve as a check. When three elevations are fixed in the adjustment, the rotation angles about the north-south and east-west axes are computed. These rotation angles serve as a further check since they should not (normally) exceed a few (e.g., 5) arcseconds.

The differences of theoretical geoidal heights are also useful in determining elevations in a small area where only one benchmark is available. The pseudoelevations for the area will be closer to the true values than if no geoid model were used and a single point were held fixed. This method should only be used when approximate elevations are desired and the technique should be used with caution since all elevations are dependent on the single fixed point.

No definite answer can be given to the question of the accuracy of GPS derived elevations since the accuracy depends upon the shape of the geoid in the particular area. Normally, in flat continental areas, the geoid is relatively smooth and elevations within a 10 km × 10 km area can be determined to

3 cm or better. In mountainous areas, the interpolated (holding three elevations fixed) elevations can be in error by several decimeters. In Europe where geoid models are more accurate, the errors might be one-half the errors experienced in the United States and Australia.

7.4.5 Computation of plane coordinates

GPS surveys performed for local engineering projects or for mapping normally require that plane coordinates be computed for all points. There are several conformal projections used for this purpose. The two most popular in the U.S. are the Transverse Mercator projection and the Lambert projection. In the U.S., each state has a different projection system (in some cases several) and programs to transform latitude and longitude to and from these projections can be purchased from the NGS. Also, most GPS software includes these transformation programs. In Europe, transformation programs are readily available from the various mapping and surveying organizations. Also, these transformations are included in most land surveying software packages.

It should be remembered that geodetic latitude and longitude are specifically referenced to a given datum. In the U.S., the older North American Datum 1927 (NAD-27) has a specific set of projections to use, while the NAD-83 uses a completely different set of projections. The projections between datums should never be mixed.

A number of transformation programs commercially available transforms both ellipsoidal and plane coordinates between datums and projections. This software is often part of Computer Aided Design (CAD) graphics package. It should be noted that these transformation programs are not intended for geodetic use; they only approximate the coordinates of the new datum. Such programs can produce coordinates with errors of up to a meter.

Special local transformations can provide quite accurate coordinates of points that do not have published values in the new system. For example, not all geodetic points have published NAD-83 values. Software such as the NGS program LEFTI use the old and new geodetic coordinates of points surrounding the old (without new values) point to compute local transformation parameters used to compute new coordinates for the old point. This type of program works quite well and provides geodetic quality coordinates.

7.5 Survey report

A final survey report is helpful to others in analyzing the conduct of a survey. In effect, a project report should document the survey so that another competent individual could recreate all computations arriving at similar answers to those obtained. This report serves as an "audit trail" for the survey. A project report should address the following topics:

1. Location of the survey and a description of the project area. A general map showing the locality is recommended.

2. Purpose of the survey and the extent that the requirements were satisfied. Also, the specifications followed should be mentioned (e.g., FGCC GPS Specifications Order A).

3. A description of the monumentation used. It should be specifically noted if underground as well as surface marks were used. A section of the report should explain which existing monuments were searched for and which ones were found. For monuments not found, an estimate of the time spent searching for the mark should be given to aid others who wish to recover that mark. A list of all control searched for, control found, and control used is helpful in analyzing the project.

4. A description of the instrumentation used should include both the GPS equipment and conventional equipment along with serial numbers. An explanation of how the tribrachs or bipods were tested for plumb should be given. If survey towers or special range poles were used, their use should be described with an explanation of how the antenna was collimated.

5. The computation scheme for the project should be described including which version of the processing software was used and which least squares adjustment was applied. An exhibit such as Table 7.5 is particularly useful in visualizing how the survey was conducted. The satellites tracked during each session should be included in this listing or in a separate exhibit. Also, an exhibit such as Table 7.6 should be included to show the quality factors for each line. The inclusion of abstracts of each vector would also be helpful.

6. The computation of coordinates for all eccentric points should be included. In the case of horizontal points, sketches and the direct computation results should be shown. For vertical points, a copy of the level records should be included in an appendix.

7. All problems encountered should be discussed and equipment failures listed. Unusual solar activity should be mentioned as well as multipath problems and other factors affecting the survey.

8. The following lists should be included in the report:

   (a) List of loop closures.

   (b) Occupation schedule (e.g., Table 7.5).

   (c) Vector statistics (e.g., Table 7.6).

   (d) Free least squares adjustment.

   (e) Portion of fixed adjustment showing rotation angles and statistics.

   (f) List of adjusted positions and plane coordinates.

   (g) Project statistics.

   (h) Copies of "original" site occupation logs.

   (i) Equipment malfunction log.

   (j) A project sketch showing all points and control with a title box, scale, and projection tic marks.

9. Finally, a copy of the original observations or the original observations translated to the receiver independent RINEX format, cf. Sect. 9.1, should be transmitted as part of the survey. For convenience, copies of the adjustment input file and vector output files would be advantageous.

When surveys are properly performed and documented, they provide a lasting contribution to the profession. Often, data can be used in later years by others to study a particular phenomenon or the work may be included in a larger project. Proper use of measurements can only be made when the survey is thoroughly documented for posterity.

8 Mathematical models for positioning

8.1 Point positioning

8.1.1 Point positioning with code ranges

The code pseudorange at an epoch t can be modeled, cf. Eq. (6.2), by

$$R_i^j(t) = \varrho_i^j(t) + c\,\Delta\delta_i^j(t)\,. \tag{8.1}$$

Here, $R_i^j(t)$ is the measured code pseudorange between the observing site i and the satellite j, $\varrho_i^j(t)$ is the geometric distance between the satellite and the observing point, and c is the speed of light. The last item to be explained is $\Delta\delta_i^j(t)$. This clock bias represents the combined clock offsets of the satellite and the receiver clock with respect to GPS time, cf. Eq. (6.1).

Examining Eq. (8.1), the desired point coordinates to be determined are implicit in the distance $\varrho_i^j(t)$, which can explicitly be written as

$$\varrho_i^j(t) = \sqrt{(X^j(t) - X_i)^2 + (Y^j(t) - Y_i)^2 + (Z^j(t) - Z_i)^2} \tag{8.2}$$

where $X^j(t)$, $Y^j(t)$, $Z^j(t)$ are the components of the geocentric position vector of the satellite for epoch t, and X_i, Y_i, Z_i are the three unknown ECEF coordinates of the observing site. Now, the clock bias $\Delta\delta_i^j(t)$ must be investigated more detailed. For the moment consider a single epoch; a single position i is automatically implied. Each satellite contributes one unknown clock bias which can be recognized from the superscript j at the clock term. Neglecting, for the present, the site i clock bias, the pseudorange equation for the first satellite would have four unknowns. These are the three site coordinates and one clock bias of this satellite. Each additional satellite adds one equation with the same site coordinates but with a new satellite clock bias. Thus, there would always be more unknowns than measurements. Even when an additional epoch is considered, new satellite clock biases must be modeled due to clock drift. Fortunately, the information for the satellite clocks is known and transmitted via the broadcast navigation message in the form of three polynomial coefficients a_0, a_1, a_2 with a reference time t_0. Therefore, the equation

$$\delta^j(t) = a_0 + a_1(t - t_0) + a_2(t - t_0)^2 \tag{8.3}$$

enables the calculation of the satellite clock bias for epoch t. It should be noted that the polynomial (8.3) removes a great deal of the satellite clock bias, but a small amount of error remains.

The combined bias term $\Delta\delta_i^j(t)$ is split into two parts by

$$\Delta\delta_i^j(t) = \delta^j(t) - \delta_i(t) \tag{8.4}$$

where the satellite related part is known by (8.3) and the receiver related term $\delta_i(t)$ remains unknown. Substituting (8.4) into (8.1) yields

$$R_i^j(t) = \varrho_i^j(t) + c\,\delta^j(t) - c\,\delta_i(t) \tag{8.5}$$

which is the equation that will be investigated with respect to the unknowns. Considering a single epoch t, there are four unknowns. These are three site coordinates and one unknown receiver clock bias $\delta_i(t)$. The four unknowns can be computed immediately if four satellites are observed simultaneously.

Equation (8.5) is now studied in a more general way. Denoting the number of satellites by n_j, and the number of epochs by n_t, then $n_j\,n_t$ observation equations are available. To obtain a unique solution, the number of unknowns must not be greater than the number of observations. Rearranging (8.5) slightly by shifting the computed satellite clock bias to the left-hand side of the equation, the relation

$$
\begin{array}{ccccc}
R_i^j(t) - c\,\delta^j(t) & = & \varrho_i^j(t) & - & c\,\delta_i(t) \\[4pt]
n_j\,n_t & \geq & 3 & + & n_t
\end{array}
\tag{8.6}
$$

is obtained. The number of measurements and the number of unknowns are shown below each corresponding term. Limiting the relation above to one epoch (i.e., $n_t = 1$) gives $n_j \geq 4$. Note that each epoch may be considered separately, and the position of site i and the clock biases for each corresponding epoch can be computed if $n_j \geq 4$ simultaneous observations are performed. Therefore, movement of receiver i is permitted. According to the definitions in Sect. 7.1.1, this is the case in kinematic applications, where the position of a moving vehicle at any arbitrary epoch is desired. This trajectory determination or navigation was the original goal of GPS. For each epoch, the position (and velocity) of i can be determined instantaneously when at least four satellites are in view.

In static applications where site i is stationary during the observation period, the situation is slightly different. In this case, in principle, the simultaneous observation of four satellites is not necessary. This can be seen from Eq. (8.6) if two satellites (i.e., $n_j = 2$) are considered. The corresponding result $n_t \geq 3$ means that the simultaneous observation of two satellites over three epochs would theoretically suffice. In practice, however, this situation would give bad results or the computation would fail because of an ill-conditioned system of observation equations unless the epochs were widely spaced (e.g., hours). A solution is also possible, if observations of three epochs for two satellites are made, followed by three additional epochs (e.g., seconds apart) for two other satellites. Such an application will be rare but is imaginable under special circumstances (e.g., in urban areas).

8.1.2 Point positioning with carrier phases

Pseudoranges can also be derived from carrier phase measurements. The mathematical model for these measurements, cf. Eq. (6.9), is

$$\Phi_i^j(t) = \frac{1}{\lambda} \varrho_i^j(t) + N_i^j + f^j \, \Delta\delta_i^j(t) \,. \tag{8.7}$$

Here, $\Phi_i^j(t)$ is the measured carrier phase, λ is the wavelength, and $\varrho_i^j(t)$ is the same as for the code range model. The time independent phase ambiguity N_i^j is an integer number and, therefore, often called the integer ambiguity or integer unknown. The term f^j denotes the frequency of the satellite signal, and $\Delta\delta_i^j(t)$ is the combined satellite and receiver clock bias.

If Eq. (8.4) is substituted into Eq. (8.7), the phase model becomes

$$\Phi_i^j(t) = \frac{1}{\lambda} \varrho_i^j(t) + N_i^j + f^j \, \delta^j(t) - f^j \, \delta_i(t) \,. \tag{8.8}$$

The satellite clock bias $\delta^j(t)$ is again assumed to be known, cf. Eq. (8.3). For n_j satellites, n_t epochs, and the single site i, there are $n_j \, n_t$ possible measurements. The number of unknowns are listed below the appropriate terms on the right-hand side of the following equation:

$$\Phi_i^j(t) - f^j \, \delta^j(t) \quad = \quad \frac{1}{\lambda} \varrho_i^j(t) \quad + \quad N_i^j \quad - \quad f^j \, \delta_i(t)$$
$$n_j \, n_t \qquad\qquad \geq \qquad 3 \quad + \quad n_j \quad + \quad n_t \,. \tag{8.9}$$

A solution for a single epoch (i.e., $n_t = 1$) is only possible when the n_j integer ambiguities are disregarded. In this case, the phase range model is equivalent to the code range model and it follows $n_j \geq 4$. This essentially means that the phase model may also be used for kinematic applications provided that the ambiguities have been resolved by initialization procedures. For static applications (where the ambiguities are to be determined), theoretically the minimum number of satellites is $n_j = 2$. This requires a minimum of $n_t = 5$ observation epochs. Practically, $n_j = 4$ satellites would give reasonable results. In this case, the minimum number of epochs is $n_t = 3$.

8.1.3   Point positioning with Doppler data

The mathematical model for Doppler data, cf. Eq. (6.10), is

$$D_i^j(t) = \dot{\varrho}_i^j(t) + c\,\Delta\dot{\delta}_i^j(t) \tag{8.10}$$

and may be considered as time derivative of a code or phase pseudorange. In this equation, $D_i^j(t)$ denotes the observed Doppler shift scaled to range rate, $\dot{\varrho}_i^j(t)$ is the instantaneous radial velocity between the satellite and the receiver, and $\Delta\dot{\delta}_i^j(t)$ is the time derivative of the combined clock bias term.

The radial velocity for a stationary receiver, cf. Eq. (4.45),

$$\dot{\varrho}_i^j(t) = \frac{\varrho^j(t) - \varrho_i}{\|\varrho^j(t) - \varrho_i\|} \cdot \dot{\varrho}^j(t) \tag{8.11}$$

relates the unknown position vector ϱ_i of the receiver to the instantaneous position vector $\varrho^j(t)$ and velocity vector $\dot{\varrho}^j(t)$ of the satellite. These vectors can be calculated from the satellite's ephemerides. The contribution of the satellite clock to $\Delta\dot{\delta}_i^j(t)$ is given by, cf. Eq. (8.3),

$$\dot{\delta}^j(t) = a_1 + 2a_2(t - t_0) \tag{8.12}$$

and is known. Summarizing, one can state that the observation equation (8.10) contains four unknowns. These unknowns are the three receiver coordinates ϱ_i and the receiver clock drift $\dot{\delta}_i(t)$. Hence, compared to the code range model, the Doppler equation contains the receiver clock drift instead of the receiver clock offset.

The concept of a combined code pseudorange and Doppler data processing for positioning is mentioned by Ashjaee et al. (1989). In this case, there is a total of five unknowns. These unknowns are the three point coordinates, the receiver clock offset, and the receiver clock drift. Each satellite contributes two equations, one code pseudorange and one Doppler equation. Therefore, three satellites are sufficient to solve for the five unknowns.

The similarity of the pseudorange and the Doppler equation gives rise to the question of a linear dependence of the equations. However, it can be shown that the lines of constant pseudoranges and the lines of constant Doppler are orthogonal, cf. Jorgensen (1980), Hatch (1982), Ashjaee et al. (1989). The pseudoranges are measured along the line of sight between receiver and satellite, and the Doppler, according to Jorgensen (1980), "provides information along the direction of the component of relative velocity that is perpendicular to the line of sight". Thus, pseudorange and Doppler equations are independent.

8.2 Relative positioning

The objective of relative positioning is to determine the coordinates of an unknown point with respect to a known point which, for most applications, is stationary. In other words, relative positioning aims at the determination of the vector between the two points which is often called a "baseline". In Fig. 8.1, A denotes the (known) reference point, B the unknown point, and $\underline{b}_{AB}$ the baseline vector. Introducing the corresponding position vectors $\underline{X}_A$, $\underline{X}_B$, the relation

$$\underline{X}_B = \underline{X}_A + \underline{b}_{AB} \tag{8.13}$$

may be formulated, and the components of the baseline vector $\underline{b}_{AB}$ are

$$\underline{b}_{AB} = \begin{bmatrix} X_B - X_A \\ Y_B - Y_A \\ Z_B - Z_A \end{bmatrix} = \begin{bmatrix} \Delta X_{AB} \\ \Delta Y_{AB} \\ \Delta Z_{AB} \end{bmatrix} . \tag{8.14}$$

The mathematical models for the code range and phase range, cf. (8.6) and (8.9) respectively, may be applied analogously where the only difference is the inclusion of the known coordinates of the reference point. These coordinates must be given in the WGS-84 system and are usually approximated by a code range solution.

Relative positioning is most effective if simultaneous observations are made at both the reference and the unknown point. Simultaneity means that the observation time tags for the two points are the same. Assuming such simultaneous observations at the two points A and B to satellites j and k, linear combinations can be formed leading to single-differences, double-differences, and triple-differences. Most postprocessing software uses these three difference techniques, so their basic mathematical modeling is shown in the following sections.

8.2.1 Phase differences

Single-differences
Two points and one satellite are involved. Denoting the points by A and B

A $\underline{b}_{AB}$ B

Fig. 8.1. Relative positioning

and the satellite by j and using Eq. (8.9), the phase equations for the two points are

$$\Phi_A^j(t) - f^j \, \delta^j(t) = \frac{1}{\lambda} \, \varrho_A^j(t) + N_A^j - f^j \, \delta_A(t)$$

$$\Phi_B^j(t) - f^j \, \delta^j(t) = \frac{1}{\lambda} \, \varrho_B^j(t) + N_B^j - f^j \, \delta_B(t) \tag{8.15}$$

and the difference of the two equations is

$$\Phi_B^j(t) - \Phi_A^j(t) = \frac{1}{\lambda} \left[\varrho_B^j(t) - \varrho_A^j(t) \right] + N_B^j - N_A^j$$

$$- f^j \left[\delta_B(t) - \delta_A(t) \right] . \tag{8.16}$$

Equation (8.16) is referred to as the single-difference equation. This equation stresses one aspect of the solution for the unknowns on the right-hand side. A system of such equations would lead to a rank deficiency even in the case of an arbitrarily large redundancy. This can be seen from the coefficients of the ambiguities and of the receiver clock biases. In both cases, the absolute values of the coefficients for the two points are the same. This means that the adjustment design matrix has linearly dependent columns and a rank deficiency exists. Therefore, the relative quantities

$$N_{AB}^j = N_B^j - N_A^j$$

$$\delta_{AB}(t) = \delta_B(t) - \delta_A(t) \tag{8.17}$$

are introduced. Using additionally the shorthand notations

$$\Phi_{AB}^j(t) = \Phi_B^j(t) - \Phi_A^j(t)$$

$$\varrho_{AB}^j(t) = \varrho_B^j(t) - \varrho_A^j(t) , \tag{8.18}$$

and substituting (8.17) and (8.18) into (8.16) gives

$$\Phi_{AB}^j(t) = \frac{1}{\lambda} \, \varrho_{AB}^j(t) + N_{AB}^j - f^j \, \delta_{AB}(t) \tag{8.19}$$

which is the final form of the single-difference equation. Compared to the phase equation (8.9), the satellite clock bias has canceled.

Double-differences
Assuming the two points A, B, and the two satellites j, k to be involved, two single-differences according to Eq. (8.19) may be formed:

$$\Phi_{AB}^j(t) = \frac{1}{\lambda} \, \varrho_{AB}^j(t) + N_{AB}^j - f^j \, \delta_{AB}(t)$$

$$\Phi_{AB}^k(t) = \frac{1}{\lambda} \, \varrho_{AB}^k(t) + N_{AB}^k - f^k \, \delta_{AB}(t) . \tag{8.20}$$

To get a double-difference, these single-differences are subtracted. Assuming equal frequencies $f^j = f^k$ for the satellite signals, the result is

$$\Phi^k_{AB}(t) - \Phi^j_{AB}(t) = \frac{1}{\lambda}\left[\varrho^k_{AB}(t) - \varrho^j_{AB}(t)\right] + N^k_{AB} - N^j_{AB}.\qquad(8.21)$$

Using in analogous way to (8.18) shorthand notations for the satellites j and k, the final form of the double-difference equation is

$$\Phi^{jk}_{AB}(t) = \frac{1}{\lambda}\varrho^{jk}_{AB}(t) + N^{jk}_{AB}.\qquad(8.22)$$

The canceling effect of the receiver clock biases is the reason why double-differences are used. This cancellation resulted from the assumptions of simultaneous observations and equal frequencies of the satellite signals.

Symbolically, the convention

$$*^{jk}_{AB} = *^k_{AB} - *^j_{AB}\qquad(8.23)$$

has been introduced where the asterisk may be replaced by Φ, ϱ, or N. Note that these terms comprising two subscripts and two superscripts are actually composed of four terms. The symbolic notation

$$*^{jk}_{AB} = *^k_B - *^j_B - *^k_A + *^j_A\qquad(8.24)$$

characterizes in detail the terms in the double-difference equation:

$$\begin{aligned}\Phi^{jk}_{AB}(t) &= \Phi^k_B(t) - \Phi^j_B(t) - \Phi^k_A(t) + \Phi^j_A(t)\\[4pt]\varrho^{jk}_{AB}(t) &= \varrho^k_B(t) - \varrho^j_B(t) - \varrho^k_A(t) + \varrho^j_A(t)\\[4pt]N^{jk}_{AB} &= N^k_B \quad - N^j_B \quad - N^k_A \quad + N^j_A.\end{aligned}\qquad(8.25)$$

Triple-differences

So far only one epoch t has been considered. To eliminate the time independent ambiguities, Remondi (1984) has suggested to difference double-differences between two epochs. Denoting the two epochs by t_1 and t_2, then

$$\begin{aligned}\Phi^{jk}_{AB}(t_1) &= \frac{1}{\lambda}\varrho^{jk}_{AB}(t_1) + N^{jk}_{AB}\\[4pt]\Phi^{jk}_{AB}(t_2) &= \frac{1}{\lambda}\varrho^{jk}_{AB}(t_2) + N^{jk}_{AB}\end{aligned}\qquad(8.26)$$

are the two double-differences, and

$$\Phi^{jk}_{AB}(t_2) - \Phi^{jk}_{AB}(t_1) = \frac{1}{\lambda}\left[\varrho^{jk}_{AB}(t_2) - \varrho^{jk}_{AB}(t_1)\right]\qquad(8.27)$$

is the triple-difference which may be written in the simplified form

$$\Phi_{AB}^{jk}(t_{12}) = \frac{1}{\lambda}\, \varrho_{AB}^{jk}(t_{12}) \tag{8.28}$$

if the symbolic formula

$$* (t_{12}) = *(t_2) - *(t_1) \tag{8.29}$$

is applied to the terms Φ and ϱ. It should be noted that both $\Phi_{AB}^{jk}(t_{12})$ and $\varrho_{AB}^{jk}(t_{12})$ are actually composed of eight terms each. Resubstituting (8.27) and either (8.24) or (8.25) yields

$$\begin{aligned}\Phi_{AB}^{jk}(t_{12}) = \quad & \Phi_{B}^{k}(t_2) - \Phi_{B}^{j}(t_2) - \Phi_{A}^{k}(t_2) + \Phi_{A}^{j}(t_2) \\ & - \Phi_{B}^{k}(t_1) + \Phi_{B}^{j}(t_1) + \Phi_{A}^{k}(t_1) - \Phi_{A}^{j}(t_1)\end{aligned} \tag{8.30}$$

and

$$\begin{aligned}\varrho_{AB}^{jk}(t_{12}) = \quad & \varrho_{B}^{k}(t_2) - \varrho_{B}^{j}(t_2) - \varrho_{A}^{k}(t_2) + \varrho_{A}^{j}(t_2) \\ & - \varrho_{B}^{k}(t_1) + \varrho_{B}^{j}(t_1) + \varrho_{A}^{k}(t_1) - \varrho_{A}^{j}(t_1)\,.\end{aligned} \tag{8.31}$$

There are two main advantages of the triple-differences which are related. These are the canceling effect for the ambiguities and, thus, the immunity of the triple-differences to changes in the ambiguities. Such changes are called cycle slips and are treated in more detail in Sect. 9.1.2.

8.2.2   Correlations of the phase combinations

In general, there are two groups of correlations, (1) the physical and (2) the mathematical correlations. The phases from one satellite received at two points, for example $\Phi_{A}^{j}(t)$ and $\Phi_{B}^{j}(t)$, are physically correlated since they refer to the same satellite. Usually, the physical correlation is not taken into account. Therefore, main interest is directed to the mathematical correlations introduced by differencing.

The assumption may be made that the phase errors show a random behavior resulting in a normal distribution with the expectation value of zero and the variance σ^2. Measured (or raw) phases are, therefore, linearly independent or uncorrelated. Introducing a vector $\underline{\Phi}$ containing the phases, then

$$\text{cov}(\underline{\Phi}) = \sigma^2\, \underline{I} \tag{8.32}$$

is the covariance matrix for the phases where $\underline{I}$ is the unit matrix.

Single-differences

Considering the two points A, B and the satellite j at epoch t gives

$$\Phi^j_{AB}(t) = \Phi^j_B(t) - \Phi^j_A(t) \tag{8.33}$$

as the corresponding single-difference. Forming a second single-difference for the same two points but with another satellite k for the same epoch yields

$$\Phi^k_{AB}(t) = \Phi^k_B(t) - \Phi^k_A(t). \tag{8.34}$$

The two single-differences may be computed from the matrix-vector relation

$$\underline{SD} = \underline{C}\,\underline{\Phi} \tag{8.35}$$

where

$$\underline{SD} = \begin{bmatrix} \Phi^j_{AB}(t) \\ \Phi^k_{AB}(t) \end{bmatrix}$$

$$\underline{C} = \begin{bmatrix} -1 & 1 & 0 & 0 \\ 0 & 0 & -1 & 1 \end{bmatrix} \qquad \underline{\Phi} = \begin{bmatrix} \Phi^j_A(t) \\ \Phi^j_B(t) \\ \Phi^k_A(t) \\ \Phi^k_B(t) \end{bmatrix}. \tag{8.36}$$

The covariance law applied to Eq. (8.35) gives

$$\mathrm{cov}(\underline{SD}) = \underline{C}\,\mathrm{cov}(\underline{\Phi})\,\underline{C}^T \tag{8.37}$$

and, by substituting Eq. (8.32),

$$\mathrm{cov}(\underline{SD}) = \underline{C}\,\sigma^2\,\underline{I}\,\underline{C}^T = \sigma^2\,\underline{C}\,\underline{C}^T \tag{8.38}$$

is obtained for the covariance of the single-differences. Taking $\underline{C}$ from (8.36), the matrix product

$$\underline{C}\,\underline{C}^T = 2 \begin{bmatrix} 1 & 0 \\ 0 & 1 \end{bmatrix} = 2\,\underline{I} \tag{8.39}$$

may be substituted into (8.38) leading to

$$\mathrm{cov}(\underline{SD}) = 2\sigma^2\,\underline{I}. \tag{8.40}$$

This shows that single-differences are uncorrelated. Note that the dimension of the unit matrix in (8.40) corresponds to the number of single-differences at epoch t, whereas the factor 2 does not depend on the number of single-differences. Considering more than one epoch, the covariance matrix is again a unit matrix with the dimension equivalent to the total number of single-differences.

Double-differences
Now, three satellites j, k, ℓ with j as reference satellite are considered. For the two points A, B and epoch t, the double-differences

$$\Phi_{AB}^{jk}(t) = \Phi_{AB}^{k}(t) - \Phi_{AB}^{j}(t)$$
$$\Phi_{AB}^{j\ell}(t) = \Phi_{AB}^{\ell}(t) - \Phi_{AB}^{j}(t)$$

(8.41)

can be derived from the single-differences. These two equations can be written in the matrix-vector form

$$\underline{DD} = \underline{C}\,\underline{SD}$$

(8.42)

where

$$\underline{DD} = \begin{bmatrix} \Phi_{AB}^{jk}(t) \\ \Phi_{AB}^{j\ell}(t) \end{bmatrix}$$

$$\underline{C} = \begin{bmatrix} -1 & 1 & 0 \\ -1 & 0 & 1 \end{bmatrix} \qquad \underline{SD} = \begin{bmatrix} \Phi_{AB}^{j}(t) \\ \Phi_{AB}^{k}(t) \\ \Phi_{AB}^{\ell}(t) \end{bmatrix}$$

(8.43)

have been introduced. The covariance matrix for the double-differences is given by

$$\mathrm{cov}(\underline{DD}) = \underline{C}\,\mathrm{cov}(\underline{SD})\,\underline{C}^T$$

(8.44)

and substituting (8.40) leads to

$$\mathrm{cov}(\underline{DD}) = 2\sigma^2\,\underline{C}\,\underline{C}^T$$

(8.45)

or, explicitly, using $\underline{C}$ from (8.43)

$$\mathrm{cov}(\underline{DD}) = 2\sigma^2 \begin{bmatrix} 2 & 1 \\ 1 & 2 \end{bmatrix}.$$

(8.46)

This shows that double-differences are correlated. The weight or correlation matrix $\underline{P}(t)$ is obtained from the inverse of the covariance matrix

$$\underline{P}(t) = [\mathrm{cov}(\underline{DD})]^{-1} = \frac{1}{2\sigma^2}\frac{1}{3}\begin{bmatrix} 2 & -1 \\ -1 & 2 \end{bmatrix}$$

(8.47)

where two double-differences at one epoch were used. Generally, with n_{DD} being the number of double-differences at epoch t, the correlation matrix is given by

$$\underline{P}(t) = \frac{1}{2\sigma^2} \frac{1}{n_{DD}+1} \begin{bmatrix} n_{DD} & -1 & -1 & \cdots \\ -1 & n_{DD} & -1 & \cdots \\ -1 & & & \\ \vdots & & \cdots & n_{DD} \end{bmatrix} \qquad (8.48)$$

where the dimension of the matrix is $n_{DD} \times n_{DD}$. For a better illustration, assume four double-differences. In this case, the correlation matrix is the 4×4 matrix

$$\underline{P}(t) = \frac{1}{2\sigma^2} \frac{1}{5} \begin{bmatrix} 4 & -1 & -1 & -1 \\ -1 & 4 & -1 & -1 \\ -1 & -1 & 4 & -1 \\ -1 & -1 & -1 & 4 \end{bmatrix}. \qquad (8.49)$$

So far only one epoch has been considered. For epochs $t_1, t_2, t_3, \ldots$ the correlation matrix becomes a block-diagonal matrix

$$\underline{P}(t) = \begin{bmatrix} \underline{P}(t_1) & & & \\ & \underline{P}(t_2) & & \\ & & \underline{P}(t_3) & \\ & & & \ddots \end{bmatrix} \qquad (8.50)$$

where each "element" of the matrix is itself a matrix. The matrices $\underline{P}(t_1)$, $\underline{P}(t_2)$, $\underline{P}(t_3), \ldots$ do not necessarily have to be of the same dimension because there may be different numbers of double-differences at different epochs.

Triple-differences
The triple-difference equations are slightly more complicated because several different cases must be considered. The covariance of a single triple-difference is computed by applying the covariance propagation law to the relation, cf. Eqs. (8.30) and (8.33),

$$\Phi_{AB}^{jk}(t_{12}) = \Phi_{AB}^{k}(t_2) - \Phi_{AB}^{j}(t_2) - \Phi_{AB}^{k}(t_1) + \Phi_{AB}^{j}(t_1). \qquad (8.51)$$

Now, two triple-differences with the same epochs and sharing one satellite are considered. The first triple-difference using the satellites j, k is given by Eq. (8.51). The second triple-difference corresponds to the satellites j, ℓ:

$$\Phi_{AB}^{jk}(t_{12}) = \Phi_{AB}^{k}(t_2) - \Phi_{AB}^{j}(t_2) - \Phi_{AB}^{k}(t_1) + \Phi_{AB}^{j}(t_1)$$

$$\Phi_{AB}^{j\ell}(t_{12}) = \Phi_{AB}^{\ell}(t_2) - \Phi_{AB}^{j}(t_2) - \Phi_{AB}^{\ell}(t_1) + \Phi_{AB}^{j}(t_1). \qquad (8.52)$$

By introducing

$$TD = \begin{bmatrix} \Phi_{AB}^{jk}(t_{12}) \\ \Phi_{AB}^{j\ell}(t_{12}) \end{bmatrix}$$

$$C = \begin{bmatrix} 1 & -1 & 0 & -1 & 1 & 0 \\ 1 & 0 & -1 & -1 & 0 & 1 \end{bmatrix} \qquad SD = \begin{bmatrix} \Phi_{AB}^{j}(t_1) \\ \Phi_{AB}^{k}(t_1) \\ \Phi_{AB}^{\ell}(t_1) \\ \Phi_{AB}^{j}(t_2) \\ \Phi_{AB}^{k}(t_2) \\ \Phi_{AB}^{\ell}(t_2) \end{bmatrix} \qquad (8.53)$$

the vector-matrix relation

$$TD = C\,SD \qquad (8.54)$$

can be formed, and the covariance for the triple-difference follows from

$$\mathrm{cov}(TD) = C\,\mathrm{cov}(SD)\,C^T \qquad (8.55)$$

or, by substituting (8.40),

$$\mathrm{cov}(TD) = 2\sigma^2\,C\,C^T \qquad (8.56)$$

is obtained which, using (8.53), yields

$$\mathrm{cov}(TD) = 2\sigma^2 \begin{bmatrix} 4 & 2 \\ 2 & 4 \end{bmatrix} \qquad (8.57)$$

for the two triple-differences (8.52). The tedious derivation may be abbreviated by setting up the following symbolic table

Epoch	t_1			t_2		
SD for Sat	j	k	ℓ	j	k	ℓ
$TD^{jk}(t_{12})$	1	-1	0	-1	1	0
$TD^{j\ell}(t_{12})$	1	0	-1	-1	0	1

$$(8.58)$$

where the point names A, B have been omitted. It can be seen that the triple-difference $TD^{jk}(t_{12})$, for example, is composed of the two single-differences (with the signs according to the table) for the satellites j and k at epoch t_1 and of the two single-differences for the same satellites but epoch t_2. Accordingly, the same applies for the other triple-difference $TD^{j\ell}(t_{12})$. Thus, the coefficients of (8.58) are the same as those of matrix C in Eq. (8.53). Finally, the product $C\,C^T$, appearing in Eq. (8.56), is also aided by referring to the table above. All combinations of inner products of the two rows (one row represents one triple-difference) must be taken. The inner product (row 1 · row 1) yields the first-row, first-column element of $\underline{C}\,C^T$, the inner product (row 1 · row 2) yields the first-row, second-column element of $\underline{C}\,C^T$, etc. Based on the general formula (8.51) and the table (8.58), arbitrary cases may be derived easily and systematically. The subsequent table shows the second group of triple-difference correlations if adjacent epochs t_1, t_2, t_3 are taken. Two cases are considered:

Epoch		t_1			t_2			t_3		$\underline{C}\,C^T$	
SD for Sat	j	k	ℓ	j	k	ℓ	j	k	ℓ		
$TD^{jk}(t_{12})$	1	−1	0	−1	1	0	0	0	0	4	−2
$TD^{jk}(t_{23})$	0	0	0	1	−1	0	−1	1	0	−2	4
$TD^{jk}(t_{12})$	1	−1	0	−1	1	0	0	0	0	4	−1
$TD^{j\ell}(t_{23})$	0	0	0	1	0	−1	−1	0	1	−1	4

$$(8.59)$$

It can be seen from (8.59) that an exchange of the satellites for one triple-difference causes a change of the sign in the off-diagonal elements of the matrix $\underline{C}\,C^T$. Therefore, the correlation of $TD^{kj}(t_{12})$ and $TD^{j\ell}(t_{23})$ produces $+1$ as off-diagonal element. Based on a table such as (8.59), each case may be handled with ease. According to Remondi (1984), pp. 142–143, computer program adaptions require only a few simple rules.

8.2.3 Static relative positioning

In a static survey of a single baseline vector between points A and B, the two receivers must stay stationary during the entire observation session. In the following, the single-, double-, and triple-differencing are investigated with respect to the number of observation equations and unknowns. It is assumed that the two sites A and B are able to observe the same satellites at the same epochs. The practical problem of satellite blockage is not considered here. The number of epochs is again denoted by n_t, and n_j denotes the number of satellites.

The undifferenced phase as shown in Eq. (8.9) (where the satellite clock is assumed to be known) is not included here, because there would be no connection (no common unknown) between point A and point B. The two data sets could be solved separately, which would be equivalent to point positioning.

A single-difference may be expressed for each satellite and for each epoch. The number of measurements is, therefore, $n_j\, n_t$. The number of unknowns is written below the corresponding terms of the single-difference equation, cf. Eq. (8.19):

$$\Phi^j_{AB}(t) = \frac{1}{\lambda}\, \varrho^j_{AB}(t) + N^j_{AB} - f^j\, \delta_{AB}(t)$$

$$n_j\, n_t \;\geq\; \quad 3 \quad + n_j + \quad n_t\,.$$

(8.60)

From above, the relation

$$n_t \geq \frac{n_j + 3}{n_j - 1}$$

(8.61)

may be derived. What are, theoretically, the minimum requirements for a solution? One satellite does not provide a solution because the denominator of (8.61) becomes zero. With two satellites, $n_t \geq 5$ results, and for the normal case of four satellites $n_t \geq \frac{7}{3}$ or, consequently, $n_t \geq 3$ is obtained.

For double-differences, the relationship of measurements and unknowns is achieved using the same logic. Note that for one double-difference two satellites are necessary. For n_j satellites, therefore, $n_j - 1$ double-differences are obtained at each epoch so that the total number of double-differences is $(n_j - 1)\, n_t$. The number of unknowns is written below the corresponding terms of the double-difference equation, cf. Eq. (8.22):

$$\Phi^{jk}_{AB}(t) \;=\; \frac{1}{\lambda}\, \varrho^{jk}_{AB}(t) + \quad N^{jk}_{AB}$$

$$(n_j - 1)\, n_t \geq \quad 3 \quad + (n_j - 1)\,.$$

(8.62)

From above, the relation

$$n_t \geq \frac{n_j + 2}{n_j - 1}$$

(8.63)

is obtained. Hence, the minimum number of satellites $n_j = 2$ yields $n_t \geq 4$. In the case of four satellites, a minimum of two epochs is required. To avoid linearly dependent equations when forming double-differences, a reference satellite is used, against which the measurements of the other satellites are differenced. For example, take the case where measurements are made to the satellites $6, 9, 11, 12$, and 6 is used as reference satellite. Then, at each epoch the following double-differences can be formed: (9-6), (11-6), and (12-6). Other double-differences are linear combinations and, thus, linearly dependent. For instance, the double-difference (11-9) can be formed by subtracting (11-6) and (9-6).

The triple-difference model includes only the three unknown point coordinates. For a single triple-difference, two epochs are necessary. Consequently, in the case of n_t epochs, $n_t - 1$ linearly independent epoch combinations are possible. Thus,

$$\Phi_{AB}^{jk}(t_{12}) \quad = \frac{1}{\lambda}\, \varrho_{AB}^{jk}(t_{12})$$

$$(n_j - 1)(n_t - 1) \geq \quad 3 \tag{8.64}$$

are the resulting equations. From above, the relation

$$n_t \geq \frac{n_j + 2}{n_j - 1} \tag{8.65}$$

is obtained. This yields $n_t \geq 4$ epochs when the minimum number of satellites $n_j = 2$ is introduced. For $n_j = 4$ satellites $n_t \geq 2$ epochs are required.

This completes the discussion on static relative positioning. As shown, each of the mathematical models: single-difference, double-difference, triple-difference, may be used. The relationships between the number of observation equations and the number of unknowns will be referred to again in the discussion of the kinematic case.

8.2.4   Kinematic relative positioning

In kinematic relative positioning, the receiver on the known point A of the baseline vector remains fixed. The second receiver moves, and its position is to be determined for arbitrary epochs. The models for single-, double-, and triple-difference implicitly contain the motion in the geometric distance. Considering point B and satellite j, the geometric distance in the static case is given by, cf. (8.2),

$$\varrho_B^j(t) = \sqrt{(X^j(t) - X_B)^2 + (Y^j(t) - Y_B)^2 + (Z^j(t) - Z_B)^2} \tag{8.66}$$

and in the kinematic case by

$$\varrho_B^j(t) = \sqrt{(X^j(t) - X_B(t))^2 + (Y^j(t) - Y_B(t))^2 + (Z^j(t) - Z_B(t))^2} \tag{8.67}$$

where the time dependence for point B appears. In this mathematical model, three coordinates are unknown at each epoch. Thus, the total number of unknown site coordinates is $3\,n_t$ for n_t epochs. The relations between the number of observations and the number of unknowns for the kinematic case follow from static single-, double-, and triple-difference models, cf. Eqs. (8.60), (8.62), (8.64):

$$\text{Single-difference:} \quad n_j\, n_t \qquad\qquad \geq 3\, n_t + n_j + n_t$$

$$\text{Double-difference:} \quad (n_j - 1)\, n_t \qquad \geq 3\, n_t + (n_j - 1) \qquad (8.68)$$

$$\text{Triple-difference:} \quad (n_j - 1)(n_t - 1) \geq 3\, n_t\,.$$

The continuous motion of the roving receiver restricts the available data for the determination of its position to one epoch. But none of the above models provides a useful solution for $n_t = 1$. Thus, these models are modified: the number of unknowns is reduced by eliminating the ambiguity unknowns. Omitting these in the single- and double-difference case leads to the modified observation requirements

$$\text{Single-difference:} \quad n_j \geq 4$$

$$\text{Double-difference:} \quad n_j \geq 4 \qquad\qquad (8.69)$$

for any n_t. Triple-differences could be used if the coordinates of the roving receiver were known at the reference epoch. In this case, the relationship would be $(n_j - 1)(n_t - 1) \geq 3\,(n_t - 1)$ which leads to

$$\text{Triple-difference:} \quad n_j \geq 4 \ . \qquad\qquad (8.70)$$

Hence, all of the models end up again with the fundamental requirement of four simultaneously observable satellites.

Omitting the ambiguities for single- and double-difference means that they must be known. The corresponding equations are simply obtained by rewriting (8.60) and (8.62) with the ambiguities shifted to the left-hand side. The single-differences become

$$\Phi^j_{AB}(t) - N^j_{AB} = \frac{1}{\lambda}\, \varrho^j_{AB}(t) - f^j\, \delta_{AB}(t) \qquad\qquad (8.71)$$

and the double-differences

$$\Phi^{jk}_{AB}(t) - N^{jk}_{AB} = \frac{1}{\lambda}\, \varrho^{jk}_{AB}(t) \qquad\qquad (8.72)$$

where the unknowns now appear only on the right-hand sides. For the triple-difference, reducing the number of unknown points by one presupposes one known position.

Thus, all of the equations can be solved if one position of the moving receiver is known. Preferably (but not necessarily), this will be the starting point of the moving receiver. The baseline related to this starting point is also denoted as the starting vector. With a known starting vector, the ambiguities are determined and are known for all subsequent positions of the roving receiver as long as no loss of signal lock occurs and a minimum of four satellites is in view.

Static initialization
Three methods are available for the determination of the starting vector. In the first method, the moving receiver is initially placed at a known point, creating a known starting vector. The ambiguities can then be calculated from the double-difference model (8.62) as real values and are then fixed to integers. A second method is to perform a static determination of the starting vector. The third initialization technique is the antenna swap method according to B. Remondi. The antenna swap is performed as follows: (1) denote the reference mark as A and the starting position of the moving receiver as B, (2) a few measurements are taken in this configuration, and (3) with continuous tracking, the receiver at A is moved to B, while the receiver at B is moved to A, (4) where again a few measurements are taken. This is sufficient to precisely determine the starting vector in a very short time (e.g., 30 seconds). Usually, the antenna swap is completed by (5) moving the receivers to their starting positions. Detailed explanations and formulas are given in Remondi (1986) and Hofmann-Wellenhof and Remondi (1988).

Kinematic initialization
Special applications require kinematic GPS without static initialization since the moving object whose position is to be calculated is in a permanent motion (e.g., an airplane while flying). Translated to model equations, this means that the most challenging case is the determination of the ambiguities on-the-fly (OTF). The solution requires an instantaneous ambiguity resolution or an instantaneous positioning (i.e., for a single epoch). This strategy sounds very simple and it actually is. The main problem is to find the position as fast and as accurately as possible. This is achieved by starting with approximations for the position and improving them by least squares adjustments or search techniques as described in Sect. 9.1.3.

For more insight, one of the many approaches is presented here. This method was proposed by Remondi (1991a) and is an easily understood and fairly efficient method.

The double-difference

$$\Phi_{AB}^{jk}(t) = \frac{1}{\lambda}\,\varrho_{AB}^{jk}(t) + N_{AB}^{jk} \tag{8.73}$$

for one receiver at A and the second receiver at B for the two satellites j and k at epoch t is defined in (8.62). Since now kinematic GPS is considered, this equation is slightly reformulated to account for the motion of one of the receivers. Therefore, the receivers are numbered 1 and 2 and those terms which are purely receiver dependent get the same indices. Thus,

$$\Phi_{12}^{jk}(t) = \frac{1}{\lambda} \varrho_{AB}^{jk}(t) + N_{12}^{jk} \tag{8.74}$$

shows that the measured phases and the ambiguities are receiver dependent, whereas the distances depend on the locations of sites A and B. Receiver 1 is now assumed to be stationary at site A, while receiver 2 moves and is assumed at site C at an epoch t_i. The double-difference equation

$$\Phi_{12}^{jk}(t_i) = \frac{1}{\lambda} \varrho_{AC}^{jk}(t_i) + N_{12}^{jk} \tag{8.75}$$

reflects this situation. In an undisturbed environment, the ambiguity N_{12}^{jk} is time independent and, thus, does not change during the observation. Unlike the static initialization with a known starting vector, here the position of the reference site B is unknown. Therefore, an approximate value for B must be computed and improved by a search technique. For the approximation, Remondi (1991a) proposes a carrier-smoothed code range solution. According to Eq. (6.25), the code range at an initial epoch t can be calculated from the code range at epoch t_i by subtracting the carrier phase difference measured between these epochs. Thus,

$$R_B^j(t) = R_B^j(t_i) - \lambda \left[\Phi_B^j(t_i) - \Phi_B^j(t) \right] + \varepsilon \tag{8.76}$$

follows where a noise term ε has been added. This equation may be interpreted as a mapping of epoch t_i to epoch t and allows an averaging (i.e., smoothing) of the initial code range. By means of such smoothed code ranges to at least $j = 4$ satellites, the position of B is calculated as described in Sect. 8.1.1. Afterwards, a search technique supplemented by Doppler observables is initialized to improve the position of B so that the ambiguities in (8.74) can be fixed to integer values. The integer ambiguities are then substituted into (8.75) and enable the calculation of site C at an epoch t_i.

8.2.5   Mixed-mode relative positioning

The combination of static and kinematic relative positioning implies a noncontinuous motion. The moving receiver stops at the points being surveyed. Hence, there are generally measurement data of more than one epoch per point. The trajectory between the stop points is of no interest to land surveyors, and the corresponding data may be discarded if the remaining data are problem free. Nevertheless, the tracking while in motion must not be interrupted; otherwise a new initialization (i.e., determination of a starting vector) must be performed.

Pseudokinematic relative positioning deserves special treatment. The notation is somehow misleading because the method is more static than kinematic. However, the name has been chosen by its inventor and will be used here. This method should better be called intermittent static or broken static, cf. Remondi (1990b). The pseudokinematic technique requires that each point to be surveyed is reoccupied. There is no requirement to maintain lock between the two occupations. This means that, in principle, the receiver may be turned off while moving.

The pseudokinematic observation data are collected and processed in the same way as static observations. The data collected while the receiver was moving are ignored. Since each site is reoccupied, the pseudokinematic method can be identified with static surveying with large data gaps, cf. Kleusberg (1990a). The mathematical model, e.g., for double-differences, corresponds to Eq. (8.62) where generally two sets of phase ambiguities must be resolved since the point is occupied at different times. Following a proposal by Remondi (1990b), processing of the data could start with a triple-difference solution for the few minutes of data collected during the two occupations of a site. Based on this solution, the connection between the two ambiguity sets is computed. This technique will only work in cases where the triple-difference solution is sufficiently good; Remondi (1990b) claims roughly 30 cm. After the successful ambiguity connection, the normal double-difference solutions are performed.

The time span between the two occupations is an important factor affecting accuracy. The solution depends on the change in the satellite-receiver geometry. Willis and Boucher (1990) investigate the accuracy improvements by an increasing time span between the two occupations. As a rule of thumb, the minimum time span should be one hour.

9 Data processing

9.1 Data preprocessing

9.1.1 Data handling

Download
The observables as well as the navigation message and additional information are generally stored in a binary (and receiver dependent) format. The downloading of the data from the receiver is necessary before processing can begin.

Most GPS manufacturers have designed a data management system which they recommend for processing data. Individual manufacturers' software is fully documented in their manuals and will not be covered here. In the following sections, a general universal processing scheme is provided which describes the basic principles used.

Data management
During a multisession and multibaseline GPS survey, a large amount of data in the Gigabyte range may be collected. In order to archive and to process these data in a reasonable time, an appropriate data structure has to be used. Among different concepts, one based on site and session tables is described here.

Assume a GPS survey including six points and using four receivers. With two overlapping points, two sessions are needed according to Eq. (7.8). In the corresponding site and session table, cf. Table 9.1, the occupation of a site in a session is marked by an asterisk. This table immediately shows

Table 9.1. Site and session table

Site	Session a	Session b
P1	*	*
P2	*	
P3		*
P4		*
P5	*	
P6	*	*

which sites have been included in a certain session, or, inversely, during
which sessions a certain site has been occupied. The first question is more
relevant, as it determines which baselines can be computed from a certain
session. For this reason, computer storage based on sessions is preferable.

The header of each session file should contain the session identifier and
a list of the occupied sites. The header is followed by data blocks. The first
block could contain the navigation messages for all satellites tracked during
that session. For each site, an additional block could be reserved to store
the following data:

1. Measured data (e.g., carrier phases, code ranges, meteorological data).

2. Intermediate results (e.g., navigation solution, diagnostic messages).

3. Supplementary information (e.g., site description, receiver, field crew).

Figure 9.1, for example, represents the file for the first session of the survey.
According to Knuth (1978), this type of storage is called a linear list where
the data are addressed by the use of pointers. To find the data for a certain
site, one has simply to search in the header for the site identifier, and the
corresponding data are accessed by the pointer.

Data exchange
Although the binary receiver data may have been converted into computer
independent ASCII format during downloading, the data are still receiver
dependent. In this case, the data management previously described is appropriate only when (in each session) one receiver type is used. Also, each GPS
processing software has its own format which necessitates the conversion of
specific data into a software independent format when they are processed
with a different type of program.

Header	Session: a Sites: P1, P2, P5, P6
	Satellite data
	P1 site data
Data blocks	P2 site data
	P5 site data
	P6 site data

Fig. 9.1. Data management by a linear list

From the preceding, one may conclude that a receiver independent format
of GPS data promotes data exchange. This has been realized by the Receiver
Independent Exchange (RINEX) format. This format was first defined by
Gurtner et al. (1989b) and has been published in a second version by Gurtner
and Mader (1990). The format consists of three types of ASCII files: (1) the
observation data file containing the range data, (2) the meteorological data
file, and (3) the navigation message file. The records of the files have variable
lengths with a maximum of 80 characters per line. Each file is composed of
a header section and a data section. The header section contains generic file
information, and the data section contains the actual data. The observation
and meteorological data files must be created for each site of the session,
while the navigation message file is site independent. A detailed description
of RINEX (version 2) is given in Tables 9.2 to 9.7.

Table 9.2. RINEX observation data file (header section)

Record	Description	Format
1	Format version	I6, 14X
	File type ("O" for observation data)	A1, 19X
	Satellite system ("G" or blank for GPS)	A1, 19X
2	Name of program creating current file	A20
	Name of agency creating current file	A20
	Date of file creation	A20
Option	Comment(s)	A60
3	Marker name	A60
Option	Marker number	A60
4	Name of observer and name of agency	A20, A40
5	Receiver number, type, and version	3A20
6	Antenna number and type	2A20
7	Approximate marker position (X, Y, Z)	3F14.4
8	Antenna eccentricities (H, E, N)	3F14.4
9	Wavelength factor for L1 and L2 (1=full cycle)	2I6
10	Number of observation types	I6
	Observation types (L=phase; C, P=code range; D=Doppler; T=Integrated Doppler)	9(4X, A2)
Option	Observation interval in seconds	I6
11	Time of first observation (year with 4 digits, month, day, hour, minute, second)	5I6, F12.6
Option	Additional comment(s)	A60
12	End of header indicator	60X

Table 9.3. RINEX observation data file (data section)

Record	Description	Format
1	Epoch (year with 2 digits, month, day, hour, minute, second)	5I3, F11.7
	Flag (0=o.k., 1=power failure, > 1=event)	I3
	Number of satellites in current epoch	I3
	List of PRNs in current epoch (if more than 12 satellites continued in next record)	12(A1, I2)
	Receiver clock offset in seconds (optional)	F12.9
2	Five observations (phase in cycles, code range in meters, Doppler in Hertz)	5(F14.3,
	Loss of lock indicator for phases (0=o.k.)	I1,
	Signal strength (9=maximum, 0=not known)	I1)
3	Continuation if more than five observations	F14.3, 2I1
Record 2 is repeated for each satellite in current epoch		

Table 9.4. RINEX meteorological data file (header section)

Record	Description	Format
1	Format version	I6, 14X
	File type ("M" for meterological data)	A1, 19X
Option	Additional comment(s)	A60
2	Number of observations	I6
	Types of observations (PR=pressure, TD=dry temperature, HR=relative humidity)	4(4X, A2)
5	End of header indicator	60X

Table 9.5. RINEX meteorological data file (data section)

Record	Description	Format
1	Epoch (year with 2 digits, month, day, hour, minute, second)	6I3
	Meteorological data	4F6.1

Table 9.6. RINEX navigation message file (header section)

Record	Description	Format
1	Format version	I6, 14X
	File type ("N" for navigation data)	A1, 19X
Option	Additional comment(s)	A60
2	End of header indicator	60X

Table 9.7. RINEX navigation message file (data section)

Record	Description	Format
1	Satellite PRN number	I2
	Epoch (year with 2 digits, month, day, hour, minute, second)	5I3, F5.1
	Clock bias (s), drift, drift rate (s^{-1})	3D19.12
2	Age of data ephemerides (s)	3X, D19.12
	Sine term for r-correction (m)	D19.12
	Mean motion difference (rad s^{-1})	D19.12
	Mean anomaly (rad)	D19.12
3	Cosine term for u-correction (rad)	3X, D19.12
	Eccentricity	D19.12
	Sine term for u-correction (rad)	D19.12
	Square root of semimajor axis ($\sqrt{m}$)	D19.12
4	Time of ephemerides (seconds of GPS week)	3X, D19.12
	Cosine term for i-correction (rad)	D19.12
	Node's longitude (rad)	D19.12
	Sine term for i-correction (rad)	D19.12
5	Inclination (rad)	3X, D19.12
	Cosine term for r-correction (m)	D19.12
	Argument of perigee (rad)	D19.12
	Rate of node's longitude (rad s^{-1})	D19.12
6	Rate of inclination (rad s^{-1})	3X, D19.12
	Codes on L2 channel	D19.12
	GPS week	D19.12
	L2 P data flag	D19.12
7	Satellite's accuracy and health	3X, 2D19.12
	Ionospheric group delay (seconds)	D19.12
	Age of data clock (seconds)	D19.12
8	Transmission time of message, 3 spares	3X, 4D19.12

At present, RINEX is the most favored format. As a consequence, some receiver manufacturers produce software for the conversion of their receiver dependent format into RINEX. The U.S. National Geodetic Survey (NGS) has acted as a coordinator for these efforts. For a detailed description of the RINEX format, the reader is referred to the cited literature.

RINEX uses the file naming convention "ssssdddf.yyt". The first four characters of the sequence (ssss) are the site identifier, the next three (ddd) indicate the day of year, and the eighth character (f) is the session number. The first two file extension characters (yy) denote the last two digits of the current year, and the file type (t) is given by the last character. The satellite designation is in the form "snn". The first character (s) is an identifier of the satellite system, and the remaining two digits denote the satellite number (e.g., the PRN number). Thus, the RINEX format enables the possible combination of different satellite observations such as GPS and TRANSIT.

9.1.2   Cycle slip detection and repair

Definition of cycle slips

When a receiver is turned on, the fractional beat phase (i.e., the difference between the satellite transmitted carrier and a receiver generated replica signal) is observed and an integer counter is initialized. During tracking, the counter is incremented by one cycle whenever the fractional phase changes from 2π to 0. Thus, at a given epoch, the observed accumulated phase $\Delta\varphi$, cf. Remondi (1984) or Remondi (1985), is the sum of the fractional phase φ and the integer count n. The initial integer number N of cycles between the satellite and the receiver is unknown. This phase ambiguity N remains constant as long as no loss of the signal lock occurs. In this event, the integer counter is reinitialized which causes a jump in the instantaneous accumulated phase by an integer number of cycles. This jump is called cycle slip which, of course, is restricted to phase measurements.

A graphical representation of a cycle slip is given in Fig. 9.2, cf. Hofmann-Wellenhof and Lichtenegger (1988), p. 98. When the measured phases are plotted versus time, a fairly smooth curve should be obtained. In the case of a cycle slip, a sudden jump appears in the plotted curve.

Three sources for cycle slips can be distinguished. First, cycle slips are caused by obstructions of the satellite signal due to trees, buildings, bridges, mountains, etc. This source is the most frequent one. The second source for cycle slips is a low SNR due to bad ionospheric conditions, multipath, high receiver dynamics, or low satellite elevation. A third source is a failure in the receiver software, cf. Hein (1990b), which leads to incorrect signal processing. Cycle slips could also be caused by malfunctioning satellite oscillators, but

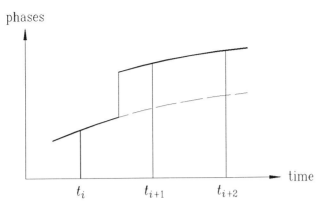

Fig. 9.2. Graphical representation of a cycle slip

these cases are rare.

As seen from Fig. 9.2, cycle slip detection and repair requires the location of the jump (i.e., cycle slip) and the determination of its size. Detection is accomplished by a testing quantity. In the example given, this is the measured raw phase. Repairs of cycle slips are made by correcting all subsequent phase observations for this satellite and this carrier by a fixed amount. The determination of the cycle slip size and the correction of the phase data is often denoted as cycle slip "fixing".

Testing quantities
The formulation of testing quantities is based on measured carrier phases and code ranges. For a single site, the testing quantities are raw phases, phase combinations, combinations of phases and code ranges, or combinations of phases and integrated Doppler frequencies. Table 9.8 summarizes a number of candidate testing quantities for a single site. Single receiver tests are important because they enable in situ cycle slip detection and repair by the receiver's internal software. When two sites are involved, single-, double-, and triple-differences provide testing quantities.

The measured raw phase $\Phi_i^j(t)$ can be modeled by

$$\lambda \, \Phi_i^j(t) = \varrho_i^j(t) + \lambda \, N_i^j + c \, \Delta \delta_i^j(t) - \frac{A_i^j(t)}{f^2} + \ldots \tag{9.1}$$

where i and j denote the site and the satellite respectively. The term $A_i^j(t)$ has been substituted for $(40.3 \, \text{TVEC}/\cos z')$ according to Eq. (6.59). Note that the phase model contains a number of time dependent terms on the right-hand side which may prevent cycle slip detection.

Table 9.8. Testing quantities to detect cycle slips for a single site

Required data	Testing quantity
Single frequency phase ($L1$ or $L2$)	Raw phase
Dual frequency phases ($L1$ and $L2$)	Phase combination (ionospheric residual)
Single frequency phase and code range	Phase and code range combination
Single frequency phase and Doppler	Phase and integrated Doppler combination

The model for the dual frequency phase combination is developed considering a single site and a single satellite. Thus, the sub- and superscripts in Eq. (9.1) may be omitted; whereas, the frequency dependency is shown explicitly by the subscripts $L1$ and $L2$:

$$\lambda_{L1}\,\Phi_{L1}(t) = \varrho(t) + \lambda_{L1}\,N_{L1} + c\,\Delta\delta(t) - \frac{A(t)}{f_{L1}^2} + \dots$$

$$\lambda_{L2}\,\Phi_{L2}(t) = \varrho(t) + \lambda_{L2}\,N_{L2} + c\,\Delta\delta(t) - \frac{A(t)}{f_{L2}^2} + \dots$$

$$(9.2)$$

In the difference of the two equations,

$$\lambda_{L1}\,\Phi_{L1}(t) - \lambda_{L2}\,\Phi_{L2}(t) = \lambda_{L1}\,N_{L1} - \lambda_{L2}\,N_{L2} - \frac{A(t)}{f_{L1}^2} + \frac{A(t)}{f_{L2}^2},$$

$$(9.3)$$

the frequency independent terms (i.e., the geometric distance and the clock error) vanish. Dividing (9.3) by λ_{L1} provides

$$\Phi_{L1}(t) - \frac{\lambda_{L2}}{\lambda_{L1}}\,\Phi_{L2}(t) = N_{L1} - \frac{\lambda_{L2}}{\lambda_{L1}}\,N_{L2} - \frac{A(t)}{\lambda_{L1}}\left(\frac{1}{f_{L1}^2} - \frac{1}{f_{L2}^2}\right)$$

$$(9.4)$$

which may be slightly transformed by introducing

$$\frac{\lambda_{L2}}{\lambda_{L1}} = \frac{f_{L1}}{f_{L2}}$$

$$(9.5)$$

which follows from $c = \lambda f$. Therefore,

$$\Phi_{L1}(t) - \frac{f_{L1}}{f_{L2}} \Phi_{L2}(t) = N_{L1} - \frac{f_{L1}}{f_{L2}} N_{L2} - \frac{A(t)}{\lambda_{L1}} \left(\frac{1}{f_{L1}^2} - \frac{1}{f_{L2}^2} \right)$$

(9.6)

is obtained, and

$$\Phi_{L1}(t) - \frac{f_{L1}}{f_{L2}} \Phi_{L2}(t) = N_{L1} - \frac{f_{L1}}{f_{L2}} N_{L2} - \frac{A(t)}{\lambda_{L1} f_{L1}^2} \left(1 - \frac{f_{L1}^2}{f_{L2}^2} \right)$$

(9.7)

is the final form of the dual frequency combination. This model is often denoted as the ionospheric residual, cf. Goad (1986). The right-hand side of Eq. (9.7) shows that the ionospheric residual does not contain time varying terms except for the ionospheric refraction. In comparison to the influence on the raw phases in Eq. (9.1), the influence of the ionosphere on the dual frequency combination is reduced by a factor $(1 - (f_{L1}/f_{L2})^2)$. Substituting the appropriate values for f_{L1} and f_{L2} yields a reduction of 65%, cf. Goad (1986).

If there are no cycle slips, the temporal variations of the ionospheric residual would be small for normal ionospheric conditions and for short baselines. Indicators of cycle slips are sudden jumps in successive values of the ionospheric residual. The remaining problem is to determine whether the cycle slip was on $L1$, $L2$, or both. This will be investigated in the next paragraph.

Note that the ionospheric residual

$$\Phi_{L1}(t) - \frac{f_{L1}}{f_{L2}} \Phi_{L2}(t)$$

is a scaled difference of dual frequency phases just as the ionospheric-free linear combination

$$\Phi_{L1}(t) - \frac{f_{L2}}{f_{L1}} \Phi_{L2}(t),$$

cf. Eq. (6.80). These two expressions differ, essentially, by the reciprocal nature of the Φ_{L2} coefficients.

Another testing quantity follows from a phase and code range combination. Modeling the carrier phase and the code pseudoranges by

$$\lambda \Phi_i^j(t) = \varrho_i^j(t) + \lambda N_i^j + c \Delta \delta_i^j(t) - \Delta^{\text{Iono}}(t) + \Delta^{\text{Trop}}(t)$$

$$R_i^j(t) = \varrho_i^j(t) + c \Delta \delta_i^j(t) + \Delta^{\text{Iono}}(t) + \Delta^{\text{Trop}}(t)$$

(9.8)

and forming the difference

$$\lambda\,\Phi_i^j(t) - R_i^j(t) = \lambda\,N_i^j - 2\,\Delta^{\mathrm{Iono}}(t) \tag{9.9}$$

provides a formula where the time dependent terms (except the ionospheric refraction) vanish from the right-hand side. Thus, the phase and code range combination could also be used as testing quantity. The ionospheric influence may either be modeled, cf. for example Beutler et al. (1987b), or neglected. The change of $\Delta^{\mathrm{Iono}}(t)$ will be fairly small between closely spaced epochs; this might justify neglecting the ionospheric term. It may also be neglected when using double-differences.

The simple testing quantity (9.9) has a shortcoming which is related to the noise level. Bastos and Landau (1988) show a noise level in the range of ten cycles for time series of the phase and code range combinations. This noise is mainly caused by the noise level of the code measurements and to a minor extent by the ionosphere. The noise of code measurements is larger than the noise for phase measurements because resolution and multipath are proportional to the wavelength. Traditionally, the measurement resolution was $\lambda/100$; today's receiver hardware are achieving improved measurement resolutions approaching $\lambda/1000$. In other words, this would lead to code range noise levels of a few centimeters. Hence, the phase and code range combination would be an ideal testing quantity for cycle slip detection.

Allison and Eschenbach (1989) compare differences of measured phases with phase differences derived from integrated Doppler which has the advantage of being immune from cycle slips. The list of testing quantities in Table 9.8 is not complete. Bock and Shimada (1989) propose the wide lane signal, cf. Eq. (6.16), as testing quantity.

When the data of two sites are combined, single-, double-, or triple-differences can be used for cycle slip detection, cf. for example Goad (1985), Remondi (1985), Hilla (1986), Beutler et al. (1987c). This means that, in a first step, unrepaired phase combinations are used to process an approximate baseline vector. The corresponding residuals are then tested. Quite often several iterations are necessary to improve the baseline solution. Note that triple-differences can achieve convergence and rather high accuracy without fixing cycle slips.

Detection and repair
Each of the described testing quantities allows the location of cycle slips by checking the difference of two consecutive epoch values. This also yields an approximate size of the cycle slip. To find the correct size, the time series of the testing quantity must be investigated in more detail. Note that in

the case of phases, phase and code range combinations, phase and Doppler combinations, single-, double-, and triple-differences, the detected cycle slip must be an integer. This is not true for the ionospheric residual.

One of the methods for cycle slip detection is the scheme of differences. The principle can be seen from an example given in Lichtenegger and Hofmann-Wellenhof (1989). Assume $y(t_i)$, $i = 1, 2, \ldots, 7$ as a time series for a signal which contains a jump of ε at epoch t_4:

t_i	$y(t_i)$	y^1	y^2	y^3	y^4
t_1	0				
		0			
t_2	0		0		
		0		ε	
t_3	0		ε		-3ε
		ε		-2ε	
t_4	ε		$-\varepsilon$		3ε
		0		ε	
t_5	ε		0		$-\varepsilon$
		0		0	
t_6	ε		0		
		0			
t_7	ε				

In this scheme, y^1, y^2, y^3, y^4 denote the first-order, second-order, third-order, and fourth-order differences. The important property in the context of data irregularities is the amplification of a jump in higher-order differences and, thus, the improved possibility of detecting the jump. The theoretical reason implied is the fact that differences are generated by subtractive filters. These are high-pass filters damping low frequencies and eliminating constant parts. High frequency constituents such as a jump are amplified. Replacing the signal $y(t_i)$ for example by the phase and assuming ε to be a cycle slip, the effect of the scheme of differences becomes evident. Any of the described testing quantities may be used as signal for the scheme of differences.

A method to determine the size of a cycle slip is to fit a curve through the testing quantities before and after the cycle slip. The size of the cycle slip is found from the shift between the two curves. The fits may be obtained from a simple linear regression, cf. Mader (1986), or from more realistic least squares models, cf. Beutler et al. (1984) or Cross and Ahmad (1988). These methods are generally called interpolation techniques. Other possibilities are prediction methods such as the Kalman filtering. At a certain epoch, the function value (i.e., one of the testing quantities) for the next epoch is predicted based on the information obtained from preceding function values. The predicted value is then compared with the observed value to detect a cycle slip. The application of Kalman filtering for cycle slip detection is proposed by, e.g., Goad (1986) and demonstrated in detail by, e.g., Landau (1988). More details on the Kalman filtering are provided in Sect. 9.2.2.

When a cycle slip has been detected (by one of the methods previously discussed), the testing quantities can be corrected by adding the size of the cycle slip to each of the subsequent quantities. Hilla (1986) and Cross and Ahmad (1988) report the details of this process.

The assignment of the detected cycle slip to a single phase observation is ambiguous in the case the testing quantities were phase combinations. An exception is the ionospheric residual. Under special circumstances, this testing quantity permits a unique separation, cf. Lichtenegger and Hofmann-Wellenhof (1989). Consider Eq. (9.7) and assume ambiguity changes ΔN_{L1} and ΔN_{L2} caused by cycle slips. Consequently, a jump ΔN in the ionospheric residual would be detected. This jump is equivalent to

$$\Delta N = \Delta N_{L1} - \frac{f_{L1}}{f_{L2}} \Delta N_{L2} \qquad (9.10)$$

where ΔN is no longer an integer. Equation (9.10) represents a diophantine equation for the two integer unknowns ΔN_{L1} and ΔN_{L2}. One equation and two unknowns; hence, there is no unique solution. This can be seen by solving for integer values ΔN_{L1} and ΔN_{L2} such that ΔN becomes zero. To get $\Delta N = 0$, the condition

$$\Delta N_{L1} = \frac{f_{L1}}{f_{L2}} \Delta N_{L2} = \frac{154}{120} \Delta N_{L2} \qquad (9.11)$$

must be fulfilled which may be rewritten as

$$\Delta N_{L1} = \frac{77}{60} \Delta N_{L2} \,. \qquad (9.12)$$

As an example, this means that $\Delta N_{L1} = 77$ and $\Delta N_{L2} = 60$ cannot be distinguished from $\Delta N_{L1} = 154$ and $\Delta N_{L2} = 120$ since both solutions satisfy Eq. (9.12). However, the solution would be unambiguous if ΔN_{L1} is less than 77 cycles. The consideration so far assumed error free measurements. To be more realistic, the effect of measurement noise must be taken into account. A simple model for the phase measurement noise is

$$m_\Phi = \pm 0.01 \text{ cycles} \qquad (9.13)$$

which corresponds to a resolution of $\lambda/100$. The same model is applied to both carriers $L1$ and $L2$ and, thus, frequency dependent noise such as multipath is neglected. The assumption is not correct for codeless or quasi-codeless receivers since additional noise is introduced during signal processing, cf. Table 5.4.

The value ΔN, in principle, is derived from two consecutive ionospheric residuals. Hence,

$$\Delta N = \Phi_{L1}(t + \Delta t) - \frac{f_{L1}}{f_{L2}} \Phi_{L2}(t + \Delta t)$$
$$- \left[\Phi_{L1}(t) - \frac{f_{L1}}{f_{L2}} \Phi_{L2}(t) \right] \tag{9.14}$$

and applying to this equation the error propagation law gives

$$m_{\Delta N} = \pm 2.3 \, m_\Phi = \pm 0.023 \, \text{cycles} \, . \tag{9.15}$$

The 3σ-error, therefore, yields approximately ± 0.07 cycles. This may be interpreted as the resolution of ΔN. The conclusion is that two ΔN calculated by (9.10) and using arbitrary integers ΔN_{L1} and ΔN_{L2} must differ by at least 0.07 cycles in order to be uniquely separable. A systematic investigation of the lowest values for ΔN_{L1}, ΔN_{L2} is given in Table 9.9. For ΔN_{L1} and ΔN_{L2}, the values $0, \pm 1, \pm 2, \ldots, \pm 5$ have been permutated and ΔN calculated by (9.10). Table 9.9 is sorted with increasing ΔN in column one. In the second column, the difference of the respective two neighboring function values ΔN is given. To shorten the length of the table, only the negative function values ΔN and zero are displayed. For supplementing with positive function values, the three signs in a row must be reversed.

Those rows in Table 9.9 being marked with an asterisk do not fulfill the criterion of an at least 0.07 cycle difference. For these values, an unambiguous separation is not possible because the measurement noise is larger than the separation value. Consider the next to the last row in Table 9.9. A jump in the ionospheric residual of about 0.14 cycle could result from the pair of cycle slips $\Delta N_{L1} = -4$, $\Delta N_{L2} = -3$ or $\Delta N_{L1} = 5$, $\Delta N_{L2} = 4$; however, notice that for the marked lines either ΔN_{L1} or ΔN_{L2} equals 5 (plus or minus). Therefore, omitting the values for $\Delta N_{L1} = \pm 5$ and $\Delta N_{L2} = \pm 5$ creates uniqueness in the sense of separability. Up to ± 4 cycles the function values ΔN are discernible by 0.12 cycles.

The conclusions reached for the cycle slip method based on the dual frequency data combination are as follows. Based on the measurement noise assumption in (9.13), the separation of the cycle slips is unambiguously possible for up to ± 4 cycles. A smaller measurement noise increases the separability. For larger cycle slips, another method should be used in order to avoid making a wrong choice in ambiguous situations. Westrop et al. (1989)

Table 9.9. Resulting ΔN by permutating ΔN_{L1} and ΔN_{L2}

ΔN	Diff.	ΔN_{L1}	ΔN_{L2}		ΔN	Diff.	ΔN_{L1}	ΔN_{L2}	
−11.42		−5	5		−3.72		−5	−1	
−10.42	1.00	−4	5		−3.56	0.16	−1	2	
−10.13	0.29	−5	4		−3.42	0.14	3	5	
−9.42	0.71	−3	5		−3.28	0.14	−2	1	
−9.13	0.29	−4	4		−3.13	0.15	2	4	
−8.85	0.28	−5	3		−3.00	0.13	−3	0	
−8.42	0.43	−2	5		−2.85	0.15	1	3	
−8.13	0.29	−3	4		−2.72	0.13	−4	−1	
−7.85	0.28	−4	3		−2.56	0.16	0	2	
−7.56	0.29	−5	2		−2.44	0.12	−5	−2	
−7.42	0.14	−1	5		−2.42	0.02	4	5	*
−7.13	0.29	−2	4		−2.28	0.14	−1	1	
−6.85	0.28	−3	3		−2.13	0.15	3	4	
−6.56	0.29	−4	2		−2.00	0.13	−2	0	
−6.42	0.14	0	5		−1.85	0.15	2	3	
−6.28	0.14	−5	1		−1.52	0.13	−3	−1	
−6.13	0.15	−1	4		−1.56	0.16	1	2	
−5.85	0.28	−2	−3		−1.44	0.12	−4	−2	
−5.56	0.29	−3	2		−1.42	0.02	5	5	*
−5.42	0.14	1	5		−1.28	0.14	0	1	
−5.28	0.14	−4	1		−1.15	0.13	−5	−3	*
−5.13	0.15	0	4		−1.13	0.02	4	4	
−5.00	0.13	−5	0		−1.00	0.13	−1	0	
−4.85	0.15	−1	3		−0.85	0.15	3	3	
−4.56	0.29	−2	2		−0.72	0.13	−2	−1	
−4.42	0.14	2	5		−0.56	0.16	2	2	
−4.28	0.14	−3	1		−0.44	0.12	−3	−2	
−4.13	0.15	1	4		−0.28	0.16	1	1	
−4.00	0.13	−4	0		−0.15	0.13	−4	−3	
−3.85	0.15	0	3		−0.13	0.02	5	4	*
−3.72	0.13	−5	−1		0.00	0.13	0	0	

mention a phase and code range combination but cite possible failures since the code range noise can be larger than ±4 cycles.

Most often, there will be more than one cycle slip. In these cases, each cycle slip must be detected and corrected in turn. The corrected phases, single-, double- or triple-differences are then used to process the baseline.

9.1.3 Ambiguity resolution

The ambiguity inherent with phase measurements depends upon both the receiver and the satellite. There is no time dependency as long as tracking is maintained without interruption. In the model for the phase,

$$\Phi = \frac{1}{\lambda}\varrho + f\,\Delta\delta + N - \frac{1}{\lambda}\Delta^{\text{Iono}}\,, \tag{9.16}$$

the ambiguity is denoted by N. As soon as the ambiguity is determined as an integer value, the ambiguity is said to be resolved or fixed, cf. Counselman and Abbot (1989). This is very important for the solution of the baseline vectors since, in general, the ambiguity resolution strengthens the baseline solution, cf. Goad (1985). There are, however, some exceptional situations. Rothacher et al. (1989) demonstrate an example where the solutions with fixed ambiguities and floating ambiguities (i.e., real values) agree within a few millimeters. Nevertheless, resolution of the ambiguities generally improves vector accuracy.

Only a few key principles from the numerous kinds of ambiguity resolution techniques will be demonstrated. Many variations may be derived from these basic methods.

Resolving ambiguities with single frequency phase data
When phase measurements for only one frequency ($L1$ or $L2$) are available, the most direct approach is as follows. The measurements are modeled by Eq. (9.16), and the linearized equations are processed. Depending on the model chosen, a number of unknowns (e.g., point coordinates, clock parameters, etc.) is estimated along with N in a common adjustment. In this geometric approach, the unmodeled errors affect all estimated parameters. Therefore, the integer nature of the ambiguities is lost and they are estimated as real values. Many error sources affect the closeness of the estimated ambiguities to their integer values. Some of these sources are: the incomplete phase model, the baseline length (because of varying atmospheric conditions), and orbital errors. To fix ambiguities to integer values, a sequential adjustment could be performed, cf. Blewitt (1987). After an initial adjustment, the ambiguity with a computed value closest to an integer and with minimum standard error is considered to be determined most reliably. This bias is then fixed, and the adjustment is repeated (with one less unknown) to fix another ambiguity and so on. When using double-differences over short baselines, this approach is usually successful. The critical factor is the ionospheric refraction which must be modeled and which may prevent a correct resolution of all ambiguities.

Resolving ambiguities with dual frequency phase data
The situation for the ambiguity resolution changes significantly when using dual frequency phase data. There are many advantages implied in dual frequency data because of the various possible linear combinations that can be

formed. Wide lane and narrow lane techniques have been proposed, e.g., by Counselman et al. (1979), Hatch (1982), Hatch and Larson (1985). Denoting the $L1$ and $L2$ phase data Φ_{L1} and Φ_{L2}, then, according to Eq. (6.16),

$$\Phi_w = \Phi_{L1} - \Phi_{L2} \tag{9.17}$$

is the wide lane signal. The frequency of this signal is $f_w = 347.82\,\text{MHz}$ and the corresponding wavelength $\lambda_w = 86.2\,\text{cm}$. This is a significant increase compared to the original wavelengths of 19.0 and 24.4 cm. The increased wide lane wavelength λ_w provides an increased ambiguity spacing. This is the key to easier resolution of the integer ambiguities. To show the principle, consider the phase models for the carriers $L1$ and $L2$:

$$\begin{aligned}
\Phi_{L1} &= \frac{1}{\lambda_{L1}}\varrho + f_{L1}\,\Delta\delta + N_{L1} - \frac{1}{\lambda_{L1}}\Delta^{\text{Iono}}(f_{L1}) \\
\Phi_{L2} &= \frac{1}{\lambda_{L2}}\varrho + f_{L2}\,\Delta\delta + N_{L2} - \frac{1}{\lambda_{L2}}\Delta^{\text{Iono}}(f_{L2})\,.
\end{aligned} \tag{9.18}$$

Replacing λ by frequency f via $\lambda = c/f$ and substituting for the ionospheric term $\Delta^{\text{Iono}}(f) = A/f^2$ correspondingly leads to

$$\begin{aligned}
\Phi_{L1} &= \frac{f_{L1}}{c}\varrho + f_{L1}\,\Delta\delta + N_{L1} - \frac{A}{c\,f_{L1}} \\
\Phi_{L2} &= \frac{f_{L2}}{c}\varrho + f_{L2}\,\Delta\delta + N_{L2} - \frac{A}{c\,f_{L2}}\,.
\end{aligned} \tag{9.19}$$

The difference of the two equations gives

$$\Phi_w = \frac{f_w}{c}\varrho + f_w\,\Delta\delta + N_w - \frac{A}{c}\left(\frac{1}{f_{L1}} - \frac{1}{f_{L2}}\right) \tag{9.20}$$

with the wide lane quantities

$$\Phi_w = \Phi_{L1} - \Phi_{L2}$$

$$f_w = f_{L1} - f_{L2}$$

$$N_w = N_{L1} - N_{L2}\,.$$

The adjustment based on the wide lane model gives wide lane ambiguities N_w which are more easily resolved than the base carrier ambiguities. To compute the ambiguities for the measured phases (e.g., for $L1$), divide the first equation of (9.19) by f_{L1} and (9.20) by f_w, and form the difference of the two equations. This gives

$$\frac{1}{f_{L1}} \Phi_{L1} - \frac{1}{f_w} \Phi_w = \frac{N_{L1}}{f_{L1}} - \frac{N_w}{f_w} - \frac{A}{c f_{L1}^2} + \frac{A}{c f_w} \left(\frac{1}{f_{L1}} - \frac{1}{f_{L2}} \right),$$

(9.21)

and the desired ambiguity N_{L1} follows explicitly after rearranging and multiplying the equation above by f_{L1}:

$$N_{L1} = \Phi_{L1} - (\Phi_w - N_w) \frac{f_{L1}}{f_w} + \frac{A}{c f_{L1}} - \frac{A}{c f_w} \left(1 - \frac{f_{L1}}{f_{L2}} \right).$$

(9.22)

The terms reflecting the ionospheric influence may be grouped as

$$\frac{A}{c} \frac{f_w f_{L2} - f_{L1} f_{L2} + f_{L1}^2}{f_{L1} f_w f_{L2}}$$

(9.23)

which is equivalent to

$$\frac{A}{c} \frac{f_w f_{L2} + f_{L1} (f_{L1} - f_{L2})}{f_{L1} f_w f_{L2}}.$$

(9.24)

The term in parentheses is replaced by the wide lane frequency which then cancels. Thus,

$$\frac{A}{c} \frac{f_{L2} + f_{L1}}{f_{L1} f_{L2}}$$

(9.25)

results from the ionospheric terms. Therefore, the phase ambiguity N_{L1} in (9.22) can be calculated from the wide lane ambiguity by

$$N_{L1} = \Phi_{L1} - (\Phi_w - N_w) \frac{f_{L1}}{f_w} + \frac{A}{c} \frac{f_{L1} + f_{L2}}{f_{L1} f_{L2}}$$

(9.26)

and in an analogous way for N_{L2} by replacing $L1$ by $L2$ and vice versa in the equation above. Note that the distance ϱ and the clock bias term $\Delta\delta$ have dropped out. These terms are, however, implicitly contained in N_w, cf. Eq. (9.20). The ionospheric term is most annoying. This term will cancel for short baselines with similar ionospheric refraction at both endpoints (using differenced phases). For long baselines or irregular ionospheric conditions, however, the ionospheric term may cause problems.

Linear combinations other than wide lane have been considered such as the ionospheric-free linear combination Φ_{L3}. The disadvantage of this combination is that the corresponding ambiguity is no longer an integer. This is a kind of circulus vitiosus: either the ambiguities may be resolved where the ionosphere is a problem or the ionospheric influence is eliminated which destroys the integer nature of the ambiguities. Wübbena (1989) shows the use of other linear combinations ranging from narrow lane with a 10.7 cm wavelength to extra wide laning with a 172.4 cm wavelength.

Resolving ambiguities by combining dual frequency carrier phase and code data

The most unreliable factor of the wide lane technique described in the previous paragraph is the influence of the ionosphere which increases with baseline length. This drawback can be eliminated by a combination of phase and code data. Consider the models for dual frequency carrier phases and code ranges

$$\Phi_{L1} = \frac{\varrho}{c} f_{L1} - \frac{\kappa}{f_{L1}} + N_{L1} + f_{L1} \Delta\delta \tag{9.27}$$

$$\Phi_{L2} = \frac{\varrho}{c} f_{L2} - \frac{\kappa}{f_{L2}} + N_{L2} + f_{L2} \Delta\delta \tag{9.28}$$

$$R_{L1} = \frac{\varrho}{c} f_{L1} + \frac{\kappa}{f_{L1}} \qquad + f_{L1} \Delta\delta \tag{9.29}$$

$$R_{L2} = \frac{\varrho}{c} f_{L2} + \frac{\kappa}{f_{L2}} \qquad + f_{L2} \Delta\delta \tag{9.30}$$

where both are expressed in cycles of the corresponding carrier. The ionospheric term has been simplified by substituting $\kappa = A/c$. Note that four equations are available with four unknowns for each epoch. The unknowns are $(\varrho/c + \Delta\delta)$, κ, and the ambiguities N_{L1}, N_{L2} and may be expressed explicitly as a function of the measured quantities by inverting the system represented by (9.27) through (9.30).

The stepwise calculation of the ambiguities makes use of the wide lane ambiguity $N_w = N_{L1} - N_{L2}$. The derivation of this ambiguity is lengthy, and the impatient reader may continue with (9.42).

By forming the differences between the corresponding carrier and code phases

$$\Phi_{L1} - R_{L1} = -\frac{2\kappa}{f_{L1}} + N_{L1}$$

$$\Phi_{L2} - R_{L2} = -\frac{2\kappa}{f_{L2}} + N_{L2}, \tag{9.31}$$

the geometric distance and the clock bias term are eliminated. The difference of the two equations above yields

$$\Phi_w - R_{L1} + R_{L2} = 2\kappa \left(\frac{1}{f_{L2}} - \frac{1}{f_{L1}} \right) + N_w \tag{9.32}$$

where the wide lane signal Φ_w and the wide lane ambiguity N_w have been substituted. Introducing a common denominator for the expression in the parentheses gives

$$\Phi_w - R_{L1} + R_{L2} = 2\kappa \, \frac{f_{L1} - f_{L2}}{f_{L1} \, f_{L2}} + N_w \, . \tag{9.33}$$

Now, the ionospheric term κ can be calculated by dividing the code ranges (9.29) by f_{L1} and (9.30) by f_{L2}:

$$\begin{aligned}
\frac{R_{L1}}{f_{L1}} &= \frac{\varrho}{c} + \frac{\kappa}{f_{L1}^2} + \Delta\delta \\
\frac{R_{L2}}{f_{L2}} &= \frac{\varrho}{c} + \frac{\kappa}{f_{L2}^2} + \Delta\delta
\end{aligned} \tag{9.34}$$

and, by subtracting the two equations from each other,

$$\frac{R_{L1}}{f_{L1}} - \frac{R_{L2}}{f_{L2}} = \kappa \left(\frac{1}{f_{L1}^2} - \frac{1}{f_{L2}^2} \right) . \tag{9.35}$$

This may be written

$$\frac{f_{L2} \, R_{L1} - f_{L1} \, R_{L2}}{f_{L1} \, f_{L2}} = \kappa \, \frac{f_{L2}^2 - f_{L1}^2}{f_{L1}^2 \, f_{L2}^2} \tag{9.36}$$

or

$$\frac{f_{L2} \, R_{L1} - f_{L1} \, R_{L2}}{f_{L1} \, f_{L2}} = \kappa \, \frac{(f_{L2} - f_{L1}) \, (f_{L2} + f_{L1})}{f_{L1} \, f_{L2}} \tag{9.37}$$

where the denominator cancels. Finally, rewriting the equation and dividing by $f_{L1} + f_{L2}$ yields

$$\frac{f_{L2} \, R_{L1} - f_{L1} \, R_{L2}}{f_{L1} + f_{L2}} = -\kappa \, \frac{f_{L1} - f_{L2}}{f_{L1} \, f_{L2}} \tag{9.38}$$

which may now be substituted into (9.33) to eliminate κ. This step in detail gives

$$\Phi_w - R_{L1} + R_{L2} = -2 \, \frac{f_{L2} \, R_{L1} - f_{L1} \, R_{L2}}{f_{L1} + f_{L2}} + N_w \tag{9.39}$$

which may be rearranged to

$$\begin{aligned}
N_w = \Phi_w + \frac{1}{f_{L1} + f_{L2}} \, &[(-R_{L1} + R_{L2})(f_{L1} + f_{L2}) \\
&+ 2 f_{L2} \, R_{L1} - 2 f_{L1} \, R_{L2}]
\end{aligned} \tag{9.40}$$

or

$$N_w = \Phi_w + \frac{1}{f_{L1} + f_{L2}} [-R_{L1} f_{L1} + R_{L2} f_{L2}$$
$$+ f_{L2} R_{L1} - f_{L1} R_{L2}] \qquad (9.41)$$

and finally

$$N_w = \Phi_w - \frac{f_{L1} - f_{L2}}{f_{L1} + f_{L2}} (R_{L1} + R_{L2}). \qquad (9.42)$$

This rather elegant equation allows for the determination of the wide lane ambiguity N_w for each epoch and each site. It is independent of the baseline length and of the ionospheric effects. Even if all modeled systematic effects cancel out in (9.42), the multipath effect remains and affects phase and code differently. Multipath is almost exclusively responsible for a variation of N_w by several cycles from epoch to epoch, cf. Dong and Bock (1989). These variations may be overcome by averaging over a longer period.

Having calculated the wide lane ambiguities, the use of (9.26) would lead to the ambiguities of the undifferenced phases which are effected by the ionospheric refraction. This can be avoided by the following procedure. Start again with the phase equations

$$\Phi_{L1} = \frac{f_{L1}}{c} \varrho + f_{L1} \Delta\delta + N_{L1} - \frac{\kappa}{f_{L1}}$$
$$\Phi_{L2} = \frac{f_{L2}}{c} \varrho + f_{L2} \Delta\delta + N_{L2} - \frac{\kappa}{f_{L2}} \qquad (9.43)$$

and multiply the first equation by f_{L1} and the second by f_{L2}. The resulting equations are then differenced and, thus,

$$f_{L2} \Phi_{L2} - f_{L1} \Phi_{L1} = \frac{\varrho}{c} (f_{L2}^2 - f_{L1}^2) + \Delta\delta (f_{L2}^2 - f_{L1}^2)$$
$$+ f_{L2} N_{L2} - f_{L1} N_{L1} \qquad (9.44)$$

is obtained. Introducing the wide lane ambiguity by $N_{L2} = N_{L1} - N_w$ leads to

$$f_{L2} \Phi_{L2} - f_{L1} \Phi_{L1} = \frac{\varrho}{c} (f_{L2}^2 - f_{L1}^2) + \Delta\delta (f_{L2}^2 - f_{L1}^2)$$
$$- f_{L2} N_w + N_{L1} (f_{L2} - f_{L1}) \qquad (9.45)$$

or, with $f_w = f_{L1} - f_{L2}$,

$$N_{L1} = \frac{f_{L1}}{f_w} \Phi_{L1} - \frac{f_{L2}}{f_w} (\Phi_{L2} + N_w) - (\frac{\varrho}{c} + \Delta\delta)(f_{L1} + f_{L2}) \qquad (9.46)$$

which is an ionospherically free equation for the determination of the N_{L1} ambiguities. Note that N_w has been determined by (9.42). A final remark concerning the formula above is appropriate. Combining the terms containing N_w and N_{L1} into a single term (for the ionospherically free model), destroys the terms' integer nature. This integer nature can be preserved by separately calculating the ambiguities, first N_w using (9.42) and then N_{L1} by (9.46).

The approach described is not the only one. Hatch (1982), Bender and Larden (1985), Melbourne (1985), Wübbena (1985), Hatch (1986) show other procedures combining carrier phase and code data. This technique is also appropriate for instantaneous ambiguity resolution in kinematic applications, cf. Hatch (1990).

According to Euler and Goad (1991) and Euler and Landau (1992), the ambiguity resolution for the combination of dual frequency code data with a very low noise level and phase data will be possible "under all circumstances" within a few epochs of data. High quality code data has already been obtained by some receivers. The need of the dual frequency data also requires a receiver being able to compensate for A-S.

If there is at least one redundant (fifth) satellite available, least squares techniques can be applied. Loomis (1989) uses the redundant satellite information in the state vector and employs a Kalman filter technique. The number of states is matched to the number of satellites and varies from 8 to 12 for 4 to 8 satellites in view. Three states account for the position, one for the receiver clock, and the remaining one for the integer ambiguities. Hwang (1990) shows a variation of the Loomis (1989) approach.

When comparing various methods, consideration of the number of measured epochs necessary for the solution is important. Hatch (1990) mentions that a single epoch solution is usually possible for short baselines if seven or more satellites can be tracked. The latter requirement is the most demanding restriction of this method. Following Loomis (1989), a very long convergence time for the correct ambiguity solution is necessary. On the other hand, this technique does not rely on dual frequency data. The other methods fall somewhere in between with regard to the number of epochs necessary.

Search techniques
The covariance information resulting from the adjusted (real value) ambiguities may be used to aid the search technique. All integer values within an appropriate region centered about the real value solution are considered as candidates for the ambiguity. Then, all possible combinations of these ambiguities are considered as known values and substituted into subsequent

adjustments. From the set of solutions, that integer combination giving the smallest root mean square (rms) error for the position is taken as the "best" solution. This solution is the one chosen when the ratio of the rms between the "best" and "next best" solution is greater than two to three. This method is only practical for a single baseline.

Previously, another search technique was mentioned, namely the sequential fixing of the ambiguities. This method is possible but time consuming. A slightly more sophisticated method is the fast ambiguity resolution approach (FARA). The development of the search technique used by FARA is given, e.g., in Frei and Beutler (1989), Frei (1991), and summarized in Frei and Schubernigg (1992). Following the latter publication, the main characteristics are (1) to use statistical information from the initial adjustment to select the search range, (2) to use information of the variance-covariance matrix to reject ambiguity sets that are not acceptable from the statistical point of view, and (3) to apply statistical hypothesis testing to select the correct set of integer ambiguities.

Following Erickson (1992a), the FARA algorithm may be partitioned into four steps: computing the float carrier phase solution, choosing ambiguity sets to be tested, computing a fixed solution for each ambiguity set, and statistically testing the fixed solution with the smallest variance.

In the first step, real values for double-difference ambiguities are estimated based on carrier phase measurements and calculated by an adjustment procedure which also computes the cofactor matrix of the unknown parameters and the a posteriori variance of unit weight (a posteriori variance factor). Thus, the variance-covariance matrix of the unknown parameters and the standard deviations of the ambiguities may also be computed.

In the second step, the criteria for the ambiguity ranges to be investigated are based on confidence intervals of the real values of the ambiguities. Therefore, the quality of the initial solution of the first step affects the possible ambiguity ranges. In more detail, if σ_N represents the standard deviation of the ambiguity N, then $\pm k\,\sigma_N$ is the search range for this ambiguity where k is derived statistically from Student's t-distribution. This is the first criterion for selecting possible ambiguity sets.

A second criterion is the use of the correlation of the ambiguities. Assuming the double-difference ambiguities N_i and N_j and the difference

$$N_{ij} = N_j - N_i \,, \tag{9.47}$$

the standard deviation follows from the error propagation law as

$$\sigma_{N_{ij}} = \sqrt{\sigma_{N_i}^2 - 2\sigma_{N_i N_j} + \sigma_{N_j}^2} \tag{9.48}$$

where $\sigma_{N_i}^2$, $\sigma_{N_i N_j}$, and $\sigma_{N_j}^2$ are contained in the variance-covariance matrix of the parameters. The search range for the ambiguity difference N_{ij} is $k_{ij}\, \sigma_{N_{ij}}$ where k_{ij} is analogous to the search range for individual double-difference ambiguities. This criterion significantly reduces the number of possible integer sets. An even more impressive reduction is achieved if dual frequency phase measurements are available. Very illustrative figures demonstrating this reduction are given in Frei and Schubernigg (1992).

In the third step, least squares adjustments with fixed ambiguities are performed for each statistically accepted ambiguity set yielding adjusted baseline components and a posteriori variance factors.

In the fourth and final step, the solution with the smallest a posteriori variance is further investigated. The baseline components of this solution are compared with the float solution. If the solution is compatible, it is accepted. As shown in Erickson (1992a), the compatibility may be checked by a χ^2-distribution which tests the compatibility of the a posteriori variance with the a priori variance. Furthermore, a Fisher test may be applied to the solution with the smallest variance and the second smallest variance to ensure their independence.

As seen from the algorithm, FARA only needs data for double-difference phases; thus, in principle, neither code data nor dual frequency data are required; however, these data will increase the number of possible ambiguity sets dramatically (see the second step of the algorithm).

Euler et al. (1990) present a very efficient and rapid search technique, based as for FARA on the a posteriori variance (resulting from the sum of the squared residual errors). First, an integer set of ambiguities is introduced in the adjustment computation as constraint leading to an initial solution and the corresponding a posteriori variance. The influence of other ambiguity sets on the initial solution and the a posteriori variance is then determined without recomputing the whole adjustment. This influence may be calculated by some simple matrix and vector operations where only a reduced matrix with the dimension of the constraint ambiguities must be inverted. Following Landau and Euler (1992), the computation time for the matrix inversion may be optimized when the Cholesky factorization method is applied which decomposes a symmetric matrix into a product of a lower and an upper triangle matrix. The impact of a changed ambiguity set on the sum of the squared residuals may be reduced by the Cholesky factorization to the computation of an inner product of two vectors. Furthermore, not even the full inner product must be computed in all cases. Based on a threshold, the computation of the inner product for some integer ambiguity sets may be interrupted (and the corresponding ambiguity set rejected) if the threshold is surpassed.

The performance of this method is demonstrated in Landau and Euler (1992) by imposing examples. Assuming six satellites and therefore five double-difference ambiguities with a ± 10 cycle uncertainty each, the total number of possible combinations is $21^5 = 4\,084\,101$. Based on a 486 PC, the computation by the Cholesky factorization took 49.1 seconds. Optimizing the Cholesky factorization by introducing the above mentioned threshold for the inner product, the computation time reduces to 0.2 seconds. For a larger search window of say ± 50 cycles, the corresponding computations amount to 1.5 days for the Cholesky factorization and 3 seconds for the optimized method. The method may be extended to dual frequency data. The appropriate formulas are given in Landau and Euler (1992).

The search techniques described so far performed the search in the ambiguity domain. An alternate technique substitutes the position as known and solves for the ambiguities as unknowns. This could be performed in the following way. Eliminate the ambiguities by forming triple-differences and obtain a first estimate for the position and its standard deviation σ by an adjustment. Now center the approximate position within a cube of dimension $8\sigma \times 8\sigma \times 8\sigma$ (i.e., $\pm 4\sigma$ in each direction and for each coordinate) and partition the cube into a regular grid. The cube, thus, contains a matrix of points where the center point is the triple-difference solution, see Fig. 9.3. Each of these grid points is considered as candidate for the correct solution. Consequently, one by one, each candidate position is substituted into the observation equation. Then the adjustment (holding the trial position fixed) is performed and the ambiguities are computed. When all points within the cube have been considered, select the solution where the estimated real values of the ambiguities appear as close as possible to integer values. Now, fix the ambiguities to these integer values and compute (holding the ambiguities fixed) the final position which will, in general, be slightly different from the corresponding grid point of the cube.

Ambiguity function method
The same principle of the gridded cube is used for the ambiguity function method. Counselman and Gourevitch (1981) proposed the principle of the

Fig. 9.3. Search technique

ambiguity function, and Remondi (1984), Remondi (1990a), Mader (1990) further investigated the concept. The idea should become clear from the following description. Assume a model for the single-difference phase represented by

$$\Phi^j_{AB}(t) = \frac{2\pi}{\lambda}\left[\varrho^j_{AB}(t) + \lambda\,N^j_{AB} - c\,\delta_{AB}(t)\right] \tag{9.49}$$

for the points A and B, and the satellite j where the dimension cycle has been replaced by radians. Assuming point A as known and B as a candidate from the gridded cube, the known term may be shifted to the left-hand side of the equation:

$$\Phi^j_{AB}(t) - \frac{2\pi}{\lambda}\,\varrho^j_{AB}(t) = 2\pi\,N^j_{AB} - 2\pi\,f\,\delta_{AB}(t)\,. \tag{9.50}$$

The key is to circumvent the ambiguities N^j_{AB}. A special effect occurs if the term $2\pi\,N^j_{AB}$ is used as the argument of a cosine or sine function because N^j_{AB} is an integer. Therefore, the whole expression (9.50) is placed into the complex plane by raising both the left- and right-hand side to the power of e^i where $i = \sqrt{-1}$ is the imaginary unit. In detail,

$$e^{i\{\Phi^j_{AB}(t) - \frac{2\pi}{\lambda}\varrho^j_{AB}(t)\}} = e^{i\{2\pi\,N^j_{AB} - 2\pi\,f\,\delta_{AB}(t)\}} \tag{9.51}$$

which may be written as

$$e^{i\{\Phi^j_{AB}(t) - \frac{2\pi}{\lambda}\varrho^j_{AB}(t)\}} = e^{i\,2\pi\,N^j_{AB}}\,e^{-i\,2\pi\,f\,\delta_{AB}(t)}\,. \tag{9.52}$$

It is illustrative to consider this situation in the complex plane, cf. Fig. 9.4.

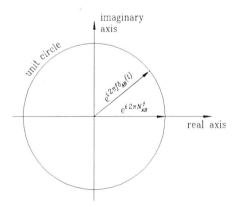

Fig. 9.4. Vector representation in the complex plane

Note the equivalence

$$e^{i\alpha} = \cos\alpha + i\sin\alpha \tag{9.53}$$

which may be represented as a unit vector with the components $\cos\alpha$ and $\sin\alpha$ if a real axis and an imaginary axis are used. Therefore,

$$e^{i\,2\pi\,N_{AB}^{j}} = \cos(2\pi\,N_{AB}^{j}) + i\,\sin(2\pi\,N_{AB}^{j}) = 1 + i\cdot 0 \tag{9.54}$$

results because of the integer nature of N_{AB}^{j}. Hence, for one epoch and one satellite

$$e^{i\{\Phi_{AB}^{j}(t) - \frac{2\pi}{\lambda}\varrho_{AB}^{j}(t)\}} = e^{-i\,2\pi\,f\,\delta_{AB}(t)} \tag{9.55}$$

remains. Considering n_j satellites and forming the sum over these satellites for the epoch t leads to

$$\sum_{j=1}^{n_j} e^{i\{\Phi_{AB}^{j}(t) - \frac{2\pi}{\lambda}\varrho_{AB}^{j}(t)\}} = n_j\,e^{-i\,2\pi\,f\,\delta_{AB}(t)}\ . \tag{9.56}$$

Considering more than one epoch, one must account for the fact that the clock error $\delta_{AB}(t)$ varies with time. A glance at Fig. 9.4 should recall that $e^{-i\,2\pi\,f\,\delta_{AB}(t)}$ is a unit vector. Thus, when $\|e^{-i\,2\pi\,f\,\delta_{AB}(t)}\| = 1$ is applied to (9.56), one gets

$$\left\|\sum_{j=1}^{n_j} e^{i\{\Phi_{AB}^{j}(t) - \frac{2\pi}{\lambda}\varrho_{AB}^{j}(t)\}}\right\| = n_j\cdot 1 \tag{9.57}$$

where the clock error has now vanished.

Take for example four satellites and an error free situation (i.e., neither measurement errors nor model errors, and correct coordinates for the points A and B). In this case, the evaluation of the left-hand side of (9.57) should yield 4 where $\Phi_{AB}^{j}(t)$ are the single-differences of measured phases and $\varrho_{AB}^{j}(t)$ can be calculated from the known points and satellite positions. However, if point B was chosen incorrectly then the result must be less than 4. In reality, this maximum can probably never be achieved precisely because of measurement errors and incomplete modeling. Thus, the task is restricted to obtaining the maximum of (9.57) by varying B.

With highly stable receiver clocks and close epoch spacing it is theoretically possible to include more than one epoch within the absolute value. Using n_t epochs, the contribution of all epochs may be summed up by

$$\sum_{t=1}^{n_t}\left\|\sum_{j=1}^{n_j} e^{i\{\Phi_{AB}^{j}(t) - \frac{2\pi}{\lambda}\varrho_{AB}^{j}(t)\}}\right\| = n_t\,n_j \tag{9.58}$$

where for simplicity the same number of satellites at all epochs is assumed. Following Remondi (1984) and Remondi (1990a), the left-hand side (i.e., the double sum) is denoted as an ambiguity function. Analogous to the case with one epoch, the maximum of the ambiguity function must be found. In general it will, as before, be less than the theoretical value $n_t\, n_j$.

The ambiguity function procedure is simple. Assume an approximate solution for point B, e.g., by triple-differences. Then, place this solution into the center of a cube, cf. Fig. 9.3, and partition the cube into grid points. Each grid point is a candidate for the final solution, and the ambiguity function (9.58) is calculated for all single-differences. The grid point yielding the maximum ambiguity function value, which should theoretically be equal to the total number of single-differences (i.e., $n_t\, n_j$), is the desired solution. Having found this solution, the ambiguities could be computed using double-differences. Also, an adjustment using double-differences might be performed to verify the position of B and the ambiguities. The computation of point B with fixed ambiguities is the final step.

It is worth noting that the ambiguity function method is completely insensitive to cycle slips. The reason can easily be seen from Eq. (9.54). Even if the ambiguity changes by an arbitrary integer amount ΔN^j_{AB}, then $e^{i\, 2\pi\, (N^j_{AB}+\Delta N^j_{AB})}$ is still a unit vector and the subsequent equations, therefore, remain unchanged. Other methods require that cycle slips be repaired before computing the ambiguity.

Remondi (1984) shows detailed examples of how to speed up the procedure, how to choose the density of the grid points within the cube, and how to find the correct maximum if there are many relative maxima for the ambiguity function. These considerations are significant, since the computational burden could, otherwise, become overwhelming. For illustrative purposes, assume a $6\,\mathrm{m} \times 6\,\mathrm{m} \times 6\,\mathrm{m}$ cube with a one centimeter grid. Then $(601)^3 \approx 2.17 \cdot 10^8$ possible solutions must be checked with the ambiguity function (9.58).

Particularly for kinematic applications, the determination of the ambiguities must be performed as fast as possible. This is achieved by the on-the-fly (OTF) ambiguity resolution techniques. These techniques have common aspects like, e.g., the determination of an initial solution; they differ only in how these aspects are carried out. A summary of the main aspects is given in Table 9.10 which is closely related to Erickson (1992b). A feature unique to the ambiguity function method and not mentioned in the table is the insensitivity with respect to cycle slips. As far as the search technique (domain, space, reduction of trials) is concerned, there are also combinations of several characteristics proposed, see, e.g., Abidin et al. (1992). Illustrative graphic representations of search spaces support an easier understanding of

Table 9.10. Characteristics and options for OTF ambiguity resolution techniques

Initial solution	• Code solution for position X, Y, Z and its accuracy σ_X, σ_Y, σ_Z • Carrier solution for X, Y, Z and N_j and accuracies σ_X, σ_Y, σ_Z, σ_{N_j}
Search domain	• Test points (three-dimensional space) • Ambiguity sets (n-dimensional integer space where n is the number of ambiguities)
Search space	• $k\,\sigma_X$, $k\,\sigma_Y$, $k\,\sigma_Z$ • $k\,\sigma_{N_j}$
Determination of k	• Empirically • Statistically
Reduction of trials	• Grid search (fine, coarse) • Double-difference plane intersection • Statistically (correlation of ambiguities for example)
Selection criterion	• Maximum ambiguity function • Minimum variance σ_0^2
Acceptance criterion	• Ratio of largest and second largest ambiguity function • Ratio of smallest and second smallest variance σ_0^2
Observation period	• Instantaneous potential • Some minutes
Data required	• Single or dual frequency • Phase only or phase and code

the reduction of trials, see Hatch (1991), Erickson (1992a), Frei and Schubernigg (1992), Abidin (1993).

The double-difference plane intersection to reduce the number of trials requires a brief explanation. Positions are derived from three double-differences with sets of possible ambiguities. Geometrically, each (linearized) double-difference with its trial ambiguity defines a plane in three-dimensional space, see Hatch (1990). Thus, the intersection of three planes yields a possible solution position. The grid spacing amounts to the carrier wavelength and is equivalent to the grid spacing in the ambiguity search domain.

Minimizing the variance σ_0^2 as selection criterion is in principle the same as minimizing the sum of the squared residuals. If the position of the receiver is eliminated by a mapping function, as proposed by Walsh (1992), the residuals reflect the ambiguities only.

9.2 Adjustment, filtering, and smoothing

9.2.1 Least squares adjustment

Standard adjustment
There are numerous adjustment techniques that can be used, but least squares adjustment with parameters is the only one discussed here. It is based on equations where the observations are expressed as a function of unknown parameters. A Taylor series expansion is usually performed in the case of nonlinear functions. This requires approximate values for the parameters. The Taylor series expansion must be truncated after the second term to obtain a linear function with respect to the unknowns. The resulting linear observation model can be represented in a matrix-vector notation as

$$\underline{\ell} = \underline{A}\,\underline{x} \tag{9.59}$$

where

$\underline{\ell}$ ...   vector of observations
$\underline{A}$ ...   design matrix
$\underline{x}$ ...   vector of unknowns.

By introducing in addition the definitions

σ_0^2 ...   a priori variance

$\underline{\Sigma}$ ...   covariance matrix,

the cofactor matrix of observations is

$$\underline{Q}_\ell = \frac{1}{\sigma_0^2}\,\underline{\Sigma}\,, \tag{9.60}$$

and

$$\underline{P} = \underline{Q}_\ell^{-1} \tag{9.61}$$

is the weight matrix. Assuming n observations and u unknown parameters leads to a design matrix $\underline{A}$ comprising n rows and u columns. For $n > u$, the system (9.59) is overdetermined and, in general, nonconsistent because of observational errors or noise. To assure consistency, the noise vector $\underline{n}$ is added to the vector of observations and Eq. (9.59) converts to

$$\underline{\ell} + \underline{n} = \underline{A}\,\underline{x}\,. \tag{9.62}$$

The solution of this system becomes unique by the least squares principle $\underline{n}^T \underline{P}\, \underline{n} = \text{minimum}$. The application of this minimum principle on the observation equations (9.62) leads to the normal equations

$$\underline{A}^T \underline{P}\, \underline{A}\, \underline{x} = \underline{A}^T \underline{P}\, \underline{\ell} \tag{9.63}$$

with the solution

$$\underline{x} = (\underline{A}^T \underline{P}\, \underline{A})^{-1} \underline{A}^T \underline{P}\, \underline{\ell} \tag{9.64}$$

which can be simplified to

$$\underline{x} = \underline{G}^{-1} \underline{g} \tag{9.65}$$

where $\underline{G} = \underline{A}^T \underline{P}\, \underline{A}$ and $\underline{g} = \underline{A}^T \underline{P}\, \underline{\ell}$.

   The cofactor matrix $\underline{Q}_x$ follows from $\underline{x} = \underline{G}^{-1} \underline{A}^T \underline{P}\, \underline{\ell}$ by the covariance propagation law as

$$\underline{Q}_x = (\underline{G}^{-1} \underline{A}^T \underline{P})\, \underline{Q}_\ell\, (\underline{G}^{-1} \underline{A}^T \underline{P})^T \tag{9.66}$$

and reduces to

$$\underline{Q}_x = \underline{G}^{-1} = (\underline{A}^T \underline{P}\, \underline{A})^{-1} \tag{9.67}$$

by substituting $\underline{Q}_\ell = \underline{P}^{-1}$.

Sequential adjustment
Assume a partitioning of the observation model (9.62) into two subsets:

$$\underline{\ell} = \begin{bmatrix} \ell_1 \\ \ell_2 \end{bmatrix} \qquad \underline{n} = \begin{bmatrix} n_1 \\ n_2 \end{bmatrix} \qquad \underline{A} = \begin{bmatrix} A_1 \\ A_2 \end{bmatrix}. \tag{9.68}$$

Using the first set only, a preliminary solution $\underline{x}_{(0)}$ can be calculated according to (9.64) and (9.67) by

$$\begin{aligned}
\underline{x}_{(0)} &= (\underline{A}_1^T \underline{P}_1 \underline{A}_1)^{-1} \underline{A}_1^T \underline{P}_1 \ell_1 = \underline{G}_1^{-1} \underline{g}_1 \\
\underline{Q}_{x_{(0)}} &= (\underline{A}_1^T \underline{P}_1 \underline{A}_1)^{-1} = \underline{G}_1^{-1}.
\end{aligned} \tag{9.69}$$

Provided that there is no correlation between the two subsets of observations, the weight matrix

$$\underline{P} = \begin{bmatrix} P_1 & 0 \\ 0 & P_2 \end{bmatrix} \tag{9.70}$$

is a block-diagonal matrix. The matrix $\underline{G}$ and the vector $\underline{g}$ for the adjustment of the full set of observations result from adding the corresponding matrices and vectors for the two subsets:

$$\underline{G} = \underline{A}^T \underline{P}\,\underline{A} = (\underline{A}_1^T \underline{P}_1\,\underline{A}_1 + \underline{A}_2^T \underline{P}_2\,\underline{A}_2) = \underline{G}_1 + \underline{G}_2$$
$$\underline{g} = \underline{A}^T \underline{P}\,\underline{\ell} = (\underline{A}_1^T \underline{P}_1\,\underline{\ell}_1 + \underline{A}_2^T \underline{P}_2\,\underline{\ell}_2) = \underline{g}_1 + \underline{g}_2 \,. \tag{9.71}$$

If the change of the preliminary solution $\underline{x}_{(0)}$ due to the additional observation set $\underline{\ell}_2$ is denoted as $\Delta\underline{x}$, then

$$(\underline{G}_1 + \underline{G}_2)(\underline{x}_{(0)} + \Delta\underline{x}) = \underline{g}_1 + \underline{g}_2 \tag{9.72}$$

is the appropriate formulation of the adjustment. This equation can be slightly rearranged to

$$(\underline{G}_1 + \underline{G}_2)\,\Delta\underline{x} = \underline{g}_1 + \underline{g}_2 - (\underline{G}_1 + \underline{G}_2)\,\underline{x}_{(0)} \tag{9.73}$$

where the right-hand side, cf. Eq. (9.69), can be simplified because of the relation $\underline{g}_1 - \underline{G}_1\,\underline{x}_{(0)} = \underline{0}$ so that

$$(\underline{G}_1 + \underline{G}_2)\,\Delta\underline{x} = \underline{g}_2 - \underline{G}_2\,\underline{x}_{(0)} \tag{9.74}$$

results. Resubstituting from (9.71) $\underline{g}_2 = \underline{A}_2^T \underline{P}_2\,\underline{\ell}_2$ and $\underline{G}_2 = \underline{A}_2^T \underline{P}_2\,\underline{A}_2$ yields

$$(\underline{G}_1 + \underline{G}_2)\,\Delta\underline{x} = \underline{A}_2^T \underline{P}_2\,\underline{\ell}_2 - \underline{A}_2^T \underline{P}_2\,\underline{A}_2\,\underline{x}_{(0)} \tag{9.75}$$

or

$$(\underline{G}_1 + \underline{G}_2)\,\Delta\underline{x} = \underline{A}_2^T \underline{P}_2\,(\underline{\ell}_2 - \underline{A}_2\,\underline{x}_{(0)}) \tag{9.76}$$

and

$$\Delta\underline{x} = (\underline{G}_1 + \underline{G}_2)^{-1}\underline{A}_2^T \underline{P}_2\,(\underline{\ell}_2 - \underline{A}_2\,\underline{x}_{(0)}) \tag{9.77}$$

or, finally,

$$\Delta\underline{x} = \underline{K}\,(\underline{\ell}_2 - \underline{A}_2\,\underline{x}_{(0)}) \tag{9.78}$$

where

$$\underline{K} = (\underline{G}_1 + \underline{G}_2)^{-1}\underline{A}_2^T \underline{P}_2 \,. \tag{9.79}$$

Note that formally in (9.78) the term $\underline{A}_2\,\underline{x}_{(0)}$ can be considered as prediction for the observations $\underline{\ell}_2$.

The goal of the next step is the computation of the change $\Delta \underline{Q}$ with respect to the preliminary cofactor matrix $\underline{Q}_{x_{(0)}}$. Starting point is the relation

$$\underline{G}\,\underline{Q}_x = (\underline{G}_1 + \underline{G}_2)\,(\underline{Q}_{x_{(0)}} + \Delta \underline{Q}) = \underline{I} \qquad (9.80)$$

where $\underline{I}$ denotes the unit matrix. This equation is reformulated as

$$(\underline{G}_1 + \underline{G}_2)\,\Delta \underline{Q} = \underline{I} - (\underline{G}_1 + \underline{G}_2)\,\underline{Q}_{x_{(0)}} \qquad (9.81)$$

and, since $\underline{G}_1\,\underline{Q}_{x_{(0)}} = \underline{I}$, this reduces to

$$(\underline{G}_1 + \underline{G}_2)\,\Delta \underline{Q} = -\underline{G}_2\,\underline{Q}_{x_{(0)}} \qquad (9.82)$$

or

$$\Delta \underline{Q} = -(\underline{G}_1 + \underline{G}_2)^{-1}\underline{G}_2\,\underline{Q}_{x_{(0)}} \qquad (9.83)$$

and, by using $\underline{G}_2 = \underline{A}_2^T\,\underline{P}_2\,\underline{A}_2$, the relation

$$\Delta \underline{Q} = -(\underline{G}_1 + \underline{G}_2)^{-1}\underline{A}_2^T\,\underline{P}_2\,\underline{A}_2\,\underline{Q}_{x_{(0)}} \qquad (9.84)$$

follows. Comparing this equation with (9.79), $\underline{K}$ may be substituted and

$$\Delta \underline{Q} = -\underline{K}\,\underline{A}_2\,\underline{Q}_{x_{(0)}} \qquad (9.85)$$

results. Matrix $\underline{K}$, which is denoted as gain matrix, satisfies the very remarkable relation

$$\underline{K} = (\underline{G}_1 + \underline{G}_2)^{-1}\underline{A}_2^T\,\underline{P}_2 = \underline{G}_1^{-1}\underline{A}_2^T(\underline{P}_2^{-1} + \underline{A}_2\,\underline{G}_1^{-1}\underline{A}_2^T)^{-1}\,. \qquad (9.86)$$

This relation is based on a formula found by Bennet (1965). For additional information cf. also Moritz (1980), Eqs. (19-12) and (19-13). The point of this equation is its application to the inversion of modified matrices of the type $(\underline{C} + \underline{D})$ where $\underline{C}^{-1}$ is known a priori. The identity of (9.86) may be proved by multiplying both sides from left by $(\underline{G}_1 + \underline{G}_2)$ and from right by $(\underline{P}_2^{-1} + \underline{A}_2\,\underline{G}_1^{-1}\underline{A}_2^T)$.

It is essential to learn from Eq. (9.86) that the first form for $\underline{K}$ implies the inversion of a $u \times u$ matrix if u is the number of unknown parameters; whereas, for the second form, an inversion of an $n_2 \times n_2$ matrix is necessary when n_2 denotes the number of observations for the second subset. Therefore, the second form is advantageous as long as $n_2 < u$.

A final remark should conclude the section on the sequential adjustment. Formally, if the substitution $\underline{A}_1 = \underline{I}$ and $\underline{\ell}_1 = \underline{x}_{(0)}$ is performed, then the model for the sequential adjustment is formulated as

$$\underline{x}_{(0)} + \underline{n}_1 = \quad \underline{x}$$
$$\underline{\ell}_2 \; + \underline{n}_2 = \underline{A}_2\, \underline{x}\,. \tag{9.87}$$

Model (9.87) reflects that the preliminary estimates $\underline{x}_{(0)}$ for the unknown parameters are introduced into the sequential adjustment as observations. This approach is often used in the context with Kalman filtering, see for example Munck (1989).

9.2.2 Kalman filtering

Introduction
Consider a dynamic system such as a moving vehicle. The unknown parameters, e.g., the coordinates and the velocity, form the elements of the "state vector". This time dependent vector may be predicted for any instant t by means of "system equations". The predicted values can be improved or updated by observations containing information on some components of the state vector.

The whole procedure is known as Kalman filtering. It corresponds to the sequential adjustment in the static case, cf. Egge (1985). Consequently, optimal estimations of the unknowns on the basis of all observations up to the epoch t are obtained. Note, however, there is no need to store these data for the subsequent epochs.

Prediction
The time dependent state vector $\underline{x}(t)$ comprising the unknown parameters of the dynamic system may be modeled by a system of differential equations of the first order as

$$\underline{\dot{x}}(t) = \underline{F}(t)\,\underline{x}(t) + \underline{w}(t) \tag{9.88}$$

where

$\qquad \underline{\dot{x}}(t) \quad \ldots \quad$ time derivative of the state vector

$\qquad \underline{F}(t) \quad \ldots \quad$ dynamics matrix

$\qquad \underline{w}(t) \quad \ldots \quad$ driving noise.

For the following, at the initial epoch t_0, the state vector $\underline{x}(t_0)$ and its cofactor matrix $\underline{Q}_{x_0}$ are assumed to be known. A general solution for the system equation (9.88) only exists if the matrix $\underline{F}(t)$ contains periodic or constant coefficients. For the latter case, this solution can be written as

$$
\underline{x}(t) = \underline{T}(t, t_0)\, \underline{x}(t_0) + \int_{t_0}^{t} \underline{T}(t, \tau)\, \underline{w}(\tau)\, d\tau \tag{9.89}
$$

$$
= \underline{T}(t, t_0)\, \underline{x}(t_0) + \underline{e}(t),
$$

cf. Schwarz (1983), Eq. (47). Here, $\underline{T}$ represents the transition matrix.

The state vector at any instant can also be expressed by a Taylor series expansion. Thus,

$$
\underline{x}(t) = \underline{x}(t_0) + \underline{\dot{x}}(t_0)\,(t - t_0) + \frac{1}{2}\,\underline{\ddot{x}}(t_0)\,(t - t_0)^2 + \ldots \tag{9.90}
$$

is obtained. Substituting (9.88) and neglecting the driving noise $\underline{w}(t)$ gives (where the dynamics matrix is assumed to be constant)

$$
\underline{x}(t) = \underline{x}(t_0) + \underline{F}(t_0)\,\underline{x}(t_0)\,(t - t_0) + \frac{1}{2}\,\underline{F}(t_0)^2\,\underline{x}(t_0)\,(t - t_0)^2 + \ldots \tag{9.91}
$$

which, by comparing with (9.89), may be written in the form

$$
\underline{x}(t) = \underline{T}(t, t_0)\, \underline{x}(t_0). \tag{9.92}
$$

Consequently, by introducing the substitution $\Delta t = t - t_0$, the transition matrix is obtained as an infinite series with respect to $\underline{F}$ by

$$
\underline{T}(t, t_0) = \underline{I} + \underline{F}(t_0)\,\Delta t + \frac{1}{2}\,\underline{F}(t_0)^2\,\Delta t^2 + \ldots \tag{9.93}
$$

$$
= \sum_{n=0}^{\infty} \frac{1}{n!}\,\underline{F}(t_0)^n\,\Delta t^n.
$$

The cofactor matrix $\underline{Q}_x$ of the state vector $\underline{x}(t)$ can be calculated via (9.89) by using the law of covariance propagation yielding

$$
\underline{Q}_x = \underline{T}(t, t_0)\, \underline{Q}_{x_0}\, \underline{T}^T(t, t_0) + \underline{Q}_e. \tag{9.94}
$$

Studying Eqs. (9.89) and (9.94), it may be concluded that the essential problems of the Kalman filtering are the definition of the transition matrix $\underline{T}$ and of the cofactor matrix $\underline{Q}_e$.

Update
Starting at the initial epoch t_0, the state vector $\underline{x}(t)$ can be predicted for any arbitrary future epoch t by the system equations (9.89). Taking into account

the system noise $\underline{e}(t)$, it is assumed that at epoch t observations $\underline{\ell}(t)$ and the corresponding cofactors $\underline{Q}_{\ell}$ are available. These data may be related to the updated state vector $\underline{\hat{x}}(t)$ – possibly after a necessary linearization – by the equation

$$\underline{\ell}(t) = \underline{A}\,\underline{\hat{x}}(t)\,. \tag{9.95}$$

Considering both the predicted state vector $\underline{x}(t)$ and the observations $\underline{\ell}(t)$ as stochastic quantities leads to the sequential adjustment problem

$$\begin{aligned} \underline{x}(t) + \underline{n}_x &= \underline{\hat{x}}(t) \\ \underline{\ell}(t) + \underline{n}_\ell &= \underline{A}\,\underline{\hat{x}}(t)\,. \end{aligned} \tag{9.96}$$

This system is equivalent to (9.87). Therefore, the solution can be taken immediately from (9.78) and (9.85) by matching the notations to the present situation, and it follows

$$\underline{\hat{x}}(t) = \underline{x}(t) + \Delta\underline{x}(t) = \underline{x}(t) + \underline{K}\left[\underline{\ell}(t) - \underline{A}\,\underline{x}(t)\right] \tag{9.97}$$

$$\underline{\hat{Q}}_x = \underline{Q}_x + \Delta\underline{Q}_x = (\underline{I} - \underline{K}\,\underline{A})\,\underline{Q}_x\,.$$

The gain matrix $\underline{K}$ is now given as

$$\underline{K} = \underline{Q}_x\,\underline{A}^T(\underline{Q}_\ell + \underline{A}\,\underline{Q}_x\,\underline{A}^T)^{-1}\,, \tag{9.98}$$

cf. also Eq. (9.86).

Example
Consider a vehicle moving on a straight line with constant velocity v where the motion is affected by the random acceleration a. Also, assume that the (one-dimensional) position $p(t_0)$ and the velocity $v(t_0)$ as well as the corresponding variances σ_p^2, σ_v^2 and that of the noise, σ_a^2, are known at the initial epoch t_0. Furthermore, it is assumed that the position of the vehicle is observed at an epoch $t = t_0 + \Delta t$ and that the observation has the variance σ_ℓ^2 at this epoch.

The state vector consists of the position and the velocity of the vehicle. Thus, for the initial epoch, one obtains

$$\underline{x}(t_0) = \begin{bmatrix} p(t_0) \\ v(t_0) \end{bmatrix} \quad \text{and} \quad \underline{\dot{x}}(t_0) = \begin{bmatrix} \dot{p}(t_0) \\ \dot{v}(t_0) \end{bmatrix} = \begin{bmatrix} v(t_0) \\ 0 \end{bmatrix}\,. \tag{9.99}$$

The substitution of these vectors and of the random acceleration a into (9.88) yields the dynamics matrix and the driving noise vector for epoch t_0:

$$\underline{F}(t_0) = \begin{bmatrix} 0 & 1 \\ 0 & 0 \end{bmatrix} \quad \underline{w}(t_0) = a\begin{bmatrix} 0 \\ 1 \end{bmatrix}\,. \tag{9.100}$$

The transition matrix according to Eq. (9.93) is

$$\underline{T}(t, t_0) = \begin{bmatrix} 1 & \Delta t \\ 0 & 1 \end{bmatrix} . \tag{9.101}$$

Assuming a constant acceleration during the integration interval Δt, then from (9.89) the noise vector is obtained as

$$\underline{e}(t) = a \begin{bmatrix} \dfrac{\Delta t^2}{2} \\ \Delta t \end{bmatrix} . \tag{9.102}$$

Note that under the present assumptions the elements of the predicted state vector $\underline{x}(t)$ would also result from the formulas of accelerated motion.

The cofactor matrix $\underline{Q}_x$ of the predicted state vector $\underline{x}(t)$ follows from Eq. (9.94) as

$$\underline{Q}_x = \begin{bmatrix} \sigma_p^2 + \Delta t^2 \sigma_v^2 + \frac{1}{4} \Delta t^4 \sigma_a^2 & \Delta t \sigma_v^2 + \frac{1}{2} \Delta t^3 \sigma_a^2 \\ \Delta t \sigma_v^2 + \frac{1}{2} \Delta t^3 \sigma_a^2 & \sigma_v^2 + \Delta t^2 \sigma_a^2 \end{bmatrix}$$

$$= \begin{bmatrix} Q_{11} & Q_{12} \\ Q_{12} & Q_{22} \end{bmatrix} . \tag{9.103}$$

Since the observation equation is $\ell(t) + n(t) = \hat{p}(t)$, the matrix $\underline{A}$ in (9.96) shrinks to the row vector

$$\underline{A} = \begin{bmatrix} 1 & 0 \end{bmatrix} , \tag{9.104}$$

and the gain matrix reduces to the column vector

$$\underline{K} = \frac{1}{Q_{11} + \sigma_1^2} \begin{bmatrix} Q_{11} \\ Q_{12} \end{bmatrix} . \tag{9.105}$$

Now, the updated state vector $\hat{\underline{x}}(t)$ and the corresponding cofactor matrix $\hat{\underline{Q}}_x$ can be calculated by Eqs. (9.97).

9.2.3 Smoothing

The process of improving previous estimates for the state vector by a new measurement is called smoothing. Since smoothing is performed backwards in time, it is (contrary to the real-time Kalman filtering) a postmission process. One smoothing technique is presented here for the sake of completeness. For further details the reader is referred to the literature, e.g., Schwarz and Arden (1985). Using the notations

$$\underline{x}(t) \quad \ldots \quad \text{predicted state vector}$$

$$\underline{\hat{x}}(t) \quad \ldots \quad \text{updated state vector}$$

$$\underline{\overset{\circ}{x}}(t) \quad \ldots \quad \text{smoothed state vector}$$

then, following Schwarz (1983), Eqs. (61), (63), (64), a formula for optimal smoothing is

$$\underline{\overset{\circ}{x}}(t_i) = \underline{\hat{x}}(t_i) + \underline{D}(t_{i+1}, t_i) \left[\underline{\overset{\circ}{x}}(t_{i+1}) - \underline{x}(t_{i+1})\right] \tag{9.106}$$

where the gain matrix is

$$\underline{D}(t_{i+1}, t_i) = \underline{\hat{Q}}_{x_i} \, \underline{T}(t_{i+1}, t_i) \, \underline{Q}_{x_{i+1}}^{-1} \,. \tag{9.107}$$

At the epoch of the last update measurement, the updated state vector is set identical to the smoothed one, and the backwards algorithm can be started. From Eq. (9.106) it may be concluded that the process requires the predicted and updated vectors and the cofactor matrices at the update epochs as well as the transition matrices between the updates. This implies, in general, a large amount of data. This is probably the reason why optimal smoothing is very often replaced by empirical methods.

9.3 Adjustment of mathematical GPS models

9.3.1 Linearization

When the models of Chap. 8 are considered, the only term comprising unknowns in nonlinear form is ϱ. This section explains in detail how ϱ is linearized. The basic formula from Eq. (8.2)

$$\begin{aligned} \varrho_i^j(t) &= \sqrt{(X^j(t) - X_i)^2 + (Y^j(t) - Y_i)^2 + (Z^j(t) - Z_i)^2} \\ &\equiv f(X_i, Y_i, Z_i) \end{aligned} \tag{9.108}$$

shows the unknown point coordinates X_i, Y_i, Z_i in nonlinear form. Assuming approximate values X_{i0}, Y_{i0}, Z_{i0} for the unknowns, an approximate distance $\varrho_{i0}^j(t)$ can be calculated by

$$
\begin{aligned}
\varrho_{i0}^j(t) &= \sqrt{(X^j(t) - X_{i0})^2 + (Y^j(t) - Y_{i0})^2 + (Z^j(t) - Z_{i0})^2} \\
&\equiv f(X_{i0}, Y_{i0}, Z_{i0}) .
\end{aligned}
\tag{9.109}
$$

Having available approximate values, the unknowns X_i, Y_i, Z_i can be decomposed by

$$
\begin{aligned}
X_i &= X_{i0} + \Delta X_i \\
Y_i &= Y_{i0} + \Delta Y_i \\
Z_i &= Z_{i0} + \Delta Z_i
\end{aligned}
\tag{9.110}
$$

where now ΔX_i, ΔY_i, ΔZ_i are new unknowns. This means that the original unknowns have been split into a known part (represented by the approximate values X_{i0}, Y_{i0}, Z_{i0}) and an unknown part (represented by ΔX_i, ΔY_i, ΔZ_i). The advantage of this splitting-up is that the function $f(X_i, Y_i, Z_i)$ is replaced by an equivalent function $f(X_{i0} + \Delta X_i, Y_{i0} + \Delta Y_i, Z_{i0} + \Delta Z_i)$ which can now be expanded into a Taylor series with respect to the approximate point. This leads to

$$
\begin{aligned}
f(X_i, Y_i, Z_i) &\equiv f(X_{i0} + \Delta X_i, Y_{i0} + \Delta Y_i, Z_{i0} + \Delta Z_i) \\
&= f(X_{i0}, Y_{i0}, Z_{i0}) + \frac{\partial f(X_{i0}, Y_{i0}, Z_{i0})}{\partial X_{i0}} \Delta X_i \\
&+ \frac{\partial f(X_{i0}, Y_{i0}, Z_{i0})}{\partial Y_{i0}} \Delta Y_i + \frac{\partial f(X_{i0}, Y_{i0}, Z_{i0})}{\partial Z_{i0}} \Delta Z_i + \ldots
\end{aligned}
\tag{9.111}
$$

where the expansion is truncated after the linear term; otherwise, the unknowns ΔX_i, ΔY_i, ΔZ_i would appear in nonlinear form. The partials are obtained from (9.109) by

$$
\begin{aligned}
\frac{\partial f(X_{i0}, Y_{i0}, Z_{i0})}{\partial X_{i0}} &= -\frac{X^j(t) - X_{i0}}{\varrho_{i0}^j(t)} \\
\frac{\partial f(X_{i0}, Y_{i0}, Z_{i0})}{\partial Y_{i0}} &= -\frac{Y^j(t) - Y_{i0}}{\varrho_{i0}^j(t)} \\
\frac{\partial f(X_{i0}, Y_{i0}, Z_{i0})}{\partial Z_{i0}} &= -\frac{Z^j(t) - Z_{i0}}{\varrho_{i0}^j(t)}
\end{aligned}
\tag{9.112}
$$

and are the components of the unit vector pointing from the satellite towards the approximate site. The substitution of Eqs. (9.109) and (9.112) into Eq. (9.111) gives

$$\varrho_i^j(t) = \varrho_{i0}^j(t) - \frac{X^j(t) - X_{i0}}{\varrho_{i0}^j(t)} \Delta X_i - \frac{Y^j(t) - Y_{i0}}{\varrho_{i0}^j(t)} \Delta Y_i$$
$$- \frac{Z^j(t) - Z_{i0}}{\varrho_{i0}^j(t)} \Delta Z_i \tag{9.113}$$

where the equivalence of $f(X_i, Y_i, Z_i)$ with $\varrho_i^j(t)$ has been used for the left-hand side. The equation above is now linear with respect to the unknowns ΔX_i, ΔY_i, ΔZ_i.

9.3.2   Linear model for point positioning with code ranges

The model is given only in its elementary form and, thus, apart from the geometry only the clocks are modeled. The ionosphere, troposphere, and other minor effects are neglected. According to Eq. (8.5), the model for point positioning with code ranges is given by

$$R_i^j(t) = \varrho_i^j(t) + c\,\delta^j(t) - c\,\delta_i(t) \tag{9.114}$$

which can be linearized by substituting (9.113):

$$R_i^j(t) = \varrho_{i0}^j(t) - \frac{X^j(t) - X_{i0}}{\varrho_{i0}^j(t)} \Delta X_i - \frac{Y^j(t) - Y_{i0}}{\varrho_{i0}^j(t)} \Delta Y_i$$
$$- \frac{Z^j(t) - Z_{i0}}{\varrho_{i0}^j(t)} \Delta Z_i + c\,\delta^j(t) - c\,\delta_i(t). \tag{9.115}$$

Leaving the terms containing unknowns on the right-hand side, the equation above is rewritten as

$$R_i^j(t) - \varrho_{i0}^j(t) - c\,\delta^j(t) = -\frac{X^j(t) - X_{i0}}{\varrho_{i0}^j(t)} \Delta X_i$$
$$- \frac{Y^j(t) - Y_{i0}}{\varrho_{i0}^j(t)} \Delta Y_i - \frac{Z^j(t) - Z_{i0}}{\varrho_{i0}^j(t)} \Delta Z_i - c\,\delta_i(t) \tag{9.116}$$

where the satellite clock bias is assumed to be known. This assumption makes sense because satellite clock correctors can be received from the navigation message. Model (9.116) comprises (for the epoch t) four unknowns, namely $\Delta X_i, \Delta Y_i, \Delta Z_i, \delta_i(t)$. Consequently, four satellites are needed to solve the problem. The shorthand notations

$$
\begin{aligned}
\ell^j \;&=\; R_i^j(t) - \varrho_{i0}^j(t) - c\,\delta^j(t) \\[2mm]
a_{Xi}^j &= -\,\frac{X^j(t) - X_{i0}}{\varrho_{i0}^j(t)} \\[2mm]
a_{Yi}^j &= -\,\frac{Y^j(t) - Y_{i0}}{\varrho_{i0}^j(t)} \\[2mm]
a_{Zi}^j &= -\,\frac{Z^j(t) - Z_{i0}}{\varrho_{i0}^j(t)}
\end{aligned}
\tag{9.117}
$$

help to simplify the representation of the system of equations. Assuming now four satellites numbered from 1 to 4, then

$$
\begin{aligned}
\ell^1 &= a_{Xi}^1\,\Delta X_i + a_{Yi}^1\,\Delta Y_i + a_{Zi}^1\,\Delta Z_i - c\,\delta_i(t) \\
\ell^2 &= a_{Xi}^2\,\Delta X_i + a_{Yi}^2\,\Delta Y_i + a_{Zi}^2\,\Delta Z_i - c\,\delta_i(t) \\
\ell^3 &= a_{Xi}^3\,\Delta X_i + a_{Yi}^3\,\Delta Y_i + a_{Zi}^3\,\Delta Z_i - c\,\delta_i(t) \\
\ell^4 &= a_{Xi}^4\,\Delta X_i + a_{Yi}^4\,\Delta Y_i + a_{Zi}^4\,\Delta Z_i - c\,\delta_i(t)
\end{aligned}
\tag{9.118}
$$

is the appropriate system of equations. Note that the superscripts are the satellite numbers and not exponents! Introducing

$$
\underline{A} = \begin{bmatrix}
a_{Xi}^1 & a_{Yi}^1 & a_{Zi}^1 & -c \\
a_{Xi}^2 & a_{Yi}^2 & a_{Zi}^2 & -c \\
a_{Xi}^3 & a_{Yi}^3 & a_{Zi}^3 & -c \\
a_{Xi}^4 & a_{Yi}^4 & a_{Zi}^4 & -c
\end{bmatrix}
\qquad
\underline{x} = \begin{bmatrix}
\Delta X_i \\
\Delta Y_i \\
\Delta Z_i \\
\delta_i(t)
\end{bmatrix}
\qquad
\underline{\ell} = \begin{bmatrix}
\ell^1 \\
\ell^2 \\
\ell^3 \\
\ell^4
\end{bmatrix},
$$

$$
\tag{9.119}
$$

the set of linear equations can be written in the matrix-vector form

$$
\underline{\ell} = \underline{A}\,\underline{x}\,.
\tag{9.120}
$$

For this first example of a linearized GPS model, the resubstitution of the vector ℓ and the matrix A using (9.117) is given explicitly for one epoch t:

$$
\ell = \begin{bmatrix}
R_i^1(t) - \varrho_{i0}^1(t) - c\,\delta^1(t) \\[6pt]
R_i^2(t) - \varrho_{i0}^2(t) - c\,\delta^2(t) \\[6pt]
R_i^3(t) - \varrho_{i0}^3(t) - c\,\delta^3(t) \\[6pt]
R_i^4(t) - \varrho_{i0}^4(t) - c\,\delta^4(t)
\end{bmatrix}
$$

$$
A = \begin{bmatrix}
-\dfrac{X^1(t) - X_{i0}}{\varrho_{i0}^1(t)} & -\dfrac{Y^1(t) - Y_{i0}}{\varrho_{i0}^1(t)} & -\dfrac{Z^1(t) - Z_{i0}}{\varrho_{i0}^1(t)} & -c \\[12pt]
-\dfrac{X^2(t) - X_{i0}}{\varrho_{i0}^2(t)} & -\dfrac{Y^2(t) - Y_{i0}}{\varrho_{i0}^2(t)} & -\dfrac{Z^2(t) - Z_{i0}}{\varrho_{i0}^2(t)} & -c \\[12pt]
-\dfrac{X^3(t) - X_{i0}}{\varrho_{i0}^3(t)} & -\dfrac{Y^3(t) - Y_{i0}}{\varrho_{i0}^3(t)} & -\dfrac{Z^3(t) - Z_{i0}}{\varrho_{i0}^3(t)} & -c \\[12pt]
-\dfrac{X^4(t) - X_{i0}}{\varrho_{i0}^4(t)} & -\dfrac{Y^4(t) - Y_{i0}}{\varrho_{i0}^4(t)} & -\dfrac{Z^4(t) - Z_{i0}}{\varrho_{i0}^4(t)} & -c
\end{bmatrix} .
$$

$$(9.121)$$

From the linear system (9.120), the coordinate differences ΔX_i, ΔY_i, ΔZ_i and the receiver clock error $\delta_i(t)$ for epoch t result. The desired point coordinates are finally obtained by (9.110).

Recall that the selection of the approximate values for the coordinates was completely arbitrary; they could even be set equal to zero (but this might require an iteration).

Point positioning with code ranges is applicable for each epoch separately. Therefore, this model may also be used in kinematic applications.

9.3.3 Linear model for point positioning with carrier phases

The procedure is the same as in the previous section. In Eq. (8.8), the linearization is performed for $\varrho_i^j(t)$, and known terms are shifted to the left-hand side. Multiplying the equation by λ and using $c = \lambda f$, the result is

$$
\lambda\,\Phi_i^j(t) - \varrho_{i0}^j(t) - c\,\delta^j(t) = -\frac{X^j(t) - X_{i0}}{\varrho_{i0}^j(t)}\,\Delta X_i
$$

$$
-\frac{Y^j(t) - Y_{i0}}{\varrho_{i0}^j(t)}\,\Delta Y_i - \frac{Z^j(t) - Z_{i0}}{\varrho_{i0}^j(t)}\,\Delta Z_i + \lambda\,N_i^j - c\,\delta_i(t)
$$

$$(9.122)$$

where, compared to point positioning with code ranges, the number of unknowns is now increased by the ambiguities. Considering again four satellites, the system follows as

$$\underline{\ell} = \begin{bmatrix} \lambda\,\Phi_i^1(t) - \varrho_{i0}^1(t) - c\,\delta^1(t) \\ \lambda\,\Phi_i^2(t) - \varrho_{i0}^2(t) - c\,\delta^2(t) \\ \lambda\,\Phi_i^3(t) - \varrho_{i0}^3(t) - c\,\delta^3(t) \\ \lambda\,\Phi_i^4(t) - \varrho_{i0}^4(t) - c\,\delta^4(t) \end{bmatrix}$$

$$\underline{A} = \begin{bmatrix} -\dfrac{X^1(t)-X_{i0}}{\varrho_{i0}^1(t)} & -\dfrac{Y^1(t)-Y_{i0}}{\varrho_{i0}^1(t)} & -\dfrac{Z^1(t)-Z_{i0}}{\varrho_{i0}^1(t)} & \lambda & 0 & 0 & 0 & -c \\ -\dfrac{X^2(t)-X_{i0}}{\varrho_{i0}^2(t)} & -\dfrac{Y^2(t)-Y_{i0}}{\varrho_{i0}^2(t)} & -\dfrac{Z^2(t)-Z_{i0}}{\varrho_{i0}^2(t)} & 0 & \lambda & 0 & 0 & -c \\ -\dfrac{X^3(t)-X_{i0}}{\varrho_{i0}^3(t)} & -\dfrac{Y^3(t)-Y_{i0}}{\varrho_{i0}^3(t)} & -\dfrac{Z^3(t)-Z_{i0}}{\varrho_{i0}^3(t)} & 0 & 0 & \lambda & 0 & -c \\ -\dfrac{X^4(t)-X_{i0}}{\varrho_{i0}^4(t)} & -\dfrac{Y^4(t)-Y_{i0}}{\varrho_{i0}^4(t)} & -\dfrac{Z^4(t)-Z_{i0}}{\varrho_{i0}^4(t)} & 0 & 0 & 0 & \lambda & -c \end{bmatrix}$$

$$\underline{x}^T = \begin{bmatrix} \Delta X_i & \Delta Y_i & \Delta Z_i & N_i^1 & N_i^2 & N_i^3 & N_i^4 & \delta_i(t) \end{bmatrix}$$

$$(9.123)$$

where the matrix-vector notation has been used. Obviously, the four equations do not solve for the eight unknowns. This reflects the fact that point positioning with phases in this form cannot be solved epoch by epoch. Each additional epoch increases the number of unknowns by a new clock term. Thus, for two epochs there are eight equations and nine unknowns (still an underdetermined problem). For three epochs there are 12 equations and 10 unknowns, thus, a slightly overdetermined problem. The 10 unknowns in the latter example are the coordinate increments ΔX_i, ΔY_i, ΔZ_i for the unknown point, the integer ambiguities N_i^1, N_i^2, N_i^3, N_i^4 for the four satellites, and the receiver clock biases $\delta_i(t_1)$, $\delta_i(t_2)$, $\delta_i(t_3)$ for the three epochs.

With the shorthand notations for the coefficients of the coordinate increments

$$a_{Xi}^j(t_k) = -\frac{X^j(t_k) - X_{i0}}{\varrho_{i0}^j(t_k)}$$

$$a_{Yi}^j(t_k) = -\frac{Y^j(t_k) - Y_{i0}}{\varrho_{i0}^j(t_k)} \qquad (9.124)$$

$$a_{Zi}^j(t_k) = -\frac{Z^j(t_k) - Z_{i0}}{\varrho_{i0}^j(t_k)},$$

the matrix-vector scheme for the example above is given by

$$
\underline{\ell} =
\begin{bmatrix}
\lambda\,\Phi_i^1(t_1) - \varrho_{i0}^1(t_1) - c\,\delta^1(t_1) \\
\lambda\,\Phi_i^2(t_1) - \varrho_{i0}^2(t_1) - c\,\delta^2(t_1) \\
\lambda\,\Phi_i^3(t_1) - \varrho_{i0}^3(t_1) - c\,\delta^3(t_1) \\
\lambda\,\Phi_i^4(t_1) - \varrho_{i0}^4(t_1) - c\,\delta^4(t_1) \\
\lambda\,\Phi_i^1(t_2) - \varrho_{i0}^1(t_2) - c\,\delta^1(t_2) \\
\lambda\,\Phi_i^2(t_2) - \varrho_{i0}^2(t_2) - c\,\delta^2(t_2) \\
\lambda\,\Phi_i^3(t_2) - \varrho_{i0}^3(t_2) - c\,\delta^3(t_2) \\
\lambda\,\Phi_i^4(t_2) - \varrho_{i0}^4(t_2) - c\,\delta^4(t_2) \\
\lambda\,\Phi_i^1(t_3) - \varrho_{i0}^1(t_3) - c\,\delta^1(t_3) \\
\lambda\,\Phi_i^2(t_3) - \varrho_{i0}^2(t_3) - c\,\delta^2(t_3) \\
\lambda\,\Phi_i^3(t_3) - \varrho_{i0}^3(t_3) - c\,\delta^3(t_3) \\
\lambda\,\Phi_i^4(t_3) - \varrho_{i0}^4(t_3) - c\,\delta^4(t_3)
\end{bmatrix}
\qquad
\underline{x} =
\begin{bmatrix}
\Delta X_i \\
\Delta Y_i \\
\Delta Z_i \\
N_i^1 \\
N_i^2 \\
N_i^3 \\
N_i^4 \\
\delta_i(t_1) \\
\delta_i(t_2) \\
\delta_i(t_3)
\end{bmatrix}
$$

$$
\underline{A} =
\begin{bmatrix}
a_{Xi}^1(t_1) & a_{Yi}^1(t_1) & a_{Zi}^1(t_1) & \lambda & 0 & 0 & 0 & -c & 0 & 0 \\
a_{Xi}^2(t_1) & a_{Yi}^2(t_1) & a_{Zi}^2(t_1) & 0 & \lambda & 0 & 0 & -c & 0 & 0 \\
a_{Xi}^3(t_1) & a_{Yi}^3(t_1) & a_{Zi}^3(t_1) & 0 & 0 & \lambda & 0 & -c & 0 & 0 \\
a_{Xi}^4(t_1) & a_{Yi}^4(t_1) & a_{Zi}^4(t_1) & 0 & 0 & 0 & \lambda & -c & 0 & 0 \\
a_{Xi}^1(t_2) & a_{Yi}^1(t_2) & a_{Zi}^1(t_2) & \lambda & 0 & 0 & 0 & 0 & -c & 0 \\
a_{Xi}^2(t_2) & a_{Yi}^2(t_2) & a_{Zi}^2(t_2) & 0 & \lambda & 0 & 0 & 0 & -c & 0 \\
a_{Xi}^3(t_2) & a_{Yi}^3(t_2) & a_{Zi}^3(t_2) & 0 & 0 & \lambda & 0 & 0 & -c & 0 \\
a_{Xi}^4(t_2) & a_{Yi}^4(t_2) & a_{Zi}^4(t_2) & 0 & 0 & 0 & \lambda & 0 & -c & 0 \\
a_{Xi}^1(t_3) & a_{Yi}^1(t_3) & a_{Zi}^1(t_3) & \lambda & 0 & 0 & 0 & 0 & 0 & -c \\
a_{Xi}^2(t_3) & a_{Yi}^2(t_3) & a_{Zi}^2(t_3) & 0 & \lambda & 0 & 0 & 0 & 0 & -c \\
a_{Xi}^3(t_3) & a_{Yi}^3(t_3) & a_{Zi}^3(t_3) & 0 & 0 & \lambda & 0 & 0 & 0 & -c \\
a_{Xi}^4(t_3) & a_{Yi}^4(t_3) & a_{Zi}^4(t_3) & 0 & 0 & 0 & \lambda & 0 & 0 & -c
\end{bmatrix}.
$$

$$(9.125)$$

The solution of this overdetermined system is performed by the least squares adjustment procedure as described in Sect. 9.2.

9.3.4   Linear model for relative positioning

The previous sections have shown linear models for both code ranges and carrier phases. For the case of relative positioning, the investigation is restricted to carrier phases, since it should be obvious how to change from the more expanded model of phases to a code model. Furthermore, the linearization and setup of the system of linear equations remains, in principle, the same for phases and phase combinations and could be performed analogously for each model. Therefore, the double-difference is selected for treatment in detail. The model for the double-difference of Eq. (8.22), multiplied by λ, is

$$\lambda\,\Phi^{jk}_{AB}(t) = \varrho^{jk}_{AB}(t) + \lambda\,N^{jk}_{AB} \tag{9.126}$$

where the term ϱ^{jk}_{AB}, containing the geometry, is composed as

$$\varrho^{jk}_{AB}(t) = \varrho^{k}_{B}(t) - \varrho^{j}_{B}(t) - \varrho^{k}_{A}(t) + \varrho^{j}_{A}(t) \tag{9.127}$$

which reflects the fact of four measurement quantities for a double-difference. Each of the four terms must be linearized according to (9.113) yielding

$$
\begin{aligned}
\varrho^{jk}_{AB}(t) = {} & \varrho^{k}_{B0}(t) - \frac{X^{k}(t) - X_{B0}}{\varrho^{k}_{B0}(t)}\,\Delta X_{B} - \frac{Y^{k}(t) - Y_{B0}}{\varrho^{k}_{B0}(t)}\,\Delta Y_{B} \\
& \qquad\qquad\qquad\qquad\qquad - \frac{Z^{k}(t) - Z_{B0}}{\varrho^{k}_{B0}(t)}\,\Delta Z_{B} \\
& - \varrho^{j}_{B0}(t) + \frac{X^{j}(t) - X_{B0}}{\varrho^{j}_{B0}(t)}\,\Delta X_{B} + \frac{Y^{j}(t) - Y_{B0}}{\varrho^{j}_{B0}(t)}\,\Delta Y_{B} \\
& \qquad\qquad\qquad\qquad\qquad + \frac{Z^{j}(t) - Z_{B0}}{\varrho^{j}_{B0}(t)}\,\Delta Z_{B} \\
& - \varrho^{k}_{A0}(t) + \frac{X^{k}(t) - X_{A0}}{\varrho^{k}_{A0}(t)}\,\Delta X_{A} + \frac{Y^{k}(t) - Y_{A0}}{\varrho^{k}_{A0}(t)}\,\Delta Y_{A} \\
& \qquad\qquad\qquad\qquad\qquad + \frac{Z^{k}(t) - Z_{A0}}{\varrho^{k}_{A0}(t)}\,\Delta Z_{A} \\
& + \varrho^{j}_{A0}(t) - \frac{X^{j}(t) - X_{A0}}{\varrho^{j}_{A0}(t)}\,\Delta X_{A} - \frac{Y^{j}(t) - Y_{A0}}{\varrho^{j}_{A0}(t)}\,\Delta Y_{A} \\
& \qquad\qquad\qquad\qquad\qquad - \frac{Z^{j}(t) - Z_{A0}}{\varrho^{j}_{A0}(t)}\,\Delta Z_{A}\,.
\end{aligned}
$$

$$\tag{9.128}$$

To achieve a linear system in the form $\underline{\ell} = A \underline{x}$, it is helpful to introduce the abbreviations

$$a_{XA}^{jk}(t) = + \frac{X^k(t) - X_{A0}}{\varrho_{A0}^k(t)} - \frac{X^j(t) - X_{A0}}{\varrho_{A0}^j(t)}$$

$$a_{YA}^{jk}(t) = + \frac{Y^k(t) - Y_{A0}}{\varrho_{A0}^k(t)} - \frac{Y^j(t) - Y_{A0}}{\varrho_{A0}^j(t)}$$

$$a_{ZA}^{jk}(t) = + \frac{Z^k(t) - Z_{A0}}{\varrho_{A0}^k(t)} - \frac{Z^j(t) - Z_{A0}}{\varrho_{A0}^j(t)}$$

$$\tag{9.129}$$

$$a_{XB}^{jk}(t) = - \frac{X^k(t) - X_{B0}}{\varrho_{B0}^k(t)} + \frac{X^j(t) - X_{B0}}{\varrho_{B0}^j(t)}$$

$$a_{YB}^{jk}(t) = - \frac{Y^k(t) - Y_{B0}}{\varrho_{B0}^k(t)} + \frac{Y^j(t) - Y_{B0}}{\varrho_{B0}^j(t)}$$

$$a_{ZB}^{jk}(t) = - \frac{Z^k(t) - Z_{B0}}{\varrho_{B0}^k(t)} + \frac{Z^j(t) - Z_{B0}}{\varrho_{B0}^j(t)}$$

and for the left-hand side

$$\ell_{AB}^{jk}(t) = \lambda \, \Phi_{AB}^{jk}(t) - \varrho_{B0}^k(t) + \varrho_{B0}^j(t) + \varrho_{A0}^k(t) - \varrho_{A0}^j(t) \tag{9.130}$$

which comprises both the measurement quantities and all terms computed from the approximate values. Using the abbreviations (9.129) and (9.130), the linear observation equation is given by

$$\ell_{AB}^{jk}(t) = \; a_{XA}^{jk}(t) \, \Delta X_A + a_{YA}^{jk}(t) \, \Delta Y_A + a_{ZA}^{jk}(t) \, \Delta Z_A$$

$$+ \, a_{XB}^{jk}(t) \, \Delta X_B + a_{YB}^{jk}(t) \, \Delta Y_B + a_{ZB}^{jk}(t) \, \Delta Z_B + \lambda \, N_{AB}^{jk}$$

$$\tag{9.131}$$

which reflects the general case with two unknown baseline points. However, the coordinates of one point (e.g., A) must be known for relative positioning. More specifically, the known point A reduces the number of unknowns by three because of

$$\Delta X_A = \Delta Y_A = \Delta Z_A = 0 \tag{9.132}$$

and leads to a slight change in the left-hand side term

$$\ell_{AB}^{jk}(t) = \lambda \, \Phi_{AB}^{jk}(t) - \varrho_{B0}^k(t) + \varrho_{B0}^j(t) + \varrho_A^k(t) - \varrho_A^j(t) . \tag{9.133}$$

Assuming now four satellites j, k, l, m and two epochs t_1, t_2, the matrix-vector system

$$
\underline{\ell} = \begin{bmatrix} \ell_{AB}^{jk}(t_1) \\ \ell_{AB}^{jl}(t_1) \\ \ell_{AB}^{jm}(t_1) \\ \ell_{AB}^{jk}(t_2) \\ \ell_{AB}^{jl}(t_2) \\ \ell_{AB}^{jm}(t_2) \end{bmatrix} \qquad \underline{x} = \begin{bmatrix} \Delta X_B \\ \Delta Y_B \\ \Delta Z_B \\ N_{AB}^{jk} \\ N_{AB}^{jl} \\ N_{AB}^{jm} \end{bmatrix}
$$

$$
\underline{A} = \begin{bmatrix}
a_{XB}^{jk}(t_1) & a_{YB}^{jk}(t_1) & a_{ZB}^{jk}(t_1) & \lambda & 0 & 0 \\
a_{XB}^{jl}(t_1) & a_{YB}^{jl}(t_1) & a_{ZB}^{jl}(t_1) & 0 & \lambda & 0 \\
a_{XB}^{jm}(t_1) & a_{YB}^{jm}(t_1) & a_{ZB}^{jm}(t_1) & 0 & 0 & \lambda \\
a_{XB}^{jk}(t_2) & a_{YB}^{jk}(t_2) & a_{ZB}^{jk}(t_2) & \lambda & 0 & 0 \\
a_{XB}^{jl}(t_2) & a_{YB}^{jl}(t_2) & a_{ZB}^{jl}(t_2) & 0 & \lambda & 0 \\
a_{XB}^{jm}(t_2) & a_{YB}^{jm}(t_2) & a_{ZB}^{jm}(t_2) & 0 & 0 & \lambda
\end{bmatrix}
$$

(9.134)

is obtained which represents a determined and, thus, solvable system. Note that for one epoch the system has more unknowns than equations.

9.4   Network adjustment

9.4.1   Single baseline solution

The previous sections described the linearization of the observation equations. The adjustment itself (i.e., the solution of the system of linear equations) is a purely mathematical task to be solved by the computer. It is not the objective of this GPS text to investigate different solution strategies. Extensive details on this subject can be found in Leick (1990). Here, only some remarks are appropriate.

The adjustment principle $\underline{n}^T \underline{P} \, \underline{n} = $ minimum necessitates for the solution the implementation of the weight matrix $\underline{P}$. As shown in Sect. 8.2.2, phases and single-differences are uncorrelated, whereas double-differences and triple-differences are correlated. The implementation of the double-difference correlation can be accomplished fairly easily. Alternatively, the double-differences can be decorrelated by using a Gram-Schmidt orthonormalization, cf. Remondi (1984). The implementation of the correlation of the triple-differences is more difficult. Furthermore, it is questionable if it is worthwhile to put much effort in a correct triple-difference correlation computation where the noise of the triple-differences always prevents a refined solution.

In the case of an observed network, the use of the single baseline method usually implies a baseline by baseline computation for all possible combinations. If n_i denotes the number of observing sites, then $n_i(n_i-1)/2$ baselines can be calculated. Note that only $n_i - 1$ of them are theoretically independent. The redundant baselines can either be used for misclosure checks or for an additional adjustment of the baseline vectors.

There are other approaches. McArthur et al. (1985) propose three different methods. One of them is the same as the previously mentioned one. The second method restricts the selection to $n_i - 1$ vectors. This means that the optimal baseline configuration must be chosen. The third method is a variation of the first one and encompasses more than one session. All possible baselines are computed for each session. Finally, the resulting vectors of all sessions are subject to a common adjustment.

The disadvantage of the simple single baseline solution from the theoretical point of view is that it is not correct. This is due to the correlation of the simultaneously observed baselines. By solving baseline by baseline, this correlation is ignored. The intercorrelation between baselines is discussed in the next section.

9.4.2 Multipoint solution

In contrast to the baseline by baseline solution, here all points in the network are considered at once. The key difference compared to the single baseline solution is that in the multipoint approach the correlations between the baselines are taken into account.

The principal correlations have been shown in Sect. 8.2.2. The same theoretical aspects also apply to the extended case of a network. The examples are kept as simple as possible to avoid the burden of lengthy formulas.

Single-difference example for a network
Consider three points A, B, C, a single satellite j, and a single epoch t. Thus, two independent baselines can be defined. Taking A as reference site,

for the two baselines $A–B$ and $A–C$ the two single-differences

$$\Phi^j_{AB}(t) = \Phi^j_B(t) - \Phi^j_A(t)$$
$$\Phi^j_{AC}(t) = \Phi^j_C(t) - \Phi^j_A(t)$$

$$(9.135)$$

can be set up for the one satellite at epoch t. By introducing the vector $\underline{SD}$ for the single-differences, the vector $\underline{\Phi}$ for the phases, and a matrix $\underline{C}$ as

$$\underline{SD} = \begin{bmatrix} \Phi^j_{AB}(t) \\ \Phi^j_{AC}(t) \end{bmatrix} \qquad \underline{C} = \begin{bmatrix} -1 & 1 & 0 \\ -1 & 0 & 1 \end{bmatrix} \qquad \underline{\Phi} = \begin{bmatrix} \Phi^j_A(t) \\ \Phi^j_B(t) \\ \Phi^j_C(t) \end{bmatrix},$$

$$(9.136)$$

the relation $\underline{SD} = \underline{C}\,\underline{\Phi}$ can be formed. To find the correlation, the covariance propagation law is applied by $\mathrm{cov}(\underline{SD}) = \underline{C}\,\mathrm{cov}(\underline{\Phi})\,\underline{C}^T$ leading to

$$\mathrm{cov}(\underline{SD}) = \sigma^2\,\underline{C}\,\underline{C}^T \qquad\qquad (9.137)$$

because of $\mathrm{cov}(\underline{\Phi}) = \sigma^2\,\underline{I}$, cf. Eq. (8.32). Substituting matrix $\underline{C}$ from (9.136) and evaluating the matrix operation yields

$$\mathrm{cov}(\underline{SD}) = \sigma^2 \begin{bmatrix} 2 & 1 \\ 1 & 2 \end{bmatrix} \qquad\qquad (9.138)$$

which shows, as is to be expected, a correlation of the single-differences of the two baselines. Recall that single-differences of a single baseline are uncorrelated as discovered in Sect. 8.2.2 but single-differences of two baselines with a common point are correlated.

Double-difference example for a network
Since double-differences are already correlated for a single baseline, a correlation must be expected for the network too. Nevertheless, the subsequent slightly larger example will demonstrate the increasing complexity. Assume again three points A, B, C with A as reference site for the two baselines $A–B$ and $A–C$. Consider a single epoch t for four satellites j, k, ℓ, m where j is taken as the reference satellite for the double-differences.

Formulating generally, there are $(n_i - 1)(n_j - 1)$ independent double-differences for n_i points and n_j satellites. For the given example, $n_i = 3$ and

$n_j = 4$ and, thus, 6 double-differences can be written. Based on Eq. (8.25), these are

$$\Phi_{AB}^{jk}(t) = \Phi_B^k(t) - \Phi_B^j(t) - \Phi_A^k(t) + \Phi_A^j(t)$$

$$\Phi_{AB}^{j\ell}(t) = \Phi_B^\ell(t) - \Phi_B^j(t) - \Phi_A^\ell(t) + \Phi_A^j(t)$$

$$\Phi_{AB}^{jm}(t) = \Phi_B^m(t) - \Phi_B^j(t) - \Phi_A^m(t) + \Phi_A^j(t)$$

$$\Phi_{AC}^{jk}(t) = \Phi_C^k(t) - \Phi_C^j(t) - \Phi_A^k(t) + \Phi_A^j(t) \qquad (9.139)$$

$$\Phi_{AC}^{j\ell}(t) = \Phi_C^\ell(t) - \Phi_C^j(t) - \Phi_A^\ell(t) + \Phi_A^j(t)$$

$$\Phi_{AC}^{jm}(t) = \Phi_C^m(t) - \Phi_C^j(t) - \Phi_A^m(t) + \Phi_A^j(t)$$

for the assumptions made. As in the previous example, a matrix-vector relation is desired. By introducing

$$\underline{C} = \begin{bmatrix} 1 & -1 & 0 & 0 & -1 & 1 & 0 & 0 & 0 & 0 & 0 & 0 \\ 1 & 0 & -1 & 0 & -1 & 0 & 1 & 0 & 0 & 0 & 0 & 0 \\ 1 & 0 & 0 & -1 & -1 & 0 & 0 & 1 & 0 & 0 & 0 & 0 \\ 1 & -1 & 0 & 0 & 0 & 0 & 0 & 0 & -1 & 1 & 0 & 0 \\ 1 & 0 & -1 & 0 & 0 & 0 & 0 & 0 & -1 & 0 & 1 & 0 \\ 1 & 0 & 0 & -1 & 0 & 0 & 0 & 0 & -1 & 0 & 0 & 1 \end{bmatrix}$$

$$\underline{DD} = \begin{bmatrix} \Phi_{AB}^{jk}(t) \\ \Phi_{AB}^{j\ell}(t) \\ \Phi_{AB}^{jm}(t) \\ \Phi_{AC}^{jk}(t) \\ \Phi_{AC}^{j\ell}(t) \\ \Phi_{AC}^{jm}(t) \end{bmatrix} \qquad \underline{\Phi} = \begin{bmatrix} \Phi_A^j(t) \\ \Phi_A^k(t) \\ \Phi_A^\ell(t) \\ \Phi_A^m(t) \\ \Phi_B^j(t) \\ \Phi_B^k(t) \\ \Phi_B^\ell(t) \\ \Phi_B^m(t) \\ \Phi_C^j(t) \\ \Phi_C^k(t) \\ \Phi_C^\ell(t) \\ \Phi_C^m(t) \end{bmatrix}, \qquad (9.140)$$

the relation

$$\underline{DD} = \underline{C}\,\underline{\Phi} \qquad (9.141)$$

is valid. The covariance follows by

$$\mathrm{cov}(\underline{DD}) = \underline{C}\,\mathrm{cov}(\underline{\Phi})\,\underline{C}^T \tag{9.142}$$

which reduces to

$$\mathrm{cov}(\underline{DD}) = \sigma^2\,\underline{C}\,\underline{C}^T \tag{9.143}$$

because of the uncorrelated phases. Explicitly, the matrix product

$$\underline{C}\,\underline{C}^T = \begin{bmatrix} 4 & 2 & 2 & 2 & 1 & 1 \\ 2 & 4 & 2 & 1 & 2 & 1 \\ 2 & 2 & 4 & 1 & 1 & 2 \\ 2 & 1 & 1 & 4 & 2 & 2 \\ 1 & 2 & 1 & 2 & 4 & 2 \\ 1 & 1 & 2 & 2 & 2 & 4 \end{bmatrix} \tag{9.144}$$

is a full matrix as expected. Finally, the weight matrix

$$\underline{P} = \frac{1}{12} \begin{bmatrix} 6 & -2 & -2 & -3 & 1 & 1 \\ -2 & 6 & -2 & 1 & -3 & 1 \\ -2 & -2 & 6 & 1 & 1 & -3 \\ -3 & 1 & 1 & 6 & -2 & -2 \\ 1 & -3 & 1 & -2 & 6 & -2 \\ 1 & 1 & -3 & -2 & -2 & 6 \end{bmatrix} \tag{9.145}$$

is the inverse of (9.144). Ashkenazi et al. (1987) show that the weight matrix can be composed by a Kronecker matrix product. Beutler et al. (1986) and Beutler et al. (1987a) give detailed instructions for a computer implementation and also show some results of network campaigns where the correlations have either been totally neglected, introduced in a single baseline mode, or calculated correctly. For small networks with baselines not exceeding 10 km, the differences of the three methods are in the range of a few millimeters. Clearly, the solution without any correlation deviates from the theoretically correct values by a greater amount. It is estimated that the single baseline method deviates from the multibaseline (correlated) solution by a maximum of 2σ.

9.4.3   Single baseline versus multipoint solution

The previous paragraphs have shown the difference between the single baseline and the multipoint solution from the theoretical point of view and mentioned a few results from GPS campaigns as shown by Beutler et al. (1987c). This section presents some arguments for using one or the other method.

- The correlation is not modeled correctly with the single baseline solution because correlations between baselines are neglected.

- The computer program is, without doubt, much simpler for the single baseline approach.

- With modern software and hardware, the computational time is not a real problem.

- Cycle slips are more easily detected and repaired in the multipoint mode, cf. Beck et al. (1989).

- It takes less effort in the single baseline mode to isolate bad measurements and possibly to eliminate them.

- The economic implementation of the full correlation for a multipoint solution only works properly for networks with the same observation pattern at each receiver site. In the event of numerous data outages it is better to calculate the covariance matrix from the scratch.

- Even in the case of the multipoint approach, it becomes questionable if the correlations can be modeled properly. A very illustrative example is given in Beutler et al. (1990) where single and dual frequency receivers are combined in a network. For the dual frequency receivers, the ionospheric-free combination $L3$ is formed from $L1$ and $L2$ and processed together with the $L1$ data of the single frequency receivers. Thus, a correlation is introduced because of the $L1$ data. A proper modeling of the correlation biases the ionospheric-free $L3$-baseline by the ionosphere of the $L1$-baseline, an effect which is definitely undesirable.

The factors listed illustrate the difficulty in deciding which method (i.e., single baseline versus multipoint solution) to use.

9.5   Dilution of Precision

The geometry of the visible satellites is an important factor in achieving high quality results especially for point positioning and kinematic surveying. The geometry changes with time due to the relative motion of the satellites. A measure for the geometry is the Dilution of Precision (DOP) factor.

First, the specific case of four satellites is considered. The linearized observation equations for the point positioning model with code ranges are given by Eq. (9.120), and the solution for the (four) unknowns follows from the inverse relation $\underline{x} = \underline{A}^{-1}\,\underline{\ell}$. The design matrix $\underline{A}$ is given by Eq. (9.121)

$$
\underline{A} =
\begin{bmatrix}
-\dfrac{X^1(t) - X_{i0}}{\varrho^1_{i0}(t)} & -\dfrac{Y^1(t) - Y_{i0}}{\varrho^1_{i0}(t)} & -\dfrac{Z^1(t) - Z_{i0}}{\varrho^1_{i0}(t)} & -c \\[2ex]
-\dfrac{X^2(t) - X_{i0}}{\varrho^2_{i0}(t)} & -\dfrac{Y^2(t) - Y_{i0}}{\varrho^2_{i0}(t)} & -\dfrac{Z^2(t) - Z_{i0}}{\varrho^2_{i0}(t)} & -c \\[2ex]
-\dfrac{X^3(t) - X_{i0}}{\varrho^3_{i0}(t)} & -\dfrac{Y^3(t) - Y_{i0}}{\varrho^3_{i0}(t)} & -\dfrac{Z^3(t) - Z_{i0}}{\varrho^3_{i0}(t)} & -c \\[2ex]
-\dfrac{X^4(t) - X_{i0}}{\varrho^4_{i0}(t)} & -\dfrac{Y^4(t) - Y_{i0}}{\varrho^4_{i0}(t)} & -\dfrac{Z^4(t) - Z_{i0}}{\varrho^4_{i0}(t)} & -c
\end{bmatrix}
$$

$$(9.146)$$

where the first three elements in each row are the components of the unit vectors $\Delta\underline{\varrho}^j$, $j = 1, 2, 3, 4$ pointing from the four satellites to the observing site. The solution fails if the design matrix is singular or, equivalently, its determinant becomes zero. The determinant is proportional to the scalar triple product

$$\left((\Delta\underline{\varrho}^4 - \Delta\underline{\varrho}^1),\ (\Delta\underline{\varrho}^3 - \Delta\underline{\varrho}^1),\ (\Delta\underline{\varrho}^2 - \Delta\underline{\varrho}^1) \right)$$

which can geometrically be interpreted by the volume of a body. This body is formed by the intersection points of the site-satellite vectors with the unit sphere centered at the observing site. The larger the volume of this body, the better the satellite geometry. Since good geometry should mirror a low DOP value, the reciprocal value of the volume of the geometric body is directly proportional to DOP, cf. for example Milliken and Zoller (1980). The critical configuration is given when the body degenerates to a plane. This is the case when the vectors $\Delta\underline{\varrho}^j$ form a cone with the observing site as apex, cf. Wunderlich (1992).

More generally, DOP can be calculated from the inverse of the normal equation matrix of the solution. The cofactor matrix $\underline{Q}_X$ follows from

$$\underline{Q}_X = (\underline{A}^T \underline{A})^{-1} \,. \tag{9.147}$$

In this case, the weight matrix has been assumed to be a unit matrix. The cofactor matrix $\underline{Q}_X$ is a 4×4 matrix where three components are contributed by the site position X, Y, Z and one component by the receiver clock. Denoting the elements of the cofactor matrix as

$$
\underline{Q}_X = \begin{bmatrix} q_{XX} & q_{XY} & q_{XZ} & q_{Xt} \\ q_{XY} & q_{YY} & q_{YZ} & q_{Yt} \\ q_{XZ} & q_{YZ} & q_{ZZ} & q_{Zt} \\ q_{Xt} & q_{Yt} & q_{Zt} & q_{tt} \end{bmatrix} ,
\tag{9.148}
$$

the diagonal elements are used for the following DOP definitions:

$$
\text{GDOP} = \sqrt{q_{XX} + q_{YY} + q_{ZZ} + q_{tt}} \quad \ldots \quad \text{geometric dilution of precision}
$$

$$
\text{PDOP} = \sqrt{q_{XX} + q_{YY} + q_{ZZ}} \quad \ldots \quad \text{position dilution of precision}
$$

$$
\text{TDOP} = \sqrt{q_{tt}} \quad \ldots \quad \text{time dilution of precision.}
$$

$$
\tag{9.149}
$$

It should be noted that the previous DOP explanation using the geometric body refers to GDOP.

These definitions deserve brief explanations in order to avoid confusion. Quite often the elements under the square root are displayed as quadratic terms. This depends on the designation of the elements of the cofactor matrix. Here, the diagonal elements of the cofactor matrix have been denoted as q_{XX}, q_{YY}, q_{ZZ}, and q_{tt}, thus no superscripts appear in the DOP definitions. If the diagonal elements are denoted as, e.g., q_X^2, q_Y^2, q_Z^2, q_t^2, then of course the superscripts also appear in the DOP definitions. The general rule used here is: when computing DOP values, the elements of the cofactor matrix are not squared (e.g., for GDOP the square root of the trace must be calculated).

The DOPs in (9.149) are expressed in the equatorial ECEF system. When the topocentric local coordinate system with its axes along the local north, east, and vertical is used, the global cofactor matrix $\underline{Q}_X$ must be transformed into the local cofactor matrix $\underline{Q}_x$ by the law of covariance propagation. Denoting now as $\underline{Q}_X$ that part of the cofactor matrix that contains the geometrical components (disregarding the time-correlated components), the transformation is

$$
\underline{Q}_x = \underline{R}\,\underline{Q}_X\,\underline{R}^T = \begin{bmatrix} q_{xx} & q_{xy} & q_{xh} \\ q_{xy} & q_{yy} & q_{yh} \\ q_{xh} & q_{yh} & q_{hh} \end{bmatrix}
\tag{9.150}
$$

where the rotation matrix $\underline{R} = [\underline{i}, \, \underline{j}, \, \underline{k}]^T$ contains the axes of the local coordinate system as given in Eq. (7.6).

In addition to the local PDOP, two further DOP definitions are given. HDOP, the dilution of precision in the horizontal position, and VDOP, denoting the corresponding value for the vertical component, the height:

$$\text{HDOP} = \sqrt{q_{xx} + q_{yy}} \quad \dots \quad \text{horizontal dilution of precision}$$

$$\text{VDOP} = \sqrt{q_{hh}} \qquad \dots \quad \text{vertical dilution of precision.}$$

(9.151)

The discussion, so far, involves only single epoch point positioning. When designing a survey, it is helpful to know DOP for the full (observation) session. The procedure is to compute the DOP values on an epoch by epoch basis for the desired period. The time increment between epochs can be matched to the specific purposes of the planned survey. In Fig. 9.5, PDOP is shown for an entire day and was computed for 15-minute increments. No measured data are necessary to calculate DOP values! The satellite positions can be calculated either from almanac data or from an appropriate orbit file. Note that DOP computations are not restricted to point positioning but can also be applied to relative positioning. Starting with the design matrix for a baseline vector determination, the cofactor matrix can be computed. These DOP values can be considered as relative DOP values.

The purposes of DOP are twofold. First, it is useful in planning a survey and, second, it may be helpful in interpreting processed baseline vectors. For example, data with poor DOP could possibly be omitted.

Finally, the correlation of DOP with the positioning accuracy is considered. Denoting the measurement accuracy by σ_0 (i.e., the standard de-

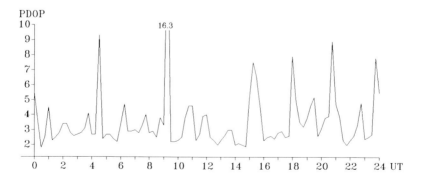

Fig. 9.5. PDOP for Graz, Austria, on October 1, 1993 (cut off elevation: 15 degrees)

viation), the positioning accuracy σ follows from the product of DOP and measurement accuracy, thus

$$\sigma = \text{DOP}\,\sigma_0\,. \tag{9.152}$$

Applying this formula to the specific DOP definitions,

GDOP σ_0 ...   geometric accuracy in position and time

PDOP σ_0 ...   accuracy in position

TDOP σ_0 ...   accuracy in time

HDOP σ_0 ...   accuracy in the horizontal position

VDOP σ_0 ...   accuracy in vertical direction

results, cf. Wells et al. (1987). The list of DOP definitions is not restricted to those given here. The meaning of other DOP definitions can be derived from the associated acronyms.

10 Transformation of GPS results

10.1 Introduction

The reference frame of GPS is the World Geodetic System 1984 (WGS-84). When using GPS, the coordinates of terrestrial sites, for example, are obtained in the same reference frame. The surveyor is not, usually, interested in coordinates of the terrestrial points referring to a global frame; rather, the results are preferred in a local coordinate frame either as geodetic (i.e., ellipsoidal) coordinates, as plane coordinates, or as vectors combined with other terrestrial data. Since the WGS-84 is a geocentric system and the local system usually is not, certain transformations are required. The subsequent sections deal with the transformations most frequently used.

10.2 Coordinate transformations

10.2.1 Cartesian coordinates and ellipsoidal coordinates

Denoting the Cartesian (rectangular) coordinates of a point in space by X, Y, Z and assuming an ellipsoid of revolution with the same origin as the Cartesian coordinate system, the point can also be expressed by the ellipsoidal coordinates φ, λ, h, see Fig. 10.1. The relation between the Cartesian coordinates and the ellipsoidal coordinates is given by Eq. (3.6):

$$
\begin{aligned}
X &= (N + h)\cos\varphi\cos\lambda \\
Y &= (N + h)\cos\varphi\sin\lambda \\
Z &= \left(\frac{b^2}{a^2}N + h\right)\sin\varphi
\end{aligned}
\tag{10.1}
$$

where N is the radius of curvature in prime vertical which can be obtained by

$$
N = \frac{a^2}{\sqrt{a^2\cos^2\varphi + b^2\sin^2\varphi}},
\tag{10.2}
$$

and a, b are the semiaxes of the ellipsoid. Recall that the Cartesian coordinates related to the WGS-84 are also denoted ECEF coordinates and that

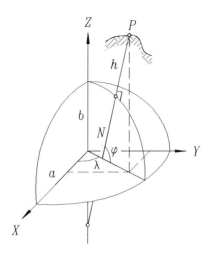

Fig. 10.1. Cartesian coordinates X, Y, Z and
ellipsoidal coordinates φ, λ, h

the origins of the ECEF coordinate system and of the WGS-84 ellipsoid are
identical (i.e., geocentric).

The formulas (10.1) transform ellipsoidal coordinates φ, λ, h into Cartesian coordinates X, Y, Z. For GPS applications, the inverse transformation
is more important since the Cartesian coordinates are given and the ellipsoidal coordinates sought. Thus, the task is now to compute the ellipsoidal
coordinates φ, λ, h from the Cartesian coordinates X, Y, Z. Usually, this
problem is solved iteratively although a solution in closed form is possible.
From X and Y the radius of a parallel,

$$p = \sqrt{X^2 + Y^2} = (N + h) \cos \varphi \,, \tag{10.3}$$

can be computed. This equation is rearranged as

$$h = \frac{p}{\cos \varphi} - N \tag{10.4}$$

so that the ellipsoidal height appears explicitly. Introducing by

$$e^2 = \frac{a^2 - b^2}{a^2} \tag{10.5}$$

the first numerical eccentricity, the relation $b^2/a^2 = 1 - e^2$ follows which can
be substituted into the equation for Z in (10.1). The result

$$Z = (N + h - e^2 N) \sin \varphi \tag{10.6}$$

can be written as

$$Z = (N + h)\left(1 - e^2\,\frac{N}{N + h}\right)\sin\varphi \qquad\qquad (10.7)$$

equivalently. Dividing this expression by Eq. (10.3) gives

$$\frac{Z}{p} = \left(1 - e^2\,\frac{N}{N + h}\right)\tan\varphi \qquad\qquad (10.8)$$

which yields

$$\tan\varphi = \frac{Z}{p}\left(1 - e^2\,\frac{N}{N + h}\right)^{-1}. \qquad\qquad (10.9)$$

For the longitude λ, the equation

$$\tan\lambda = \frac{Y}{X} \qquad\qquad (10.10)$$

is obtained from Eq. (10.1) by dividing the first and the second equation.

The longitude λ can be directly computed from Eq. (10.10). The height h and the latitude φ are determined by Eqs. (10.4) and (10.9). The problem is that both equations depend on the latitude and the height. A solution can be found iteratively by the following steps:

1. Compute $p = \sqrt{X^2 + Y^2}$.

2. Compute an approximate value $\varphi_{(0)}$ from
$$\tan\varphi_{(0)} = \frac{Z}{p}(1 - e^2)^{-1}.$$

3. Compute an approximate value $N_{(0)}$ from
$$N_{(0)} = \frac{a^2}{\sqrt{a^2\cos^2\varphi_{(0)} + b^2\sin^2\varphi_{(0)}}}.$$

4. Compute the ellipsoidal height by
$$h = \frac{p}{\cos\varphi_{(0)}} - N_{(0)}.$$

5. Compute an improved value for the latitude by
$$\tan\varphi = \frac{Z}{p}\left(1 - e^2\,\frac{N_{(0)}}{N_{(0)} + h}\right)^{-1}.$$

6. Check for another iteration step: if $\varphi = \varphi_{(0)}$ then the iteration is completed otherwise set $\varphi_{(0)} = \varphi$ and continue with step 3.

There exist numerous other computation methods. One example for the transformation of X, Y, Z into φ, λ, h without iteration but with an inherent approximation is

$$\varphi = \arctan \frac{Z + e'^2\, b\, \sin^3\theta}{p - e^2\, a\, \cos^3\theta}$$

$$\lambda = \arctan \frac{Y}{X} \tag{10.11}$$

$$h = \frac{p}{\cos\varphi} - N$$

where

$$\theta = \arctan \frac{Z\, a}{p\, b} \tag{10.12}$$

is an auxiliary quantity and

$$e'^2 = \frac{a^2 - b^2}{b^2} \tag{10.13}$$

is the second numerical eccentricity. Actually, there is no reason why these formulas are less popular than the iterative procedure. Bowring (1976) shows that there does not arise a significant discrepancy for all practical purposes. A computation method with neither iteration nor approximation is, e.g., given by Zhu (1993).

For a numerical example, consider a point with $\varphi = 47°$, $\lambda = 15°$, and $h = 2\,000$ m referring to the WGS-84 ellipsoid. Using the WGS-84 parameters, see Sect. 3.2.1, the desired ECEF coordinates result from (10.1) as $X = 4\,210\,520.621$ m, $Y = 1\,128\,205.600$ m, $Z = 4\,643\,227.495$ m. It is recommended to perform also the inverse transformation.

10.2.2   Ellipsoidal coordinates and plane coordinates

In contrast to the previous section, only points on the ellipsoid are considered. Thus, ellipsoidal latitute φ and longitude λ are of interest here. The objective is to map a point φ, λ on the ellipsoid into a point x, y on a plane.

There are many kinds of map projections, some being more popular than others. In principle,

$$x = x(\varphi, \lambda;\, a,\, b)$$

$$y = y(\varphi, \lambda;\, a,\, b) \tag{10.14}$$

is the general formulation of the desired map projection. Geodetic applications require conformal projections be used. Conformality means that an angle on the ellipsoid is preserved after mapping it into the plane. More precisely, the angle included by two geodesics on the ellipsoid is preserved if the two geodesics are conformally mapped into the plane. The drawback is, the geodesics on the ellipsoid mapped into the plane are in general no longer geodesics (i.e., straight lines) but curved lines.

Some of the most important conformal mappings of the ellipsoid into the plane are subsequently interpreted geometrically although they are defined analytically. Detailed formulas for many conformal mappings can be found, e.g., in Richardus and Adler (1972) or in Hofmann-Wellenhof et al. (1994).

- Conical projection. Consider a cone which is tangent to the ellipsoid at the standard parallel. After development of the conical surface, the meridians are straight lines converging at a point called apex. This point is also the center of circles which represent the projected parallels. Note that the standard parallel is mapped without distortion. One example for this projection is the conformal Lambert projection.

- Cylindrical projection. This is a special case of the conical projection if the apex is moved to infinity so that the cone becomes a cylinder which is tangent at the equator. In transverse position, the cylinder is tangent at a standard meridian. After development of the cylindrical surface, the standard meridian is mapped without distortion. Two examples for this projetion are the Transverse Mercator projection and the Universal Transverse Mercator (UTM) system. Because both projections are widely used, more details on these mappings are given below.

- Azimuthal projection. This is also a special case of the conical projection if the apex is moved to the pole so that the cone becomes a plane which is tangent at the pole. The pole is the center of circles representing the parallels and of straight lines representing the meridians. More generally, the projection plane can be defined as tangent plane at any point on the ellipsoid. One example for this projection is the stereographic projection.

Transverse Mercator projection

This mapping method is also referred to as Gauss-Krüger projection. The ellipsoid is partitioned into 120 zones of 3° longitude each where the central meridian is in the center of each zone. The central meridian is mapped into the plane without scale distortion and represents the y-axis (north direction). The x-axis is the mapping of the equator. The central meridian of the zone and the equator are special cases since all other meridians and parallels are mapped as curved lines. Because of conformality, the mapped images of the meridians and parallels are orthogonal to each other.

The numbering of the zones is related either to Greenwich or to Ferro. By definition, the latter is situated $17°40'$ W with respect to Greenwich.

For the Transverse Mercator (or Gauss-Krüger) projection, the mapping of an ellipsoidal point φ, λ into a point y, x of the plane is given by the series expansions

$$y = B(\varphi) + \frac{t}{2} N \cos^2\varphi \; \ell^2$$

$$+ \frac{t}{24} N \cos^4\varphi \left(5 - t^2 + 9\eta^2 + 4\eta^4\right)\ell^4$$

$$+ \frac{t}{720} N \cos^6\varphi \left(61 - 58\, t^2 + t^4 + 270\,\eta^2 - 330\, t^2\eta^2\right)\ell^6$$

$$+ \frac{t}{40\,320} N \cos^8\varphi \left(1385 - 3111\, t^2 + 543\, t^4 - t^6\right)\ell^8 + \ldots$$

$$(10.15)$$

$$x = N \cos\varphi \; \ell + \frac{1}{6} N \cos^3\varphi \left(1 - t^2 + \eta^2\right)\ell^3$$

$$+ \frac{1}{120} N \cos^5\varphi \left(5 - 18\, t^2 + t^4 + 14\,\eta^2 - 58\, t^2\eta^2\right)\ell^5$$

$$+ \frac{1}{5040} N \cos^7\varphi \left(61 - 479\, t^2 + 179\, t^4 - t^6\right)\ell^7 + \ldots$$

where

$$
\begin{aligned}
&B(\varphi) && \ldots && \text{arc length of meridian} \\
&N = \frac{a^2}{b\sqrt{1 + \eta^2}} && \ldots && \text{radius of curvature in prime vertical} \\
&\eta^2 = e'^2 \cos^2\varphi && \ldots && \text{auxiliary quantity} \\
&e'^2 = (a^2 - b^2)/b^2 && \ldots && \text{second numerical eccentricity} \\
&t = \tan\varphi && \ldots && \text{auxiliary quantity} \\
&\ell = \lambda - \lambda_0 && \ldots && \text{longitude difference} \\
&\lambda_0 && \ldots && \text{longitude of the central meridian}
\end{aligned}
$$

are used. By convention, y is given first followed by x because the pair of coordinates (y, x) corresponds to (φ, λ). The arc length of meridian $B(\varphi)$ is the ellipsoidal distance from the equator to the point to be mapped and can be computed by the series expansion

$$B(\varphi) = \alpha \left[\varphi + \beta \sin 2\varphi + \gamma \sin 4\varphi + \delta \sin 6\varphi + \varepsilon \sin 8\varphi + \ldots \right]$$

(10.16)

where

$$\alpha = \frac{a+b}{2}\left(1 + \frac{1}{4}n^2 + \frac{1}{64}n^4 + \ldots\right)$$

$$\beta = -\frac{3}{2}n + \frac{9}{16}n^3 - \frac{3}{32}n^5 + \ldots$$

$$\gamma = \frac{15}{16}n^2 - \frac{15}{32}n^4 + \ldots$$

(10.17)

$$\delta = -\frac{35}{48}n^3 + \frac{105}{256}n^5 - \ldots$$

$$\varepsilon = \frac{315}{512}n^4 + \ldots$$

and

$$n = \frac{a-b}{a+b}.$$

(10.18)

As examples,

Bessel ellipsoid	WGS-84 ellipsoid
$\alpha =$ $6\,366\,742.5203$ m	$\alpha =$ $6\,367\,449.1458$ m
$\beta = -2.511\,274\,56 \cdot 10^{-3}$	$\beta = -2.518\,827\,92 \cdot 10^{-3}$
$\gamma =$ $2.627\,71 \cdot 10^{-6}$	$\gamma =$ $2.643\,54 \cdot 10^{-6}$
$\delta = -3.42 \cdot 10^{-9}$	$\delta = -3.45 \cdot 10^{-9}$
$\varepsilon =$ $5 \cdot 10^{-12}$	$\varepsilon =$ $5 \cdot 10^{-12}$

(10.19)

are the parameters for the Bessel ellipsoid and the WGS-84 ellipsoid. Despite the slightly different definition, the parameters for the WGS-84 ellipsoid can also be used for the GRS-80 ellipsoid. For the precision shown, there is no significant difference in the coefficients.

Consider the following numerical example where the arc length of the meridian on the Bessel ellipsoid should be calculated. For $\varphi = 47°$, the result is $B(\varphi) = 5\,206\,717.123$ m.

The inverse Gauß-Krüger projection is the mapping of a point y, x in the plane to a point φ, λ on the ellipsoid. The mapping formulas are given by the series expansions

$$\varphi = \varphi_f + \frac{t_f}{2N_f^2}\left(-1 - \eta_f^2\right)x^2$$

$$+ \frac{t_f}{24\,N_f^4}\left(5 + 3t_f^2 + 6\eta_f^2 - 6t_f^2\,\eta_f^2 - 3\eta_f^4 - 9t_f^2\,\eta_f^4\right)x^4$$

$$+ \frac{t_f}{720\,N_f^6}\left(-61 - 90\,t_f^2 - 45\,t_f^4 - 107\,\eta_f^2 + 162\,t_f^2\,\eta_f^2 \right.$$
$$\left. +45\,t_f^4\,\eta_f^2\right)x^6$$

$$+ \frac{t_f}{40\,320\,N_f^8}\left(1385 + 3633\,t_f^2 + 4095\,t_f^4 + 1575\,t_f^6\right)x^8 + \dots$$

$$(10.20)$$

$$\lambda = \lambda_0 + \frac{1}{N_f\cos\varphi_f}\,x + \frac{1}{6N_f^3\cos\varphi_f}\left(-1 - 2t_f^2 - \eta_f^2\right)x^3$$

$$+ \frac{1}{120\,N_f^5\cos\varphi_f}\left(5 + 28\,t_f^2 + 24\,t_f^4 + 6\eta_f^2 + 8t_f^2\,\eta_f^2\right)x^5$$

$$+ \frac{1}{5040\,N_f^7\cos\varphi_f}\left(-61 - 662\,t_f^2 - 1320\,t_f^4 - 720\,t_f^6\right)x^7 + \dots$$

where the terms with the subscript f must be calculated based on the footpoint latitude φ_f. For the footpoint latitude, the series expansion is given by

$$\varphi_f = \bar{y} + \bar{\beta}\,\sin 2\bar{y} + \bar{\gamma}\,\sin 4\bar{y} + \bar{\delta}\,\sin 6\bar{y} + \bar{\varepsilon}\,\sin 8\bar{y} + \dots \qquad (10.21)$$

where

$$\bar{\alpha} = \frac{a + b}{2}\left(1 + \frac{1}{4}\,n^2 + \frac{1}{64}\,n^4 + \dots\right)$$

$$\bar{\beta} = \frac{3}{2}\,n - \frac{27}{32}\,n^3 + \frac{269}{512}\,n^5 + \dots$$

$$\bar{\gamma} = \frac{21}{16}\,n^2 - \frac{55}{32}\,n^4 + \dots \qquad\qquad\qquad (10.22)$$

$$\bar{\delta} = \frac{151}{96}\,n^3 - \frac{417}{128}\,n^5 + \dots$$

$$\bar{\varepsilon} = \frac{1097}{512}\,n^4 + \dots$$

and the relation

$$\bar{y} = \frac{y}{\bar{\alpha}} \tag{10.23}$$

are used. Note that the coefficient $\bar{\alpha}$ is identical to α in (10.17). As examples,

Bessel ellipsoid	WGS-84 ellipsoid
$\bar{\alpha} = 6\,366\,742.5203$ m	$\bar{\alpha} = 6\,367\,449.1458$ m
$\bar{\beta} = 2.511\,273\,24 \cdot 10^{-3}$	$\bar{\beta} = 2.518\,826\,58 \cdot 10^{-3}$
$\bar{\gamma} = 3.678\,79 \cdot 10^{-6}$	$\bar{\gamma} = 3.700\,95 \cdot 10^{-6}$
$\bar{\delta} = 7.38 \cdot 10^{-9}$	$\bar{\delta} = 7.45 \cdot 10^{-9}$
$\bar{\varepsilon} = 17 \cdot 10^{-12}$	$\bar{\varepsilon} = 17 \cdot 10^{-12}$

$$(10.24)$$

are the parameters for the Bessel ellipsoid and the WGS-84 ellipsoid. Without loss of accuracy, the coefficients for the WGS-84 may also be used for the GRS-80 ellipsoid.

For a numerical example consider the coordinate $y = 5\,206\,717.123$ m referring to the Bessel ellipsoid and compute the associated footpoint latitude. The result is $\varphi_f = 47°$.

Universal Transverse Mercator (UTM) system
The UTM system is a modification of the Transverse Mercator system. First, the ellipsoid is partitioned into 60 zones with a width of 6° longitude each. Second, a scale factor of 0.9996 is applied to the conformal coordinates in the plane. The reason for this factor is to avoid fairly large distortions in the outer areas of a zone.

The zone numbering starts with M1 for the central meridian $\lambda_0 = 177°$ W and continues with M2 for the central meridian $\lambda_0 = 171°$ W. Thus, the central meridian $\lambda_0 = 3°$ W would be the zone M30.

For a numerical example, consider a point on the WGS-84 ellipsoid with $\varphi = 47°$ N and $\lambda = 16°$ E and compute the UTM coordinates. The result is obtained by the formulas (10.15) after multiplication by the scale factor. Related to the central meridian $\lambda_0 = 15°$ (i.e., zone M33), the final result $y = 5\,205\,649.348$ m, $x = 76\,025.312$ m is obtained. It is recommended to perform the inverse mapping which demonstrates that millimeter accuracy is achieved.

10.2.3 Height transformation

In the previous section, a point on the ellipsoid was mapped into the plane and vice versa. The ellipsoidal height could be completely ignored. In this

Fig. 10.2. Definition of heights

section, the primary interest is the height. The formula

$$h = H + N \tag{10.25}$$

where

$$
\begin{array}{lll}
h & \dots & \text{ellipsoidal height} \\
H & \dots & \text{orthometric height} \\
N & \dots & \text{geoidal height (undulation)}
\end{array} \tag{10.26}
$$

is the relationship between the ellipsoid and the geoid. As shown in Fig. 10.2, this formula is an approximation but is sufficiently accurate for all practical purposes. The angle ε expresses the deflection of the vertical between the slightly curved plumb line and the ellipsoidal normal. This angle does not exceed 30 arcseconds in most areas.

Positioning with GPS results in X, Y, Z coordinates. After application of the transformation (10.11), the ellipsoidal heights are obtained. If, additionally, one of the two remaining terms in (10.25) is given, the other one can be calculated. Thus, if the geoid is known, orthometric heights can be derived. On the other hand, if orthometric heights are known, geoidal heights can be derived.

A short explanation is given below for readers not familiar with the ellipsoid and the geoid.

Ellipsoid

An ellipsoid of revolution is an approximation of the earth's surface. This surface is formed by choosing a proper sized ellipse and rotating it about its minor axis. The earth ellipsoid is a convenient mathematical surface which has been subdivided by latitude and longitude to form a coordinate system. Distances and azimuths can be computed on this ellipsoid to millimeter accuracy and hundredths of an arcsecond. The ellipsoid only approximates the real earth's surface. As long as geodesists were performing horizontal surveys (e.g., triangulation) separate from vertical surveys (leveling), the difference between the ellipsoid and the true earth's surface (or the geoid) was not significant. This changed with the advent of space geodesy (TRANSIT, GPS) which yields both horizontal and vertical information. Now, the geometrically defined (i.e., ellipsoidal) heights obtained from space geodesy must be combined with physically defined (i.e., orthometric) heights. The ellipsoidal heights refer to the ellipsoid, and the orthometric heights to the geoid. The difference between these two surfaces will undoubtedly occupy geodesists for the next several years (maybe decades), but for the present, surveyors must learn to correct GPS heights (i.e., ellipsoidal heights) to obtain useable elevations.

It should be noted that there is a distinction between locally best-fitting (nongeocentric) ellipsoids and a global (geocentric) ellipsoid. Different local ellipsoids are primarily used because certain sized ellipsoids fit a particular portion of the earth better than a global ellipsoid. In fact, the ellipsoid chosen for an area – for example the Clarke ellipsoid for the former North American Datum 1927 (NAD-27) – was picked to minimize the difference between that ellipsoid and the geoid in that area. The center of a local ellipsoid does not coincide with the center of the true earth, but is displaced from the true center by up to some 100 meters.

Fortunately, only one global ellipsoid is used today. When it became possible to connect the datums of the various continents, geodesists decided to choose a single global reference ellipsoid. The present Geodetic Reference System 1980 (GRS-80) was chosen after much discussion. Recall that the WGS-84 used for GPS is virtually identical with the GRS-80. The center of the GRS-80 ellipsoid now coincides with the true center of the earth, and its surface provides an average fit of the geoid. The fit of this new surface to the geoid (often called sea level surface) is not an improvement for all places on the earth. For example, the old Clarke ellipsoid surface only differs by small amounts from the geoid surface for the U.S.; whereas, the new GRS-80 ellipsoid is approximately 30 m lower than the geoid in the eastern U.S. Surveyors using the old NAD-27 datum were accustomed to reduce their distance measurements to "sea level" when actually they were correcting lengths to map them onto the ellipsoid. Now, they must add approximately 30 m to the elevation to obtain the correct height to use for the reduction to the ellipsoid.

Geoid
The geoid is defined physically and is the surface that is used to represent the actual shape of the earth. Drawings of the geoid show it as a bumpy surface with hills and valleys similar to a topographic model.

The center of the geoid coincides with the true center of the earth and its surface is an equipotential surface. The geoid can be visualized by imagining that the earth were completely covered by water. This water surface would (in theory) be an equipotential surface since the water would flow to compensate for any height difference that would occur. In actuality, the sea level differs slightly from a true equipotential surface due to "bumps" formed by different temperatures, ocean currents, etc.

The geoid is the surface chosen for leveling datums. In many countries, the geoid that most nearly coincides with the average sea level value (measured by tide gauges) is chosen as the zero elevation. Because of this choice, the datum is often referred to as the sea level datum. This does not mean, however, that the zero elevation will coincide with the average level of sea level along a coastline. In fact, differences of about a meter exist between the zero elevation and the average sea level at any given point. The average sea level at a given point along the coast is affected by many factors so that average sea levels along the coast do not form an equipotential surface.

The geoidal surface is very irregular and it is virtually impossible to realize an exact mathematical model for the geoid. Geodesists, however, have developed a good approximation of the geoid through the use of spherical harmonics. The most popular mathematical model of the continental U.S. geoid was produced by R. Rapp of Ohio State University. Similarly, H. Sünkel of Graz University of Technology and others have produced geoid models for European countries.

10.3 Datum transformations

The coordinate transformations in the previous section dealt with the transition from one type of coordinates to another type of coordinates for the same point. Cartesian coordinates X, Y, Z have been transformed into ellipsoidal coordinates φ, λ, h, and two-dimensional ellipsoidal surface coordinates φ, λ have been transformed into plane coordinates y, x. Finally, the ellipsoidal height has been transformed either to the orthometric height or to the geoidal height.

A (geodetic) datum defines the relationship between a global and a local three-dimensional Cartesian coordinate system; therefore, a datum transformation transforms one coordinate system of a certain type to another coordinate system of the same type. This is one of the primary tasks when combining GPS data with terrestrial data, i.e., the transformation of geocentric WGS-84 coordinates to local terrestrial coordinates. As mentioned earlier, the terrestrial system uses a locally best-fitting ellipsoid, e.g., the Clarke ellipsoid or the GRS-80 ellipsoid in the U.S. and the Bessel ellipsoid in many parts of Europe. The local ellipsoid is linked to a nongeocentric

Cartesian coordinate system where the origin coincides with the center of the ellipsoid. Plane coordinates such as Gauss-Krüger coordinates are obtained by mapping the local ellipsoid into the plane.

10.3.1 Three-dimensional transformation

Consider two sets of three-dimensional Cartesian coordinates forming the vectors $\underline{X}$ and $\underline{X}_T$, cf. Fig. 10.3. The transformation between the two sets can be formulated by the relation

$$\underline{X}_T = \underline{c} + \mu\,\underline{R}\,\underline{X} \tag{10.27}$$

which is denoted as Helmert transformation where $\underline{c}$ is the translation (or shift) vector, μ is a scale factor, and $\underline{R}$ is a rotation matrix.

The components of the shift vector

$$\underline{c} = \begin{bmatrix} c_1 \\ c_2 \\ c_3 \end{bmatrix}, \tag{10.28}$$

account for the coordinates of the origin of the $\underline{X}$ system in the $\underline{X}_T$ system. Note that a single scale factor is considered. More generally (but with GPS not necessary), three scale factors, one for each axis, could be used. The rotation matrix is an orthogonal matrix which is composed of three successive rotations

$$\underline{R} = \underline{R}_3\{\alpha_3\}\,\underline{R}_2\{\alpha_2\}\,\underline{R}_1\{\alpha_1\}\,. \tag{10.29}$$

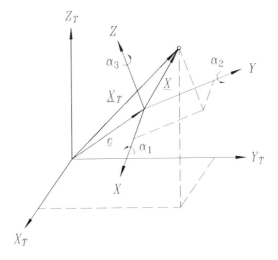

Fig. 10.3. Three-dimensional transformation

Explicitly,

$$
\underline{R} = \begin{bmatrix}
\cos\alpha_2 \cos\alpha_3 & \cos\alpha_1 \sin\alpha_3 & \sin\alpha_1 \sin\alpha_3 \\
& +\sin\alpha_1 \sin\alpha_2 \cos\alpha_3 & -\cos\alpha_1 \sin\alpha_2 \cos\alpha_3 \\
-\cos\alpha_2 \sin\alpha_3 & \cos\alpha_1 \cos\alpha_3 & \sin\alpha_1 \cos\alpha_3 \\
& -\sin\alpha_1 \sin\alpha_2 \sin\alpha_3 & +\cos\alpha_1 \sin\alpha_2 \sin\alpha_3 \\
\sin\alpha_2 & -\sin\alpha_1 \cos\alpha_2 & \cos\alpha_1 \cos\alpha_2
\end{bmatrix}
$$

$$(10.30)$$

is obtained.

In the case of known transformation parameters $\underline{c}$, μ, $\underline{R}$, a point from the $\underline{X}$ system can be transformed into the $\underline{X}_T$ system by (10.27).

If the transformation parameters are unknown, they can be determined with the aid of common (identical) points. This means that the coordinates of the same point are given in both systems. Since each common point (given by $\underline{X}_T$ and $\underline{X}$) yields three equations, two common points and one additional common component (e.g., height) are sufficient to solve for the seven unknown parameters. In practice, redundant common point information is used and the unknown parameters are calculated by an adjustment procedure.

Since in Eq. (10.27) the parameters are mixed nonlinearly, a linearization must be performed where approximate values (μ), $(\underline{R})$, $(\underline{c})$ are required. In the case of a datum transformation between WGS-84 and a local system, the approximation $(\mu) = 1$ is appropriate and the relation

$$\mu = (\mu) + d\mu = 1 + d\mu \tag{10.31}$$

is obtained. Furthermore, the rotation angles α_i in (10.30) are small and may be considered as differential quantities $d\alpha_i$. Introducing these quantities into (10.30), setting $\cos d\alpha_i = 1$ and $\sin d\alpha_i = d\alpha_i$, and neglecting second-order terms gives

$$
\underline{R} = \begin{bmatrix}
1 & d\alpha_3 & -d\alpha_2 \\
-d\alpha_3 & 1 & d\alpha_1 \\
d\alpha_2 & -d\alpha_1 & 1
\end{bmatrix} = \underline{I} + d\underline{R} \tag{10.32}
$$

where $\underline{I}$ is the unit matrix and $d\underline{R}$ is a (skewsymmetric) differential rotation matrix. Thus, the approximation $(\underline{R}) = \underline{I}$ is appropriate. Finally, the shift vector is split up in the form

$$\underline{c} = (\underline{c}) + d\underline{c} \tag{10.33}$$

where the approximate shift vector

$$(\underline{c}) = \underline{X}_T - \underline{X} \tag{10.34}$$

follows by substituting the approximations for the scale factor and the rotation matrix into Eq. (10.27).

Introducing the Eqs. (10.31), (10.32), (10.33) into (10.27) and skipping details which can be found for example in Hofmann-Wellenhof et al. (1994) gives the linearized model for a single point i. This model can be written in the form

$$\underline{X}_{T_i} - \underline{X}_i - (\underline{c}) = \underline{A}_i\, d\underline{p} \tag{10.35}$$

where the left-hand side of the equation is known and may formally be considered as an observation. The design matrix $\underline{A}$ and the vector $d\underline{p}$, containing the unknown parameters, are given by

$$\underline{A}_i = \begin{bmatrix} 1 & 0 & 0 & X_i & 0 & -Z_i & Y_i \\ 0 & 1 & 0 & Y_i & Z_i & 0 & -X_i \\ 0 & 0 & 1 & Z_i & -Y_i & X_i & 0 \end{bmatrix} \tag{10.36}$$

$$d\underline{p} = \begin{bmatrix} dc_1 & dc_2 & dc_3 & d\mu & d\alpha_1 & d\alpha_2 & d\alpha_3 \end{bmatrix}^T.$$

Recall that Eq. (10.35) is now a system of linear equations for point i. For n common points, the design matrix A is

$$\underline{A} = \begin{bmatrix} \underline{A}_1 \\ \underline{A}_2 \\ \vdots \\ \underline{A}_n \end{bmatrix}. \tag{10.37}$$

In detail, for three common points the design matrix is

$$\underline{A} = \begin{bmatrix} 1 & 0 & 0 & X_1 & 0 & -Z_1 & Y_1 \\ 0 & 1 & 0 & Y_1 & Z_1 & 0 & -X_1 \\ 0 & 0 & 1 & Z_1 & -Y_1 & X_1 & 0 \\ 1 & 0 & 0 & X_2 & 0 & -Z_2 & Y_2 \\ 0 & 1 & 0 & Y_2 & Z_2 & 0 & -X_2 \\ 0 & 0 & 1 & Z_2 & -Y_2 & X_2 & 0 \\ 1 & 0 & 0 & X_3 & 0 & -Z_3 & Y_3 \\ 0 & 1 & 0 & Y_3 & Z_3 & 0 & -X_3 \\ 0 & 0 & 1 & Z_3 & -Y_3 & X_3 & 0 \end{bmatrix} \tag{10.38}$$

which leads to a slightly overdetermined system. A least squares adjustment yields the parameter vector $d\underline{p}$ and the adjusted values by (10.31), (10.32), (10.33). Once the seven parameters of the Helmert similarity transformation are determined, formula (10.27) can be used to transform other than the common points.

For a specific example, consider the task of transforming GPS coordinates of a network to (three-dimensional) coordinates of a (nongeocentric) local system. The GPS coordinates are denoted by $(X, Y, Z)_\text{GPS}$ and the local coordinates are the plane coordinates $(y, x)_\text{LS}$ and the ellipsoidal height h_LS. To get the transformation parameters, it is assumed that for some points (common points) the coordinates in both systems are available. The solution of the task is obtained by the following algorithm:

1. For the available common points, transform the plane coordinates $(y, x)_\text{LS}$ into the ellipsoidal surface coordinates $(\varphi, \lambda)_\text{LS}$ by using the adequate mapping formulas.

2. For the available common points, transform the ellipsoidal coordinates $(\varphi, \lambda, h)_\text{LS}$ into the Cartesian coordinates $(X, Y, Z)_\text{LS}$ by (10.1).

3. Determine the seven parameters of a Helmert transformation by using the coordinates $(X, Y, Z)_\text{GPS}$ and $(X, Y, Z)_\text{LS}$ of the common points.

4. For network points other than the common points, transform the coordinates $(X, Y, Z)_\text{GPS}$ into $(X, Y, Z)_\text{LS}$ via Eq. (10.27) using the transformation parameters determined in the previous step.

5. Transform the Cartesian coordinates $(X, Y, Z)_\text{LS}$ computed in the previous step into ellipsoidal coordinates $(\varphi, \lambda, h)_\text{LS}$ by (10.11) or by the iteration procedure.

6. Map the ellipsoidal surface coordinates $(\varphi, \lambda)_\text{LS}$ computed in the previous step into plane coordinates $(y, x)_\text{LS}$ by the appropriate mapping formulas.

The advantage of the three-dimensional approach is that no a priori information is required for the seven parameter Helmert transformation. This means that no information about the three shifts, one scale, and three rotation parameters between the two systems is necessary. The disadvantage of the method is that for the common points ellipsoidal heights (and, thus, geoidal heights) are required. However, as reported by Schmitt et al. (1991), the effect of incorrect heights of the common points often has a negligible affect on the plane coordinates (y, x). For example, incorrect heights may cause a tilt of a 20 km × 20 km network by an amount of 5 m in space; however, the effect on the plane coordinates is only approximately 1 mm.

For large areas, the height problem can be solved by adopting approximate ellipsoidal heights for the common points and performing a three-dimensional affine transformation instead of the similarity transformation, cf. Schödlbauer et al. (1989).

10.3.2 Two-dimensional transformation

In this section, two-dimensional coordinates are considered. The two different sets of plane coordinates are represented by $\underline{x}$ and $\underline{x}_T$, cf. Fig. 10.4. The two-dimensional datum transformation is defined by

$$\underline{x}_T = \underline{c} + \mu\,\underline{R}\,\underline{x} \tag{10.39}$$

with a scale factor μ, the shift vector

$$\underline{c} = \begin{bmatrix} c_1 \\ c_2 \end{bmatrix} \tag{10.40}$$

and the rotation matrix

$$\underline{R} = \begin{bmatrix} \cos\alpha & -\sin\alpha \\ \sin\alpha & \cos\alpha \end{bmatrix} \tag{10.41}$$

which comprises a single rotation angle. Hence, Eq. (10.39) is the two-dimensional Helmert transformation with four parameters: the two transla-

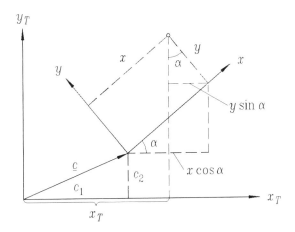

Fig. 10.4. Two-dimensional transformation

tion components c_1, c_2, the scale factor μ, and the rotation angle α. Substituting (10.40) and (10.41) into (10.39) gives the transformed components explicitly:

$$x_T = c_1 + \mu\, x\, \cos\alpha - \mu\, y\, \sin\alpha$$
$$y_T = c_2 + \mu\, x\, \sin\alpha + \mu\, y\, \cos\alpha\,. \tag{10.42}$$

These simple formulas can be verified by the geometry given in Fig. 10.4 where the contributing terms for x_T (without scale factor) are indicated.

In the case of known transformation parameters $\underline{c}$, μ, $\underline{R}$, a point in the $\underline{x}$ system can be transformed into the $\underline{x}_T$ system by (10.39).

If the transformation parameters are unknown, they can be determined – analogously to the three-dimensional case – using common points. Two common points, each yielding two equations, are sufficient to solve for the four unknown parameters. In practice, redundant common point information is used and the unknown parameters are calculated by least squares adjustment.

As seen from (10.42), the unknowns appear again in nonlinear form. However, using the auxiliary unknowns

$$p = \mu\, \cos\alpha$$
$$q = \mu\, \sin\alpha\,, \tag{10.43}$$

linear equations

$$x_T = c_1 + p\,x - q\,y$$
$$y_T = c_2 + q\,x + p\,y \tag{10.44}$$

with respect to the unknowns are obtained. In the case of redundant common points, the solution is obtained by the conventional least squares adjustment procedure where the coordinates x_T and y_T are formally considered as observations. The scale factor and the rotation angle are determined from the auxiliary unknowns by

$$\mu = \sqrt{p^2 + q^2}$$
$$\tan\alpha = \frac{q}{p}\,. \tag{10.45}$$

For a specific example, consider the task of transforming GPS coordinates of a network to (two-dimensional) coordinates of a (nongeocentric) local system. The GPS coordinates are denoted by $(X, Y, Z)_{\text{GPS}}$ and the plane coordinates in the local system are denoted by $(y, x)_{\text{LS}}$. To get the transformation parameters, it is assumed that for some points (common points) the coordinates in both systems are known. Note that no height information in the local system is available. The solution of the task is obtained by the following algorithm:

1. For all available network points, transform the Cartesian coordinates $(X, Y, Z)_{\text{GPS}}$ into ellipsoidal coordinates $(\varphi, \lambda, h)_{\text{GPS}}$ by (10.11) or by the iteration procedure. Note that the ellipsoid of the local datum should be used.

2. For all available network points, disregard the ellipsoidal heights h_{GPS} and map the ellipsoidal surface coordinates $(\varphi, \lambda)_{\text{GPS}}$ computed in the previous step into plane coordinates $(y, x)_{\text{GPS}}$ by using the appropriate mapping formulas and the ellipsoid of the local datum.

3. Determine the four parameters of a two-dimensional Helmert transformation by using the coordinates $(y, x)_{\text{GPS}}$ and $(y, x)_{\text{LS}}$ of the common points.

4. For network points other than the common points, transform the coordinates $(y, x)_{\text{GPS}}$ into $(y, x)_{\text{LS}}$ via Eq. (10.39) using the transformation parameters determined in the previous step.

This data transformation works well (even without using height information) for small sized networks, low elevations, and for areas where geoidal heights do not change. The coordinates $(y, x)_{\text{GPS}}$, however, depend on the dimension and on the displacement of the local ellipsoid. These dependencies may lead to a distortion of the point clusters which, in principle, is not matched by a similarity transformation, cf. Lichtenegger (1991). A numerical example is given in Schmitt et al. (1991) and shows that the use of the WGS-84 ellipsoid and the two-dimensional Helmert transformation leads to unacceptable discrepancies in the range of 8 mm to 15 mm for a network covering an area of 200 km × 200 km.

One way to overcome the problem is to apply other transformations such as the affine transformation between the two coordinate sets in the plane. Another way is to transform the $(y, x)_{\text{LS}}$ coordinates of common points approximately to $(X, Y, Z)_{\text{LS}}$ by using approximate ellipsoidal heights. Now, the parameters of a three-dimensional similarity transformation can be derived which enable the approximate transformation of all GPS coordinates into the local datum. This transformation could also be achieved by applying an approximate shift vector to the GPS coordinates. The approximate coordinates are then mapped into the plane, and the final similarity transformation is performed in two-dimensional space.

10.3.3 One-dimensional transformation

One of the distinct features of GPS is that three-dimensional (3D) coordinates are obtained in a common frame. There is no separation between the horizontal coordinates and the height of a point because all three components are calculated together by the same procedure. In classical geodesy, horizontal coordinates and heights were obtained independently.

Now, the question arises why in the previous section a two-dimensional (2D) transformation and now a one-dimensional (1D) transformation are discussed. The answer lies in historical data. Many countries have excellent horizontal control points available but often fairly poor ellipsoidal heights because of lack of geoidal heights. Thus, it is appropriate to use the 2D transformation if height information is not available. Similarly, the 1D transformation can be used to transform heights without detailed knowledge of the geoid.

Symbolically, the 1D transformation is obtained by 3D $\ominus$ 2D. In more detail, the parameters for the 1D transformation are obtained by "subtracting" the parameters of the 2D transformation from the parameters of the 3D transformation. This looks like

$$
\left.\begin{array}{llllllll}
\text{3D} & c_1 & c_2 & c_3 & \mu & \alpha_1 & \alpha_2 & \alpha_3 \\
\text{2D} & c_1 & c_2 & & \mu & & & \alpha_3 \\
\hline
\text{1D} & & & c_3 & & \alpha_1 & \alpha_2 &
\end{array}\right\} \ominus
\tag{10.46}
$$

where for the 2D transformation the rotation angle has been given the corresponding subscript. In other words, the 3D transformation is composed of a 2D transformation for the horizontal coordinates and a 1D transformation for the heights.

Concentrating now on the 1D transformation, from the parameters in (10.46) it can be seen that the transformation consists of a shift along the vertical axis, a tilt (rotation) about the north-south axis, and a tilt about the east-west axis. These three unknowns are determined by using the height information of at least three common points.

Transformation using heights
Assume that for some (common) points in a GPS network the orthometric heights or elevations H_i and the ellipsoidal heights h_i are known. The mathematical model for the one-dimensional transformation is given by

$$
H_i - h_i = \Delta h - y_i \, d\alpha_1 + x_i \, d\alpha_2
\tag{10.47}
$$

where Δh is a vertical shift, and $d\alpha_1$ and $d\alpha_2$ are rotation angles about the x-axis and the y-axis. Formally, Eq. (10.47) corresponds to the third component of the three-dimensional similarity transformation without taking into account a scale factor. Additionally, the equation is now expressed in the local coordinate frame with the position coordinates x_i and y_i. These coordinates are required with only low accuracy and can be taken, e.g., from a map. Geometrically, the model equation (10.47) may be interpreted as the equation of a plane which enables the interpolation of geoidal heights $N = h - H$ in other than the common points. The interpolation could be extended to a higher-order surface to take into account more irregular geoid structures.

When a geoid model is available, the ellipsoidal heights h_i could be transformed into approximate elevations (H_i). Normally, there are discrepancies between the heights H_i and (H_i) due to the combined effects of the GPS systematic errors and the errors in the geoid modeling, see Collins (1989).

The FGCC specifications for GPS surveys require that surveys to be included into the national network be tied to a minimum of four benchmarks well-distributed geometrically throughout the project area (e.g., corners of project area). The additional benchmarks (ties) enable a least squares adjustment of the model equations (10.47) and provide the necessary check on the computation of the rotation of the ellipsoid to the geoid. A good practice is to perform the rotation using three of the elevations and to check the rotated elevation of the fourth point against the true elevation. The two values should agree within a few centimeters under normal conditions. An additional check on the correctness of the transformation is provided by inspecting the magnitude of the two rotation angles computed by the least squares adjustment. Normally, these angles should be less than 5 arcseconds, although they can on occasion be greater.

Usually, the elevations of points in a network of small size, let us say $10\,\text{km} \times 10\,\text{km}$, can be determined with an accuracy of about $3\,\text{cm}$. In cases where the generalized model adequately describes the variation of the geoidal heights, much larger areas can be surveyed using this method with comparable accuracies being achieved.

Transformation using height differences
In the preceding paragraph, the importance of geoidal heights has been stressed. The ellipsoidal height determined by GPS can be transformed to the orthometric height if the geoidal height is known.

There are times, however, when it is only required to measure changes in elevation. For example, when it is desired to measure the subsidence rate of a point (e.g., oil platform). In such cases, the importance of a well-known geoid diminishes because relative heights are considered. For two points then

$$
\begin{aligned}
H_1 &= h_1 - N_1 \\
H_2 &= h_2 - N_2
\end{aligned}
\tag{10.48}
$$

are the height relations and

$$
H_2 - H_1 = h_2 - h_1 - (N_2 - N_1)
\tag{10.49}
$$

is the height difference or height change between the points 1 and 2. Here, only the difference of the geoidal heights affects the result. Thus, if the geoidal heights are constant in a local area, meaning that the separation between the geoid and the ellipsoid is constant, they can be ignored. Similarly, if the geoid has a constant slope with the ellipsoid, the heights can be computed accurately by rotating the GPS heights into the geoidal surface as previously described.

10.4   Combining GPS and terrestrial data

The combination of data sets from two or more different sources is strictly an adjustment problem. This section, however, is restricted to basic considerations, and only a few aspects are covered here; otherwise the text would become a treatment on adjustment theory and not a GPS book.

As earlier, the GPS coordinates referred to WGS-84 are denoted by the subscript "GPS" and the Cartesian coordinates referred to a local datum are denoted by the subscript "LS".

The position vectors $\underline{X}_{\mathrm{GPS}}$ in a network are provided by GPS observations. The position vectors $\underline{X}_{\mathrm{LS}}$ may be derived from terrestrial observations. Considering such measurements from say point A to point B, the spatial distance is denoted by s, the azimuth by a, and the zenith angle by z. The vector $\underline{b}$ between the two points can be represented in the horizon system of A by

$$
\underline{b} =
\begin{bmatrix}
s \sin z \cos a \\
s \sin z \sin a \\
s \cos z
\end{bmatrix} .
\tag{10.50}
$$

The rotation of this vector into the equatorial system is described by

$$
\underline{b}_{\mathrm{LS}} = \underline{R}\,\underline{b}
\tag{10.51}
$$

where the column vectors of the rotation matrix $\underline{R}$ are the vectors $\underline{i}$, $\underline{j}$, $\underline{k}$ of Eq. (7.6). Thus, starting with the position vector $\underline{X}_{A_{\mathrm{LS}}}$ for point A, the position vector $\underline{X}_{B_{\mathrm{LS}}}$ for point B is obtained by

$$\underline{X}_{B_{\mathrm{LS}}} = \underline{X}_{A_{\mathrm{LS}}} + \underline{b}_{\mathrm{LS}} \tag{10.52}$$

where subsequently the point subscripts are omitted.

The relation between position vectors in the local system and the WGS-84 system is given by the three-dimensional Helmert transformation

$$\underline{X}_{\mathrm{GPS}} = \underline{c} + \mu\,\underline{R}\,\underline{X}_{\mathrm{LS}}\,. \tag{10.53}$$

The discussion of the adjustment of this model is kept as brief as possible.

Assuming the coordinates of both systems as stochastic, a noise vector can be added to both vectors $\underline{X}_{\mathrm{GPS}}$ and $\underline{X}_{\mathrm{LS}}$. The relation in this form is

$$\underline{X}_{\mathrm{GPS}} + \underline{n}_{\mathrm{GPS}} = \underline{c} + \mu\,\underline{R}(\underline{X}_{\mathrm{LS}} + \underline{n}_{\mathrm{LS}}) \tag{10.54}$$

and is called Gauss-Helmert model. From the adjustment point of view, it is advantageous to denote the adjusted coordinates in the local datum by $\underline{\hat{X}}_{\mathrm{LS}}$. The model is now reformulated as

$$\begin{aligned} \underline{X}_{\mathrm{LS}} + \underline{n}_{\mathrm{LS}} &= \underline{\hat{X}}_{\mathrm{LS}} \\ \underline{X}_{\mathrm{GPS}} + \underline{n}_{\mathrm{GPS}} &= \underline{c} + \mu\,\underline{R}\,\underline{\hat{X}}_{\mathrm{LS}} \end{aligned} \tag{10.55}$$

and is called Gauss-Markov model.

The method based on (10.55) has one implicit drawback. A position vector $\underline{X}_{\mathrm{LS}}$ may only be used as observation if all three measurement quantities s, z, and a are available. A different approach is shown for example in Jäger and van Mierlo (1991). Here, terrestrial observations are gathered in a vector $\underline{\ell}$. Adding the corresponding noise, the model can be written in the form

$$\underline{\ell}_{\mathrm{LS}} + \underline{n} = \underline{\ell}(\underline{\hat{X}}_{\mathrm{LS}})\,. \tag{10.56}$$

In Hofmann-Wellenhof et al. (1994), distances, vertical angles, azimuths, (nonoriented) directions, ellipsoidal height differences, and baseline vectors are considered as measurements. Each measurement is explicitly given as a function of the unknown parameters along with its linearized form so that it may be used directly in an adjustment by parameters.

In principle, any type of geodetic measurement can be employed if the integrated geodesy adjustment model is used. The basic concept is that any geodetic measurement can be expressed as a function of one or more position vectors $\underline{X}$ and of the gravity field W of the earth. The usually nonlinear function must be linearized where the gravity field W is split into the normal potential U of an ellipsoid and the disturbing potential T, thus, $W = U + T$. Applying a minimum principle leads to the collocation formulas, cf. Moritz (1980), Chap. 11.

Many examples integrating GPS and other data can be found in technical publications. For example, Hein et al. (1989) combine GPS and gravity data. Hein (1990a) computes orthometric heights by combining GPS and gravity data. Grant (1988) attempts to detect earth deformations from a combination of GPS and terrestrial data. Delikaraoglou and Lahaye (1990) cite further contributions.

10.5   Fiducial point concept

Although the use of the GPS fiducial point concept is primarily to improve satellite orbits, cf. for example Ashkenazi et al. (1990), it nevertheless should be considered in the section on transformations. Fiducial points are sites whose positions are accurately known from a (GPS independent) method such as VLBI or SLR. The concept of fiducial points is quite simple: during a GPS campaign, at least three fiducial points in the area of the campaign are also equipped with receivers (apart from the points to be determined). The geometry of the fiducial points with respect to the remaining points has a strong effect on the GPS accuracy in this region, cf. Lichten et al. (1989). The measurements of the fiducial points serve two purposes: the data are used for baseline determinations and also for orbit improvements, cf. Davidson et al. (1985).

Regarding transformations, the $(X, Y, Z)_{\text{GPS}}$ coordinates can be transformed into the frame of the fiducial points by a three-dimensional similarity transformation. In accordance with Sect. 10.3.1, the coordinates of at least three fiducial points are necessary in both systems to determine the transformation parameters.

11 Software modules

11.1 Introduction

The policy used throughout this book of not endorsing commercial products is also adhered in this chapter. There are no references given, although publications of authors describing various software packages have been used. The main goal of this chapter is to provide potential GPS users with information concerning the various features of different software modules. The following sections cannot give a complete list of all imaginable features, but they will be a help in determining which features are worthwhile. However, the main consideration is that the software (and the corresponding receiver) should match the personal requirements. Most applications do not require all given features.

Each of the following paragraphs describing various terms is kept as brief as possible. More extensive descriptions are found in other chapters of this book. A summary table is provided at the end of each section. The goal of these tables is twofold. First, they can be used as a checklist when comparing different software and, second, they can support for the development of a new software.

Most software modules are designed to run on PC-type computers, although this will undoubtedly change as better computers become available. Some software is used in the receiver, while other software operates interactively between the PC and the receiver (or with another equipment).

Table 11.1 gives an overview of the modules described in the following sections. Only keywords are given here to keep the table as concise and compact as possible.

Table 11.1. Software modules

- Planning
- Data transfer
- Data processing
- Quality control
- Network computations
- Data base management
- Utilities
- Flexibility

11.2   Planning

Satellite visibility
In the planning stage of a survey, it is often necessary to have a visibility table listing the locations of the satellites. Also, rise and set times of the satellites are useful. In addition to the visibility table, a (polar) sky plot of the individual satellites is useful. A helpful option is the ability of entering site obstructions at both ends of a baseline to determine the "combined" visibility.

   With the final constellation, a 24-hour window is available; thus, satellite visibility software is not as important today as in the past.

Satellite geometry
The DOP values are highly correlated with satellite geometry and, thus, the number of visible satellites. A table or a plot of DOP helps to select observation windows with good geometry. This is of importance especially for kinematic surveys.

Simulations
Simulations can be used to plan a survey. The distribution of the sites, the observation window, and the session length all contribute to the design matrix from which the cofactor matrix can be computed. Considering the various goals for a survey with respect to optimization, in some cases maximum accuracy is desired, while in other cases minimum cost is the objective. Software might also support the planning of vehicle routes to save time and resources.

Table 11.2. Module on planning

Planning
• Satellite visibility
- elevation and azimuth lists
- rise and set times
- sky plot
- site obstruction
• Satellite geometry
- list of DOP
- plot of DOP
• Simulations
- cofactor matrix
- optimization

11.3 Data transfer

Downloading data
Upon completion of a survey, the data stored in each receiver must usually be downloaded to a computer. There are several possibilities for downloading these data depending on the storage device. One technique is to copy the data onto a cassette or floppy disk, using a cable or a radio link. Another method is to copy files from the receiver directly to a computer disk.

The transferred data should be verified for consistency and integrity. This could be performed either after downloading or before decoding.

Decoding data
The downloaded data are often decoded from a special compact receiver format to a general binary format. Software that yields the navigation message (e.g., broadcast ephemerides), the measured quantities (i.e., code ranges, carrier phases, and Doppler data), and other information (e.g., field log) is used to provide files required by the processing software.

An important software feature is the ability to convert the data into the RINEX format. Most data exchanges are based on this format so that data from two different types of receivers can be used for processing.

Table 11.3. Module on data transfer

Data transfer
• Downloading data
- storage device
- copying technique
- transfer checks
• Decoding data
- binary format
- RINEX format

11.4 Data processing

Baseline definition
For projects where more than a single baseline vector has been measured there are different combinations of baselines that can be computed. The processing software should offer the choice of calculating single baseline vectors (with all possible combinations) or of calculating multipoint vectors

(where for n sites, there are $n - 1$ independent baselines). User interaction for a reformulation of baselines must be possible. The ability to combine various sessions is also useful.

Ephemerides

The broadcast ephemerides must be converted to an orbit file where the coordinates of the satellites are available for selected epochs. Satellite coordinates at other epochs are normally interpolated from a few selected epochs. In addition to the broadcast ephemerides, an option for using the precise orbit is essential for high-accuracy surveys.

Code data processing

Before a baseline vector can be computed, the coordinates of each endpoint of the line are normally first determined using the code pseudoranges. In addition to the three-dimensional positions, the receiver clock offset is obtained. For stations with known coordinates, the receiver clock information is more precise.

Useful modules have been designed to differentially postprocess code data from two or more sites.

Phase data processing

There are numerous options available for processing phase data. The raw phases can be used or they can be combined to form single-, double-, or triple-differences, for either one or two frequencies. There is also a variety of data combinations. Dual frequency phases may be combined to form the ionospheric-free, the wide lane, or the narrow lane signal. In addition, phase and code range or phase and Doppler combinations are possible.

Covariance matrices

Correct modeling of the covariances can be fairly complex for various data combinations. Software should cover the most common cases such as covariances for double-differences in both the single baseline and the multipoint mode.

Parameter estimation

Optimal software should provide flexibility in selecting the parameters to be adjusted and the way that the adjustment will be performed. The following options are some that optimal software should contain:

- Computation of baseline vectors. This includes static, kinematic, and pseudokinematic surveys. A choice of using the single baseline or multipoint mode should be available. As previously mentioned, the ability to combine various sessions is also useful.

- Ambiguities. In the first adjustment, the ambiguities are calculated as real values (i.e., float solution). Subsequently, the ambiguities are fixed as integer values using different techniques. In succeeding adjustments, the ambiguities are substituted as known values (i.e., fixed solution). The ability to bias integers one at a time can prove useful.

- Atmosphere. There should be various choices for modeling the atmosphere. In addition to a standard atmosphere model, various models for the ionosphere and the troposphere allow optimizing data processing, especially for long baselines.

- Orbit. Some insight is necessary to judge the efficiency of orbit computations. The result should be the six orbital elements of the satellites and the corresponding partial derivatives (osculating ellipses). Sometimes only three degrees of freedom are assigned to the orbit by a shift vector.

Table 11.4. Module on data processing

Data processing
• Baseline definition
- single baseline
- multibaselines
- combination of various sessions
• Ephemerides
- broadcast ephemerides
- precise ephemerides
• Code data processing
- single point solution
- DGPS
• Phase data processing
- raw phase
- phase differences
- data combinations
• Covariance matrices
• Parameter estimation
- computation of baseline vectors
- ambiguities
- atmosphere
- orbit

11.5   Quality control

Data analysis
Reliable software should provide sophisticated data analysis. Gross errors should automatically be detected and eliminated. Automatic cycle slip detection and repair is essential. Plot options are an excellent tool to visualize errors such as cycle slips. A listing of the repaired cycle slips can also be helpful for understanding the quality of the data.

Statistical data
In addition to the parameter estimation, a posteriori site variance-covariance matrices and interpoint variance-covariance matrices should be produced.

Observation residuals resulting from the baseline adjustment can also be used for checking the homogeneity of the data. A plot of these residuals quickly shows outliers, and critical measurements can be isolated.

Loop closures
Computing loop misclosures is the most direct method of performing quality control checks. The best loop software allows the user to choose arbitrary loops by specifying various routes by node identifiers.

Table 11.5. Module on quality control

Quality control
• Data analysis
- gross error detection
- cycle slip detection and repair
- listings and plots
• Statistical data
- a posteriori site covariance matrices
- interpoint covariance matrices
- residuals
- plots
• Loop closures

11.6   Network computations

Adjustment of GPS networks
The final results of a baseline vector computation are the differences in ECEF

coordinates. The coordinates of points are then determined by combining these coordinate differences in a network adjustment where one (or more) point is held fixed. Recall that the residuals as well as loop misclosures are suitable quality control factors.

Datum and coordinate transformation
A seven parameter similarity transformation (i.e., Helmert transformation) is generally performed in order to shift, scale, and rotate the entire network to fixed control. Appropriate software is an essential part of GPS surveying. Datum transformations should include frequently used coordinate frames (e.g., NAD-83, NAD-27, state plane).

The software should also transform ECEF coordinates to latitude, longitude, and height and map geodetic coordinates into the plane (e.g., UTM, Lambert projection, Gauss-Krüger projection).

Hybrid data combination
More flexible network adjustment programs that adjust both GPS vectors and conventionally measured angles, distances, and elevation differences are useful when GPS and conventional measurements are combined. The combination of GPS results with any other kind of data is optimally performed by the least squares collocation method.

Table 11.6. Module on network computations

Network computations
• Adjustment of GPS networks
• Datum and coordinate transformation
• Hybrid data combination

11.7 Data base management

Archiving data and survey results
The data of GPS surveys should be organized in a data base. This permits retrieval of the data for additional computation. For example, recomputation using precise orbits instead of broadcast orbits or using a changed pattern of the fiducial stations should be possible.

Also the results of the processing should be archived in the data base. This ensures an easy access to the data for any purpose. File compaction programs can be used to good advantage in archiving data.

Interface to other data bases
To interface with national control points, a plot of both the national network reference points and the project points is useful in determining which points should be selected as tie points.

To interface with Geographic Information Systems (GIS), geodetic data are included as overlay or CAD file. This permits the viewing of point locations and provides users with a clear understanding of actual site locations.

Table 11.7. Module on data base management

Data base management
• Archiving data and survey results
• Interface to other data bases
- national control points
- GIS

11.8   Utilities

File editing
Occasionally, editing of a data file is necessary. For example, noisy data might be eliminated, data from fragmented files might be combined, or large files might be split into smaller files.

Time conversions
In addition to GPS time, there are other time systems desirable such as the Gregorian date, the modified Julian date, and others.

Documentation of results
The final project documentation should contain a complete list of the results. Various plots are helpful to understand the survey results.

Table 11.8. Module on utilities

Utilities
• File editing
• Time conversions
• Documentation of results

11.9   Flexibility

This section partly repeats items previously mentioned and stresses some additional aspects which may help evaluate the versatility and flexibility of a particular software package.

- Computer compatibility. There are some minimum computer requirements; however, software should run on a wide variety of computers. As far as possible, the software should be computer independent.

- Processing time. Computation time is of course a crucial question and is (apart from computer performance) dependent on the complexity of the software. Using a single baseline as a test criterion is a good method of timing various programs.

- Real-time applications. Software and hardware combinations that are capable of operating in real time are becoming more important. These applications include real-time differential navigation and "stake-out" surveying. Communication links are critical to this type of GPS use.

- Memory amount.

- Limitations. What are the limits for the number of sites, satellites, and sessions?

- Data. It should be possible to add one or more data sets at a point to create a larger single data set. For example, combining two sessions at a point. An option for reformatting the observation data into the RINEX format is essential. It should also be possible to process both single and dual frequency data using the same software. Combining data from different receivers (also for a single baseline) and possibly of different satellite types is highly desirable. Software should be capable of processing several sessions in either batch or manual mode.

- Orbit. It is critical that the software is capable of using both the broadcast and precise ephemerides. The possibility of computing the six Keplerian elements and their variations with time is a feature that is useful for both research and many practical purposes.

- Parameter estimation. Is it possible to select the number of parameters for the vector computation or the adjustments or is it restricted to fixed parameters?

- Transformations and map projections. Are coordinate transformations widely offered? Transformations from the global system to a local datum are necessary. Map projections should also be available.

- User interactivity. There should be an option to change the amount of (necessary) user interactivity. For normal processing, the user does not need or want much interactivity.

- User friendliness. How much time is necessary to learn how to use the software? Does it need an expert with lots of computer experience? Does it offer help routines?

Table 11.9. Module on flexibility

Flexibility
• Computer compatibility
• Processing time
• Real-time applications
- single point positioning
- differential GPS
- relative positioning
• Memory amount
• Limitations on the number of
- sites
- satellites
- sessions
• Data
- additional data
- conversion to RINEX format
- combination of single and dual frequency data
- combination of different receiver types
- combination of different satellite types
- combination of various sessions
• Orbit
- broadcast ephemerides
- precise ephemerides
- modeling of orbital elements
• Parameter estimation
- number of parameters
- selectable parameters
• Transformations and map projections
• User interactivity option
• User friendliness

12 Applications of GPS

12.1 General uses of GPS

The general overall uses of GPS are numerous. In this chapter, an arbitrary grouping of global, regional, and local uses has been selected. A further additional arbitrary classification of navigation and survey uses is made to help organize the discussion of GPS applications.

Application of DGPS is adequate for local, regional and even global applications. At present, the main application is at sea, but the use of DGPS by aircraft and for land navigation is inevitable. Today's navigation of civil aircraft is based on a variety of systems such as radio altimeters and inertial systems which form the Flight Management System (FMS). DGPS will support these systems and can also be used to supplement the Instrument Landing System (ILS) which is at present the international standard for approaching and landing. An overview of the present DGPS performance on position with SA on is given in Table 12.1. The accuracy of the heights is worse by a factor 1.5 to 2.

Before describing surveying applications in detail, an overview of the present achievable accuracies in relative positioning is given in Table 12.2. The partitioning of this table is performed by the two groups of (conventional) static and kinematic surveys. The accuracies shown are based on the baseline length, the number of satellites, and the session duration. The accuracies of Table 12.2 can be considered as being average, because better and worse results might be achieved under certain circumstances. It should be noted that a fairly reasonable DOP value is presupposed. Furthermore, it is assumed that the satellite signal is not disturbed by anomalous ionospheric conditions.

Table 12.1. Accuracies for DGPS

Observable	Station separation	Accuracy in position
Code range	10 km	4 – 8 m
	500 km	5 – 10 m
Smoothed code ranges	10 km	0.3 – 3 m
	500 km	4 – 7 m
Carrier phases	10 km	0.03 – 0.20 m

Table 12.2. Accuracies for relative positioning

Frequency	Baseline [km]	Satellites	Session [min]	Accuracy [ppm]
STATIC SURVEYS				
Single	1	4	30	5 – 10
		5	15	
	5	4	60	5
		5	30	
	10	4	90	4
		5	60	
	20	4	120	3
		5	90	
Dual	50	4	10	1.0
	100	5	60	0.1
	500	5	120	0.1 – 0.01
KINEMATIC SURVEYS				
Single	3	5	0.1	10
		3	3	
Dual	10	5	0.1	3

12.1.1 Global uses

Navigation

This was the planned primary use of GPS. Both military and civilian uses of the system in this mode are similar in that users wish to know their spatial locations as precisely as possible. For example, all types of aircraft and vessels will use GPS for en route navigation, and the denial of accuracy does not materially affect this use. The global 100 m level of accuracy achievable even with activated SA is not a problem for en route positioning. But as aircraft are ready for landing or as vessels enter restricted waters, accuracy becomes more critical, cf. Table 12.3. Another factor critical to aircraft navigation is the high level of integrity demanded, for example, by the Federal Aviation Administration (FAA). This agency has specified a status warning time of 30 seconds for en route navigation and 10 seconds during approach and landing. This level of integrity is achieved by either Receiver Autonomous Integrity Monitoring (RAIM) which is an internal quality control of the actual GPS solution, or by GPS Integrity Channels (GIC) which use signals from a source external to GPS, cf. Montgomery (1991). In the spring of 1994, FAA has officially accepted GPS as part of the U.S. airspace system.

Table 12.3. Current air user requirements in meters

Phase	Category	Position	Height
En route	–	≥ 100	≥ 100
Approach	I	17.1	4.1
and	II	5.2	1.7
landing	III	4.0	0.6

Surveying

Global application of GPS provides a powerful geodetic tool. This science is involved in monitoring global changes over time which is the key for understanding long-term geodynamical phenomena. Applications include measuring crustal deformations, postglacial rebound, volcanic uplift, plate tectonics, and earth rotation. Until now, Very Long Baseline Interferometry (VLBI) and Satellite Laser Ranging (SLR) techniques have been used for this purpose. GPS is not presently capable of replacing these techniques but it will be used to augment them and provide more cost effective solutions to geodetic problems.

Timing and communications

Another global use of GPS is in global determination of accurate time. High accuracy timing has many scientific applications such as coordinating seismic monitoring and other global geophysical measurements. With SA on, inexpensive GPS receivers operating on known stations provide a timing accuracy of about 0.3 microsecond (95% probability level) with only one satellite in view. With more sophisticated techniques, one can globally synchronize clocks even more precisely. Presently, the achievable accuracy of time transfer via GPS is some tens of nanoseconds; however, one nanosecond is considered possible.

Global communication depends upon precise coordination to pack as many data bits into a given period of time as possible. GPS should make it possible to increase the overall efficiency of communication, allowing many more users per unit of time than is presently possible.

12.1.2 Regional uses

Navigation

The regional applications of GPS navigation are enormous and include: exploration, transportation management, structural monitoring, and various types of automation.

The denial of full system accuracy by SA can be overcome by differential navigation, i.e., DGPS. This involves placing fixed GPS receivers at known locations in a project area and broadcasting range corrections to receivers within the area. The DGPS technique is also being used for hydrographic surveys. The U.S. Coast Guard (USCG) is in the process of testing differential navigation networks to assist vessels approaching the coast. Additionally, private firms have set up similar networks in heavily trafficked areas and sell a precise navigation service. Differential navigation eliminates the effect of denial of accuracy virtually.

There are numerous uses of GPS in managing regional resource and controlling activities within large areas. One example is the Geographic Information System (GIS) which is a computer based geographically oriented data base that helps manage resources on both regional and local levels. The GIS also provides a means of making rapid informed decisions for planning, development, and tracking of infrastructure. Normally, a GIS is initialized by performing base mapping to create a digital data file that contains all map information. The digital file usually contains roads, buildings, vegetation types, property lines, soil types, and other critical data which can be displayed in various overlays on a computer screen. GPS often plays a key role in providing ground control for the base mapping. The coordinates of photo-identifiable points are determined by GPS, and these points are used to control the scale and orientation of the map. GPS can also be used to update GIS information and enter new information in the file. This is accomplished by placing the GPS receiver over the point one wishes to include in the GIS to determine its location and then keying in an object code for the item so that it is tagged with time and coordinates.

The GIS is an excellent example of the use of GPS in its various modes: (1) point positioning, (2) precise surveying, (3) differential positioning, and (4) combinations of the methods.

The point positioning mode would be used to help locate existing survey marks (or photo-targets) whose coordinates had been previously determined, or whose coordinates had been scaled from a large-scale map. Inexpensive hand-held receivers are being used to locate control points that have defied recovery because land features have greatly changed. Also, this method facilitates locating property corners whose coordinates have been computed from surveyed bearings and distances from a known point.

Next, the precise survey mode is used to measure the vectors between the known control points (both horizontal and vertical) and selected photo-targets or photo-identifiable points. These points are used in the photogrammetric map compilation to scale and orient the photograph to the chosen datum. The static, pseudokinematic, and kinematic modes could all be used during this phase of the work. Recently, the kinematic method has also been used to determine the coordinates of the photocenter by placing one GPS receiver in the aircraft and a second on a ground datum point. For this application, dual frequency receivers being able to resolve cycle slips or interruptions to the received signal during flight are useful. This is accomplished by using smoothed code pseudoranges to compute the vector between fixed and airborne receiver using the differential navigation technique. The integer bias of the wide lane phase and, finally, the integer ambiguity of the base (19 cm) carrier is resolved to reinitialize the airborne receiver on-the-fly. This technique significantly reduces the amount of ground control needed to produce a metric map.

After the map has been produced and the GIS data base is initialized, changes and corrections often must be made to update the data base. It would be inordinately expensive to refly and remap the area, so that GPS can further be used to determine the coordinates of additional points to be placed in the data base. For example, instrumented vans are being used to collect information as they drive along the highway. Videocameras and other devices collect data while GPS keeps track of the position of the van, and, thus, the various features are collected.

The positional accuracy of the roving GPS receiver can be improved by the use of DGPS. Several state highway departments are using this technique to develop a data base of all important road features so they can better manage their resources.

Surveying

Geodesists have long desired to measure crustal movements for various scientific purposes. One use would be to predict earthquakes by measuring certain precursor ground movement. GPS is an ideal tool for such studies in that the equipment is relatively inexpensive, portable, and highly accurate. For example, the NGS has measured an array of widely spaced points in the eastern part of the U.S. (Eastern Strain Network) using dual frequency GPS receivers. This array or network will be periodically resurveyed so that crustal movement can be measured. Typically, this information can be used to provide nuclear plant siting information as well as providing a general purpose high accuracy network. The NGS network is tied into or referenced to GPS receivers located at VLBI tracking sites, so the Eastern Strain Network also provides a multipurpose high precision network. Various other groups have measured similar networks to determine both continental and island crustal motion throughout the world. For example, the Japanese have established an array of permanent GPS tracking stations to provide near real-time crustal motion monitoring. Another example is the geodynamic goal of the Austrian GPS Reference network (AGREF) presented by

Stangl et al. (1991).

GPS is the first measuring device that can be used to accurately measure height differences in real time. Studies by the NGS have shown that repeat measurements between stable and subsiding points provide accurate measures of the subsidence. Industry has used GPS to measure the subsidence among groups of offshore oil platforms by making repeat surveys. One example is the subsidence measurement of several North Sea oil platforms with respect to other platforms that were thought to be in a more stable area. Monthly GPS surveys showed measurable height changes, and trends in the results positively proved which platforms were subsiding (relative to other platforms). In this particular case, GPS was probably the only method to make the determination.

As GPS equipment decreases in price, it is expected that receivers will be permanently mounted on structures and at selected sites and used to measure both subsidence and crustal deformation.

12.1.3   Local uses

The difference between regional and local uses of GPS is quite arbitrary because a small state GIS could either be considered regional or local in scope. Also, the difference between navigation and surveying will decrease as navigation becomes more accurate. Nevertheless, the grouping is kept for convenience.

Navigation
As stated earlier, the air user accuracy requirements are fairly high during approach and landing, cf. Table 12.3. In order to achieve these accuracies in the navigation mode, fixed receivers must broadcast range corrections (and carrier phase) to incoming aircraft so that they can compute more accurate positions (by DGPS) as they approach the runway. GPS aided approach and landing will be an economical answer to airport control.

The use of GPS in its point positioning mode is becoming popular for emergency vehicle management. For example, if emergency vehicles were equipped with a C/A-code pseudoranging receiver and a radio transceiver, the position of each vehicle could be determined by GPS as it travels to a designated area, and the transceiver could send this position to a central dispatcher. The location of all vehicles could then be displayed on a screen so that at any given instant the dispatcher could see where his resources are positioned. If, for example, one of the roads were blocked, the dispatcher could reroute the vehicle or he could dispatch a closer vehicle. There is little doubt that such GPS based Automatic Vehicle Location (AVL) systems will be installed in all major cities in the world in the near future.

Surveying
The GIS discussed in the previous section is also being developed for cities
and towns so this use will not be covered further. A typical local use of GPS
is local property and site survey. Some surveyors are using GPS to place all
projects surveyed on a single datum (e.g., NAD-83). An economical way to
do this is to place an antenna at a fixed central location (e.g., office) and to
determine the precise coordinates of this point by measuring vectors from
the nearby fixed control points. After the coordinates of the fixed central
site have been determined, one receiver is left there and is run continuously
during those times where field crews are engaged in survey activities. Each
survey crew takes one or two additional receivers and places them on points
in the local scheme being surveyed. For example, a topographic site survey
and boundary determination requires the establishment of many temporary
and permanent points all connected by conventional survey measurements.
Two GPS receivers placed on two widely spaced points in this local scheme
could collect data during the time the survey crew made conventional measurements with little additional manpower cost. Upon completion of the
conventional survey and simultaneous GPS measurements, the coordinates
of all points in the scheme would be determined and also all bearings in the
scheme would be precisely related to true north.

An additional local application of GPS is to perform topographic surveys
by using the kinematic mode. In areas of relatively few obstructions, a roving
GPS receiver can either be carried or placed on a vehicle (e.g., all terrain
vehicle) and the terrain traversed by a series of cross sections. The horizontal
position and the height of points can typically be determined every second,
so a high density of point determinations will result even when the receiver
is vehicle mounted and travels at high speed. The processing and plotting
of the kinematic cross sections is automated so that the field to finish time
can be minimized.

Several organizations are using GPS kinematic surveying to determine
the coordinates of the photocenter during aerial mapping flights. There is
also consideration being given to use three or more antennas connected to
the GPS receiver to determine the orientation angles of the aircraft. Both
aspects are treated in more detail in the following two sections.

12.2 Attitude determination

Attitude is defined as the orientation of a specific coordinate system (body-
fixed frame) in a land vehicle, ship, or aircraft with respect to a global or

local coordinate system or reference frame. Three parameters are commonly used to define the attitude. These are the Euler angles for roll, pitch, and yaw (or heading). In the case of an aircraft, the roll angle measures the rotation of the aircraft about the fuselage axis, the pitch angle measures the rotation about the wing axis, and the yaw angle measures the rotation about the vertical axis. If all three angles are zero, the aircraft is flying exactly straight and level, and heading north, cf. Graas and Braasch (1992).

The attitude of a body-fixed platform may be derived from the relative positions of GPS antennas located at various positions of this platform. Since the plane of the platform is uniquely defined by three points or by two (non coincident) vectors, three antennas forming two independent baselines are the minimum for attitude determination. The two (three-dimensional) baselines provide six equations to determine the three Euler angles of the platform. In the case of a rigid platform, three conditions exist: the norm of the baselines and the spatial angle between them are invariant against attitude variations.

As stated above, three antennas are required for three-dimensional attitude determination. Two antennas are needed if only heading and pitch are desired. This corresponds to the determination of azimuth and elevation in a local coordinate system. If four antennas are used, the nonrigidity of the platform may be taken into account. Furthermore, if the four antennas are mounted, for example, one on each wing tip of an aircraft, and the remaining two atop the fuselage, then the roll angle can be determined independently from heading and the pitch angle. In practice, the movement of the aircraft's wings during flight may completely obviate the precise determination of the roll angle.

For the mathematical formulation of attitude determination, the position vector of an antenna in the local reference frame is denoted by $\underline{X}_R$ and the corresponding position vector in the body frame by $\underline{X}_B$. The reference frame coordinates are GPS coordinates which have been transformed from the global to the local frame by formulas similar to Eq. (7.7). The body frame coordinates are known from initialization.

In the (general) case of a nonrigid platform, the relationship between the vectors $\underline{X}_R$ and $\underline{X}_B$ may be described by an affine transformation. The introduction of baseline vectors $\Delta\underline{X}$ instead of position vectors $\underline{X}$ eliminates a shift vector, and the affine transformation is given by

$$\Delta\underline{X}_B = \underline{M}\,\Delta\underline{X}_R \tag{12.1}$$

where $\underline{M}$ is a 3×3 matrix with all nine elements as unknowns. Therefore, three baselines (or four antennas) are needed to solve the linear system for the unknowns.

In the case of a rigid platform, the relationship between the vectors $\Delta \underline{X}_R$ and $\Delta \underline{X}_B$ may be described by a similarity transformation in the form

$$\Delta \underline{X}_B = \underline{R} \, \Delta \underline{X}_R \tag{12.2}$$

where $\underline{R}$ is a rotation matrix composed of the three Euler angles. This matrix corresponds to Eq. (10.30) if the angles α_1, α_2, α_3 are identified with roll, pitch, and yaw respectively. No scale factor is considered because of the assumed rigidity. The minimum of two baselines provides six equations for the three unknown Euler angles. Thus, the problem is overdetermined and may be solved by least squares adjustment, cf. Sect. 10.3.1.

The solution for a multiantenna array with n independent baselines may also be found by writing Eq. (12.2) as

$$\underline{A}_B = \underline{R} \, \underline{A}_R \tag{12.3}$$

where $\underline{A}_B$ is a $3 \times n$ matrix with the baseline vectors in the body frame as column vectors. The corresponding matrix $\underline{A}_R$ contains the baseline vectors in the local reference frame. Solving for the rotation matrix involves multiplying Eq. (12.3) by the (generalized) inverse of the matrix $\underline{A}_R$. The result is given by, cf. Graas and Braasch (1991),

$$\underline{R} = \underline{A}_B \, \underline{A}_R^T (\underline{A}_R \underline{A}_R^T)^{-1} \, . \tag{12.4}$$

Denoting the elements of the matrix $\underline{R}$ by R_{ij}, the Euler angles are obtained from

$$\sin \alpha_2 = R_{31}$$
$$\sin \alpha_1 = -\frac{R_{32}}{\cos \alpha_2} \tag{12.5}$$
$$\sin \alpha_3 = -\frac{R_{21}}{\cos \alpha_2}$$

which may immediately be seen from Eq. (10.30).

The azimuth a and the zenith angle z (corresponding to heading and the pitch angle) may be derived from one baseline only. If the components of the baseline vector in the local reference frame are denoted by ΔX, ΔY, ΔZ, then the equations

$$\tan a = \frac{\Delta Y}{\Delta X}$$
$$\tan z = \frac{\sqrt{\Delta X^2 + \Delta Y^2}}{\Delta Z} \tag{12.6}$$

are valid, cf. Eq. (7.7). Note that in this case no a priori knowledge of the body frame is required, cf. Lu et al. (1993).

Some GPS manufacturers have already designed a multiantenna platform for attitude determination, cf. e.g. Quin et al. (1992). This platform consists of four microstrip antennas connected to a 24-channel single frequency receiver. Six channels are assigned to each antenna so that up to six satellites may be tracked. One antenna is used to determine position and velocity of the platform. The baselines between the primary antenna and the other three antennas are used for attitude determination. An accuracy of ± 1 mm in the relative position of the antennas can be achieved by using double-differences of carrier phases. This accuracy corresponds to an inclination of one milliradiant or 0.057 degrees when the antenna separation is 1 m. The type of error which most limits the (theoretical) accuracy of attitude determination is multipath. This effect can be reduced by installing a common ground plane for all antennas. The redundant fourth antenna allows internal checks. When the antennas are mounted on a rigid platform, conditions for the relative positions of the antennas can be introduced which further improves reliability, cf. Ferguson et al. (1991).

12.3   Airborne GPS for photo-control

Now that the GPS constellation provides 24-hour coverage, the use of GPS in aircraft (and other vehicles) to provide positions for photographs is becoming more widely used. Several government organizations as well as private firms now routinely use GPS for precise positioning. The development of accurate (10 cm) C/A-code receivers and dual band full wavelength receivers has accelerated the use of GPS for decimeter accuracy positioning.

The most simple use of the system is to perform DGPS using the C/A-code pseudorange. This technique is extremely robust in that temporary loss of lock does not affect the accuracy of subsequent positions. Furthermore, initialization on the ground prior to flight is unnecessary. Sub-meter accuracies are obtainable (with proper receivers and software) and provide adequate control for small-scale mapping and control of orthophoto maps.

The more recent and precise positioning method for photo-aircraft is to use dual frequency full wavelength receivers and software that provide on-the-fly resolution of the integer ambiguities. Because the full wavelength carrier phase is available on both frequencies, the (86 cm) wide lane observable can be formed. A few epochs of precise code range data combined with Kalman filtering permit the solution of the initial vector between the fixed base station and the roving airborne receiver. This knowledge is then used to define a "search box" which contains the solution of the wide lane ambiguities. The smaller the search box, the faster the ambiguity is resolved. Once the wide lane ambiguity has been resolved, the $L1$ ambiguity can be quickly found. Factors which affect the speed and reliability of this method are:

- Pseudorange bias and noise.

- Carrier phase bias and noise.

- Multipath.

- Baseline separation.

- Satellite geometry.

Although the on-the-fly software can be initialized while the aircraft is in motion, the intial integer resolution can be accomplished more rapidly with the aircraft parked on the ground. Normally, only a minute or two are required for this initialization. If the airborne receiver then tracks the satellites during takeoff and climbing, there is a greater chance of success of the mission.

The GPS receiver must be capable of recording the precise time of each aerial exposure. Specially equipped aerial cameras provide a time pulse for the precise instant of exposure of the photograph. This time is then recorded by the GPS receiver so that the coordinates at that instant can be interpolated for the adjacent regular GPS receiver epochs. Normally, receivers are set to record data every 0.5 to 2 seconds. The shorter interval provides more data so that the software can recover more rapidly from temporary loss of lock, and also provides more accurate photo positions since the aircraft trajectory is more correctly defined. A short data rate can fill up the memory during a photographic mission day so that for longer days or briefer epochs an external recording device such as a laptop computer is maybe needed.

The best position for the airborne GPS antenna is directly over the camera. This configuration reduces the error that can occur due to an incorrectly applied offset. A number of research studies investigates the use of multiple antennas and receivers to provide both redundant observations and aircraft attitude information, see Cooper et al. (1994), Blankenberg (1994). At present, the best method of determining the aircraft's attitude is to compute the roll, pitch, and yaw from the photogrammetric block adjustment.

A number of photogrammetric analytical block adjustments have been adapted to accept the airborne GPS data. In addition to providing aircraft attitude information, these adjustments can be used to verify the GPS coordinates. For example, blocks with fixed (ground) control at the corner points will flag any photo-position that is in error. Typically, agreement between the block solution and the GPS positions is at the 5 to 10 centimeter level.

The solution of airborne GPS heights is performed using the ellipsoidal height of the base (ground) station so that all airborne heights are in the ellipsoidal system. Elevations relative to the geoid are normally desired so that the geoidal heights must be applied to the airborne heights (along with the distance from the antenna to the camera). The most accurate method of determining the local geoidal height is to make a ground survey where vertical control points are occupied. The locally derived geoidal heights can then be applied to the appropriate photo-heights to obtain the proper elevation.

GPS controlled photography is also suitable for large-scale mapping. In this instance, greater care should be exercised to ensure that the derived positions meet the desired accuracy requirements. In particular, the ground base station from which the airborne positions are derived should be located as close to the center of the project area as possible. This location will reduce the distance between the aircraft and the base station during the actual photography resulting in the greatest precision (due to reduction of unknown ionospheric and tropospheric errors). Furthermore, this base station site will provide the most accurate determination of the geoidal height. As a practical matter, it is best to have two ground stations to provide redundancy of data. One good scenario is to locate one receiver on the project site and the second receiver at an airport near the site. Furthermore, ground sites should be free from obstructions and in low multipath environments.

Processing of airborne data is similar to ground kinematic data. With on-the-fly software it is possible to process the data both forward and backward so that the optimum solution of the data can be made. The two solutions can be either averaged or combined in an optimum way to give the best solution. Also, when two ground stations are used, these solutions may be combined to give optimal results.

The GPS airborne control method is extremely cost effective in that a great portion of local control needed for photo-mapping can be eliminated. In many areas where access to the site is limited, the airborne control method will make difficult mapping tasks routine.

12.4   Interoperability of GPS

12.4.1   GPS and Inertial Navigation Systems

One of the main disadvantages of using GPS for surveying, land navigation, and feature coordinate tagging is the temporary outage as the receiver passes under bridges or other obstructions. For example, a highway data collection van would experience loss of positioning when the van passed under trees overhanging the highway. Various devices have been used to compensate for this disadvantage. One simple dead reckoning system to use is an odometer and a (flux gate) magnetic compass to assist in interpolating the position of vehicles during satellite outages, cf. Byman and Koskelo (1991). More sophisticated approaches involve combining GPS with Inertial Navigation Systems (INS).

Basically, an INS consists of two components: (1) gyros to stabilize space or locally oriented axes and (2) accelerometers placed on them to measure accelerations (i.e., velocity rates). Hence, when mounting such an INS on a moving vehicle, one can continuously measure the accelerations along the stabilized axes. Starting from a known position and integrating the observables twice over time yields differences in position which determine the trajectory of the vehicle. This simple principle becomes fairly complicated in practice, and the reader is referred to the voluminous literature, see Schwarz and Lachapelle (1990).

The error of an (unaided) INS generally increases with the square of time due to the double integration over time. What are the advantages of INS compared to GPS? First, inertial systems are autonomous and independent of external sources. Also, there is no visibility problem as with GPS. Second, INS provides accuracy similar to GPS when used over short time intervals with data rates of generally 64 Hz. Hence, INS can serve as an interpolator for GPS gaps.

When GPS is combined with a precise INS, it is possible to reinitialize the GPS integer cycle count after a temporary loss of lock. For example, it is critical to maintain continuous count of integer cycles when performing a kinematic survey with C/A-code receivers. Accurate inertial systems could overcome the loss of cycle count problem by being able to predict an accurate change in carrier phase and, thus, cycle count during signal outages or massive cycle slips. The difficulty in using inertial systems for this purpose is their high cost and lack of field worthiness. Many experts feel that inertial systems have become redundant for surveying with the advent of on-the-fly technology.

12.4.2 GPS and GLONASS

The GLONASS is the Russian equivalent of GPS. The system is expected to be completely deployed in 1995 and will be composed of 24 satellites (including three active spares) equally spaced in three orbital planes with 64.8 degree nominal inclination. The nearly circular orbits with altitudes of 19 100 km and a period of 11.25 hours are similar to GPS. In contrast to GPS, the broadcast carrier frequencies are satellite-specific. The individual carrier frequencies f_{L1}^j and f_{L2}^j for satellite j are defined by

$$f_{L1}^j = 1602.0000 \, \text{MHz} + j \cdot 0.5625 \, \text{MHz}$$

$$f_{L2}^j = 1246.0000 \, \text{MHz} + j \cdot 0.4375 \, \text{MHz}$$

$$(12.7)$$

where $j = 1, \ldots, 24$, cf. Kleusberg (1990b). The C/A- and P-code modulated onto the carriers are the same for all satellites, and the code frequencies are about half the corresponding GPS values. Also, the structure of the navigation message is different from GPS. Furthermore, GLONASS is using different coordinate and time systems.

It should be noted that GLONASS has some advantages compared to GPS. Currently, GLONASS signals experience no SA degradation. Therefore, the data transmission rates in differential applications can be lowered. All GLONASS satellites are equipped with retroreflectors for laser tracking, while at this time only one GPS satellite (i.e., PRN 05, launched in mid 1993) has this feature.

Today, receivers have been produced that have dual GPS-GLONASS capability. These multichannel receivers are capable of tracking any combination of GPS and GLONASS satellites. For details on this subject, the reader is referred to the literature. The utility of such receivers for navigation is still questionable although the obstacles may be surmountable. However, the added satellites would be of significant use in surveying applications. In a normal survey environment, there are many obstructions that block satellite signals in certain portions of the sky. The addition of GLONASS satellites could significantly improve the possibility that a given line could be surveyed. There is much to be determined before all aspects of combined GPS-GLONASS systems are known.

The joint use of GPS and GLONASS is the basis for the future Global Navigation Satellite System (GNSS). This system has some major advantages, cf. Shebshayevich (1991). These are improvements in geometry, availability, integrity, and reliability.

12.4.3   GPS and other sensors

Experiments are also being proposed to place GPS receivers on low-altitude satellites with various other sensing devices such as laser altimeters and synthetic aperture radar. Inclusion of GPS to determine positions of various events logged by such equipment will add to the data's value and in most cases reduce the costs of data collection.

One special use is to include GPS capability in earth sensing satellites. Accurate positioning of such satellites will greatly reduce the cost of determining coordinates of points appearing in the various images.

Several manufacturers also plan to combine GPS and conventional survey instruments. Today, the state-of-the-art surveying instruments measure angles and distances electronically so that the addition of GPS capability fits well with the total survey concept. Such a system would be particularly useful once a network of active control points were established because continuous accurate positioning would then be possible by computing vectors to the surrounding active control points.

12.4.4   GPS and the Federal Radionavigation Plan

The U.S. Department of Transportation (DoT) operates navigation systems for both civil and military use, whereas the U.S. Department of Defense (DoD) mainly operates systems for national defense.

In 1980, DoD and DoT jointly produced the Federal Radionavigation Plan (FRP) in order to select a mix of common-use navigation systems. These efforts should increase accuracy, coverage and reliability, while costs are reduced. Since 1980, DoT is conducting open meetings for all users of radionavigation systems provided by the U.S. Government to revise and update the FRP every two years. The present plan was issued in 1992, the next version will be available in 1994.

Today, nine different systems are considered in the FRP. These are the Long-range navigation system Loran-C, the Omega system with worldwide coverage, the Very High Frequency Omnidirectional Range and Distance Measuring Equipment (VOR/DME), Tactical Air Navigation (TACAN), the Instrument Landing System (ILS), the Microwave Landing System (MLS), Transit, radiobeacons, and GPS. For details about these systems, the reader is referred to, e.g., Langley (1992) or Schrödter (1994).

It is also the responsibility of the FRP to study the feasibility of replacing some of the existing systems by GPS, particularly since Initial Operational Capability has been declared. For short-range navigation such as airport-approach and landing, DGPS is appropriate.

12.5   Installation of control networks

GPS is in fact a geodetic tool in that it provides precise vector measurements over long as well as short distances. Virtually all GPS processing software employs a three-dimensional model, and results are given in geodetic latitude, longitude, and ellipsoidal height in the WGS-84 which for vectors is (virtually) the same as NAD-83. If the GPS datum does not correspond to the national datum, a three-dimensional similarity transformation must be performed. Afterwards, the ellipsoidal values are mapped onto a projection so that land surveyors who are more familiar with plane coordinates can use the survey results.

GPS provides reference datums by two methods: the passive control networks and the active control networks.

12.5.1 Passive control networks

Virtually all civilized areas have some type of geodetic control networks generally surveyed by triangulation, traverse (or a combination of the two methods), and by spirit leveling. In many cases, the horizontal control network is separate from the vertical control network with perhaps 10% of these points in common. These control networks were used to scale and orient maps to provide a unified reference frame for large-scale projects, and to provide a common datum for property surveys. Geodetic control networks basically serve two functions: (1) they provide a "seamless" datum spanning large areas and (2) they provide a reference framework which appears to be errorless to its users (surveyors).

The apparent errorless aspect of a geodetic network is accomplished by employing state-of-the-art instrumentation and using the utmost care in making observations. Historically, geodetic survey instruments were manufactured by specialists, and observers were rigorously trained in their use. Horizontal accuracies of 1:250 000 of the distance and vertical accuracies on a few millimeters per kilometer were typically obtained.

The advent of GPS changed the concept of what constituted a geodetic control network. The first surveys performed in 1983 were carried out with internal accuracies approaching 1 ppm, and disagreed with the existing control networks by 10 to 20 ppm, in many cases. This discrepancy was not surprising to the geodesists responsible for establishing the control networks, but it did concern GPS surveyors because they could not obtain accurate position checks of their work. Eventually, the concept of "supernets" or sparse arrays of high accuracy control networks established by GPS began to evolve. Many such supernets are now being established in the U.S. and in other countries by state governments. These supernets will supersede the traditional lower accuracy control network.

Horizontal control
In addition to being less accurate than required by the users, the existing control networks have another disturbing feature that dooms them to ex-

tinction. The points in the two-dimensional network are normally located on the highest point in the area and are often not easily occupiable by GPS. Also, existing control points are located in heavily treed areas or at sites that are difficult to reach. Since most of the future geodetic (horizontal) surveys will be performed by GPS, the existing network points are (in many cases) inadequate.

The solution to this problem was found by establishing an array of new control points spaced between 25 and 100 km at locations suitable for GPS occupation. In most cases, these points are located at sites that are vehicle accessible and where they will not be disturbed. The internal accuracy of the supernets is normally 0.1 ppm so that in effect they appear to be errorless to users.

The global accuracy of supernets is controlled by referencing them to VLBI points. The international VLBI framework of points provides the ultimate geodetic framework, inasmuch as the interrelationship of these points is known to a higher accuracy than any other global array of points. The supernet observations using dual frequency receivers are made simultaneously with observations at the VLBI sites. In fact, these observations are routinely made by the CIGNET stations, cf. Sect. 4.4.1. Since the positions of the points in a state supernet are known to a few centimeters accuracy with respect to the VLBI stations, it is possible to establish networks in adjoining states at separate times. The seamless feature required for a true geodetic network is, therefore, easily achieved because there is relatively little error in the common boundary between the adjacent states. This feature of GPS supernets is particularly important because the surveys can be performed as needed and do not have to proceed in an orderly progression as conventional surveys.

Vertical control

GPS is a three-dimensional survey system in that it measures a vector between points with roughly the same degree of accuracy in all three components. Therefore, GPS is able to determine elevations as well as latitude and longitude. However, there is a problem in using GPS to establish elevations, since the height differences measured with GPS are referenced to an ellipsoid and not to the geoid to which conventionally leveled heights refer. As explained in more detail in Sect. 10.2.3, the difference between the ellipsoid and geoid differs for every point on the earth and can be found from existing global or local geoid models. One way to model the local or regional geoid is to run levels to a point of known ellipsoidal height. This is normally done for points in a supernet so that each point has an accurate ellipsoidal height and elevation. Based on this, geodesists are able to refine their geoidal height prediction model to provide a more accurate determination. Many geodesists feel that prediction models in the future generally will have accuracies of a few centimeters in areas where supernets have been established.

Vertical accuracies of a few centimeters can also be presently achieved by connecting or referencing a GPS survey to supernet points. Since the supernet points have well-known elevations, and interpolation is done between these known points, the elevations of the new points can be accurately determined. Additionally, accuracies of such surveys are improved when a good model of geoidal heights is used.

12.5.2 Active control networks

For DGPS applications, the monitor stations can be arranged in networks which are called "Active control networks" or "Wide-area differential GPS" (WADGPS) systems. These networks improve the integrity and reliability of DGPS. Just as the supernets are making the existing control networks obsolete, the development of active control networks will possibly make the supernets obsolete.

One example for such an active control network is the Canadian Active Control System (ACS). This system has been developed since 1985. When completely deployed, it will consist of about twenty regularly distributed monitor stations (with the master control station in Ottawa) which continuously track all visible satellites. The operation is fully automated. Thus, satellite tracking, collection of dual frequency and ground meteorological data, performance of self-diagnostic tests, and the communication with the master control station in full duplex mode are performed automatically. The master control station coordinates the observing stations, processes the data, and manages the dissemination of the results. For more details, the reader is referred to Delikaraoglou et al. (1990).

Professional DGPS services like SkyFix, cf. Mack (1991), with worldwide coverage have been installed. An overview on such services can be found in Sluiter (1993). The U.S. Coast Guard plans to provide DGPS service, free of charge, for harbor approach of maritime navigation. This system should be operational in 1996 and achieve an accuracy better than 10 meters at the 95% probability level, cf. Olsen (1992). A similar service is planned for maritime use in Europe, cf. Speckter (1991). Some 50 DGPS monitor stations will provide an almost complete coastal coverage in Europe including parts of the Mediterranean Sea.

Another prototype of an active control network is the system developed by the Texas Highway Department. The plan is to continuously track all satellites from nine sites located throughout the state and then use the phase data to compute vectors from these fixed sites to other receivers surveying the various highway projects. The Texas system is a good example of the advantages and disadvantages of this concept. The advantage is that survey crews do not have to search for and occupy control points near their project area. They simply occupy the points they need coordinates for at the given project site. The vectors from the fixed stations surrounding the project site are combined with the (short) interstation vectors to give the "best fit" solution for that particular survey. The cost effectiveness of this approach is positive when numerous crews take advantage of the system so that the cost of maintaining the fixed sites is spread over a large number of units. The disadvantage of the Texas system (at this time) is that the Highway Department is not prepared to provide its internal service to the public, as it is not funded to perform this service. The active control network of the Highway Department is a single user private network which may have to be duplicated by various other users. This is not the only example of such duplication. Several other organizations are also setting up various types of active control points to serve their particular needs. Only time will tell how this problem will be resolved.

In practice, any moderately sized organization (e.g., company) will be able to establish its own tracking network. For example, a firm could place three receivers at equally spaced points that would cover its operations area. The precise coordinates of these fixed sites could be determined by combining a day's observation with data from the CIGNET stations. Once the coordinates of the local tracking stations have been determined, they can be used as tracking stations themselves. A local tracking station can be as simple as an antenna mounted on the roof and a GPS receiver placed in a drawer and connected to a modem. At the end of the survey day, users would call each local tracker and download desired files. Recalibration of local networks could be performed periodically by recomputing the vectors from the CIGNET stations. The use of local tracking networks may be advantageous since the accuracy of the broadcast ephemerides is significantly degraded by SA. Local surveys are unaffected by this degradation because surveyed vectors can be computed by using orbit relaxation software that only uses the broadcast orbit to initialize the computations.

13 Future of GPS

13.1 New application aspects

The future uses of GPS are limited only by one's imagination. Many of the present uses were described in various articles written as early as 1982 when this new system first demonstrated its high accuracy. With the reduction of equipment costs and the complete satellite coverage, many more applications will develop. This includes terrestrial, marine, and aviation applications.

Some examples for applications on land are vehicle navigation and information systems including the establishment of Vehicle Traffic Systems (VTS) or Intelligent Vehicle/Highway Systems (IVHS). There will be also numerous applications in survey and geodesy as well as precise time determination and time transfer. One land application which has been mentioned is the use of GPS to automate various types of machinery. For example, it should be possible to automate the grading and paving equipment used for road building. Equipment could be run around the clock without operators with GPS performing all motion operations based upon a digital terrain model stored in the equipment's computer.

Marine applications will include vessel navigation and information systems, precise harbor entrance systems, and oceanography in general. DGPS will mostly be used for these purposes, and dense networks of monitor stations are to be established along the coasts. For example, the USCG plans to equip more than 50 monitor stations with state-of-the-art receivers for data collection and DGPS corrections dissemination.

For aviation, GPS will be integrated into other navigation systems like INS to fullfil the high reliability and integrity requirements. Applications will cover the fields of en route navigation and surveillance, approaching and landing, collision avoidance, and proximity warning. Aircraft could be operated in an automated mode with takeoffs and landings being performed by integrating GPS and computer units.

The use of GPS will increasingly also be extended to space for precise positioning of satellites (e.g., earth remote sensing satellites like ERS-1 and TOPEX/Poseidon), for attitude determination of spacecraft, and for missile navigation, cf. McDonald (1991) and Exon (1993).

Table 13.1 gives an insight into the expected growth of GPS users between 1990 and 2000. One can immediately read from the table the dominant role which GPS will likely play in future navigation.

Table 13.1. Growth of GPS users between
1990 and 2000 after Langley (1992)

Users	1990	2000
Civil aviation	500	70 000
Civil land	2 500	150 000
Civil maritime	4 000	250 000
Military	2 500	30 000
Total	9 500	500 000

13.2   Improved constellation

The future Global Navigation Satellite System (GNSS) combines satellite-based navigation systems such as GPS and GLONASS. The inclusion of geostationary satellites and so-called econosats (i.e., small and low-cost navigation satellites), cf. McDonald (1993), is also considered.

13.2.1   Next generation GPS satellites

The construction of 20 Block IIR satellites has already been contracted; while the Block IIF or follow-on satellites are presently being designed. These next generation satellites will have many improvements over the present Block II/IIA satellites. It is planned to include the capability to transmit data between satellites to make the system more independent. This capability will allow the satellites to essentially position themselves without extensive ground tracking. The advantages of these satellites are:

- Navigation accuracy is maintained for six months without ground support. No survivable control and no user modifications are required.

- Uplink jamming concerns are minimized.

- One upload per spacecraft per month instead of one or even more per day is performed.

- Need for overseas stations to support navigation uploads is reduced.

- Improved navigation accuracy is achieved.

These features mainly benefit the military use of the system, since civilians will still be required to provide their own ephemerides for accurate surveys.

13.2.2   GLONASS satellites

In addition to the GPS constellation, the GLONASS constellation will provide a like number of satellites which can be used in combination with the GPS satellites. Because of the similarity of the two systems, it will be possible to include the GLONASS measurements in a combined solution forming triple- and double-differences between the satellite pairs. The main benefit to surveyors will be the increase in sky coverage, making it possible to measure lines that would otherwise be obstructed. Also, the increased number of measurements makes the kinematic method much more viable than it is with just the GPS constellation. For example, Remondi (1991a) has shown that kinematic surveys can be performed without presurvey initialization when five or more satellites are available and using C/A-code receivers. On-the-fly kinematic surveying using an inexpensive C/A-code receiver (rather than the more expensive dual frequency receivers) could be used for most present land surveying tasks such as boundary, topographic, hydrographic, and construction surveys. By the integration of GLONASS, kinematic surveys can continue even after cycle slips have been experienced.

13.2.3   INMARSAT satellites

The International Maritime Satellites, a system of geosynchronous communication satellites, are planned to be equipped with repeaters which will transmit C/A-code signals on $L1$, cf. Kinal and Singh (1990), Nagle et al. (1992/93). The primary purpose of these satellites is integrity monitoring. These satellites will significantly increase the effective coverage of GPS and will be particularly useful in the kinematic surveys since satellite motion is not needed. Also, these satellites can be used as the reference satellite in static surveying. A detailed description of INMARSAT can be found in Ackroyd and Lorimer (1990), pp. 171–198.

13.2.4   Econosats

The proposed econosats would primarily be designed for civil use and would, thus, have less stringent requirements than the military GPS satellites. Consequently, small low-cost navigation satellites (thus the name econosats) are being considered to augment the GNSS. For compatibility reasons, the econosats would broadcast a signal very similar to GPS satellites; however, since there would be no need for P-code (with inherent A-S problems) only C/A-code would be modulated on the two carrier frequencies. These frequencies would actually have to be slightly offset from the present GPS carrier frequencies to avoid interference, cf. McDonald (1993).

13.3   Hardware improvements

Many of today's hardware developments were predicted by GPS pioneers. For example, the rapid cost reduction in equipment, predicted in Wells et al. (1987), in many ways parallels the development of small computers. The continued production of special computer chips will both decrease the cost and size, and increase the reliability and field worthiness.

13.3.1   Receiver cost

The first GPS receivers for commercial use cost in excess of $ 150 000 and possessed much less capability than receivers presently costing $ 20 000. Original Equipment Manufacturer (OEM) units are now (1994) being marketed at a cost of less than $ 3 000 (with demonstrated survey accuracies). If one plots the receiver cost against time, the curve shows a sharp (exponential) decline during the first few years (1983–1987) and then becomes asymptotic with the receiver prices slowly decreasing after 1987. The GPS price curve closely resembles the decrease in the price of survey totalstations or hand-held calculators. The cost analysis of GPS is somewhat complicated by the fact that the processing software is bundled in the sales price. When the cost of software is a significant portion of the receiver cost, and the receiver is mainly composed of integrated circuit chips, the cost of receivers can be appreciably lowered by quantity production. Today, the point has been reached where volume production by a manufacturer could reduce the receiver cost to a fraction of the present level.

13.3.2   Receiver capability

The present multichannel dual frequency receivers measure and record all the basic observables; that is, pseudoranges with both codes and phases on both carriers. It appears that the resolution will soon be improved to 0.1% of the wavelength (or better). This capability translates into a precision of a few centimeters in the code pseudorange, thus, providing instantaneous carrier phase ambiguity resolution. Additionally, multichannel receivers with up to 36 digital programmable channels (measuring any combination of the $L1$ and $L2$ observables) will routinely be manufactured. Multiantenna arrays connected to a single receiver will be improved for highly accurate attitude determination. It is anticipated that such receivers will be modified to determine azimuths to distant azimuth marks; thus, reducing the task of surveying a geodetic control network by 50%.

Improvements of the kinematic GPS technique will also affect the design of future GPS receivers. Automatic bandwidth adjustment and more rigorous cycle slip detection will be the norm of the future. The size (and power requirements) of receivers will also be reduced. One can easily project the present GPS "stake out" capability to imagine a small antenna mounted on top of a range pole with the electronics placed inside the pole to reduce the bulk carried by the rodman. This (no longer futuristic) receiver combined with a receiver incorporated in a conventional totalstation instrument provides the surveyor with the ultimate surveying capability. One receiver in a totalstation and a second in the rod would significantly increase the surveyor's productivity, since the totalstation could be used in those instances when the point desired was under a tree or otherwise obstructed, while the GPS capability could be used when the "rod" was in the clear. This combination would also allow the surveyor to obtain instantaneous true azimuths by initializing on the "rod" receiver prior to sighting points with the conventional angle measurements.

As the cost of receivers decrease, instruments will also be placed on structures such as bridges and dams to provide near real-time motion detection. It has been hypothesized for a number of years that instrumenting dams with GPS receivers tied into a central control network could provide a warning system to foretell dam failure.

The GLONASS satellite system was briefly discussed previously. If this system develops as planned, receivers of the future will incorporate the capability of receiving both GPS and GLONASS signals. It is worth noting that prototypes of such receivers have already been produced. Receivers with programmable digital channels will be tailored to switch channels between the two systems to gain the optimum accuracy for the satellites in view. Also, the number of channels in receivers will increase if the GLONASS system is used since there could be as many as twenty useable satellites in view from the two systems.

13.4 Software improvements

There are three basic types of GPS software: (1) preplanning software, (2) software used by the receiver to track and record the satellite data, and (3) postprocessing software. Some GPS receivers presently include partial postprocessing software in the receiver. For example, one manufacturer offers receivers capable of performing real-time differential navigation (i.e., stake out) using their normal hardware and upgraded receiver software. This trend will increase in the future and additional processing software will be included with the receiver. For example, the prior generation TRANSIT receivers had the capability of processing data from a second receiver to determine precise differential positions. It is likely that GPS receivers will also provide this capability in the near future. A similar recent development is receiver software that will notify the operator when a sufficient number of observations has been taken (when receivers are linked by radio).

The first GPS processing software (for Macrometer) required that cycle slips be fixed interactively. A reasonably good line (few cycle slips) required about one hour to process on a DEC PDP-11 computer. A major breakthrough was made when C. Goad introduced processing software which automatically repaired cycle slips and could batch process a day's data overnight using a PC. The kinematic and pseudokinematic software introduced by B. Remondi produced new and better ways to accurately compute vectors and added to the overall capabilities of the system. Today, some manufacturers are incorporating the wide lane technique to quickly determine integer carrier phase biases and, thus, shorten the time required to measure vectors (to a few minutes). New software, based on dual frequency data, will provide powerful capabilities. This software will also allow GPS and GLONASS data to be combined resulting in real-time centimeter navigation.

The CIGNET tracking network and active control points were discussed in previous chapters. In the future, these types of networks will be expanded and improved. Software will be developed so that surveyors can download data from one or more active control points in real or near real time using a mobile telephone. They will then be able to compute accurate positions on-site to any predetermined degree of accuracy. Orbit relaxation type software used for this purpose will provide centimeter accuracy positions over large areas so that the concept of survey accuracy will virtually disappear, since all GPS survey points will exceed the present first-order accuracy. The surveyor could also place a second receiver on a nearby temporary point so that the azimuth between the two points can be computed at the same time as position (scenario using the GPS totalstation and GPS rod receiver).

13.5   Conclusion

The present status of GPS is sufficiently exciting for most surveyors; however, future developments will make the present use of the system appear quite ordinary. The enlarged number of next generation satellites will meet all future requirements for navigation, surveying, timing, and additionally provide many new revolutionary uses. Substantially improved hardware and software components will provide desired results more quickly, in real time, at lower cost. Real-time data transfer systems will soon become affordable, reliable, and simple to use. Accuracy is expected to increase by at least one order of magnitude even with lower costs. In addition, GPS will achieve a higher level of integrity and its output will be more reliable due to extensive quality control. As a consequence, the differences between navigation and surveying will be less pronounced. Apart from the present tasks, new application will arise which today are undreamed of.

The future uses of GPS are virtually unlimited. Projections for the next decade are imaginable; however, its use into the next century is difficult to comprehend. The one undeniable fact is that surveyors will be fully challenged by this technology, and will receive benefits commensurate with their efforts to understand and adapt to this new system.

References

Abidin HZ (1993): On the construction of the ambiguity searching space for on-the-fly ambiguity resolution. Navigation, 40(3): 321–338.

Abidin HZ, Wells DE, Kleusberg A (1992): Some aspects of "on the fly" ambiguity resolution. In: Proceedings of the Sixth International Geodetic Symposium on Satellite Positioning, Columbus, Ohio, March 17–20, vol 2: 660–669.

Ackroyd N, Lorimer R (1990): Global navigation – a GPS user's guide. Lloyd's of London, London New York Hamburg Hong Kong.

Allison T, Eschenbach R (1989): Real-time cycle-slip fixing during kinematic surveys. In: Proceedings of the Fifth International Geodetic Symposium on Satellite Positioning, Las Cruces, New Mexico, March 13–17, vol 2: 330–337.

Arnold K (1970): Methoden der Satellitengeodäsie. Akademie, Berlin.

Ashby N (1987): Relativistic effects in the Global Positioning System. In: Relativistic effects in geodesy, Proceedings of the International Association of Geodesy (IAG) Symposia of the XIX General Assembly of IUGG, Vancouver, Canada, August 10–22, vol 1: 41–50.

Ashjaee J (1986): GPS Doppler processing for precise positioning in dynamic applications. In: The Institute of Navigation: Global Positioning System, vol 3: 54–69.

Ashjaee J (1993): An analysis of Y-code tracking techniques and associated technologies. Geodetical Info Magazine, 7(7): 26–30.

Ashjaee J, Lorenz R (1992): Precision GPS surveying after Y-code. In: Proceedings of ION GPS-92, Fifth International Technical Meeting of the Satellite Division of the Institute of Navigation, Albuquerque, New Mexico, September 16–18, 657–659.

Ashjaee J, Lorenz R, Sutherland R, Dutilloy J, Minazio J-B, Abtahi R, Eichner J-M, Kosmalska J, Helky R (1989): New GPS developments and Ashtech M-XII. In: Proceedings of ION GPS-89, The Second International Technical Meeting of the Satellite Division of the Institute of Navigation, Colorado Springs, Colorado, September 27–29, 195–198.

Ashkenazi V, Fuente C de la, Moore T, Yau J (1987): GPS processing algorithms and accuracies. Paper presented at the XIX General Assembly of the IUGG at Vancouver, Canada, August 10–22.

Ashkenazi V, Moore T, Ffoulkes-Jones G, Whalley S, Aquino M (1990): High precision GPS positioning by fiducial techniques. In: Bock Y, Leppard N (eds): Global Positioning System: an overview. Springer,

New York Berlin Heidelberg London Paris Tokyo Hong Kong, 195–202 [Mueller II (ed): IAG Symposia Proceedings, vol 102].

Avdis V, Billiris H, Hurst K, Kastens K, Paradissis D, Veis G (1990): Selection, monumentation, and documentation of GPS sites in the circum-Aegean region, Greece. Newsletter of the Space Geodetic Measurement Sites Subcommission (SGMS), 1(2): 7–9.

Bagley LC, Lamons JW (1992): NAVSTAR Joint Program Office and a status report on the GPS program. In: Proceedings of the Sixth International Geodetic Symposium on Satellite Positioning, Columbus, Ohio, March 17–20, vol 1: 21–30.

Bastos L, Landau H (1988): Fixing cycle slips in dual-frequency kinematic GPS-application using Kalman filtering. Manuscripta geodaetica, 13: 249–256.

Bauer M (1992): Vermessung und Ortung mit Satelliten. Wichmann, Karlsruhe, 2nd edition.

Bauersima I (1983): NAVSTAR/Global Positioning System (GPS) II, Radiointerferometrische Satellitenbeobachtungen. Mitteilungen der Satelliten-Beobachtungsstation Zimmerwald, Bern, vol 10.

Beck N, Duval JR, Taylor PT (1989): GPS processing methods: comparison with precise trilateration. Journal of Surveying Engineering, 115(2): 181–197.

Bender PL, Larden DR (1985): GPS carrier phase ambiguity resolution over long baselines. In: Proceedings of the First International Symposium on Precise Positioning with the Global Positioning System, Rockville, Maryland, April 15–19, vol 1: 357–361.

Bennet JM (1965): Triangular factors of modified matrices. Numerische Mathematik, 7: 217–221.

Beutler G (1991): Himmelsmechanik I. Mitteilungen der Satelliten-Beobachtungsstation Zimmerwald, Bern, vol 25.

Beutler G (1992): Himmelsmechanik II. Mitteilungen der Satelliten-Beobachtungsstation Zimmerwald, Bern, vol 28.

Beutler G, Davidson DA, Langley RB, Santerre R, Vanicek P, Wells DE (1984): Some theoretical and practical aspects of geodetic positioning using carrier phase difference observations of GPS satellites. University of New Brunswick, Canada, Technical Report vol 109.

Beutler G, Gurtner W, Bauersima I, Rothacher M (1986): Efficient computation of the inverse of the covariance matrix of simultaneous GPS carrier phase difference observations. Manuscripta geodaetica, 11: 249–255.

Beutler G, Bauersima I, Gurtner W, Rothacher M (1987a): Correlations between simultaneous GPS double difference carrier phase observations in the multistation mode: implementation considerations and first experiences. Manuscripta geodaetica, 12: 40–44.

Beutler G, Bauersima I, Gurtner W, Rothacher M, Schildknecht T, Geiger A (1987b): Atmospheric refraction and other important biases in GPS carrier phase observations. Mitteilungen der Satellitenbeobachtungsstation Zimmerwald, Bern, vol 22.

Beutler G, Bauersima I, Gurtner W, Rothacher M, Schildknecht T, Mader GL, Abell MD (1987c): Evaluation of the 1984 Alaska Global Positioning System campaign with the Bernese GPS software. Journal of Geophysical Research, 92(B2): 1295–1303.

Beutler G, Bauersima I, Gurtner W, Rothacher M, Schildknecht T (1988): Static positioning with the Global Positioning System (GPS): state of the art. In: Groten E, Strauß R (eds): GPS-techniques applied to geodesy and surveying. Springer, Berlin Heidelberg New York London Paris Tokyo, 363–380 [Bhattacharji S, Friedman GM, Neugebauer HJ, Seilacher A (eds): Lecture Notes in Earth Sciences, vol 19].

Beutler G, Gurtner W, Rothacher M, Wild U, Frei E (1990): Relative static positioning with the Global Positioning System: basic technical considerations. In: Bock Y, Leppard N (eds): Global Positioning System: an overview. Springer, New York Berlin Heidelberg London Paris Tokyo Hong Kong, 1–23 [Mueller II (ed): IAG Symposia Proceedings, vol 102].

Bevis M (1991): GPS Networks: the practical side. EOS Transactions, American Geophysical Union, 72(6): 49.

Black HD (1978): An easily implemented algorithm for the tropospheric range correction. Journal of Geophysical Research, 83(B4): 1825–1828.

Black HD, Eisner A (1984): Correcting satellite Doppler data for tropospheric effects. Journal of Geophysical Research, 89(D2): 2616–2626.

Blackwell EG (1986): Overview of differential GPS methods. In: The Institute of Navigation: Global Positioning System, vol 3: 89–100.

Blankenberg LE (1994): GPS-supported aerial triangulation – results from test flight Fredrikstad. In: Proceedings of the XX Congress of FIG (International Federation of Surveyors), Commission 5, Survey Instruments and Methods, Melbourne, Australia, March 5–12, 553.1/1–553.1/12.

Bletzacker FR (1985): Reduction of multipath contamination in a geodetic GPS receiver. In: Proceedings of the First International Symposium on Precise Positioning with the Global Positioning System, Rockville, Maryland, April 15–19, vol 1: 413–422.

Blewitt G (1987): New approaches to GPS carrier phase ambiguity resolution. Paper presented at the XIX General Assembly of the IUGG at Vancouver, Canada, August 10–22.

Bock Y, Shimada S (1989): Continuously monitoring GPS networks for deformation measurements. In: Bock Y, Leppard N (eds): Global Positioning System: an overview. Springer, New York Berlin Heidelberg London Paris Tokyo Hong Kong, 40–56 [Mueller II (ed): IAG Symposia Proceedings, vol 102].

Boucher C, Altamimi Z (1989): The initial IERS terrestrial reference frame. Observatoire de Paris, International Earth Rotation Service, Technical Note 1.

Bowen R, Swanson PL, Winn FB, Rhodus NW, Feess WA (1986): Global Positioning System Operational Control System accuracies. In: The Institute of Navigation: Global Positioning System, vol 3: 241–257.

Bowring BR (1976): Transformation from spatial to geographical coordinates. Survey Review, XXIII(181): 323–327.

Braasch MS (1990/91): A signal model for GPS. Navigation, 37(4): 363–377.

Brandt L (1992): GPS information center and civil interface. In: Proceedings of ION GPS-92, Fifth International Technical Meeting of the Satellite Division of the Institute of Navigation, Albuquerque, New Mexico, September 16–18, 23–30.

Breuer B, Campbell J, Müller A (1993): GPS-Meß- und Auswerteverfahren unter operationellen GPS-Bedingungen. Journal for Satellite-Based Positioning, Navigation and Communication, 2(3): 82–90.

Bronstein IN, Semendjajew KA (1969): Taschenbuch der Mathematik. Teubner, Leipzig.

Brouwer D, Clemence GM (1961): Methods of celestial mechanics. Academic Press, New York.

Brunner F (1984): NAVSTAR GPS – ein Satellitensystem für die Navigation und Vermessung der Zukunft. Krieg im Äther, vol XXIV.

Bucerius H (1966): Himmelsmechanik I. Bibliographisches Institut, Mannheim, BI Hochschultaschenbücher vol 143/143a.

Byman P, Koskelo I (1991): Mapping Finnish roads with differential GPS and dead reckoning. GPS World, 2(2): 38–42.

Cannon ME (1990): The contribution of GPS to the information society. CISM Journal ACSGC, 44(3): 225–231.

Cannon ME, Schwarz KP (1989): GPS semi-kinematic positioning along a well-controlled traverse. In: Proceedings of the Fifth International Geodetic Symposium on Satellite Positioning, Las Cruces, New Mexico, March 13–17, vol 2: 621–630.

Cannon ME, Schwarz KP, Wong RVC (1986): Kinematic positioning with GPS – an analysis of road tests. In: Proceedings of the Fourth International Geodetic Symposium on Satellite Positioning, Austin, Texas, April 28 – May 2, vol 2: 1251–1268.

CGSIC (1993a): Summary record of the 21st meeting of the Civil GPS Service Interface Committee (CGSIC), Falls Church, Virginia, January 25–26.

CGSIC (1993b): Summary record of the 22nd meeting of the Civil GPS Service Interface Committee (CGSIC), Salt Lake City, Utah, September 20–21.

Chan L, Schorr J (1994): Receiver survey. GPS World, 5(1): 38–56.

Chao CC (1972): A model for tropospheric calibration from daily surface and radiosonde balloon measurements. Jet Propulsion Laboratory, Pasadena, California, JPL Technical Memorandum, 391-350.

Chin M (1991): CIGNET report. GPS Bulletin, 4(2): 5–11.

Clynch JR, Coco DS (1986): Error characteristics of high quality geodetic GPS measurements: clocks, orbits, and propagation effects. In: Proceedings of the Fourth International Geodetic Symposium on Satellite Positioning, Austin, Texas, April 28 – May 2, vol 1: 539–556.

Collins J (1982): The satellite solution to surveying. Professional Surveyor, 2(6): 12–17.

Collins J (1989): Fundamentals of GPS baseline and height determinations. Journal of Surveying Engineering, American Society of Civil Engineers, 115(2): 223–235.

Cooper MAR, Cross PA, Dahl PA, Corbett S, Short T (1994): GPS kinematic positions and orientations of airborne sensors: some preliminary results. In: Proceedings of the XX Congress of FIG (International Federation of Surveyors), Commission 5, Survey Instruments and Methods, Melbourne, Australia, March 5–12, 503.1/1–503.1/10.

Counselman CC (1981): Miniature interferometer terminals for earth surveying – MITES. CSTG Bulletin vol 3, International Activities, Technology and Mission Developments.

Counselman CC, Abbot RI (1989): Method of resolving radio phase ambiguity in satellite orbit determination. Journal of Geophysical Research, 94(B6): 7058–7064.

Counselman CC, Gourevitch SA (1981): Miniature interferometer terminals for earth surveying: ambiguity and multipath with the Global Positioning System. IEEE Transactions on Geoscience and Remote Sensing, GE–19(4): 244–252.

Counselman CC, Shapiro II (1978): Miniature interferometer terminals for earth surveying. Ohio State University, Department of Geodetic Sciences, Columbus, Ohio, vol 280: 65–85.

Counselman CC, Hinteregger HF, Shapiro II (1972): Astronomical applications of differential interferometry. Science, 178: 607–608.

Counselman CC, Shapiro II, Greenspan RL, Cox DB (1979): Backpack VLBI terminal with subcentimeter capability. In: Proceedings of Radio Interferometry Techniques for Geodesy, NASA Conference Publication, vol 2115: 409–414.

Cross PA, Ahmad N (1988): Field validation of GPS phase measurements. In: Groten E, Strauß R (eds): GPS-techniques applied to geodesy and surveying. Springer, Berlin Heidelberg New York London Paris Tokyo, 349–360 [Bhattacharji S, Friedman GM, Neugebauer HJ, Seilacher A (eds): Lecture Notes in Earth Sciences, vol 19].

Davidson JM, Thornton CL, Vegos CJ, Young LE, Yunck TP (1985): The March 1985 demonstration of the fiducial network concept for GPS geodesy: a preliminary report. In: Proceedings of the First International Symposium on Precise Positioning with the Global Positioning System, Rockville, Maryland, April 15–19, vol 2: 603–611.

Davis JL, Herring TA, Shapiro II, Rogers AE, Elgered G (1985): Geodesy by radio interferometry: effects of atmospheric modeling errors on estimates of baseline lengths. Radio Science, 20(6): 1593–1607.

Decker BL (1986): World Geodetic System 1984. In: Proceedings of the Fourth International Geodetic Symposium on Satellite Positioning, Austin, Texas, April 28 – May 2, vol 1: 69–92.

Deines SD (1992): Missing relativity terms in GPS. Navigation, 39(1): 111–131.

Delikaraoglou D, Lahaye F (1990): Optimization of GPS theory, techniques and operational systems: progress and prospects. In: Bock Y, Leppard N (eds): Global Positioning System: an overview. Springer, New York Berlin Heidelberg London Paris Tokyo Hong Kong, 218–239 [Mueller II (ed): IAG Symposia Proceedings, vol 102].

Delikaraoglou D, Dragert H, Kouba J, Lochhead K, Popelar J (1990): The development of a Canadian GPS Active Control System: status of the current array. In: Proceedings of the Second International Symposium on Precise Positioning with the Global Positioning System, Ottawa, Canada, September 3–7, 190–202.

DeLoach SR, Remondi B (1991): Decimeter positioning for dredging and hydrographic surveying. In: Proceedings of the First International Symposium on Real Time Differential Applications of the Global Positioning System. TÜV Rheinland, Köln, vol 1: 258–263.

Department of Defense (1993): Global Positioning System Standard Positioning Service – signal specification.

Dierendonck AJ van, Russell SS, Kopitzke ER, Birnbaum M (1980): The GPS navigation message. In: The Institute of Navigation: Global Positioning System, vol 1: 55–73.

Dong D, Bock Y (1989): Global Positioning System network analysis with phase ambiguity resolution applied to crustal deformation studies in California. Journal of Geophysical Research, 94(B4): 3949–3966.

Easton RL (1970): Navigation system using satellites and passive ranging techniques. U.S. Patent Office, Patent no. 3,789,409.

Egge D (1985): Zur sequentiellen Auswertung von Doppler-Satellitenbeobachtungen. Wissenschaftliche Arbeiten der Fachrichtung Vermessungswesen der Universität Hannover, vol 141.

Eissfeller B (1993): Stand der GPS-Empfänger-Technologie. In: Institute of geodesy (ed): Proceedings of the Geodetic Seminar on Das Global Positioning System im praktischen Einsatz der Landes- und Ingenieurvermessung, Munich, May 12–14. Schriftenreihe der Universität der Bundeswehr München, vol 45: 29–55.

Elgered G, Johansson J, Rönnäng B (1985): Methods to correct for the tropospheric delay in satellite-earth range measurements. In: Proceedings of the Second SATRAPE Meeting, Saint-Mandé, France, November 4–6, 60–76.

Erickson C (1992a): Investigations of C/A code and carrier measurements and techniques for rapid static GPS surveys. Reports of the Department of Geomatics Engineering of the University of Calgary, vol 20044.

Erickson C (1992b): An analysis of ambiguity resolution techniques for rapid static GPS surveys using single frequency data. In: Proceedings of ION GPS-92, Fifth International Technical Meeting of the Satellite Division of the Institute of Navigation, Albuquerque, New Mexico, September 16–18, 453–462.

Essen L, Froome KD (1951): The refractive indices and dielectric constants of air and its principal constituents at 24 000 Mc/s. In: Proceedings of Physical Society, vol 64(B): 862–875.

Euler H-J, Goad CC (1991): On optimal filtering of GPS dual frequency observations without using orbit information. Bulletin Géodésique, 65: 130–143.

Euler H-J, Landau H (1992): Fast GPS ambiguity resolution on-the-fly for real-time applications. In: Proceedings of the Sixth International Geodetic Symposium on Satellite Positioning, Columbus, Ohio, March 17–20, vol 2: 650–659.

Euler H-J, Sauermann K, Becker M (1990): Rapid ambiguity fixing in small scale networks. In: Proceedings of the Second International Symposium on Precise Positioning with the Global Positioning System, Ottawa, Canada, September 3–7, 508–523.

Euler H-J, Hein GW, Landau H (1992): First experiences with a real-time differential GPS positioning system. Paper presented at the Sixth International Geodetic Symposium on Satellite Positioning at Columbus, Ohio, March 17–20.

Evans AG (1986): Comparison of GPS pseudorange and biased Doppler range measurements to demonstrate signal multipath effects. In: Proceedings of the Fourth International Geodetic Symposium on Satellite Positioning, Austin, Texas, April 28 – May 2, vol 1: 573–587.

Exon J (1993): The future of the U.S. Global Positioning System, GPS World, 4(7): 44–47.

Fantou J-C (1993): Urban positioning with GPS: a mobile communications field measurement application. GPS World, 4(7): 28–39.

Farrell WE (1972): Deformation of the earth by surface loads. Reviews of Geophysics and Space Physics, 10(3): 761–797.

Federal Geodetic Control Committee (FGCC) (1988): Geometric geodetic accuracy standards and specifications for using GPS relative positioning techniques, version 5.0.

Feigl KL, King RW, Herring TA, Rothacher M (1991): A scheme for reducing the effect of selective availability on precise geodetic measurements from the Global Positioning System. Geophysical Research Letters, 18(7): 1289–1292.

Feissel M, McCarthy DD (1994): Explanatory supplement to IERS Bulletins A and B. IERS Information.

Fell PJ (1980): Geodetic positioning using a Global Positioning System of satellites. Ohio State University, Department of Geodetic Sciences, Columbus, Ohio, vol 299.

Feltens J (1988): Several aspects of solar radiation pressure. In: Groten E, Strauß R (eds): GPS-techniques applied to geodesy and surveying. Springer, Berlin Heidelberg New York London Paris Tokyo, 487–502 [Bhattacharji S, Friedman GM, Neugebauer HJ, Seilacher A (eds): Lecture Notes in Earth Sciences, vol 19].

Ferguson KE, Veatch ER (1990): Centimeter level surveying in real-time. In: Proceedings of the Second International Symposium on Precise Positioning with the Global Positioning System, Ottawa, Canada, September 3–7, 1185–1195.

Ferguson K, Kosmalska J, Kuhl M, Eichner J-M, Kepski K, Abtahi R (1991): Three-dimensional attitude determination with the Ashtech 3DF 24-channel GPS measurement system. In the Institute of Navigation (ed): Proceedings of the National Technical Meeting "Using Synergism to Strengthen Navigation Systems", Phoenix, Arizona, January 22–24.

Finn A, Matthewman J (1989): A single frequency ionospheric refraction correction algorithm for TRANSIT and GPS. In: Proceedings of the

Fifth International Geodetic Symposium on Satellite Positioning, Las Cruces, New Mexico, March 13–17, vol 2: 737–756.

Fliegel HF, Feess WA, Layton WC, Rhodus NW (1985): The GPS radiation force model. In: Proceedings of the First International Symposium on Precise Positioning with the Global Positioning System, Rockville, Maryland, April 15–19, vol 1: 113–119.

Frei E (1991): GPS-Fast Ambiguity Resolution Approach "FARA": theory and application. Presented paper at XX General Assembly of IUGG, IAG-Symposium GM 1/4, Vienna, August 11–24.

Frei E, Beutler G (1989): Some considerations concerning an adaptive, optimized technique to resolve the initial phase ambiguities for static and kinematic GPS surveying-techniques. In: Proceedings of the Fifth International Geodetic Symposium on Satellite Positioning, Las Cruces, New Mexico, March 13–17, vol 2: 671–686.

Frei E, Beutler G (1990): Rapid static positioning based on the fast ambiguity resolution approach: the alternative to kinematic positioning. In: Proceedings of the Second International Symposium on Precise Positioning with the Global Positioning System, Ottawa, Canada, September 3–7, 1196–1216.

Frei E, Schubernigg M (1992): GPS surveying techniques using the "Fast Ambiguity Resolution Approach (FARA)". Paper presented at the 34th Australian Surveyors Congress and the 18th National Surveying Conference at Cairns, Australia, May 23–29.

Fricke W, Schwan H, Lederle T (1988): Fifth Fundamental Catalogue (FK5), Part I, The basic fundamental stars. Braun, Karlsruhe, Veröffentlichungen Astronomisches Rechen-Institut, Heidelberg, vol 32.

Friedrich M, Finsterbusch R, Murr F, Torkar KM, Riedler W (1989): Study of propagation effects for the DRS ranging system. University of Technology Graz, Department of Communications and Wave Propagation.

Geiger A (1988): Einfluss und Bestimmung der Variabilität des Phasenzentrums von GPS-Antennen. Eidgenössische Technische Hochschule Zürich, Institute of Geodesy and Photogrammetry, Mitteilungen vol 43.

Georgiadou Y, Doucet KD (1990): The issue of selective availability. GPS World, 1(5): 53–56.

Gervaise J, Mayoud M, Beutler G, Gurtner W (1985): Test of GPS on the CERN-LEP control network. In: Welsch WM, Lapine LA (eds): Proceedings of the Joint Meeting of FIG Study Groups 5B and 5C on Inertial, Doppler and GPS Measurements for National and Engineering Survey, Munich, July 1–3. Schriftenreihe der Universität der Bundeswehr München, vol 20-2: 337–358.

Gibson R (1983): A derivation of relativistic effects in satellite tracking. Naval Surface Weapons Center, Dahlgren, Virginia, Technical Report TR 83-55.

Goad CC (1985): Precise relative position determination using Global Positioning System carrier phase measurements in a nondifference mode. In: Proceedings of the First International Symposium on Precise Positioning with the Global Positioning System, Rockville, Maryland, April 15-19, vol 1: 347-356.

Goad CC (1986): Precise positioning with the GPS. CERN Accelerator School, Applied Geodesy for Particle Accelerators, Geneva, Switzerland, April 14-18.

Goad CC, Goodman L (1974): A modified Hopfield tropospheric refraction correction model. Paper presented at the American Geophysical Union Annual Fall Meeting at San Francisco, California, December 12-17.

Gouldman MW, Herman BR, Swift ER (1986): Absolute station position solutions for sites involved in the spring 1985 GPS precision baseline test. In: Proceedings of the Fourth International Geodetic Symposium on Satellite Positioning, Austin, Texas, April 28 – May 2, vol 2: 1045-1057.

Gouldman MW, Herman BR, Weedon DL (1989): Evaluation of GPS production ephemeris and clock quality. In: Proceedings of the Fifth International Geodetic Symposium on Satellite Positioning, Las Cruces, New Mexico, March 13-17, vol 1: 210-222.

Gourevitch SA, Lorenz RG, Nolan JM (1993): Z-tracking^{TM} results: implications to precision civilian applications. Personal communication.

Graas F van, Braasch MS (1991): GPS interferometric attitude and heading determination: Initial flight test results. Navigation, 38(4): 297-316.

Graas F van, Braasch MS (1992): Real-time attitude and heading determination using GPS. GPS World, 3(3): 32-39.

Grafarend EW, Schwarze V (1991): Relativistic GPS positioning. In: Caputo M, Sansò F (eds): Proceedings of the geodetic day in honor of Antonio Marussi. Accademia Nazionale dei Lincei, Rome. Atti dei Convegni Lincei, vol 91: 53-66.

Grant DB (1988): Combination of terrestrial and GPS data for earth deformation studies in New Zealand. University of New South Wales, School of Surveying, Kensington, Australia.

Graviss LP (1992): GPS development program status. In: Proceedings of ION GPS-92, Fifth International Technical Meeting of the Satellite Division of the Institute of Navigation, Albuquerque, New Mexico, September 16-18, 3-16.

Gurtner W, Mader G (1990): Receiver independent exchange format version 2. GPS Bulletin, 3(3): 1-8.

Gurtner W, Beutler G, Rothacher M (1989a): Combination of GPS observations made with different receiver types. In: Proceedings of the Fifth International Geodetic Symposium on Satellite Positioning, Las Cruces, New Mexico, March 13–17, vol 1: 362–374.

Gurtner W, Mader G, McArthur D (1989b): A common exchange format for GPS data. GPS Bulletin, 2(3): 1–11.

Hartl P, Schöller W, Thiel K-H (1985): GPS related activities of the INS. In: Welsch WM, Lapine LA (eds): Proceedings of the Joint Meeting of FIG Study Groups 5B and 5C on Inertial, Doppler and GPS Measurements for National and Engineering Survey, Munich, July 1–3. Schriftenreihe der Universität der Bundeswehr München, vol 20-2: 391–401.

Hatch R (1982): The synergism of GPS code and carrier measurements. In: Proceedings of the Third International Symposium on Satellite Doppler Positioning, New Mexico State University, February 8–12, vol 2: 1213–1231.

Hatch R (1986): Dynamic differential GPS at the centimeter level. In: Proceedings of the Fourth International Geodetic Symposium on Satellite Positioning, Austin, Texas, April 28 – May 2, vol 2: 1287–1298.

Hatch R (1990): Instantaneous ambiguity resolution. In: Schwarz KP, Lachapelle G (eds): Kinematic systems in geodesy, surveying, and remote sensing. Springer, New York Berlin Heidelberg London Paris Tokyo Hong Kong, 299–308 [Mueller II (ed): IAG Symposia Proceedings, vol 107].

Hatch R (1991): Ambiguity resolution while moving – experimental results. In: Proceedings of ION GPS-91, Fourth International Technical Meeting of the Satellite Division of the Institute of Navigation, Albuquerque, New Mexico, September 11–13, 707–713.

Hatch R, Larson K (1985): MAGNET-4100 GPS survey program processing techniques and test results. In: Proceedings of the First International Symposium on Precise Positioning with the Global Positioning System, Rockville, Maryland, April 15–19, vol 1: 285–297.

Hatch R, Keegan R, Stansell TA (1992): Kinematic receiver technology from Magnavox. In: Proceedings of the Sixth International Geodetic Symposium on Satellite Positioning, Columbus, Ohio, March 17–20, vol 1: 174–183.

Heckmann B (1985): Über die Auswirkung von relativistischen Effekten auf geodätische Messungen. Allgemeine Vermessungsnachrichten, 92(8–9): 329–336.

Hein GW (1990a): Bestimmung orthometrischer Höhen durch GPS und Schweredaten. Schriftenreihe der Universität der Bundeswehr München, vol 38-1: 291–300.

Hein GW (1990b): Kinematic differential GPS positioning: applications in airborne photogrammetry and gravimetry. In: Crosilla F, Mussio L (eds): Il sistema di posizionamento globale satellitare GPS. International Centre for Mechanical Sciences (CISM), Collana di Geodesia e Cartografia, Udine, Italy, 139–173.

Hein GW, Landau H, Baustert G (1988): Terrestrial and aircraft differential kinematic GPS positioning. In: Groten E, Strauß R (eds): GPS-techniques applied to geodesy and surveying. Springer, Berlin Heidelberg New York London Paris Tokyo, 307–348 [Bhattacharji S, Friedman GM, Neugebauer HJ, Seilacher A (eds): Lecture Notes in Earth Sciences, vol 19].

Hein GW, Leick A, Lambert S (1989): Integrated processing of GPS and gravity data. Journal of Surveying Engineering, 115(1): 15–33.

Heiskanen WA, Moritz H (1967): Physical Geodesy. Freeman, San Francisco London.

Henstridge F (1991): Getting started in GPS. Professional Surveyor, 11(4): 4–9.

Hilla SA (1986): Processing cycle slips in nondifferenced phase data from the Macrometer V-1000 receiver. In: Proceedings of the Fourth International Geodetic Symposium on Satellite Positioning, Austin, Texas, April 28 – May 2, vol 1: 647–661.

Hofmann-Wellenhof B, Lichtenegger H (eds) (1988): GPS – Von der Theorie zur Praxis. Mitteilungen der geodätischen Institute der Technischen Universität Graz, vol 62.

Hofmann-Wellenhof B, Remondi BW (1988): The antenna exchange: one aspect of high-precision GPS kinematic survey. In: Groten E, Strauß R (eds): GPS-techniques applied to geodesy and surveying. Springer, Berlin Heidelberg New York London Paris Tokyo, 261–277 [Bhattacharji S, Friedman GM, Neugebauer HJ, Seilacher A (eds): Lecture Notes in Earth Sciences, vol 19].

Hofmann-Wellenhof B, Klostius W, Pesec P (1990): Real-time relative positioning with GPS. In: Proceedings of the Second International Symposium on Precise Positioning with the Global Positioning System, Ottawa, Canada, September 3–7, 1248–1256.

Hofmann-Wellenhof B, Kienast G, Lichtenegger H (1994): GPS in der Praxis. Springer, Wien New York.

Holdridge DB (1967): An alternate expression for light time using general relativity. Jet Propulsion Laboratory, Supporting Research and Advanced Development, Space Programs Summary, 3: 37–48.

Hopfield HS (1969): Two-quartic tropospheric refractivity profile for correcting satellite data. Journal of Geophysical Research, 74(18): 4487–4499.

Hothem LD, Fronczek CJ (1983): Report on test and demonstration of Macrometer model V-1000 interferometric surveyor. FGCC Report: FGCC-IS-83-2.

Hwang PYC (1990): Kinematic GPS: resolving integer ambiguities on the fly. In: Proceedings of the IEEE Position Location and Navigation Symposium, Las Vegas, March 20–23, 579–586.

Jäger R, Mierlo J van (1991): Mathematische Modellbildungen bei der Integration von GPS-Konfigurationen in bestehende Netze. Deutscher Verein für Vermessungswesen, special issue: GPS und Integration von GPS in bestehende geodätische Netze, vol 38: 143–164.

Jahn C-H (1992): Untersuchungen über den Einsatz des Global Positioning Systems (GPS) zum Nachweis rezenter Erdkrustenbewegungen im Spaltengebiet Nordost-Islands. Wissenschaftliche Arbeiten der Fachrichtung Vermessungswesen der Universität Hannover, vol 182.

Janes HW, Langley RB, Newby SP (1989): A comparison of several models for the prediction of tropospheric propagation delay. In: Proceedings of the Fifth International Geodetic Symposium on Satellite Positioning, Las Cruces, New Mexico, March 13–17, vol 2: 777–788.

Jones T (1989): NAVSTAR Global Positioning System – status and update. In: Proceedings of the Fifth International Geodetic Symposium on Satellite Positioning, Las Cruces, New Mexico, March 13–17, vol 1: 28–52.

Joos G (1956): Lehrbuch der Theoretischen Physik. Akademische Verlagsgesellschaft Geest & Portig K-G, Leipzig, 9th edition.

Jorgensen PS (1980): Combined pseudo range and Doppler positioning for the stationary NAVSTAR user. In: Proceedings of the Position Location and Navigation Symposium, IEEE Publication 80CH1597-4: 450–458.

Jorgensen PS (1989): An assessment of ionospheric effects on the GPS user. Navigation, 36(2): 195–204.

Jünemann K (1991): Airlines requirements for a Global Navigation Satellite System with differential applications. In: Proceedings of the First International Symposium on Real Time Differential Applications of the Global Positioning System. TÜV Rheinland, Köln, vol 1: 122–135.

Kalafus R (1992): RTCM SC-104, Differential GPS standards. In: Summary record of the 20th meeting of the Civil GPS Service Interface Committee, Albuquerque, New Mexico, September 14–15.

Kaniuth K (1986): A local model for estimating the tropospheric path delay at microwave frequencies. In: Proceedings of the Fourth International Geodetic Symposium on Satellite Positioning, Austin, Texas, April 28 – May 2, vol 1: 589–601.

Kaniuth K, Stuber K, Tremel H (1989): A comparative analysis of various procedures for modelling the tropospheric delay in a regional GPS network. In: Proceedings of the Fifth International Geodetic Symposium on Satellite Positioning, Las Cruces, New Mexico, March 13–17, vol 2: 767–776.

Kasties G, Harrer S (1991): Differential GPS for real time flight path surveillance. In: Proceedings of the First International Symposium on Real Time Differential Applications of the Global Positioning System. TÜV Rheinland, Köln, vol 1: 205–237.

Kato T, Murata I, Tsuchiya A (1987): Effects of ionosphere on interferometric GPS observations. Earthquake Research Institute, University of Tokyo.

Kaula WM (1966): Theory of Satellite Geodesy. Blaisdell, Toronto.

Keegan R (1990): P-code aided Global Positioning System receiver. U.S. Patent Office, Patent no. 4,972,431.

Kinal GV, Singh JP (1990): An international geostationary overlay for GPS and GLONASS. Navigation, 37(1): 81–93.

King RW, Masters EG, Rizos C, Stolz A, Collins J (1987): Surveying with Global Positioning System. Dümmler, Bonn.

Klees R (1990): Anwendung des NAVSTAR/Global Positioning System in der kanadischen Landes-, Kataster- und Stadtvermessung. Allgemeine Vermessungsnachrichten, 97(3): 117–120, and 97(4): 138–157.

Kleusberg A (1990a): A review of kinematic and static GPS surveying procedures. In: Proceedings of the Second International Symposium on Precise Positioning with the Global Positioning System, Ottawa, Canada, September 3–7, 1102–1113.

Kleusberg A (1990b): Comparing GPS and GLONASS. GPS World, 1(6): 52.

Klobuchar J (1986): Design and characteristics of the GPS ionospheric time-delay algorithm for single-frequency users. In: Proceedings of the IEEE Position Location and Navigation Symposium, Las Vegas, November 4–7.

Knuth DE (1978): The art of computer programming – fundamental algorithms. Addison Wesley, Reading (Massachusetts) Menlo Park (California) London Amsterdam Don Mills (Ontario) Sydney, vol 1, 2nd edition.

Kozai Y (1959): On the effects of the sun and the moon upon the motion of a close earth satellite. Smithsonian Astrophysical Observatory, Special Report vol 22.

Kremer GT, Kalafus RM, Loomis PVW, Reynolds JC (1990): The effect of selective availability on differential GPS corrections. Navigation, 37(1): 39–52.

Kreyszig E (1968): Advanced engineering mathematics. Wiley, New York London Sydney, 2nd edition.

Lachapelle G (1990): GPS observables and error sources for kinematic positioning. In: Schwarz KP, Lachapelle G (eds): Kinematic systems in geodesy, surveying, and remote sensing. Springer, New York Berlin Heidelberg London Paris Tokyo Hong Kong, 17–26 [Mueller II (ed): IAG Symposia Proceedings, vol 107].

Lachapelle G (1991): Capabilities of GPS for airborne remote sensing. Canadian Journal of Remote Sensing, 17(4): 305–312.

Lachapelle G, Beck N, Héroux P (1982): NAVSTAR/GPS single point positioning using pseudo-range and Doppler observations. In: Proceedings of the Third International Symposium on Satellite Doppler Positioning, New Mexico State University, February 8–12, vol 2: 1079–1091.

Lachapelle G, Hagglund J, Falkenberg W, Bellemare P, Casey M, Eaton M (1986): GPS land kinematic positioning experiments. In: Proceedings of the Fourth International Geodetic Symposium on Satellite Positioning, Austin, Texas, April 28 – May 2, vol 2: 1327–1344.

Lachapelle G, Cannon ME, Erickson C, Falkenberg W (1992): High precision C/A code technology for rapid static DGPS surveys. In: Proceedings of the Sixth International Geodetic Symposium on Satellite Positioning, Columbus, Ohio, March 17–20, vol 1: 165–173.

Landau H (1988): Zur Nutzung des Global Positioning Systems in Geodäsie und Geodynamik: Modellbildung, Software-Entwicklung und Analyse. Schriftenreihe der Universität der Bundeswehr München, vol 36.

Landau H (1990): GPS processing techniques in geodetic networks. In: Proceedings of the Second International Symposium on Precise Positioning with the Global Positioning System, Ottawa, Canada, September 3–7, 373–386.

Landau H, Euler H-J (1992): On-the-fly ambiguity resolution for precise differential positioning. In: Proceedings of ION GPS-92, Fifth International Technical Meeting of the Satellite Division of the Institute of Navigation, Albuquerque, New Mexico, September 16–18, 607–613.

Langley RB (1991): The GPS receiver: an introduction. GPS World, 2(1): 50–53.

Langley RB (1992): The Federal Radionavigation Plan. GPS World, 3(3): 50–53.

Langley RB (1993): Communication links for DGPS. GPS World, 4(5): 47–51.

Lanyi G (1984): Tropospheric calibration in radio interferometry. In: Proceedings of the International Symposium on Space Techniques for Geodynamics, Sopron, Hungary, July 9–13, vol 2: 184–195.

Leick A (1990): GPS satellite surveying. Wiley, New York Chichester Brisbane Toronto Singapore.

Li Z, Schwarz KP, El-Mowafy A (1993): GPS multipath detection and reduction using spectral technique. Paper presented at the General Meeting of IAG at Beijing, P.R. China, August 8–13.

Lichten SM, Neilan RE (1990): Global networks for GPS orbit determination. In: Proceedings of the Second International Symposium on Precise Positioning with the Global Positioning System, Ottawa, Canada, September 3–7, 164–178.

Lichten SM, Bertiger WI, Lindqwister UJ (1989): The effect of fiducial network strategy on high-accuracy GPS orbit and baseline determination. In: Proceedings of the Fifth International Geodetic Symposium on Satellite Positioning, Las Cruces, New Mexico, March 13–17, vol 1: 516–525.

Lichtenegger H (1991): Über die Auswirkung von Koordinatenänderungen in der Referenzstation bei relativen Positionierungen mittels GPS. Österreichische Zeitschrift für Vermessungswesen und Photogrammetrie, 79(1): 49–52.

Lichtenegger H, Hofmann-Wellenhof B (1989): GPS-data preprocessing for cycle-slip detection. In: Bock Y, Leppard N (eds): Global Positioning System: an overview. Springer, New York Berlin Heidelberg London Paris Tokyo Hong Kong, 57–68 [Mueller II (ed): IAG Symposia Proceedings, vol 102].

Lindemann U, Haverland M (1991): AERONAV – an integrated navigation system for special mission aircraft. In: Proceedings of the First International Symposium on Real Time Differential Applications of the Global Positioning System. TÜV Rheinland, Köln, vol 1: 238–247.

Loomis P (1989): A kinematic GPS double-differencing algorithm. In: Proceedings of the Fifth International Geodetic Symposium on Satellite Positioning, Las Cruces, New Mexico, March 13–17, vol 2: 611–620.

Lu G, Cannon ME, Lachapelle G, Kielland P (1993): Attitude determination in a survey launch using multi-antenna GPS technology. National Technical Meeting of the Institute of Navigation, San Francisco, January 20–22.

McArthur D, Beck N, Lochhead K, Delikaraoglou D (1985): Precise relative positioning with the Macrometer V-1000 interferometric surveyor: experiences at the Geodetic Survey of Canada. In: Proceedings of the First International Symposium on Precise Positioning with the Global Positioning System, Rockville, Maryland, April 15–19, vol 2: 521–532.

McCarthy DD (ed) (1992): IERS Standards (1992). Observatoire de Paris, International Earth Rotation Service, Technical Note 13.

McDonald KD (1991): Navigation Satellite Systems - a perspective. In: Proceedings of the First International Symposium on Real Time Differential Applications of the Global Positioning System. TÜV Rheinland, Köln, vol 1: 20–35.

McDonald KD (1993): Econosats: toward an affordable Global Navigation Satellite System. GPS World, 4(9): 44–54.

MacDoran PF, Miller RB, Buennagel LA, Whitcomb JH (1985): Codeless systems for positioning with NAVSTAR-GPS. In: Proceedings of the First International Symposium on Precise Positioning with the Global Positioning System, Rockville, Maryland, April 15–19, vol 1: 181–190.

Mack G (1991): SkyFix – the performance of a professional DGPS service. In: Proceedings of the First International Symposium on Real Time Differential Applications of the Global Positioning System. TÜV Rheinland, Köln, vol 2: 616–624.

Mader GL (1986): Dynamic positioning using GPS carrier phase measurements. Manuscripta geodaetica, 11: 272–277.

Mader GL (1990): Ambiguity function techniques for GPS phase initialization and kinematic solutions. In: Proceedings of the Second International Symposium on Precise Positioning with the Global Positioning System, Ottawa, Canada, September 3–7, 1233–1247.

Marini JW, Murray CW (1973): Correction of laser range tracking data for atmospheric refraction at elevations above 10 degrees. NASA/GSCF X-591-73-351.

Melbourne WG (1985): The case for ranging in GPS-based geodetic systems. In: Proceedings of the First International Symposium on Precise Positioning with the Global Positioning System, Rockville, Maryland, April 15–19, vol 1: 373–386.

Melbourne WG, Yunck TP, Bertiger WI, Haines BJ, Davis ES (1993): Scientific applications of GPS on low earth orbiters. Journal for Satellite-Based Positioning, Navigation and Communication, 2(4): 131–145.

Melchior P (1978): The tides of the planet earth. Pergamon Press, Oxford New York Toronto Sydney Paris Frankfurt.

Merminod B, Grant DB, Rizos C (1990): Planning GPS-surveys using appropriate precision indicators. CISM Journal, 44(3): 233–249.

Meyerhoff SL, Evans AG (1986): Demonstration of the combined use of GPS pseudorange and Doppler measurements for improved dynamic positioning. In: Proceedings of the Fourth International Geodetic Symposium on Satellite Positioning, Austin, Texas, April 28 – May 2, vol 2: 1397–1409.

Milliken RJ, Zoller CJ (1980): Principle of operation of NAVSTAR and system characteristics. In: The Institute of Navigation: Global Positioning System, vol 1: 3–14.

Minkel DH (1989): Demonstration and discussion of the pseudo-kinematic method. In: Proceedings of the Fifth International Geodetic Symposium on Satellite Positioning, Las Cruces, New Mexico, March 13–17, vol 2: 577–588.

Montenbruck O (1984): Grundlagen der Ephemeridenrechnung. Sterne und Weltraum Vehrenberg, München.

Montgomery H (1991): GPS – the next generation. GPS World, 2(10): 12–16.

Moritz H (1977): Introduction to interpolation and approximation. Lecture Notes of the Second International Summer School in the Mountains, Ramsau, Austria, August 23 – September 2.

Moritz H (1980): Advanced Physical Geodesy. Wichmann, Karlsruhe.

Moritz H, Mueller II (1988): Earth rotation – theory and observation. Ungar, New York.

Mueller II (1991): International GPS Geodynamics Service. GPS Bulletin, 4(1): 7–16.

Mueller II, Archinal B (1981): Geodesy and the Global Positioning System. Paper presented at the IAG Symposium on Geodetic Networks and Computations at Munich, Germany, August 31 – September 5.

Munck JC de (1989): Kalman filtering. In: Bakker G, Munck JC de, Strang van Hees GL: Radio positioning at sea. Delft University.

Nagle JR, Dierendonck AJ van, Hua QD (1992/93): Inmarsat-3 navigation signal C/A-code selection and interference analysis. Navigation, 39(4): 445–461.

Nautical Almanac Office (1983): The astronomical almanac for the year 1984. US Government Printing Office, Washington.

Nee RDJ van (1992): Multipath effects on GPS code phase measurements. Navigation, 39(2): 177–190.

Nieuwejaar PW (1988): GPS signal structure. In: The Navstar GPS system. US Department of Commerce, National Technical Information Service, 5.1–6.

Olsen DL (1992): FRP update - what to expect in the 1992 U.S. Federal Radionavigation Plan. In: Summary record of the 20th Meeting of the Civil GPS Service Interface Committee, Albuquerque, New Mexico, September 14–15.

Oswald J, Mitchell J, Whiting L (1986): Simple differential techniques using the Trimble 4000A GPS locator. In: Proceedings of the Fourth International Geodetic Symposium on Satellite Positioning, Austin, Texas, April 28 – May 2, vol 1: 503–511.

Payne CR (1982): NAVSTAR Global Positioning System: 1982. In: Proceedings of the Third International Symposium on Satellite Doppler

Positioning, New Mexico State University, February 8–12, vol 2: 993–1021.

Perreault PD (1980): Description of the Global Positioning System (GPS) and the STI receivers. CSTG Bulletin vol 2, Technology and Mission Developments.

Pesec P, Stangl G (1990): TI-4100 PROM-type automation for unattended operation in international GPS orbit-service programs. In: Colic K, Pesec P, Sünkel H (eds) (1990): Proceedings of the First International Symposium on Gravity Field Determination and GPS-Positioning in the Alps-Adria Area. Mitteilungen der Geodätischen Institute der Technischen Universität Graz, vol 67: 336–344.

Prescott W, Davis J, Svarc J (1989): Height of L2 phase center for TI-antennas. GPS Bulletin, 2(2): 13.

Prilepin MT (1989): Improvement of accuracy of single-point determinations. In: Proceedings of the Fifth International Geodetic Symposium on Satellite Positioning, Las Cruces, New Mexico, March 13–17, vol 1: 462–473.

Quin X, Gourevitch S, Ferguson K, Kuhl M, Ladd J (1992): Dynamic short baseline calibration and attitude determination using Ashtech 3DF system. In: Proceedings of the Sixth International Geodetic Symposium on Satellite Positioning, Columbus, Ohio, March 17–20, vol 1: 190–199.

Rahnemoon M (1988): Ein Korrekturmodell für Mikrowellenmessungen zu Satelliten. German Geodetic Commission, Munich, series C, vol 335.

Reichert G (1986): A new water-vapor radiometer design. In: Proceedings of the Fourth International Geodetic Symposium on Satellite Positioning, Austin, Texas, April 28 – May 2, vol 2: 603–613.

Remondi BW (1984): Using the Global Positioning System (GPS) phase observable for relative geodesy: modeling, processing, and results. University of Texas at Austin, Center for Space Research.

Remondi BW (1985): Global Positioning System carrier phase: description and use. Bulletin Géodésique, 59: 361–377.

Remondi BW (1986): Performing centimeter-level surveys in seconds with GPS carrier phase: initial results. In: Proceedings of the Fourth International Geodetic Symposium on Satellite Positioning, Austin, Texas, April 28 – May 2, vol 2: 1229–1249.

Remondi BW (1988): Kinematic and pseudo-kinematic GPS. In: Proceedings of the Satellite Division Conference of the Institute of Navigation, Colorado Springs, Colorado, September 21–23.

Remondi BW (1989): Extending the National Geodetic Survey standard GPS orbit formats. National Information Center, Rockville, Maryland, NOAA Technical Report NOS 133, NGS 46.

Remondi BW (1990a): Pseudo-kinematic GPS results using the ambiguity function method. National Information Center, Rockville, Maryland, NOAA Technical Memorandum NOS NGS-52.

Remondi BW (1990b): Recent advances in pseudo-kinematic GPS. In: Proceedings of the Second International Symposium on Precise Positioning with the Global Positioning System, Ottawa, Canada, September 3–7, 1114–1137.

Remondi BW (1991a): Kinematic GPS results without static initialization. National Information Center, Rockville, Maryland, NOOA Technical Memorandum NOS NGS-55.

Remondi BW (1991b): NGS second generation ASCII and binary orbit formats and associated interpolation studies. Paper presented at the XX General Assembly of IUGG at Vienna, Austria, August 11–24.

Remondi BW (1991c): The Global Positioning System. The Military Engineer, 84(545): 31–36.

Remondi BW, Hofmann-Wellenhof B (1989a): Accuracy of Global Positioning System broadcast orbits for relative surveys. National Information Center, Rockville, Maryland, NOAA Technical Report NOS 132, NGS 45.

Remondi BW, Hofmann-Wellenhof B (1989b): GPS broadcast orbits versus precise orbits: a comparison study. GPS Bulletin, 2(6): 8–13.

Richardus P, Adler RK (1972): Map projections for geodesists, cartographers and geographers. North-Holland, Amsterdam London.

Rizos C, Stolz A (1985): Force modelling for GPS satellite orbits. In: Proceedings of the First International Symposium on Precise Positioning with the Global Positioning System, Rockville, Maryland, April 15–19, vol 1: 87–96.

Rizos C, Govind R, Stolz A, Luck JMcK (1987): The Australian GPS orbit determination pilot project. Australian Journal of Geodesy Photogrammetry and Surveying, 46 & 47: 17–40.

Rocken C, Meertens CM (1989): GPS antenna and receiver tests: multipath reduction and mixed receiver baselines. In: Proceedings of the Fifth International Geodetic Symposium on Satellite Positioning, Las Cruces, New Mexico, March 13–17, vol 1: 375–385.

Rocken C, Meertens C (1991): Monitoring selective availability dither frequencies and their effect on GPS data. Bulletin Géodésique, 65(3): 162–169.

Rockwell International Corporation (1984): Navstar GPS space segment. Downey, California, Interface Control Document ICD-GPS-200.

Rogers AEE, Knight CA, Hinteregger HF, Whitney AR, Counselman CC, Shapiro II, Gourevitch SA, Clark TA (1978): Geodesy by radio interferometry. Determination of a 1.24 km baseline vector with 5 millimeter repeatability. Journal of Geophysical Research, 83: 325–333.

Rothacher M, Beutler G, Gurtner W, Schildknecht T, Wild U (1989): Results of the 1984, 1986, and 1988 Alaska GPS campaigns. In: Proceedings of the Fifth International Geodetic Symposium on Satellite Positioning, Las Cruces, New Mexico, March 13–17, vol 1: 554–566.

Rutscheidt EH, Roth BD (1982): The NAVSTAR Global Positioning System. CSTG Bulletin vol 4, International Activities including Proceedings of Symposium 4e, IAG General Meeting Tokyo.

Saastamoinen II (1973): Contribution to the theory of atmospheric refraction. Bulletin Géodésique, 107: 13–34.

Scherrer R (1985): The WM GPS primer. WM Satellite Survey Company, Wild, Heerbrugg, Switzerland.

Schmitt G, Illner M, Jäger R (1991): Transformationsprobleme. Deutscher Verein für Vermessungswesen, special issue: GPS und Integration von GPS in bestehende geodätische Netze, vol 38: 125–142.

Schödlbauer A, Krack K, Glasmacher H (1989): Densification of horizontal networks by GPS. In: Proceedings of the Fifth International Geodetic Symposium on Satellite Positioning, Las Cruces, New Mexico, March 13–17, vol 2: 1090–1103.

Schrödter F (1994): GPS-Satelliten-Navigation: Technik, Systeme, Geräte, Funktionen und praktischer Einsatz. Franzis, Poing.

Schupler BR, Clark TA (1991): How different antennas affect the GPS observable. GPS World, 2(10): 32–36.

Schwarz KP (1983): Inertial surveying and geodesy. Reviews of Geophysics and Space Physics, 21(4): 878–890.

Schwarz KP (1987): Geoid profiles from an integration of GPS satellite and inertial data. Bollettino di geodesia e scienze affini, 46(2): 117–131.

Schwarz KP, Arden DAG (1985): A comparison of adjustment and smoothing methods for inertial networks. In: Schwarz KP (ed) (1985): Proceedings of the Symposium on Inertial Technology for Surveying and Geodesy, Banff, Canada, September 16–20, vol 1: 257–271.

Schwarz KP, Lachapelle G (eds) (1990): Kinematic systems in geodesy, surveying, and remote sensing. Springer, New York Berlin Heidelberg London Paris Tokyo Hong Kong, 299–308 [Mueller II (ed): IAG Symposia Proceedings, vol 107].

Schwarz KP, Cannon ME, Wong RVC (1987): The use of GPS in exploration geophysics – a comparison of kinematic models. Paper presented at the XIX General Assembly of the IUGG at Vancouver, Canada, August 10–22.

Schwiderski EW (1981): Global ocean tides, atlas of tidal charts and maps. Naval Surface Weapons Center (NSWC), Virginia.

Scott C (1993): An overview of the communication options for broadcast DGPS corrections. Australian Journal of Geodesy Photogrammetriy and Surveying, 58: 69–84.

Seeber G (1993): Satellite geodesy: foundations, methods, and applications. Walter de Gruyter, Berlin New York.

Shebshayevich VS (1991): Main problems of joint use of GLONASS and NAVSTAR in differential navigation fixing. In: Proceedings of the First International Symposium on Real Time Differential Applications of the Global Positioning System. TÜV Rheinland, Köln, vol 1: 81–85.

Sims ML (1985): Phase center variation in the geodetic TI4100 GPS receiver system's conical spiral antenna. In: Proceedings of the First International Symposium on Precise Positioning with the Global Positioning System, Rockville, Maryland, April 15–19, vol 1: 227–244.

Sluiter PG (1993): The world of DGPS. Geodetical Info Magazin, 7(7): 57–61.

Smith ID (1964): Satellite hyperbolic navigating system. U.S. Patent Office, Patent no. 3,126,545.

Snay RA (1986): Network design strategies applicable to GPS surveys using three or four receivers. Bulletin Géodésique, 60(1): 37–50.

Speckter HE (1991): Standardization and implementation of a DGPS system and service in the maritime field. In: Proceedings of the First International Symposium on Real Time Differential Applications of the Global Positioning System. TÜV Rheinland, Köln, vol 2: 687–701.

Spilker JJ (1980): GPS signal structure and performance characteristics. In: The Institute of Navigation: Global Positioning System, vol 1: 29–54.

Stangl G, Hofmann-Wellenhof B, Pesec P, Sünkel H (1991): Austrian GPS reference network – concept, realization, and first results. Paper presented at the XX General Assembly of IUGG at Vienna, Austria, August 11–24.

Stein WL (1986): NAVSTAR Global Positioning System 1986 status and plans. In: Proceedings of the Fourth International Geodetic Symposium on Satellite Positioning, Austin, Texas, April 28 – May 2, vol 1: 37–49.

Strange WE (1985): High-precision, three-dimensional differential positioning using GPS. In: Proceedings of the First International Symposium on Precise Positioning with the Global Positioning System, Rockville, Maryland, April 15–19, vol 2: 543–548.

Swift ER (1985): NSWC'S GPS orbit/clock determination system. In: Proceedings of the First International Symposium on Precise Positioning with the Global Positioning System, Rockville, Maryland, April 15–19, vol 1: 51–62.

Tallqvist S (1985): The GPS microstrip antenna properties; reduction of multipath contamination and other interference by an RF absorbent ground plane. In: Proceedings of the Second SATRAPE Meeting, Saint-Mandé, France, November 4–6, 46–59.

Tranquilla JM (1986): Multipath and imaging problems in GPS receiver antennas. In: Proceedings of the Fourth International Geodetic Symposium on Satellite Positioning, Austin, Texas, April 28 – May 2, vol 1: 557–571.

Tranquilla JM, Carr JP (1990/91): GPS multipath field observations at land and water sites. Navigation, 37(4): 393–414.

True Time, Santa Rosa, California (1993): Oscillator disciplining with selective availability truetime "Sathoptm" algorithm. (Remark: original title has been corrected because of misspellings.) Journal for Satellite-Based Positioning, Navigation and Communication, 2(4): 145–146.

Unguendoli M (1990): A rational approach to the use of a large number of GPS receivers. Bulletin Géodésique, 64(4): 303-312.

Walser F (1988): Ionosphäreneinfluss bei GPS-Messungen. Eidgenössische Technische Hochschule Zürich, Institute of Geodesy and Photogrammetry, vol 147.

Walsh D (1992): Real time ambiguity resolution while on the move. In: Proceedings of ION GPS-92, Fifth International Technical Meeting of the Satellite Division of the Institute of Navigation, Albuquerque, New Mexico, September 16–18, 473–481.

Weber L, Tiwari A (1994): An ideal link for DGPS: the Radio Data System. In: Proceedings of the XX Congress of FIG (International Federation of Surveyors), Commission 5, Survey Instruments and Methods, Melbourne, Australia, March 5–12, 504.3/1–504.3/10.

Wells D (1985): Recommended GPS terminology. In: Welsch WM, Lapine LA (eds): Proceedings of the Joint Meeting of FIG Study Groups 5B and 5C on Inertial, Doppler and GPS Measurements for National and Engineering Survey, Munich, July 1–3. Schriftenreihe der Universität der Bundeswehr München, vol 20-1: 179–207.

Wells D, Lachapelle G (1981): Impact of NAVSTAR/GPS on land and offshore positioning in the 1980s. Paper presented at Canadian Petroleum Association Colloquium III, Petroleum Mapping and Surveys in the '80s at Banff, Alberta, October 14–16.

Wells DE, Beck N, Delikaraoglou D, Kleusberg A, Krakiwsky EJ, Lachapelle G, Langley RB, Nakiboglu M, Schwarz KP, Tranquilla JM, Vanicek P (1987): Guide to GPS positioning. Canadian GPS Associates, Fredericton, New Brunswick, Canada.

Westrop J, Napier ME, Ashkenazi V (1989): Cycle slips on the move: detection and elimination. In: Proceedings of ION GPS-89, The Second

International Technical Meeting of the Satellite Division of the Institute of Navigation, Colorado Springs, Colorado, September 27–29, 31–34.

Wild U, Beutler G, Gurtner W, Rothacher M (1989): Estimating the ionosphere using one or more dual frequency GPS receivers. In: Proceedings of the Fifth International Geodetic Symposium on Satellite Positioning, Las Cruces, New Mexico, March 13–17, vol 2: 724–736.

Willis P, Boucher C (1990): High precision kinematic positioning using GPS at the IGN: recent results. In: Bock Y, Leppard N (eds): Global Positioning System: an overview. Springer, New York Berlin Heidelberg London Paris Tokyo Hong Kong, 340–350 [Mueller II (ed): IAG Symposia Proceedings, vol 102].

Wooden WH (1985): Navstar Global Positioning System: 1985. In: Proceedings of the First International Symposium on Precise Positioning with the Global Positioning System, Rockville, Maryland, April 15–19, vol 1: 23–32.

Wu S, Bertiger WI, Wu J (1990): Minimizing selective availability error on TOPEX GPS measurements. Paper presented at the Astrodynamics Conference at Portland, Oregon.

Wübbena G (1985): Software developments for geodetic positioning with GPS using TI 4100 code and carrier measurements. In: Proceedings of the First International Symposium on Precise Positioning with the Global Positioning System, Rockville, Maryland, April 15–19, vol 1: 403–412.

Wübbena G (1988): GPS carrier phases and clock modeling. In: Groten E, Strauß R (eds): GPS-techniques applied to geodesy and surveying. Springer, Berlin Heidelberg New York London Paris Tokyo, 381–392 [Bhattacharji S, Friedman GM, Neugebauer HJ, Seilacher A (eds): Lecture Notes in Earth Sciences, vol 19].

Wübbena G (1989): The GPS adjustment software package GEONAP – concepts and models. In: Proceedings of the Fifth International Geodetic Symposium on Satellite Positioning, Las Cruces, New Mexico, March 13–17, vol 2: 452–461.

Wunderlich T (1992): Die gefährlichen Örter der Pseudostreckenortung. Technical University Hannover.

Yionoulis S M (1970): Algorithm to compute tropospheric refraction effects on range measurements. Journal of Geophysical Research, 75(36): 7636–7637.

Yiu KP, Crawford R, Eschenbach R (1984): A low-cost GPS receiver for land navigation. In: The Institute of Navigation: Global Positioning System, vol 2: 44–60.

Young LE, Neilan RE, Bletzacker FR (1985): GPS satellite multipath: an experimental investigation. In: Proceedings of the First International Symposium on Precise Positioning with the Global Positioning System, Rockville, Maryland, April 15–19, vol 1: 423–432.

Zhu J (1993): Exact conversion of earth-centered, earth-fixed coordinates to geodetic coordinates. Journal of Guidance, Control, and Dynamics, 16(2): 389–391.

Zhu SY, Groten E (1988): Relativistic effects in GPS. In: Groten E, Strauß R (eds): GPS-techniques applied to geodesy and surveying. Springer, Berlin Heidelberg New York London Paris Tokyo, 41–46 [Bhattacharji S, Friedman GM, Neugebauer HJ, Seilacher A (eds): Lecture Notes in Earth Sciences, vol 19].

Subject index

B. Hofmann-Wellenhof, G. Kienast, H. Lichtenegger

GPS in der Praxis

1994. 15 Abbildungen. IX, 143 Seiten.
Broschiert DM 38,–, öS 266,–
ISBN 3-211-82609-2

Das satellitengestützte Positionierungssystem GPS wurde ursprünglich für die militärische Navigation konzipiert und entwickelt. Bald wurden aber auch die Anwendungsmöglichkeiten im zivilen Bereich erkannt. Unter anderem zählt GPS heute bereits zu den Standardmethoden der geodätischen Punktbestimmung, wobei Genauigkeiten bis in den Millimeterbereich erzielt werden können.

Dieses Buch richtet sich an alle, die eine praxisbezogene Beschreibung von GPS hinsichtlich der Beobachtung und der Auswertung suchen. Nach einer elementaren Einführung in das Prinzip von GPS werden die wichtigsten Aspekte der Beobachtung beginnend von der Planung über die Durchführung bis zur Berechnung der Basisvektoren beschrieben. Das Schwergewicht des Buches liegt in der Auswertung. Im Detail werden die Netzbildung, die Transformation der GPS-Ergebnisse in das lokale geodätische Datum sowie die gemeinsame Ausgleichung von GPS und terrestrischen Messungen behandelt, wobei zahlreiche numerische Beispiele angeführt sind. Im Anhang sind neben den Zahlenwerten für die Parameter der bekanntesten Ellipsoide auch die Formelsysteme für die gebräuchlichsten konformen Abbildungen enthalten.

Springer-Verlag Wien New York

Sachsenplatz 4–6, P.O.Box 89, A-1201 Wien · 175 Fifth Avenue, New York, NY 10010, USA
Heidelberger Platz 3, D-14197 Berlin · 3-13, Hongo 3-chome, Bunkyo-ku, Tokyo 113, Japan

Springer-Verlag
and the Environment

WE AT SPRINGER-VERLAG FIRMLY BELIEVE THAT AN international science publisher has a special obligation to the environment, and our corporate policies consistently reflect this conviction.

WE ALSO EXPECT OUR BUSINESS PARTNERS – PRINTERS, paper mills, packaging manufacturers, etc. – to commit themselves to using environmentally friendly materials and production processes.

THE PAPER IN THIS BOOK IS MADE FROM NO-CHLORINE pulp and is acid free, in conformance with international standards for paper permanency.